Tupolev Tu-154

The USSR's Medium-Range Jet Airliner

Dmitriy Komissarov

An imprint of
Ian Allan Publishing

Tupolev Tu-154:
The USSR's Medium-Range Jet Airliner
© 2007 Dmitriy Komissarov

ISBN (10) 1 85780 241 1
ISBN (13) 1 85780 241 2

Published by Midland Publishing
4 Watling Drive, Hinckley, LE10 3EY, England
Tel: 01455 254 490   Fax: 01455 254 495
E-mail: midlandbooks@compuserve.com

Midland Publishing and Aerofax are imprints of
Ian Allan Publishing Ltd

Worldwide distribution (except North America):
Midland Counties Publications
4 Watling Drive, Hinckley, LE10 3EY, England
Telephone: 01455 254 450   Fax: 01455 233 737
E-mail: midlandbooks@compuserve.com
www.midlandcountiessuperstore.com

North American trade distribution:
Specialty Press Publishers & Wholesalers Inc.
39966 Grand Avenue, North Branch, MN 55056
Tel: 651 277 1400   Fax: 651 277 1203
Toll free telephone: 800 895 4585
www.specialtypress.com

Design and concept
© 2007 Midland Publishing and
Stephen Thompson Associates
Layout by Sue Bushell

Printed in England by
Ian Allan Printing Ltd
Riverdene Business Park, Molesey Road,
Hersham, Surrey, KT12 4RG

Visit the Ian Allan Publishing website at:
www.ianallanpublishing.com

Contents

**Title page: Still retaining the Aeroflot colours
so familiar in Soviet Union days, Tu-154B-2
RA-85346 is operating for Pulkovo Airlines.**
via Author

**Below: All-white Georgian Airlines Tu-154B-2
4L-85496 is the former Presidential aircraft of
Georgia's first President Zviad Gamsakhurdia
and, later, his successor Eduard A Shevardnadze.**
Dmitriy Petrochenko

Introduction

No book about an aircraft would ever be written unless there was something special about that aircraft. So, what's special about the aircraft that is the subject of this book? Of all Soviet and Russian medium-haul airliners the Tupolev Tu-154 was built in the greatest numbers by far: 928 copies, although this total includes the two static/fatigue test airframes and about ten aircraft remain uncompleted as of this writing. True enough, the Tu-154 does not rank first among Soviet airliners as far as production is concerned, being surpassed by the Yakovlev Yak-40 (1,104 built) and the Antonov An-24 (1,028 produced in Kiev and another 180 in Ulan-Ude, which makes a total of 1,208 passenger-configured An-24s – not counting the 164 An-24T and An-24RT transports manufactured in Irkutsk). However, both of these types are in a different league, being regional airliners.

The Tu-154 is the only Soviet airliner to remain in mass production after the break-up of the Soviet Union. After all, the Ilyushin IL-76, which can boast a similar achievement, is a transport, not an airliner; the IL-86 wide-body airliner was produced on a very small scale after 1991, and the IL-96-300 and the Tu-204, which were first flown in 1988 and 1989 respectively, entered production in earnest in post-Soviet days. Moreover, the Tu-154 has been in production for 37 years now – longer than any other Soviet/Russian commercial aircraft type.

The Tu-154 is one of the bestsellers among Soviet/Russian commercial types and, as in the case of its smaller stablemate, the Tu-134, it has paved the way into some markets where the Soviet Union had not maintained a presence before. It was the first Tupolev aircraft to have such design features as leading-edge devices, thrust reversers or an auxiliary power unit. It was the first Soviet airliner to be certificated under Soviet airworthiness standards, which had not existed until 1967. Last but not least, the Tu-154 introduced new standards of comfort on medium-haul routes, and it has a well-earned reputation as a true airline workhorse.

To understand the Tu-154's background we have to travel back in time for half a century. When the British de Havilland Aircraft company brought out the 44-seat DH.106 Comet 1, which first flew on 27th July 1949 and became the world's first jet airliner to enter service on 2nd May 1952, the Soviet Union immediately felt the need to give the Western world an adequate answer – an indigenous jet airliner. This

politically important task was entrusted to the design bureau led by Andrey Nikolayevich Tupolev: OKB-156 – the nation's leading designer of commercial aircraft. The first Soviet commercial jet, which entered flight test on 17th June 1955 and performed the first revenue flight on 15th September 1956, was designated Tu-104 (NATO reporting name *Camel*). Thus was born a tradition – all subsequent Tupolev airliners were designated in the 1x4 (and later the 2x4 and 3x4) series, the Soviet answer to Boeing's 7x7 system. Designed as a 50-seater, the Tu-104 was gradually refined and the ultimate production version, the stretched-fuselage Tu-104B, seated 100.

When developing the Tu-104, in order to save time Andrey N Tupolev opted for maximum structural and systems commonality with the Tu-16 twin-turbojet medium bomber (NATO codename *Badger*) from which the wings, tail surfaces, powerplant and landing gear were borrowed. Shortly afterwards this design strategy was used again to create the mighty Tu-114 *Rossiya* (Russia; NATO codename *Cleat*) four-turboprop long-haul airliner as a derivative of the Tu-95 (NATO codename *Bear*) strategic bomber with a new fuselage mated to the existing wings, tail unit and landing gear. Predictably, this approach led to an over-strengthened and overweight airframe, but this was not the only drawback. In the case of the Tu-104 the mighty turbojets were buried in the wing roots (just like on the Comet), which led to high cabin noise levels. Nevertheless, these and other first-generation turbine-powered airliners took Aeroflot, the sole Soviet airline, to a qualitatively new level as regards service standards. Interestingly, for many years the Tu-104 was touted by the Soviet press as 'the world's first jet airliner'; no mention was made of the Comet – obviously it was acceptable to bend the facts a little for propaganda purposes.

In those years jet airliner technology developed quickly in the Soviet Union. Responding to the need to introduce jet hardware on short-haul services, the Tupolev OKB brought out the 44-seat Tu-124 (NATO codename *Cookpot*) which first flew on 30th March 1960 and entered service with Aeroflot on 2nd October 1962. Although a 'clean sheet of paper' design, it looked like a scaled-down Tu-104 with low-mounted wings, conventional swept tail surfaces and engines buried in the wing roots. What made the Tu-124 special, though, was the powerplant. This was the world's first turbofan airliner representing the second generation of

General Designer Andrey N. Tupolev, the founder of the OKB-156 design bureau which created the Soviet Union's first jet airliner. Tupolev PLC

turbine-powered commercial aircraft; it was powered by two 5,400-kgp (11,900-lbst) D-20P turbofans created by the OKB-19 aero engine design bureau headed by Pavel Aleksandrovich Solov'yov[2] – the first-ever commercial turbofan engine.[3] Later, the Tu-124 evolved into the rear-engined, T-tailed Tu-134 (née Tu-124A; NATO codename *Crusty*) on which the cabin noise problem was alleviated thanks to the new engine placement. The Tu-134, which first flew on 29th July 1963 and entered service on 9th September 1967, turned out to be one of the Tupolev OKB's most successful airliners.

Now, in the mid-1960s Aeroflot found itself operating three first-generation turbine-engined airliners on its medium-haul routes 1,500-3,500km (930-2,170 miles) long. These were the Tu-104, the Ilyushin IL-18 (NATO codename *Coot*) first flown on 4th July 1957 and the Antonov An-10 *Ookraïna* (the Ukraine; NATO codename *Cat*) first flown on 7th March 1957; the latter two types, which had been in revenue service since 20th April 1959 and 22nd July 1959 respectively, were powered by four Ivchenko AI-20 turboprops. While all three had had their share of teething troubles, eventually they had managed to build up a fairly good ser-

The Tu-104, the first Soviet medium-haul passenger jet. CCCP-42442 (c/n 920904) was a stretched Tu-104B; this version served as the starting point for the development of the Tu-154 which was to replace it. *Yefim Gordon archive*

vice record. Each of the three types had its strengths. The swept-wing, turbojet-powered Tu-104 had the highest cruising speed and offered the highest passenger comfort (notwithstanding the controversial engine placement); the An-10 offered the best field performance and soft-field capability, while the IL-18 boasted the longest range and the best operating economics. Yet, operating three very different aircraft in the same class (the design philosophy of Tupolev, Antonov and Ilyushin aircraft differed markedly) was a logistical and maintenance nightmare – no small thing, regarding the rapidly growing passenger traffic volumes which placed high demands on the regularity of flights and dispatch reliability.

Therefore, in the mid-1960s the need arose to replace the Tu-104, the IL-18 and the An-10 with one third-generation medium-haul airliner that would combine, so to say, the best of all three worlds; in particular, stringent demands were placed on field performance. Two of the three Soviet design bureaux specialising in transport aircraft took on the task, vying for the government order. The Tupolev OKB's contender was designated Tu-154, since the intervening designation, Tu-144, had already been allocated to a supersonic airliner; the competing Ilyushin project will be dealt with a while later. The Kiev-based GSOKB-473 led by Oleg Konstantinovch Antonov did not submit a contender – presumably because it was tasked with high-priority military airlifter projects which ultimately led to the An-22 Antey (Antheus; NATO codename *Cock*) and a jet airliner project would have overtaxed its resources.

For the first time in the Tupolev OKB's practice the Tu-154 was designed from the outset as a civil airliner with no military forebear. (Well, actually, as mentioned earlier, the Tu-124 and

Tu-134 were not warmed-over bombers either, but – remember the 'magic shrinking trick' with the Tu-104/Tu-124?) With the Tu-154, OKB-156 used 'pure civil' design practices, which included a prior study of the needs of both Aeroflot and potential foreign customers for the 15-20 years to come (that is, up to the early 1980s). We may just as well say now that this approach accounted in no small degree for the Tu-154's export success.

From the outset the new airliner was to incorporate a large number of novel features, drawing on the latest achievements of airliner design both in the Soviet Union and abroad. The objective was to create an aircraft that would match, or excel, the capabilities of the Boeing 727 three-turbofan medium-haul airliner which first flew on 9th February 1963.

Acknowledgements
The author wishes to thank all those who assisted and contributed (in whatever degree) to the making of this book: Aleksandr V Androsov, Aleksandr I Kirpichenko, Aleksandr V Lebedev, Stanislav I Looschchik, Viktor A Mashkin, Nikolai V Nalobin, Ivan D Nosych, Mikhail I Pronyakin, Aleksey V Romanov, Andrey D Sizykh and Boris N Terekhov (Vnukovo Airport Aviation Security), as well as Aleksandr P Boonaryov, Vladislav N Korzh, Aleksandr V Zaïtsev and Aleksandr I Zhoochkov (East Line Aviation Security) who gave ramp access at Moscow-Vnukovo and Moscow-Domodedovo, allowing valuable photos to be taken; Lydia N Anghelova, the late Ivan G Faleyev, Rudolf A Teymurazov and Natal'ya I Titova (CIS Interstate Aviation Committee) for providing access to the official records of civil Tu-154s which allowed a lot of production data (notably manufacture dates), operational details and accident reports to be included; Dmitriy Ye Kolesnik who helped resolve some queries associated with the Tu-154's design and operational service; Sergey Yu Panov who gave an insight into Tu-154 operations in the Russian Air Force;

Vladislav A Golubenko, Nikolai N Ionkin, Yuriy Kirsanov, Yuriy A Kotel'nikov and Viktor G Kravchenko who did the often risky job of spotting when the author was otherwise engaged, supplying photos and hot information on aircraft movements; Sergey S Tsvetkov and Vasiliy V Zolotov (*Mir Aviatsiï* magazine); Pyotr B Batooyev, Ernest V Katayev (*Aviatsiya* Magazine), Sergey D Komissarov, Sergey Krivchikov, Dmitriy A Petrochenko, Dmitriy Pichoogin, Ghennadiy F Petrov, Sergey Sergeyev, Igor' Sitchikhin, Aleksey M Yankitov (Nizhegorodskiye Airlines), Sergey S Yeriomin (Komiinteravia), Bob Archer, Aidan Curley, Peter G Davison, George Ditchfield, Nigel A Eastaway (Russian Aviation Research Trust), Scott Henderson, Chris Knott, Martín Novak, Pierre-Alain Petit and Bob Ogden who also provided assorted data and/or photos without which the book would have been so much the poorer; Andrey A Yurgenson who completed the line drawings used in this book; and Dmitriy S Makovenko who printed many of the photos used in this book with excellent quality.

Thanks are due to Russell Strong at Midland Publishing for taking the time and trouble to help the author with the page layout.

Special thanks go to Vladimir G Rigmant at the Tupolev Public Limited Company who supplied a lot of information on the type's history and a number of valuable original photographs.

Special thanks also go to Yefim I Gordon whose extensive archive and technical assistance with the photos was a great help.

Special thanks are also due to the editorial team of the excellent reference book *More than Half a Century of Soviet Transports* (Peter Hillman, Stuart Jessup, Adrian Morgan, Tony Morris, Guus Ottenhof and Michael Roch) who painstakingly collected data on Tu-154 operations worldwide. Not only did they kindly give permission to use this information but they also supplied this author with monthly updates to *Scramble* magazine, which has been instrumental in making the book as up-to-date as possible.

Chapter One

Genesis

A Camel with Three Humps

The first steps towards the Tu-154 were taken as early as 1963 when the preliminary design (PD) section of OKB-156 headed by Sergey Mikhaïlovich Yeger prepared the Tu-104D project. Actually to all intents and purposes this was a new aircraft, only the forward fuselage (up to and including the nosewheel well and the forward entry door), the landing gear and parts of the wing structure being retained. The circular-section fuselage had a maximum diameter of 3.5m (11ft 5¾in), which allowed six-abreast seating, and an extensively glazed navigator's station in the extreme nose, beneath which there was an RBP-4 Rubidiy-MM-2 weather/navigation radar[1] (NATO codename *Toad Stool*) in a chin radome. This 'bomber nose' was typical of nearly all Soviet airliners and transport aircraft designed in the late 1950s and early 1960s – the An-8 *Camp* twin-turboprop tactical transport, the An-10 and its transport derivative – the An-12 *Cub*, the huge An-22 four-turboprop strategic airlifter, the Tu-104 and its derivatives (the Tu-107 military transport and Tu-110 *Cooker* four-jet airliner), the Tu-114, the Tu-116 VIP transport, the Tu-124 and the Tu-134. In the case of the Tupolev aircraft this was indeed bomber heritage, since the Tu-104/-107/-110 and the Tu-114/-116 were derivatives of the Tu-16 and the Tu-95 respectively. A curious side effect of this arrangement on the Tupolev designs was that the captain and the first officer each had his own pair of throttles.

Everything else was quite different, though. Instead of two Mikulin AM-3 turbojets rated at 9,500kgp (20,940lbst) the Tu-104D was powered by three 9,580-kgp (21,120-lbst) NK-8 two-spool turbofans; this was a brand-new commercial engine developed by the OKB-276 design bureau under Nikolay Dmitriyevich Kuznetsov in Kuibyshev (now renamed back to Samara).[2] Two of the engines were housed in cylindrical nacelles flanking the rear fuselage sides, just like on the Tu-134; the third was buried in the rear fuselage and positioned further aft, breathing through a circular air intake with an S-duct passing through the fin's front

spar. In side elevation the centre engine air intake had a raked leading edge; this feature was meant to improve the engine's operating conditions. No thrust reversers were envisaged yet but, surprisingly, all three engines had multiple-lobe noise attenuation nozzles similar to the 'hushkits' fitted to some Western airliners. The reason why the author writes 'surprisingly' is that ambient noise was not an issue of particular importance in the Soviet Union – at least in those days.

The rear engine placement necessitated a new tail unit design: the conventional tail surfaces gave place to a T-tail similar to that of the Tu-124A/Tu-134. The tapered fin blending into the centre engine's air intake trunk had a fairly high aspect ratio and the fin/tailplane junction was enclosed by a prominent bullet fairing widening towards the rear.

Thanks to the rear-engine layout the Tu-104D had new aerodynamically 'clean' wings unencumbered by the engines. Still, as on the original design, the wing centre section spars encroached on the cabin, creating a raised floor with 'steps' and causing five cabin windows amidships on each side to be slightly raised above the rest. This was rather strange; on the original Tu-104 the 'steps', which were a major source of annoyance for passengers who kept tripping over them, had been caused by the spars passing over the engines; with no engines amidships it would have been logical to create a smooth cabin floor throughout, just as had been the case with the Tu-124A. Speak-

ing of windows and such, in common with the basic *Camel* the Tu-104D had cabin doors on the port side only; the window arrangement to port was door+5+door+5+11. An available project drawing does not show any emergency exits, although the basic Tu-104 had them; still, such drawings tend to be very provisional.

As with previous Tupolev swept-wing jets (both civil and military), wing sweep at quarter-chord was 35°. In common with the OKB's previous turbine-engined airliners and their bomber forebears, the main landing gear units retracted into elongated fairings protruding beyond the wing trailing edge (these fairings became a trademark feature of Tupolev aircraft designed in the 1950s and 1960s). As on the Tu-124 and Tu-134, the trailing edge occupied by large two-section flaps had a pronounced kink, running at right angles to the fuselage inboard of the landing gear fairings. In contrast, the Tu-104 and Tu-114 had constant trailing-edge sweep (although on the Tu-104B the trailing edge also featured a slight kink due to the increased chord of the outer flap sections). Large ailerons were installed outboard of the flaps. Two boundary layer fences were installed on each wing's upper surface to limit spanwise flow, delaying tip stall and improving aileron efficiency; this feature was also typical of many Tupolev aircraft.

The landing gear design was again typical of Tupolev's post-war heavy aircraft: all three units retracted aft, the four-wheel main gear bogies rotating through 180° to lie inverted in

Right: **Sergey M. Yeger, the Tu-154's first project chief.** Tupolev PLC

Far right: **Dmitriy S. Markov succeeded Yeger as the Tu-154's project chief in 1964; it was under his supervision that the aircraft materialised.** Tupolev PLC

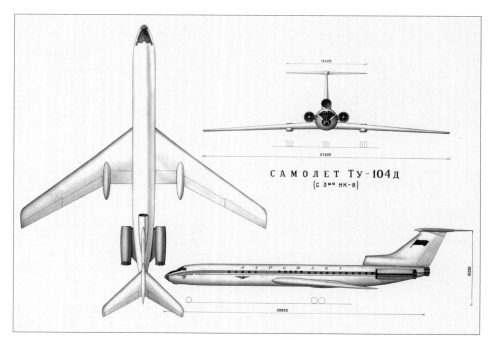

C A M O Л E T Tу - 104 Д
(C 3 ᴹᴿ HK-8)

the abovementioned fairings. Since the Tu-104's landing gear was borrowed from the Tu-16 bomber, the airliner sat fairly high above the ground.

Thus, with the exception of the landing gear design, the Tu-104D shared the general arrangement of the de Havilland DH.121 (later Hawker Siddeley HS.121) Trident, which first flew on 9th January 1962, and the Boeing 727. Now much has been said of the apparent Soviet custom of copying Western designs. However, even though industrial espionage is undeniably alive as can be, designers working on the same problem often arrive at similar solutions independently. Indeed, critics on this design aspect should be reminded of the similarity between the Trident and the 727 – and of the fact that the British accused Boeing of filching the Trident's layout (a claim which Boeing vehemently denied). Indeed, the low-wing, T-tail, rear-engine layout was very popular in the 1960s, finding use on the twin-turbofan BAC One-Eleven, Douglas DC-9 and Fokker F.28 Fellowship, the three-turbofan Yakovlev Yak-40 Codling, as well as the four-turbofan Ilyushin IL-62 Classic and Vickers VC-10.

The chosen layout offered a number of advantages. The 'clean' wings allowed relative flap area and wing efficiency to be increased. The aft fuselage and tail unit were less affected by vibration and tailplane buffet (caused by jet efflux), a phenomenon that could cause fatigue problems. Likewise, the high-set stabilisers were less affected by wing upwash, which improved longitudinal stability in cruise flight. In addition, this improved engine operating conditions thanks to the short inlet ducts, reduced foreign object damage (FOD) risk and facilitated engine maintenance and change (although in the case of the trijets the centre engine's S-duct could provoke engine surge, as the Boeing 727's testing revealed). Passenger comfort was greatly enhanced by the low

noise and vibration levels. Finally, there was no danger of engine fragments entering the cabin in the event of an uncontained engine failure.

Yet this layout also had some serious shortcomings. The wings were positioned further aft as compared to the normal layout, increasing fuselage area ahead of the centre of gravity (CG); this meant vertical tail area had to be increased to ensure adequate directional stability, with an attendant increase in structural weight. The fuselage and fin had to be reinforced, increasing empty weight and reducing the payload. CG travel was increased, and the high position of the thrust line produced a pitch-down force that increased rotation speed on take-off and elevator control forces. A highly dangerous (and as yet unknown) deep stall problem was inherent in the T-tail layout. Finally, maintenance of the tail unit became complicated, since a tall work platform was required to reach the horizontal tail.

The Tu-104D was to have a fuselage length of 39.65m (130ft 1in; the overall length is unknown), a wing span of 37.6m (123ft 4⁵⁄₁₆in) and a stabiliser span of 12.4m (40ft 8⅜in), standing 12.25m (40ft 2²⁄₃₂in) tall on the ground.

Enter the Tu-154

The Tu-104D did not last long: in 1964 the project began evolving into a new aircraft which, to underscore its newness, was allocated the designation '154' (Tu-154). The PD work lasted nearly two years, the aircraft changing appreciably in the process. Dmitriy Sergeyevich Markov was appointed the Tu-154's chief project engineer.

The very first project version bore a striking resemblance to the Tu-104D, featuring a glazed navigator's station and a chin radome. However, the maximum fuselage diameter was increased to 3.8m (12ft 5³⁄₄in) to create a roomier cabin and more capacious underfloor baggage holds; this allowed the wing centre

section spars to pass under the cabin floor, eliminating the annoying 'steps'. The flightdeck glazing was no longer identical to the Tu-104's – in fact, it strongly resembled that of the Tu-124/Tu-134, with four optically flat windshield panes, four triangular side windows and two eyebrow windows. The radar, too, was borrowed from the Tu-124/Tu-134 – it was the ROZ-1 Lotsiya (Navigational directions) weather/navigation radar[3] (NATO codename Toad Stool) enclosed by a smaller teardrop radome. The Tu-154's cabin windows were still circular and there were still no cabin doors on the starboard side; the window arrangement was door+1+10+door+1+12+small window to port and two small windows+1+10+small window+1+12+small window to starboard. The doors were now rectangular, not quasi-oval as in the earlier project.

The proportions of the Tu-154 had changed. Apart from the fatter fuselage, the wings were now located closer to the tail. In contrast, the Tu-104D's wings had been located about halfway along the fuselage length, resulting in proportions not unlike those of the future Boeing 727-200 (which appeared in 1967). The vertical tail-cum-air intake trunk still strongly resembled that of the Tu-104D but had a lower aspect ratio. The nacelles of the outer engines and their pylons were reshaped, as was the rear extremity of the fuselage which was extended to protrude beyond the rudder trailing edge; the conspicuous 'hushkit' nozzles of the Tu-104D were gone.

Another change concerned the landing gear, which was designed anew: the general arrangement was the same but the main gear bogies now had six wheels each (three pairs of wheels in tandem). Also, unlike the Tu-104, the new airliner featured semi-levered main gear suspension first used on the Tu-22 Blinder ('105A') bomber; the oleos were inclined when extended and a prominent telescopic retraction strut was attached to the front of the oleo. This allowed the main gear bogies to move aft by virtue of oleo compression in the event of hard braking or jolts, providing a very smooth touchdown and a smoother ride on the ground – which was just as well, considering the less-than-perfect runways and taxiways at many Soviet airports.

The 'glass-nosed' Tu-154 was envisaged in several layouts. One of them had a 109-seat first-class interior with ten rows of seats in the forward cabin and twelve in the rear cabin. All rows except the rearmost one had five-abreast

The first version of the Tu-154 project, which appeared in 1964, still had a Tu-104 style glazed nose and chin radome nose (although the flightdeck glazing is more like that of the Tu-124/Tu-134) but had a fatter fuselage. The doors are still on the port side only but the fin has a lower aspect ratio and the 'hushkits' are gone. This drawing shows a 109-seat first class layout with five-abreast seating; note the facing first two seat rows in each cabin with tables in between. Tupolev PLC

An early artist's impression of the Tu-154 from the project documents. The aircraft already has a 'solid' nose incorporating the radome. Of note are the position of the wings well aft on the fuselage, the Fokker F28-style smooth transition from fin leading edge to fin top (with no bullet fairing) and the absence of overwing emergency exits. Tupolev PLC

An exploded view of the Tu-154 dating back to an early design stage, as indicated by the metal upper half of the nosecone (the radome forms the lower half only). Note the three-piece wing design and the addition of overwing emergency exits and of service doors on the starboard side. Tupolev PLC

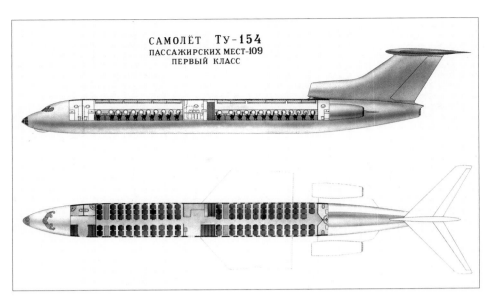

САМОЛЁТ Ту-154
ПАССАЖИРСКИХ МЕСТ-109
ПЕРВЫЙ КЛАСС

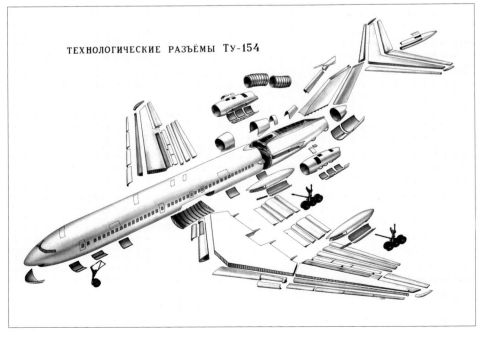

ТЕХНОЛОГИЧЕСКИЕ РАЗЪЁМЫ Ту-154

seating with an aisle offset to port (row 22 had four seats); the first row in each cabin faced aft, with tables between it and the next row. In the forward vestibule, two coat closets flanked the entry door, with toilets located opposite. A large galley with more coat closets aft of it on both sides was located amidships, opposite the rear (main) entry door, and two more toilets were placed at the rear of the cabin. Hence the small windows mentioned earlier were set rather high, since the front and rear ones were the toilet windows while the window amidships served the galley. An alternative version had six-abreast economy-class seating for 141 passengers and no central galley.

A different project version developed in parallel (which we will call No 2 for the sake of convenience) dispensed with the hitherto customary glazed navigator's station of Tupolev aircraft, featuring a more conventional 'solid' nose (the navigator now sat aft of the pilots). Unlike most commercial aircraft, however, only the lower half of the nosecone was dielectric at this stage; the upper half was a metal structure from which the revolving scanner of the ROZ-1 radar was suspended. (This arrangement had been first used by the OKB on the Tu-22 and would be used again on later military aircraft – the Tu-22M *Backfire* bomber, the Tu-160 *Blackjack* missile carrier and the Tu-134UBL *Crusty-C* crew trainer used for training pilots for both of these types.) The engine nacelles were positioned slightly lower, the aft extremity of the fuselage incorporating the No 2 engine nozzle was reshaped and the centre air intake had a vertically cut-off leading edge. The tail unit was altered, resembling that of the Boeing 727 – there was no bullet fairing projecting beyond the fin leading edge and the horizontal tail was set slightly lower (just below the top of the fin).

An alternative version (No 3) featured a different powerplant – four Solov'yov D-20P-125M

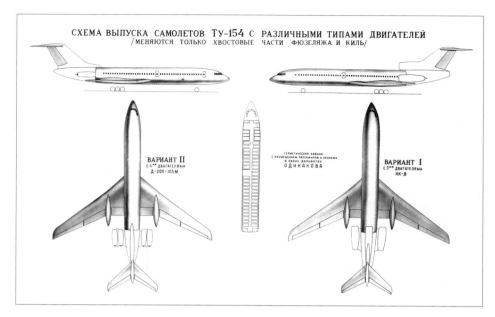

СХЕМА ВЫПУСКА САМОЛЕТОВ Ту-154 С РАЗЛИЧНЫМИ ТИПАМИ ДВИГАТЕЛЕЙ
/МЕНЯЮТСЯ ТОЛЬКО ХВОСТОВЫЕ ЧАСТИ ФЮЗЕЛЯЖА И КИЛЬ/

ВАРИАНТ II
С 4-мя ДВИГАТЕЛЯМИ
Д-20П-125М

ГЕРМЕТИЧЕСКАЯ КАБИНА
С РАЗМЕЩЕНИЕМ ПАССАЖИРОВ И ЭКИПАЖА
В ОБОИХ ВАРИАНТАХ
ОДИНАКОВА

ВАРИАНТ I
С 3-мя ДВИГАТЕЛЯМИ
NK-8

This drawing shows the alternative powerplants envisaged for the Tu-154; the version on the left has four Solov'yov D-20P-125M turbofans, while the one on the right has three NK-8s. With the exception of the rear fuselage and the vertical tail, the airframes are identical. Tupolev PLC

turbofans were arranged on the rear fuselage sides in horizontally paired nacelles, just like on the IL-62 and the VC-10. This engine was a version of the D-20P uprated from 5,400 to 5,800kgp (from 11,900 to 12,790 lbst), with a specific fuel consumption (SFC) reduced from 0.89 to 0.815kg/kgp·hr (lb/lbst·hr), and the D-20P-125 powered the Tu-134 prototypes. This brought about some structural changes (the centre air intake trunk and S-duct were replaced by a small root fillet and the fuselage had a normal tailcone). Small bullet fairings were fitted between each pair of intakes, and vertical splitters separated each pair of engine nozzles; no thrust reversers were provided. In all other respects versions 2 and 3 were identical. However, the aggregate thrust of four D-20P-125Ms (23,200kgp/51,150 lbst) was smaller than that of three NK-8s (28,740kgp/63,360 lbst), and the four-engined version was soon abandoned.

It should be noted that the choice of layout was influenced by two rather contradictory requirements – maximum fuel efficiency and maximum flight safety. The best fuel efficiency would be attained with a twin-engined aircraft, while the prevailing view in those days was that only a four-engined aircraft offered maximum reliability and safety. The designers at OKB-156 settled for a compromise – a trijet airliner.

In common with previous Tupolev jetliners, versions 2 and 3 of the Tu-154 project had neither leading-edge devices (the slightly kinked wing leading edge incorporated only de-icers) nor spoilers.

The 'radar-nosed' versions again had several interior layouts to choose from, including a 112-seat mixed-class layout and a 142-seat all-economy layout lacking the galley amidships. Available drawings (*very* provisional) suggest that service doors on the starboard side were added at this stage. One drawing shows the following window arrangement to port: door+17+door+6+emergency exit+2+exit+14; all doors and emergency exits incorporated windows (which were now rectangular with rounded corners) and the overwing emergency exits were of equal (small) size. The three baggage holds, two of which were pressurised, were accessed via doors on the starboard side.

And the Oscar Goes to...

By mid-1965, after numerous PD project versions and proposals had been considered, the outlook of the Tu-154 began to crystallise. The aircraft was to transport a payload of 16-18 tons (35,270-39,680 lb) over a distance of 2,850-4,000km (1,770-2,480 miles) with a cruising speed of 900km/h (559mph) or a payload of 5.8 tons (12,790 lb) over a distance of 5,800-7,000km (3,600-4,350 miles) with a cruising speed of 850km/h (528mph). The aircraft was to be capable of operating from Class B airfields even at its maximum take-off weight. (In the Soviet/Russian classification, Class B airfields are those with a runway length up to 2,600m (8,530ft) and Class A airfields are those with a runway length up to 3,250m (10,660ft); those with longer runways are termed as 'unclassed'.)

On 24th August 1965 the Soviet Council of Ministers (= government) issued Directive No 647-240 tasking the Tupolev OKB with designing and building the Tu-154 medium-haul airliner. The powerplant was specified as three NK-8-2 turbofans, again with a take-off rating of 9,580kgp – a lighter and more fuel-efficient version of the NK-8-4 powering the IL-62; the other stipulations of the document will be dealt with a while later.

By then the project had undergone further changes. The curious 'split nose' of parabolic shape ahead of the flightdeck windscreen gave place to a conventional 'full-face' dielectric radome having a slightly more conical shape. Four-section leading-edge slats were fitted outboard of the main gear fairings (for the first time on a Tupolev aircraft), and multi-section spoilers (one section inboard and three outboard) were located ahead of the flaps; the latter were triple-slotted – another 'first' for the OKB. The

two outer spoilers on each wing assisted the large ailerons for roll control; the remaining outer sections (immediately outboard of the main gear fairing) were airbrakes, while the innermost spoilers were actually lift dumpers deploying automatically on touchdown. The engine pylons were forward-swept and the structure around the centre engine nozzle had a strongly concave contour in side elevation (reminiscent of the forked fairing between the engine nozzles of the Mikoyan/Gurevich MiG-19 *Farmer* fighter). There were still no thrust reversers. This version reverted to the fin/tailplane bullet fairing, which now carried a 'spike' at the front incorporating an HF radio antenna; the centre engine air intake was now oval, not circular (for better integration with the fin), and had a vertical leading edge. Some project drawings show the window arrangement at this stage as door+4+large exit+12+door +4+small exit+4+small exit+19 to port and 4+large exit+10+service door+4+small exit+2+small exit+19 to starboard.

Several interior arrangements were proposed at this stage. In the so-called short-range version the cabin could be configured for either 146 passengers in an all-economy layout or 122 in a mixed-class layout. In the former case the forward cabin seated 48 six-abreast at 78cm (30¾in) seat pitch, followed by two units of three seats on the starboard side in the vestibule amidships and 92 seats at 75cm (29½in) pitch in the rear cabin. The latter had basically six-abreast seating, except for the rearmost row (four abreast) and the two rows ahead of it (five abreast with the aisle offset to port). The first two rows of seats in each cabin (and the two rows amidships) faced each other, with meal tables in between. The 122-seat layout featured a 24-seat first-class forward cabin with four-abreast seats at 102cm (40³⁄₃₂in) pitch. A toilet (to starboard) and a wardrobe (to port) were located between the forward vestibule and the forward cabin, with two more toilets at the rear extremity of the cabin. A so-called winter version seating 98 was similar to the 102-seater but the six seats amidships were removed and the No 2 vestibule was transformed into two extra wardrobes, rendering the rear entry door unusable.

The long-range version again had three varieties – an all-economy 134-seater, a 110-seat two-class arrangement and a 98-seat 'winter' version of the latter. Here, the two cabins were separated by a galley. The all-economy version had 48 seats at 78cm pitch in the forward cabin and 86 at 81cm (31⁵⁷⁄₆₄in) pitch in the rear one – six-abreast everywhere except the rearmost row (four abreast). The mixed-class version similarly had a 24-seat first-class forward cabin

These cabin layouts from the project documents show the so-called short-range version of the Tu-154 in a 146-seat all-economy layout (above) and a 122-seat mixed-class layout with a first-class forward cabin. Note the six seats amidships on the starboard side; the scrap view shows the 'winterised' version with a wardrobe replacing these six seats. Tupolev PLC

Two varieties of the so-called long-range version with a galley amidships from the same documents – a 134-seat all-economy layout and a 110-seat mixed-class layout. Again, the scrap view shows the 'winterised' version with two wardrobes aft of the galley. Tupolev PLC

The rival IL-74 project tendered by the Ilyushin OKB shared the Tu-154's three-engine, T-tail layout. The aircraft looks remarkably similar to the Hawker Siddeley Trident (note the fairing above the centre engine nozzle; the shape of the flightdeck glazing and the elliptical cabin windows reveal this is a close relative of the IL-62. Ilyushin Aircraft Complex

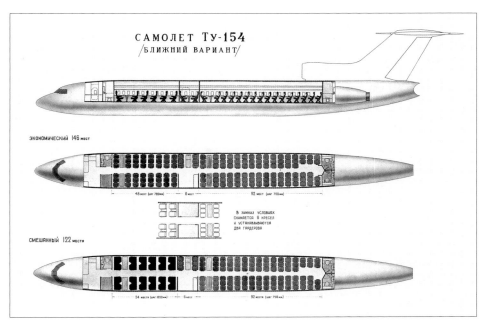

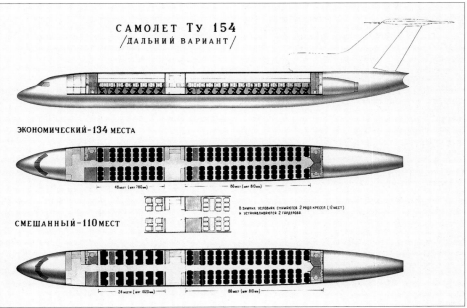

and an 86-seat economy-class rear cabin. Here, however, in the winter version the two rows immediately aft of the centre vestibule were eliminated and the aft-facing row and tables were moved aft accordingly.

A VIP version fitted with secure voice communications equipment was also envisaged. Opposite the forward entry door (meant for the crew) there were a toilet and a wardrobe. Immediately aft on the starboard side were two private sleeping compartments with sofas transformable into berths (for one and two persons respectively). A small enclosure with a communications officer's workstation was located opposite the No 1 compartment, with two armchairs and a table in between further aft (opposite the No 2 compartment). Next came the VIP cabin (called 'main passenger's cabin' in Soviet terminology) with large tables on either side; there were two-seat sofas on either side of the table to starboard, while the one to port was located between an identical sofa and a revolving armchair for 'Mr Himself'. Further aft were the galley and the second entry vestibule, with a wardrobe opposite the passenger entry door. Next came two more sleeping compartments with sofas (which, unlike the forward compartments, were mounted along the cabin walls instead of transversely) and a 44-seat cabin for the retinue with 11 four-abreast rows (the first two rows faced each other, with tables in between); three toilets were located at the aft extremity of the cabin.

Meanwhile, the OKB-240 design bureau led by Sergey Vladimirovich Il'yushin had been working on a competing design called IL-72 since 1964. The IL-72 resembled a slightly scaled-down version of the IL-62 long-haul airliner which was undergoing tests at the time – that is to say, it had low-set swept wings, a T-tail and four engines in paired nacelles flanking the rear fuselage. The wings were fitted with powerful high-lift devices (leading-edge slats and triple-slotted flaps) enabling the aircraft to operate from 2,000-m (6,560-ft) runways.

	Tu-154	IL-72	IL-74
Maximum take-off weight, kg (lb)	75,000-85,000 (165,340-187,390)	69,000-73,300 (152,120-161,600)	81,000 (178,570)
Weight empty, kg (lb)	39,600 (87,300)	35,600 (78,480)	n/a
Maximum payload, kg (lb)	14,000-16,000 (30,860-35,270)	14,000 (30,860)*	n/a
Efficient load ratio with max payload	47.2-54.1%	48.4-51.5%	n/a
Maximum tourist-class seating capacity	141	138	144
Range with max payload, km (miles)	4,550-6,450 (2,826-4,006)	4,100-4,850 (2,546-3,012)*	n/a
Range with max fuel, km (miles)	6,570-7,730 (4,080-4,801)	5,850 (3,633)	n/a
and a payload of, kg (lb)	6,000-10,000 (13,230-22,045)	7,500-10,000 (16,530-22,045)	n/a
Economical cruising speed, km/h (mph)	850-900 (527-559)	850-900 (527-559)	900 (559)
Cruise altitude, m (ft)	10,000-12,000	10,000-11,000	n/a

* Some sources say that the IL-72 was to have a range of 3,500km (2,175 miles) with a maximum payload of 18 tons (39,680 lb)
† With thrust reversers/noise attenuators
‡ Without thrust reversers/noise attenuators

A careful analysis revealed that the four-engined configuration was not a viable option for a medium-haul jet, as it entailed excessive maintenance costs reducing the aircraft's profitability. Hence the IL-72 project was abandoned in 1965 and a rework was begun which resulted in the appearance of the IL-74 airliner project in 1966. The 144-seat aircraft closely resembled its rival, the Tu-154, except for the lack of Tupolev's trademark main gear fairings (the main gear units retracted inward into the fuselage). The IL-74 was powered by three Solov'yov D-30I low-bypass turbofans rated at 6,800kgp (14,990 lbst) – an 'Ilyushinised' version of the engine powering the production Tu-134. Design specifications included a practical range of 3,900km (2,424 miles) in the 144-seat version with a 81,000-kg (178,570-lb) maximum take-off weight; in the 120-seat version the range was increased to 4,600km (2,859 miles). The aircraft was to have a cruising speed of 900km/h (559mph). The high-lift devices and the field performance were similar to the IL-72's. Comparative data for the three designs are given in the table above.

The design specifications of the two aircraft were subjected to comparative studies at the Ministry of Aircraft Industry (MAP – *Ministerstvo aviatsionnoy promyshlennosti*). Eventually the Ministry opted for the Tu-154 because this machine incorporated the latest theoretical and practical achievements of the Soviet aircraft industry and met Aeroflot's anticipated requirements for the 1970s/1980s more fully than the Ilyushin projects. Instead of the IL-74's manual controls, simple autopilot and fixed wing leading edge with a vortex generator 'dogtooth', it offered triplex fully hydraulic controls, a triplex automatic flight control system, triple-slotted flaps and slats.

On 20th-21st November 1965 the Ministry of Civil Aviation (MGA – *Ministerstvo grazhdahnskoy aviahtsii*) issued its preliminary specifications – or, to use a military term, specific operational requirement – for the Tu-154. These and the specifications set forth in the Council of Ministers directive of 24th August are compared in the table below. Interestingly, for the first time in Soviet aircraft design practice the documents specified the take-off weight.

The Tu-154 underwent more changes before the design was finally frozen. An additional LE slat section was fitted to each inner wing, with a gap (that is, a fixed portion of the leading edge) between it and the outboard sections. The innermost slat sections terminated quite a long way from the fuselage because the wing roots housed the heat exchangers and ducts of the air conditioning system. For the first time on a Tupolev aircraft, cascade-type thrust reversers were installed on the outer engines.

The list of 'firsts' was not limited to the LE devices and thrust reversers. The Tu-154 became the first Tupolev aircraft to have an auxiliary power unit (APU) for self-contained engine starting, ground power supply and air conditioning. The TA-6A APU (*toorboagregaht* – lit. 'turbo unit') was housed above the centre engine's jetpipe, breathing through two air intakes closed by doors on the sides of the fin and featuring a rear exhaust. Originally developed for the IL-62, this APU was a product of the Stoopino Machinery Design Bureau (SKBM – *Stoopinskoye konstrooktorskoye byuro mashinostroyeniya*),[4] alias KB-120, based in the town of Stoopino near Moscow.

For the first time, not only in the practice of the Tupolev OKB but in Soviet airliner design practice at large, the Tu-154 featured irreversible hydraulic actuators in all three control channels. This was a major step ahead because Andrey N Tupolev, who was known for his conservative approach, had always been distrustful of powered controls and had once remarked that 'the best hydraulic control actuator is the one which remains on the ground'. The Tu-154 was also the first Tupolev aircraft with a stable-frequency AC primary electric system featuring parallel operation of the engine-driven generators.

The aircraft featured the ABSU-154 automatic flight control system (AFCS; *avtomaticheskaya bortovaya sistema oopravleniya* – lit. 'automatic on-board control system') automating all flight modes, including landing approach. Initially this was designed to enable automatic approach in ICAO Cat I weather minima (decision altitude 60m/200ft, horizontal visibility 800m/2,620ft); later it was to be upgraded to ICAO Cat II requirements (decision altitude 30m/100ft, horizontal visibility 400m/1,300ft), facilitating night and poor-weather operations considerably. Incidentally, the Tu-154 was one of the first Tupolev aircraft to feature an integrated avionics suite. For the first time in Soviet airliner design practice the principal aircraft systems (hydraulics, electrics and so on) were made multiply redundant for maximum reliability and flight safety.

The Tu-154 had a design thrust/weight ratio of 0.35-0.36 versus 0.22-0.27 for most of the contemporary airliners. Such a high thrust/weight ratio could lead to an increased fuel burn per seat-mile, but it allowed the aircraft to operate from runways 1,500-1,800m (4,920-5,900ft) long and in hot-and-high conditions – an important asset in the Soviet Union's southern republics. Together with the carefully chosen wing airfoils this also gave the Tu-154 the highest cruising speed among contemporary airliners in the same class – up to 950km/h (590mph) – coupled with good stability and handling throughout the speed and altitude envelope.

The powerful high-lift devices not only afforded relatively low take-off and approach

	CofM Directive	MGA Specifications
Take-off weight, kg (lb)	77,000-80,000 (169,750-176,370)	77,000-80,000 (169,750-176,370)
Maximum payload, kg (lb)	18,000 (39,680)	15,000 (33,070)
Maximum seating capacity	160	160
SFC (NK-8-2 engines), kg/kgp·hr	0.76	0.76
Effective range, km (miles)	3,300-3,500	3,300-3,500
with maximum payload*	(2,050-2,174)	(2,050-2,174)
with a 15,500-kg (lb) payload	4,700-5,000 (2,919-3,105)	–
Airfield class	2	2

* at a cruising speed of 900km/h (559mph) and a cruise altitude of 11,000m (36,090ft) with 1-hour fuel reserves

This three-view pretty much reflects the final project configuration, except for the very provisional shape of the doors and the fact that no inboard leading-edge slat sections are shown. Tupolev PLC

A cutaway drawing of the Tu-154 from the project documents showing the 110-seat mixed-class layout. The engine type is already stated as NK-8-2. The inscriptions read (clockwise from the nose): flightdeck; toilet; wardrobe; galley; wardrobe; 104-seat cabin; toilets; flaps; spoilers; aileron; integral fuel tanks; entry door; 54-seat cabin (an obvious error, since the forward cabin seats 24!); entry door. Tupolev PLC

A desktop model of the Tu-154 photographed in August 1966; as is often the case with such models, the registration CCCP-65000 is fictional (in reality it belonged to a Tu-134A manufactured in December 1975!). Note the boundary layer fences 'wrapped around' the wing leading edge. S Preobrazhenskiy/ITAR-TASS

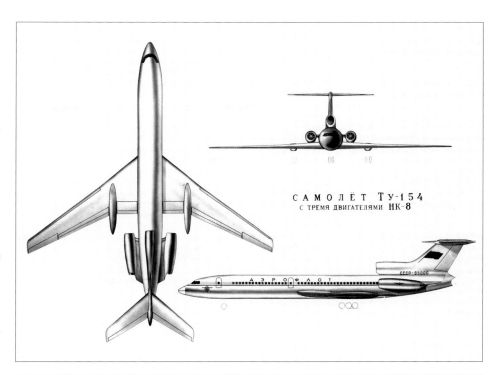

САМОЛЁТ Ту-154
С ТРЕМЯ ДВИГАТЕЛЯМИ НК-8

ПАССАЖИРСКИЙ САМОЛЕТ Ту-154
С 3-мя ТУРБОВЕНТИЛЯТОРНЫМИ ДВИГАТЕЛЯМИ НК-8-2

speeds but also gave the Tu-154 considerable possibilities for vertical manoeuvres – that is, the aircraft could both climb and descend more steeply, which reduced its noise footprint. Ambient noise was a major issue in the West, and the Soviet designers, knowing that the Tu-154 would serve destinations abroad, had to take account of this. In cruise flight the engines would operate at 70-75% of the nominal power, which would prolong engine life.

Here we may compare the Tu-154 with its US counterpart, the Boeing 727. Unlike the latter, which was designed to cruise at 7,600-9,150m (24,930-30,020ft), the Tu-154 was optimised for cruise at 11,000-12,000m (36,090-39,370ft). To this end the Soviet airliner had a greater wing area – 180m² (1,935.48ft²) versus 145m² (1,559.13ft²). Both of these factors helped reduce the cruise fuel burn. Thanks to the six-wheel main gear bogies the Tu-154's runway loading was nearly 50% lower than that of the Boeing 727-200 Advanced with its twin-wheel main gear units; in fully loaded condition it was 17,000-19,000kg (37,480-41,890lb) per unit versus 31,000-33,000kg (68,340-72,750lb). Having six wheels on each main gear unit instead of two also made the Tu-154's brakes more effective. On the other hand, the Tu-154 was more dependent on ground support equipment, since it had no integral airstairs, whereas the Boeing 727 had two.

As per the final project version the Tu-154 had the specifications as shown in the table on the following page.

At this stage the baseline version of the Tu-154 was configured as a 158-seater with 54 seats in the forward cabin and 104 in the rear one at 75cm pitch. The seats moved along the floor tracks at 30-cm (11¹³⁄₁₆in) increments, enabling alternative 110-, 122-, 146- and 134-seat versions. A 128-seat mixed-class version with 24 first-class seats four-abreast in the forward cabin was also envisaged, as was a 164-seat high-density version with a smaller galley for flights with a duration of up to two hours. In

the winter season an extra wardrobe was to be outfitted in the rear part of the cabin, replacing eight passenger seats. Finally, a VIP version was also developed for government flights.

A so-called mock-up review commission consisting of MAP and MGA representatives convened in December 1965 to inspect the full-scale wooden mock-up, hear reports on the project and point out any problems that needed to be addressed before the prototype was built. This was an obligatory stage in the development of Soviet aircraft. As was most often the case, the commission gave the go-ahead. The prototype was to be completed in the spring of 1967, the first production aircraft following in the autumn of that year.

Production was initially planned to take place at MMZ No 30 'Znamya truda' (*Moskovskiy mashinostroitel'nyy zavod* – Moscow Machinery Plant No 30 'Banner of Labour', pronounced **znahmya trooda**),[5] which was located at the now-defunct Central Airfield named after Mikhail Vasil'yevich Frunze almost smack in the middle of Moscow (the field is better known as Khodynka). However, this plant was burdened with two important programmes, manufacturing Mikoyan MiG-21 *Fishbed* tactical fighters (both for the Soviet Air Force and for export) and launching production of the new-generation MiG-23 *Flogger* tactical fighter. Therefore, MAP reassigned the Tu-154 to aircraft factory No 18 in Kuibyshev, alias KuAZ (**Kuibyshevskiy aviatsionnyy zavod** – Kuibyshev aircraft factory).[6] NK-8 production was already under way at the Kazan' aero engine plant No 27, alias KMPO (*Kazahnskoye motorostroitel'noye proizvodstvennoye obyedineniye* – Kazan' engine production association).[7]

A large-scale model of the Tu-154 in the T-101 wind tunnel at TsAGI, Zhukovskiy. RART

Final Project Specifications of the Tu-154

Wing span	37.55m (123' 2¹¹⁄₃₂")
Length overall	47.9m (157' 1⁵³⁄₆₄")
Height on ground	11.4m (37' 4¹³⁄₁₆")
Wing area, m² (ft²):	
net	180.0 (1,935.48)
gross	201.5 (2,166.66)
Normal take-off weight, kg (lb)	78,000-78,500 (171,960-173,060)
Maximum take-off weight, kg (lb)	86,000 (189,590)
Empty weight, kg (lb)	40,200 (88,620)
Payload, kg (lb):	
normal	16,000 (35,270)
maximum	18,000 (39,680)
Maximum seating capacity	164
Cruising speed at 11,000m (36,090ft), km/h (mph)	1,000 (621)
Economic cruising speed at 11,000-12,000m (36,090-39,370ft), km/h (mph)	900 (559)
Optimum cruising speed at 11,000-12,000m (for maximum range), km/h (mph)	850 (527)
Effective range at 900km/h with a 78,000-80,000-kg (171,960-176,370-lb) TOW, km (miles):	
with a 18,000-kg (39,680-lb) payload	2,850 (1,770)
with a 16,000-kg (35,270-lb) payload	3,300 (2,050)
with a 13,000-kg (28,660-lb) payload	4,000 (2,484)
with a 9,000-kg (19,840-lb) payload	4,950 (3,074)
with a 5,800-kg (12,790-lb) payload	5,600 (3,478)
Effective range at 850km/h with a 86,000-kg (189,600-lb) TOW, km (miles): *	
with a 18,000-kg payload	4,200 (2,608)
with a 16,000-kg payload	4,700 (2,919)
with a 6,000-kg (13,230-lb) payload	7,000 (4,347)
Take-off run with normal TOW, ISA, m (ft)	800-900 (2,620-2,950)
Required runway length for take-off, m (ft):	
ISA	1,250-1,500 (4,100-4,920)
at +15°C (+59°F) and 730mm Hg	1,750 (5,740)
Landing run, m (ft):	
without the aid of thrust reversers	590 (1,935)
with thrust reversers	550 (5,740)
Required runway length for landing, m (ft):	
without the aid of thrust reversers	1,220 (4,000)
with thrust reversers	970 (3,180)
Crew	3
Designated service life	30,000 hours

* with auxiliary fuel tanks in the wing centre section

Chapter Two

The Only Way is Up Now

Assembly of the Tu-154 prototype and a static test airframe began in 1968 at MMZ No 156 'Opyt', the OKB's experimental plant in Radio Street, Moscow (the name translates as either 'experiment' or 'experience'). Of course, the prototype was virtually hand-crafted and, in view of the size of the machine, it took quite a long time to complete.

It has to be said here that, unlike Western aircraft manufacturing companies, the Soviet/CIS aircraft design bureaux had no factories of their own – only very limited production facilities for prototype manufacturing. After completing the prototypes and static test airframes a Soviet OKB would turn over the manufacturing drawings to a production factory within the MAP system. Of course, the OKB would keep an eye on production and assist the factory during the learning curve, overseeing the introduction of changes on the production line – but it had no control over the factory. On the other hand, strong ties would be forged eventually, and this or that factory tended to specialise in the products of a particular OKB for technological commonality reasons. This was the case with the Kuibyshev aircraft factory – it had built Tupolev products before, whereas MMZ No 30 had not, being associated with the Ilyushin and Mikoyan bureaux (OKB-240 and OKB-155).

The prototype was registered CCCP-85000 and bore the construction number KKh1 (although some sources give the prototype's c/n as 67-KH1). This represented a departure from the normal Soviet practice of breaking the production run down into batches (in the case of Tupolev heavy aircraft the first prototype typically had the c/n 00-00 – batch zero, aircraft zero). (Note: Under the Soviet/CIS five-digit registration system in use since 1958 the first two digits are usually a type designator introduced for flight safety reasons (this allows air traffic control officers to identify the aircraft type by its registration and thus avoid placing excessive demands on the crew).[1]

The prototype had 46 cabin windows to port (entry door+18+entry door+7+exit+2+exit+15) and 42 to starboard (4+exit+10+service door+7+exit+2+exit+15). Additionally, there were three small circular windows in the cabin roof (two on the rear fuselage sides next to the outer engines and one offset to starboard just aft of the flightdeck) for the toilets. All three doors opened outward and forward on L-shaped swinging arms, moving in parallel to the fuselage side – just like the passenger doors of a typical modern coach. The foremost

emergency exit to starboard was almost as big as the service door, while the forward pair of the overwing emergency exits was smaller than the rear one (the width was identical but the sills of the forward pair were placed higher).

There were three rectangular baggage loading doors (opened by pushing inwards and sliding forward) on the starboard side. While the forward one was conventionally located halfway between the foremost emergency exit and the service door, the No 2 baggage door was immediately aft of the wing trailing edge and was partially obstructed by the wing/fuselage fairing. Hence the rear end of the latter was hinged, swinging outward through 180° to give access to the door. The door of the unpres-

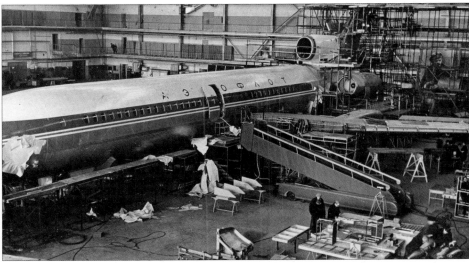

CCCP-85000, the Tu-154 prototype, takes shape in Shop 10 of the Tupolev OKB' experimental production facility (MMZ 'Opyt'). This view shows clearly the cutout for the wing torsion box, the three baggage loading doors, the attachment ribs for the engine nacelle/pylon assemblies (mounted in a nose-up attitude) and the installation of the centre engine air intake trunk. The forward cabin emergency exit and the service door amidships are of equal size, but the overwing emergency exits are not. Tupolev PLC

Another view of the prototype nearing completion in Shop 10; the machine has already received a coat of paint. Note how the doors open outward and forward while staying parallel to the fuselage side; an SPT-104 mobile gangway is parked alongside for access. Tupolev PLC

Left: The prototype at the Tupolev OKB's flight test facility in Zhukovskiy following reassembly. Note that the forward entry door is heavily outlined and the anti-glare panel on the nose extends across the radome. In keeping with the custom of the time the aircraft wears a large Tupolev OKB badge on the nose. Tupolev PLC

Centre: Another view of the prototype posing for an 'official photo session'. The rudder is still unpainted. Tupolev PLC

Bottom: Another view of CCCP-85000 at Zhukovskiy, showing the hexagonal nose gear door segment linked to the oleo strut. Tupolev PLC

Opposite page:

Top left: Front view of the Tu-154 prototype. Note the open hatch of the forward avionics bay ahead of the nosewheel well and the air intakes of the air conditioning system heat exchangers in the wing roots. The dielectric panel of the Doppler speed/drift sensor immediately aft of the radome is barely visible in this view.

Top right: The prototype's tail unit and rear fuselage; the thin spike at the front of the fin/tailplane fairing is well visible. Vortex generators are fitted to the rudder and the elevators; the curved fixture immediately aft of the rudder is for ground tests only, serving for checking the rudder travel; the APU exhaust is closed by a cover. Note the flush short-range radio navigation (SHORAN) antenna in the middle of the Soviet flag and the L-shaped aerial just above it; the dielectric portions of the fin/tailplane fairing house radio antennas.

Right: The port side of the prototype's centre fuselage. Note the 'cut here in emergency' stencils below the A of the Aeroflot titles, the sensors in the centre engine air intake and the early-model deeply recessed air intake cover on the port engine. All Tupolev PLC

surised No 3 baggage compartment was located, rather inconveniently, below the starboard engine pylon.

A peculiarity of the prototype as originally completed was the nosewheel well closed by three doors, the hexagonal forward door being attached to the nose gear oleo in similar manner to the Tu-22 bomber. Another peculiarity was the APU exhaust, which was flush with the curved fairing forming the transition between the rudder and the centre engine nozzle; it was surrounded by a heat-resistant steel plate. The APU intakes were closed by doors rotating into horizontal position on axles running down their middle. The fairing at the fin/tailplane junction had a blunt dielectric rear end and a slender spike at the front whose root portion was also dielectric; these dielectric portions concealed antennas for an HF radio.

Until the mid-1970s each type of aircraft in Aeroflot's fleet had a colour scheme of its own. The Tu-154 had a white fuselage top and vertical tail, a bright blue cheatline underlined by a red pinstripe on white, a dark blue fin/tailplane fairing, natural metal wings, horizontal tail, lower fuselage and engine nacelles, and a black anti-glare panel encroaching on the white radome. The Soviet flag was painted on the fin in a 'flying' presentation (as was customary at the time), the black Aeroflot titles were in widely spaced small letters and the airline's winged hammer and sickle logo (irreverently referred to by some people as *koo*ritsa, 'chicken'!) was carried on the engine nacelles. In common with previous Tupolev airliners the Tu-154 carried the OKB's round badge with the Cyrillic letters 'Tu' on both sides of the nose. The forward entry door and the service door were heavily outlined in red (as per ICAO requirements) but, strangely enough, the other doors and exits were not.

In the second half of 1968 the prototype was trucked to the airfield of the Flight Research Institute named after Mikhail M Gromov (LII – *Lyot*no-is*sled*ovatel'skiy insti*toot*) in the town

of Zhukovskiy south of Moscow where OKB-156, like most other Soviet aircraft design bureaux, had its flight test facility. Once the aircraft had been reassembled, ground systems checks began. Meanwhile the static test airframe commenced tests at the OKB's structural test laboratory; these lasted from November 1968 to May 1970, progressing in parallel with the flight tests.

The maiden flight took place on 3rd October 1968. The airliner was flown by captain Yuriy V Sookhov, co-pilot Nikolay N Kharitonov and flight engineer V I Yevdokimov; test programme project engineer L A Yumashev, test engineer Yu G Yefimov and electrics engineer Yu G Kooz'menko were also aboard on the first flight. After the first 12 flights and modifications made as a result of these, CCCP-85000 commenced joint trials – that is, trials held jointly by the manufacturer (the Tupolev OKB) and the customer (MGA), represented by the State Civil

Aviation Research Institute (GosNII GA – *Gosoodarstvennyy naoochno-issledovatel'skiy institoot grazhdahnskoy aviahtsii*). Stage One of the trials lasting from December 1968 to January 1971 was, in effect, the manufacturer's flight tests and was performed by the OKB at the LII airfield in Zhukovskiy. Stage Two, which corresponded to the usual state acceptance trials (the Soviet equivalent of certification trials), lasted from June to December 1971. A succession of test crews put the Tu-154 through its paces; they were captained by S T Agapov, V P Borisov, I K Vedernikov, Boris I Veremey, Yevgeniy A Goryunov, Nikolay Ye Kool'chitskiy, V M Matveyev, Andrey I Talalakin and V I Shkatov.

Three years is quite a long test cycle by Western standards. It should be noted at this point that, as distinct from the Western world, the Soviet Union had no airworthiness regulations or certification bodies and procedures

The Tu-154 prototype in an early test flight in November 1968; the camera ship was a Tu-124. Note the boundary layer fences 'wrapped around' the wing leading edge and the small windows for the toilets in the cabin roof just aft of the flightdeck and near the engine nacelle.
E Kassin/ITAR-TASS

CCCP-85000 banks away from the camera ship, showing the large ailerons and the flap track fairings. The characteristic curvature of the centre engine nozzle shroud is well visible.
E Kassin/ITAR-TASS

Another view of CCCP-85000 flying above thick overcast during an early test flight.
Tupolev PLC

The flightdeck of Tu-154 CCCP-85000 during a test flight. The crew is attired according to the mission but, surprisingly, only the flight engineer (right), the radio operator (left) and the navigator wear modern ZSh-7 'bone dome' helmets while both pilots make do with old-fashioned leather helmets. Sergey and Dmitriy Komissarov collection

until 1967. Aircraft were designed to common-sense criteria derived by trial and error, or ones read-across from general mechanical engineering standards, and tested basically to make sure they met the performance targets they were supposed to meet. The first Soviet common airworthiness regulations were drafted in the 1960s and introduced in 1967 as the NLGS (*Normy lyotnoy godnosti samolyotov* – airworthiness regulations for fixed-wing aircraft; later known retrospectively as the NLGS-1). The Tu-154 was the first Soviet aircraft to be developed to these standards, and this delayed progress considerably.

In 1969 the manufacturer's flight tests were briefly interrupted so that the Tu-154 could make its international debut at the 27th Paris Air Show. Before this could happen, however, some preparatory work was needed: the test equipment racks in the cabin had to be removed and a representative airline interior fitted. On 25th May CCCP-85000 appeared at Paris-Le Bourget, wearing the exhibit code 828. Western aviation experts and journalists and the public at large were allowed to examine the flightdeck and the comfortable cabin. By then the aircraft had logged about 100 hours in 43 flights.

Of course, the Western world had been aware of the Tu-154's existence for some time by then, and the new trijet received the NATO reporting name *Careless* (C for commercial). Inevitably, Western observers began comparing the Tu-154 with its American counterpart, and the sobriquet '727ski' came into existence. Western observers noted 'the Soviet adherence to simplified flightdeck instrumentation – very sparse looking for an aircraft of this size and complexity – in which the dominant feature was a centrally-mounted moving map display; the unusual six-wheeled main undercarriage bogies; and the general inattention to aerodynamic detail'.

On 12th August 1969 a special promotional flight was made between Moscow-Vnukovo and Moscow-Sheremet'yevo for the benefit of the press.

As the flight tests progressed, aircraft plant No 18 (KuAZ) started tooling up to build the Tu-154; the first metal for the first Kuibyshev-built example was cut in 1968. Before that, however, the Tupolev OKB was forced to make changes to the design, which had been optimised for the plant originally intended (MMZ No 30), and adapt it to the different production techniques used by the Kuibyshev plant. Inevitably, this caused delays and was detrimental to the manufacturing quality of the first production (or rather pre-production) machines. The first of these was rolled out at Kuibyshev-Bezymyanka in 1969 and the rest followed in 1970, joining the prototype in the joint trials programme. Nevertheless, KuAZ managed to sort out the first serious problems fairly quickly and manufacture an initial batch of ten Tu-154s, subsequently modifying these aircraft in accordance with the trials/evaluation results and introducing the changes on the production line.

Actually the word 'batch' is not quite applicable here. In the Soviet Union, and later the Commonwealth of Independent States (CIS), aircraft production was traditionally organised in batches, usually with the same number of airframes in each batch (although this could change as production progressed). The batch number and the number of the aircraft within the batch were reflected in the machine's construction number (manufacturer's serial number). Yet there is always an exception to the rule, and the Tu-154 was one. Tu-154 production was not split into batches; instead, the c/n consisted of a sequential three-digit line number prefixed by the year of manufacture and a letter that presumably was an in-house product code. Thus, the first pre-production example, CCCP-85701 (later reregistered CCCP-85001) was c/n 69M001 – that is, year of manufacture 1969, *izdeliye* M, and 001st Kuibyshev-built example.[2] In 1971, when the Tu-154 entered full-scale production, the product code was changed to A; for example, CCCP-85031 manufactured on 24th November 1972 is c/n 72A031.

The last three digits of the c/n are embossed on four small metal plates riveted to the inside of the small mainwheel well doors (near the main gear fulcrums). As often as not, however, they are *extremely* hard to read or completely illegible because they have been overpainted more than once during the aircraft's service life and the digits are really tiny. However, the last three digits of the c/n are also embossed on the front of both main gear oleos, together with the letter Л (the Cyrillic 'L', standing for *levaya* – left-hand) on the port strut and the letter П (the Cyrillic 'P', standing for *pravaya* – right-hand) on the starboard strut). Finally, they are stencilled on every panel in the baggage compartments, preceded by the number of the panel ('1 467', '2 467', '3 467' and so on). The full c/n (with the year of manufacture) is found only in the aircraft's record card or other papers. Sometimes, however, the actual manufacture date does not match the year suggested by the c/n – for instance, Tu-154Bs CCCP-85189 and CCCP-85190 (c/ns 76A189 and 76A190) were both manufactured on 8th June 1977, six months later than the aircraft that followed. A production list is provided in Appendix 1 at the end of the book.

Curiously, the first four pre-production machines were laid down as CCCP-85701 through -85704 and wore these registrations at the final assembly stage but were apparently reregistered CCCP-85001 through -85004 before being flown. Thus was born a tradition –

the last three digits of a Soviet Tu-154's registration matched the last three of the c/n (that is, until the Tu-154M came on the scene – see next chapter). Therefore, when export deliveries began, export aircraft started 'biting holes' in the Soviet registration sequence (thus, there was no Aeroflot aircraft registered CCCP-85036 because c/n 73A036 was a Bulgarian aircraft, LZ-BTC). The registrations CCCP-85701 through -85704 were reused much later for four Tu-154Ms.

In addition to the basic programme of the joint trials, the pre-production Tu-154s were involved in several special test programmes. Thus, CCCP-85001 and CCCP-85002 (c/n 70M002?) were used to explore the Tu-154's behaviour at high angles of attack, including stall and spin tests (these became a mandatory part of the test programme after several Tu-104s stalled and crashed at low speed). To this end CCCP-85002 was fitted with a spin recovery parachute in a fairing with a hinged hemispherical cover at the base of the fin; this required the APU to be removed and the aircraft had to rely on ground air supply for engine starting. One of the doors was modified to serve as an escape hatch for bailing out, should spin recovery become impossible.

The tests were not altogether without incident. On one occasion the latches on one of the entry doors on CCCP-85006 failed and the

Aeroflot stewardesses Svetlana Sviridova, Tat'yana Timashkova and Tat'yana Artyomova (left to right) pose for a publicity photo in the first prototype's forward cabin outfitted in a first-class configuration for demonstration purposes in November 1968. E. Kassin/ITAR-TASS

Tu-154 CCCP-85000 made the type's international debut. Wearing the exhibit code 828 near the forward entry door, the aircraft is seen here at the 1969 Paris Air Show in company with the first prototype Tu-134A (CCCP-65624, coded '827'), an IL-62 and the Royal Air Force's McDonnell Douglas F-4M-33-MC XV395.
Aerosport No 8-1969

door opened partially, thus depressurising the aircraft – luckily without any disastrous consequences.

In addition, the pre-production Tu-154s were used for publicity flights abroad. For instance, the same CCCP-85006 made the type's first appearance at Prague-Ruzyne.

The OKB kept modifying the aircraft throughout the trials programme. Changes were made to the flap control system and the ABSU-154 AFCS. The latter was first tested on a Tu-124 operated by LII (CCCP-45003; c/n 0350102?), which served as a testbed for the ABSU-154 between 1969 and 1978; concurrently the system was continuously refined, using several Tu-154s, including CCCP-85003 and Tu-154A CCCP-85055 (c/n 74A055). Several Tu-154s served for refining the powerplant and various other systems; among other things, CCCP-85005 (c/n 70M005) was a testbed for a modified navigation suite.

As already mentioned, Dmitriy S Markov had been the Tu-154's chief project engineer from the outset; it was he who held overall responsibility for the airliner, shouldering the many problems arising in the course of the Tu-154's trials and production entry. Later, when the Tupolev OKB embarked on new military programmes Markov was reassigned to bombers, Aleksandr Sergeyevich Shengardt became the Tu-154's new project chief on 25th May 1975.

The specifications and performance shown on this page were recorded at the manufacturer's flight test stage.

The tests showed that the Tu-154 basically met the performance target. On the minus side, the reliability of some design elements and systems was still inadequate; ease of maintenance during routine operations still left something to be desired, and so did the cabin layout. The main tasks facing the aircraft's designers now lay in ensuring an adequately long designated service life and introducing ICAO Cat II automatic blind landing capability (decision altitude 30m/100ft, horizontal visibility 400m/1,300ft). It may as well be said now that these two problems kept the OKB busy right up until the advent of the ultimate version, the Tu-154M.

On 17th May 1971, when the joint trials were almost completed, the Tu-154 was demonstrated to the Soviet government at Moscow/Vnukovo-2 (the government VIP terminal)

Wing span	37.55m (123' 2¹¹⁄₃₂")
Length overall	47.9m (157' 1⁵³⁄₆₄")
Height on ground	11.4m (37' 4¹³⁄₁₆")
Wing area, m² (ft²):	
net	180.0 (1,935.48)
gross	201.45 (2,166.12)
Maximum take-off weight, kg (lb)	90,000 (198,410)
Maximum payload, kg (lb)	15,500 (34,170)
Maximum seating capacity	144/152
SCF of the NK-8-2 engines, kg/kgp·hr (lb/lbst·hr)	0.79
Cruising speed at 11,000m (36,090ft), km/h (mph)	1,000 (621)
Maximum speed, km/h (mph):	
with a 63,000-kg (138,890-lb) all-up weight	982 (610)
with a 73,000-kg (160,930-lb) all-up weight	960 (596)
Effective range with a 80,000-kg (176,370-lb) TOW and 1,805kg (3,980 lb) of fuel reserves, km (miles)	4,240 (2,633)
Effective range with a 90,000-kg TOW and 3,190kg (7,030 lb) of fuel reserves, km (miles)	4,470 (2,776)
Effective range with a 90,000-kg TOW and a 15,500-kg payload, km (miles)	2,560 (1,590)
Maximum range with a 90,000-kg TOW and a 15,500-kg payload, km (miles)	2,560 (1,590)
Take-off run with a 71,500... 82,500-kg (157,630... 181,880-lb) TOW, m (ft)	730-1,100 (2,395-3,610)
Balanced field length with a 71,500... 82,500-kg TOW, m (ft)	1,070-1,550 (3,510-5,085)
Landing run with a 56,500-65,000-kg (124,560-143,300-lb) landing weight, m (ft):	
without the aid of thrust reversers	610-730 (2,000-2,395)
with thrust reversers	760-880 (2,490-2,890)

together with the IL-62M, Tu-134A and Yak-40 airliners.

The prototype was retained by the OKB, serving for several years as a 'dogship' for testing new features. Eventually it was struck off charge and finally broken up.

Following retirement in the mid-1970s, some of the pre-production airliners found further use. Thus, in 1977 Tu-154 CCCP-85005 (c/n 70M005) was put on display at the VDNKh fairground (**Vys**tavka dosti**zhen**iy na**rod**novo kho**ziay**stva – National Economy Achievements Exhibition) in Moscow, succeeding the first prototype Tu-134 (CCCP-45075) which had been there since mid-1968. Thus it became the first Tu-154 to be preserved. To this day CCCP-85005 graces the fairground's central plaza in company with another Soviet medium-haul trijet – a pre-production Yakovlev Yak-42 *Clobber* (CCCP-42304), which similarly replaced another Yakovlev product (a Yak-40 *Codling* feederliner, CCCP-19661) at the VDNKh.

Tu-154 CCCP-85000 on the north apron at Moscow-Sheremet'yevo (now Moscow/Sheremet'yevo-1) beside the recently completed 'mushroom' concourse in August 1969. Tupolev PLC

CCCP-85001 (ex-CCCP-85701 No 1), the first Tu-154 built by the production plant in Kuibyshev, pictured during tests. Like the prototype, it has L-shaped aerials on the sides of the fin (albeit located differently, in the middle of the Soviet flag). Note the circular air outlets at the base of the fin on both sides (the prototype had rectangular outlets) and the small lateral nose gear doors replacing the original forward-mounted door. Tupolev PLC

CCCP-85006, another initial production Tu-154 used in the test programme, with the high-lift devices fully extended, the flight spoilers deployed and the forward entry door open. Tupolev PLC

CCCP-85006 was also used a good deal for demonstration flights during the Tu-154's evaluation period. Sergey and Dmitriy Komissarov collection

Chapter Three

Versions

Over the years the Tu-154 has been steadily developed with a view to rectifying its initial weaknesses and improving performance; specialised versions have also appeared. These are dealt with in this chapter.

Tu-154 Medium-haul Airliner

As already mentioned, the first pre-production example of the initial version (known simply as the Tu-154) was completed in 1969, and full-scale production commenced in 1971. The MiG-23 fighter had a version known among pilots as **dvah**dsat' **tre**tiy 'bez **book**vy' – 'MiG-23 with no [suffix] letter', or sans suffixe;[1] by analogy the initial production version of the Tu-154 will be referred to hereinafter as the Tu-154 sans suffixe.

The first external change was introduced on the pre-production examples. The forward-mounted hexagonal nose gear door segment of the prototype created strong drag when the landing gear was down; therefore it was replaced by a pair of lateral doors mechanically linked to the nose gear oleo. The aircraft's registration digits were repeated on these doors to facilitate identification if the tail was not visible. The boundary layer fences were shortened so that their front ends no longer wrapped around the wing leading edge. One change that was not visible lay inside the radome: the ROZ-1 radar fitted to the prototype gave place to the Groza-154 (Thunderstorm, pronounced gro**zah**) weather radar.[2]

The production version was displayed for the first time at the 28th Paris Air Show, which opened on 20th May 1971. Tu-154 sans suffixe CCCP-85012 was shown statically with the exhibit code 452.

As soon as the Tu-154 entered production, the Tupolev OKB started improving the design.

Tu-154 sans suffixe CCCP-85012, the first of the production aircraft to be shown abroad; here it is seen at Le Bourget during the 1971 Paris Air Show. Early-production aircraft wore the same livery as the prototype. Yefim Gordon archive

Seen from a Tu-134 chase plane, Tu-154 sans suffixe CCCP-85012 shows the exhibit code 452 with which it was displayed in Paris. Aviaexport

The final Tu-154s sans suffixe, including CCCP-85041 (shown here on short finals with the flaps fully deployed and stabiliser trim evident), had a lengthened APU exhaust with a vertically cut-off end which became standard on all later Kuznetsov-powered examples.
Sergey and Dmitriy Komissarov collection

The first production machines still had the prototype's flush APU exhaust; from Tu-154 *sans suffixe* CCCP-85038 (c/n 73A038) onwards an extended APU jetpipe with a vertically cut-off rear end was introduced. The APU air intakes were redesigned at the same time. Instead of revolving on horizontal axles the intake doors were hinged along the trailing edge and opened outward to form air scoops; this made it easier to start the APU in flight by windmilling.

For some reason the ICAO Cat I blind landing capability target was not met with the Tu-154 *sans suffixe*. The initial production version with an ABSU-154 Srs 1 AFCS was cleared for automatic approach with a decision altitude of 100m (330ft) and horizontal visibility of at least 1,200m (3,940ft).

A total of 42 Tu-154s *sans suffixe* was reportedly built. However, a report on the Tu-154's programme status submitted by Sergey M Yeger to Minister of Defence Marshal Dmitriy F Ustinov on 28th February 1975 contains a self-contradictory phrase: '*The Kuibyshev aircraft factory has manufactured 92 Tu-154s – 42 examples of the Tu-154 [sans suffixe] and 50 Tu-154As; the latter version entered production **in the second half of 1974**' (my highlighting – Auth.*). A look at the production list shows that the 43rd Kuibyshev-built example, which supposedly was the Tu-154A prototype, was manufactured in mid-1973, not the second half of 1974! Also, it is not clear whether this figure of 42 includes the prototype or not (some sources indicate that CCCP-85041 was the last Tu-154 *sans suffixe*); see Tu-154A and Tu-154K sections below.

Tu-154A Medium-haul Airliner

1974 saw the service entry of the second production version – the Tu-154A. The abovementioned sources state that CCCP-85042 (c/n 73A042) was the first prototype, commencing joint trials in April 1974. This was presaged by tests of the new version's design features on Tu-154s CCCP-85000, -85002, -85003, -85032 and -85035.

The Tu-154A differed from the Tu-154 *sans suffixe* basically in being powered by NK-8-2U engines uprated from 9,580kgp (21,120lbst) to 10,500kgp (23,150lbst) for take-off, with a 2,200-kgp (4,850-lbst) cruise rating. The new version of the engine offered a lower SFC and higher reverse thrust (3,600kgp/7,940lbst) for more efficient braking; it also had a higher mass flow. To improve the engines' surge resistance a row of 12 spring-loaded blow-in

doors was added around the circumference of each engine nacelle immediately aft of the air intake de-icer. The upgraded powerplant was put through its paces on CCCP-85043 (c/n 73A043).

An additional integral tank (No 4) holding 6,600kg (14,550 lb) of fuel was provided in the wing centre section between the front and middle spars, increasing the total fuel load to 39,750kg (87,630 lb). The new tank could not be used in flight, however: the fuel from the No 4 tank could be transferred to the No 1 tank (the service tank) only on the ground. The No 4 tank was a trim tank ensuring an acceptable CG position, especially during positioning flights with no payload and an aft CG. The Tu-154A's CG travel was reduced to 18-39% of the mean aerodynamic chord (MAC) versus 16.5-44% MAC for the Tu-154 *sans suffixe*, which made for more benign handling and higher flight safety. As a bonus, if the aircraft was carrying a partial payload, the fuel from the No 4 tank could be transferred to the main tanks at the destination airport on the outbound flight, reducing the amount of fuel to be filled up for the return trip – an important asset at locations where fuel was scarce or expensive. An automatic system for adding grade 'I' special fluid[3] preventing the water content in the fuel from crystallising and clogging the fuel filters was also introduced.

The more powerful engines allowed the Tu-154A's maximum take-off weight and maximum payload to be increased by 2 tons (4,410 lb) – to 94 tons (207,230 lb) and 18 tons (39,680 lb) respectively; the maximum landing weight was increased to 78 tons (171,960 lb). With a 16-ton (35,270-lb) payload the aircraft could work medium-haul routes up to 3,300km (2,050 miles) long, cruising at 900km/h (559mph). The Tu-154A had a slightly wide flight envelope: maximum indicated airspeed during normal operations was increased from 525 to 575km/h (from 326mph/283kts to 357mph/310kts), the 525km/h limit remaining in force only if the aircraft was flying above 7,000m (22,965ft) with less than 7,150kg (15,760 lb) of fuel remaining. This allowed the aircraft to descend faster from cruise altitudes.

Changes were made to the high-lift devices: the Tu-154A featured a common (automated) flap, slat and stabiliser control system making sure that stabiliser incidence changed in concert with flap and slat movement. Fact is, the Tu-154's powerful high-lift devices coupled with its considerable CG range necessitated considerable longitudinal trimming on the approach. The need to operate the flaps, slats and stabilisers separately when the crew was pressed for time left plenty of room for errors, and forgetting to change the tailplane trim on approach could be disastrous. The new 'one-move-does-it-all' system improved flight safety considerably (the separate control mode was retained as a back-up). True enough, debugging this system took a while, by which time production had switched to the Tu-154B.

New twin-chamber shock absorbers were introduced on the main gear units, replacing the earlier single-chamber oleos; this cured the Tu-154's propensity to bouncing on touchdown, enabling smooth landings with a sink rate up to 1.5m/sec (4.9ft/sec). For greater reliability the Tu-154A had a double complement of certain avionics items – the ARK-15M automatic direction finder, the RV-5 radio altimeter and the SD-67 distance measuring equipment; a critical bank angle warning feature was added. The flightdeck glazing featured new two-speed windshield wipers. From CCCP-85088 onwards, manufactured in December 1974, the Tu-154A was equipped with new MSRP-64 primary flight data recorder and Mars-B cockpit voice recorder replacing the MSRP-12-96 FDR and MS-61B CVR of earlier aircraft. The baggage compartments featured reinforced floors and were fitted with smoke alarm sensors.

The easiest way to tell a Tu-154A from a Tu-154 *sans suffixe* was initially the tail – specifically, the fin/tailplane junction. The new model was equipped with a new *Mikron* (Micron) HF radio replacing the old 1RSB-70 radio; its antenna was housed in a fat bullet fairing at the top of the fin replacing the earlier slender spike. This new tail bullet was indeed introduced on CCCP-85043, which does seem to support the figure of 42 Tu-154s *sans suffixe*. (The auxiliary blow-in doors are pretty obvious, too, but only when the engines are running; when the doors

CCCP-85068, a typical production Tu-154A in Aeroflot's 1973-standard livery belonging to the Ukrainian Civil Aviation Directorate/Odessa United Air Detachment/90th Flight, shares a snow-covered ramp with a Lisunov Li-2 and an Antonov An-2. The aircraft has the fat bullet fairing on top of the fin but still lacks emergency exits ahead of the engine nacelles. The fairings below the forward cabin emergency exit and the service door are for the pressurisation system's outlet valves. Yefim Gordon archive

are closed, you won't have a chance to see them at all.)

For 1974 the Kuibyshev aircraft factory and the Tupolev OKB developed no fewer than 15 interior layouts for the Tu-154A which served as the basis for those of subsequent versions. Interior layouts are given, using the accepted coding system (F = first class, C = business class, CY = tourist class, Y = economy class):

- the basic 152-seat all-tourist configuration for Aeroflot (54+98 seats at 75cm pitch with a galley amidships);
- a winterised 144-seat all-tourist configuration for Aeroflot (54+90 seats with a removable wardrobe aft);
- a 158-seat all-tourist configuration with a smaller galley for Aeroflot's shorter routes (60+98 seats);
- a 152-seat all-tourist configuration with two extra emergency exits and additional cabin equipment (see below);
- a 126-seat mixed-class version (F12CY18+CY96) for Aeroflot's Central Directorate of International Services (TsUMVS – Tsentrahl'noye oopravleniye mezhdunarodnykh vozdooshnykh so'obschcheniy). The first class seating in the foremost cabin was at 1.05-m (41²¹⁄₆₄in) pitch; the seat pitch in the rear cabin was 75 or 96cm (29½ or 37⁵⁄₈in), depending on the season – that is, depending on whether a rear wardrobe was fitted or not;
- a winterised 144-seat all-tourist configuration for TsUMVS (48+96 seats with a removable wardrobe aft);
- a 158-seat all-tourist basic version with improved cabin trim for Balkan Bulgarian Airlines (54+104 seats);
- a 164-seat all-tourist configuration with a smaller galley for Balkan's shorter routes (60+104 seats);
- a 128-seat mixed-class version (F24+CY104) for Balkan Bulgarian Airlines;
- a 158-seat all-tourist basic version with improved cabin trim for Malév Hungarian Airlines;
- a 134-seat mixed-class version (F12CY18+CY104) for Malév;
- a 124-seat mixed-class basic version (F20+CY104) for Egyptair;
- a 120-seat mixed-class version (F16+CY104) for

Egyptair featuring a first class cabin divided into two sections, the first of which was a separate compartment for eight;
- a 145-seat all-tourist version (41+104 seats) for Egyptair;
- a 151-seat all-tourist version (47+104 seats) for Egyptair.

Once again, the OKB began introducing improvements as soon as the new version entered production. Early-production Tu-154As had the same window arrangement as the previous version (door+18+door+7+ exit+2+exit+15 to port and 4+exit+10+ door+7+exit+2+exit+15 to starboard). In early 1975 (from c/n 75A097 onwards), however, an extra pair of large emergency exits equipped with inflatable escape slides was added at the rear extremity of the cabin (immediately ahead of the engine nacelles) to facilitate evacuation. This necessitated some repositioning of the seats at the rear, but maximum seating capacity was unchanged – 152 in the summer and 144 in 'winterised' configuration with extra wardrobes. The window arrangement was now door+18+door+7+exit+2+ exit+13+exit to port and 4+exit+10+door+ 7+exit+2+exit+13+exit to starboard. The additional exits were provided on top of the requirements posed by Soviet and international regulations. Bearing the exhibit code 369, Tu-154A CCCP-85105 with the new window arrangement was displayed at the 31st Paris Air Show, which opened on 30th May 1975.

Like the Tu-154 sans suffixe, early-production Tu-154As were equipped with the ABSU-154 Srs 1 automatic flight control system and cleared for automatic landing approach in 30 x 1,200m weather minima. On 1st January 1975 the Kuibyshev factory began producing aircraft with an updated ABSU-154 Srs 1-1 AFCS that were ICAO Cat I compliant (decision altitude 60m/200ft, horizontal visibility 800m/2,600ft); previously built Tu-154s were modified accordingly. In the meantime the Tupolev OKB kept working on giving the Tu-154 ICAO Cat II blind landing capability (decision altitude 30m/100ft, horizontal visibility 400m/1,310ft).

With the Tu-154A the OKB began a determined effort to increase the aircraft's fatigue life. The earliest Tu-154s sans suffixe had a guaranteed service life of only 1,000 cycles until the first major overhaul (or, to use a Western term, D-check), which was totally unacceptable.

From January 1975 onwards all Tu-154As left the factory with a guaranteed service life of 12,000 flight hours and 3,000 cycles – the figures stated in the MGA preliminary specifications of 1965. The next objective was to increase the guaranteed service life to 5,000-6,000 cycles by the fourth quarter of 1976. Actually the results of destructive testing undertaken on time-expired Tu-154s sans suffixe at the Siberian Aviation Research Institute named after S A Chaplygin (SibNIA – Sibeerskiy naoochno-issledovatel'skiy institoot aviahtsii) in Novosibirsk had allowed an increase of the guaranteed service life to 17,000 hours and 4,300 cycles by February 1975. This gave good reason to believe that the 6,000-cycle guaranteed service life goal could be attained before the year's end. (Still, the required designated service life of 15,000 cycles was not achieved until the Tu-154B came on the scene.)

The OKB and Aeroflot spent a lot of effort on improving maintenance procedures at this stage. The service life of many components and subassemblies was increased to match that of the airframe, and many equipment items were henceforth operated in terms of their technical condition. The OKB developed a Minimum Equipment List (MEL) enumerating malfunctions with which the aircraft could return to its home base instead of being grounded until repairs could be made on site; this was made possible by the Tu-154's multiply redundant systems. This approach reduced downtime and improved the aircraft's economic efficiency.

In due course all surviving Tu-154s sans suffixe were updated to Tu-154B standard during overhauls. On the other hand, not all of them wore appropriate nose titles.

Tu-154K VIP Aircraft

A VIP version of the Tu-154A (and, according to some sources, the Tu-154 sans suffixe) was brought out for Aeroflot's 235th Independent Air Detachment (otdel'nyy aviaotryad) – the Soviet federal government flight. By analogy with its precursors – the Tu-124K-36, Tu-124K2-22, Tu-134K and Tu-134AK – the aircraft was designated Tu-154K, the K standing for komfort – (enhanced) comfort.

The interior was divided into two sections. The forward section was reserved for the VIPs (referred to as the main passengers), featuring a lounge, a bedroom and a wardrobe. The rear section (aft of the galley amidships) was occupied by a 28-seat rear cabin for the escorting staff and a sleeping compartment. The crew had

a small galley at the front all to itself; this was for the convenience of the VIPs (165 Imp gal) each, bringing the total fuel amount to 17,800 litres (3,916 Imp gal) or 14.2 tons (31,305 lb).

Three-section electrically powered airstairs similar to those of the Tu-134AK were mounted next to the rear entry door, stowing against the rear bulkhead of the entry vestibule when not in use. They were used when the aircraft arrived at a military base or a factory airfield where mobile boarding ramps might be unavailable.

The Tu-154K had several interior layouts. Some versions were fitted with VHF secure communications equipment; such aircraft had a large enclosure (the so-called **spetsotsek** – 'special bay') housing the radios and scramblers/descramblers and the operators' workstations in the rear cabin, which required some local structural reinforcement.

Known Tu-154Ks are CCCP-85096 and -85097 (c/ns 75A096 and 75A097) built in 1975. Both were later converted to airline configuration and passed on to regular Aeroflot units. The designation Tu-154K may also apply to three aircraft operated by the Soviet Air Force – '32 Red' (ex-CCCP-85015, c/n 71A015?), CCCP-85049 and -85050 (c/ns 73A049 and 73A050); the first and the last of these later passed to the Russian and Uzbek Air Forces. '32 Red' falls within the c/n range of the Tu-154 *sans suffixe*; this again may account for the different quotes of 41 or 42 aircraft.

Tu-154B Medium-haul Airliner (second use of designation)

Pretty soon after the Tu-154's service entry it became clear that the designers had made a blunder: the wings turned out to be insufficiently strong; the advent of the high gross weight Tu-154A only made the problem worse. After a series of structural tests SibNIA reported that the wings could fail earlier than anticipated; and indeed, fatigue cracks began appearing in the wings of quite young aircraft. This was because the wing structure was made of the relatively new V95 aluminium alloy whose properties had not yet been studied fully; its fatigue resistance turned out to be inadequate. Also, the wings had been designed to be very flexible, giving a smooth ride in turbulence; pilots and airline passengers noted that the wings flexed and 'flapped' in flight.

The root of the problem was that the required methods of calculating the service life were not yet available to the Soviet designers when the Tu-154 was being designed; pre-stressed joints and methods of structural strengthening had not yet been mastered in production, and the stresses applied to the airframe in various operational conditions had not been fully studied either. Another reason was that the Tu-154 turned out to be nearly 10,000kg (22,040 lb) over the maximum take-off weight target stipulated by the Council of Ministers directive and the MAP specs. This was due both to excess

structural weight and to the need to carry more fuel than originally intended because the NK-8-2 engines had a higher fuel burn than advertised by the manufacturer. As a result, the Tupolev OKB had taken weight reduction measures – and overdone it; while possessing the required static strength, the wings were not durable enough.

Now the OKB had no choice but to undertake a crash redesign programme (no pun intended). A new wing structure made of more durable D16 duralumin was developed; not only was it stiffer and stronger but the control

A view of the final assembly shop in Kuibyshev with Tu-154Bs on the production line; the short low-speed ailerons are visible on the nearest aircraft, as are the short boundary layer fences. Sergey and Dmitriy Komissarov collection

Nearly all Tu-154s *sans suffixe* and Tu-154As were upgraded to Tu-154B standard and received appropriate nose titles, but structurally the conversion concerned only the wings; early aircraft lacking the rearmost emergency exits, such as RA-85061, did not have them retrofitted. Yuriy Kirsanov

Opposite page, top to bottom:

Tu-154 *sans suffixe* CCCP-85032 (seen here at the 1979 Paris Air Show with the exhibit code '346' and the original long anti-glare panel) served as a testbed for some features of the Tu-154B but also for the NPK-154T flight director/navigation suite; the associated TV camera can be seen in the undernose fairing. RART

This view of CCCP-85032 preserved in the city park in Zhukovskiy (the picture was taken in 1989) shows the open plug-type entry door of patented Boeing design. Note that the radome is now white and the anti-glare panel is short. Sergey Komissarov

The rear fuselage of CCCP-85032, showing the non-standard wing/fuselage fairing and the port side conduit exiting from it. Note the absence of the thrust reverser grilles; quite simply, the engines were removed before preservation and the resulting apertures faired over! Sergey Komissarov

The wing/fuselage fairing on the starboard side obstructs the No 2 baggage door almost completely, and a portion of the fairing swings upward out of the way. Note the equal-sized overwing emergency exits. Sergey Komissarov

surfaces were redesigned as well. The ailerons were reduced to about half their original span, terminating 2m (6ft 6¾in) inboard of the wingtips; the outermost portions of the trailing edge were now fixed. On the other hand, the span of the flight and ground spoilers was increased, matching that of the flaps. Thus in cruise flight the forces generated by the spoilers for roll control were applied closer to the centreline, reducing wing flexure and fatigue build-up; this was expected to give the aircraft the specified service life of 30,000 hours and 15,000 cycles. Concurrently the trailing-edge segments of the inboard flaps were rerigged to 2° downtrim, reducing the approach speed to 180km/h (111mph/97kts). The maximum take-off weight was increased to 96,000kg (211,640 lb). The modified aircraft was designated Tu-154B.

The fuselage structure and the fin were also reinforced. All four overwing emergency exits were now of equal size (the forward pair was increased in height).

The manufacturing drawings for the redesigned wings were completed and transferred to the Kuibyshev factory by February 1975. CCCP-85120 (c/n 75A120) was to be manufactured in September of that year as the prototype of the Tu-154B, as Sergey M Yeger stated in the abovementioned report.

The Tu-154B also boasted improved avionics. A new version of the ABSU-154 AFCS (Srs 2) gave the aircraft ICAO Cat II automatic landing capability. It was introduced on the production line in January 1976 after extensive testing on Tu-154 *sans suffixe* CCCP-85003 undertaken jointly by the Tupolev OKB, LII and the Moscow Institute of Electronics and Automatic Systems (MIREA – *Moskovskiy institutoot rahdioelektroniki i avtomahtiki*). At the same time the control system was modified to cure one of the Tu-154's initial weaknesses – poor elevator response on the approach with the high-lift devices deployed. Changes were again made to the fuel system: the fuel from the No 4 tank in the wing centre section could now be used in flight.

An upgraded navigation suite was fitted (this included a new DISS-013 Trassa-A (Route-A) Doppler speed and drift sensor system replacing the earlier DISS-3P). A new AGR-72 back-up artificial horizon was introduced and the instruments and switches in the flightdeck were rearranged, allowing the aircraft to be operated by a crew of three as originally intended (the navigator was eliminated on Aeroflot examples – in theory at least). This calls for some explanation. Export Tu-154s were indeed flown by a crew of three because they were operated on European airways equipped with comprehensive navigation aids. In the Soviet Union, however, the navaids often left a lot to be desired, which is why a navigator was included in the crew for flight safety reasons. In order to simplify navigation procedures the OKB tested an upgraded navigation suite making use of the VNPK-154 processor instead of the earlier

NVU-B3 processor on Tu-154 *sans suffixe* CCCP-85005. The results proved very encouraging; however, the VNPK-154 (originally developed for the Tu-22M bomber) was out of production by then and the effort had to start anew with a digital processor.

From CCCP-85120 onwards the Tu-154B supplanted the A model on the production line; 111 examples (up to and including CCCP-85230, c/n 77A230 manufactured on 31st August 1977) were built as such. Most of the Tu-154s *sans suffixe* and Tu-154As in airline service were progressively returned to the manufacturer and rewinged. Such aircraft were referred to as Tu-154Bs and wore appropriate nose titles. Actually, however, they were neither fish nor fowl, combining Tu-154B-style wings with the original fuselage featuring overwing emergency exits of unequal size and, in the case of many aircraft, no rear emergency exits.

Like its predecessor, the Tu-154B was produced in two main versions as regards the cabin layout – a 152-seater and a 'winterised' 144-seater. A 124-seat mixed-class variant and an all-tourist 136-seater were supplied to TsUMVS. 138-, 140- and 146-seat versions were also available.

In 1977 Tu-154B CCCP-85207 was demonstrated at the 33rd Paris Air Show (which opened on 9th June) with the exhibit code 344.

Tu-154 CCCP-85032 Development Aircraft

Tu-154 *sans suffixe* CCCP-85032 (c/n 72A032) was apparently purpose-built for the Tupolev OKB as a development aircraft intended for verifying several new features. This theory is supported by the fact that, despite the construction number commencing 72, the aircraft was manufactured on 12th June 1973 – six months later than it should have been. By comparison, the preceding aircraft (CCCP-85031, c/n 72A031) was released by the factory on 24th November 1972.

As already mentioned, the Tu-154 has outward-opening entry and service doors moving in parallel to the fuselage on L-shaped arms. On one occasion this door design had led to decompression when the door latches failed. Therefore the Tupolev OKB decided to utilise plug-type doors opening outward and forward through 180°; the doors featured inflatable escape slides which were deployed automatically by rip cords (the cord was disengaged before opening the door normally). Developed and patented by the Boeing Aircraft Co, this type of door had been first used on the Boeing 707, and the Soviet Union had bought a licence to use it.

Accordingly CCCP-85032 was fitted with Boeing-type doors. However, tests quickly showed that the American design was unsuitable for the Tu-154. The doors were placed too high above the fuselage waterline; as a result, the hinge line was not vertical as it should be, making it hard to open and close the heavy door. Therefore, CCCP-85032 remained a one-off in this respect.[4]

The doors were not the only unique feature. CCCP-85032 had equal-sized overwing emergency exits as later introduced on the Tu-154B but lacked the latter's rear emergency exits (as befits a Tu-154 *sans suffixe*). The wing/fuselage fairings were extended aft so that the starboard fairing obstructed the rear baggage door almost completely instead of just encroaching on it a little; hence a portion of the fairing equal in width to the baggage door swung upward (not forward, as on standard aircraft) to provide access. A thick conduit ran from the rear end of the port wing/fuselage fairing to a point in line with the middle of the port engine nacelle.

Last but not least, the aircraft had a non-standard NPK-154T flight director/navigation suite (*navigatsionno-pilotazhnyy kompleks*); this included an optoelectronic system developed by the French companies Thomson-CSF and SFIM jointly with Soviet designers to facilitate night and poor-weather approach. The sys-

tem's optical sensor (video camera, hence the T for *televizionnaya kahmera*) was installed in a small teardrop fairing with a sloping window located immediately aft of the radome instead of the usual dielectric panel associated with the Doppler speed/drift sensor system. Four Penetron cathode-ray tube (CRT) displays were mounted on the instrument panels.

CCCP-85032 was displayed at the 34th Paris Air Show (which opened on 7th June 1979) with the exhibit code 346 – obviously for the sake of the modernised avionics suite. Upon retirement in the 1980s the aircraft was preserved in a city park in Zhukovskiy a short way from the main gate of the LII airfield; its interior was opened to the public on festive occasions like Aviation Day. Unfortunately this unique aircraft was burned by vandals in June 1993 and had to be scrapped.

Tu-154B-1 Medium-haul Airliner

When Aeroflot set about increasing revenues from its Tu-154 operations, it was decided to launch production of a 160-seat version of the Tu-154B for use on domestic routes. Since the changes were only minor and did not warrant a new suffix letter, the 160-seater was designated Tu-154B-1. A 144-seat mixed-class version of the Tu-154B-1 also existed for the TsUMVS.
Outwardly the Tu-154B-1 differed from the 'pure B' in having an extra window aft of the service door to admit some daylight into the galley, creating more comfortable working conditions for the flight attendants. The window arrangement to starboard was now 4+exit+ 10+door+1+7+exit+2+exit+13+exit.

Production of the new version began with CCCP-85231 (c/n 77A231) manufactured on 1st September 1977 and lasted one year and one day. 64 Tu-154B-1s (up to and including CCCP-85294, c/n 78A294 manufactured on 1st September 1978) were built as such, including VIP examples (see Tu-154 'Salon'). Many of the Tu-154Bs previously built were updated to this standard. The Tu-154B-1 was also exported to Bulgaria and Romania.

CCCP-85267, a brand-new Tu-154B-1 with appropriate nose titles. The aircraft was delivered to the Volga CAD/1st Kuibyshev UAD/368th Flight. Tupolev PLC

Another aspect of Tu-154B-1 CCCP-85267. Tupolev PLC

Anonymous-looking Tu-154B-2 RA-85523 belonging to Tupolev-Aerotrans sits at the Tupolev PLC's flight test facility in Zhukovskiy in 2004. Note the extra window aft of the service door introduced on the Tu-154B-1. Yefim Gordon

Tu-154B-2 RA-85452 of Aeroflot-Don taxies out for take-off from runway 20 at Moscow-Vnukovo on 5th September 2001 past the unfinished maintenance hangar and several half-dead aircraft of the defunct Vnukovo Airlines. Note the open APU air intake and the open auxiliary blow-in doors on the engine nacelle. Author

Pictured here at Oslo-Fornebu in May 1991, when it brought Soviet President Mikhail S. Gorbachov for the Nobel Peace Prize handover ceremony, Tu-154B-2 'Salon' CCCP-85604 was one of several equipped with the Surgut secure HF communications suite. Such aircraft are identifiable by the dorsal canoe fairing and the extra blade aerials atop the fin and under the rear fuselage. When operated by the 235th Independent Flight Detachment (the Soviet federal government flight), CCCP-85604 wore 'Sovetskiy Soyuz' (Soviet Union) titles and the Soviet coat of arms, plus small Aeroflot titles on the nose. Sergey Komissarov

Uzbekistan Government Tu-154B-2 'Salon' UK 85600 is shown on approach to Moscow-Domodedovo. Most VIP-configured Tu-154s are outwardly indistinguishable from their sister ships in regular airline service. This one wears one of several versions of Uzbekistan Airways' livery; the Uzbekistan coat-of-arms aft of the flightdeck is the only giveaway that it is not just an ordinary airliner. Yuriy Kirsanov

Tu-154B-2 Medium-haul Airliner

At its own initiative the Tupolev OKB developed what it called a convertible variant of the Tu-154B designated Tu-154B-2. Lest the reader should get the wrong idea, this was *not* a quick-change passenger/cargo or combi version with a large cargo door; rather, the aircraft was to be quickly convertible from a 160-seater to a 180-seater for high-density routes by removing the galley. The conversion could be performed within two or two and a half hours by the personnel of a typical airport maintenance facility.

The Tu-154B-2 did have a notable difference from the preceding versions: the forward pair of wheels on each main gear bogie was steerable; these wheels were actuated by small hydraulic rams in concert with the nosewheels to reduce the wear and tear on the tyres during tight turns.

The prototype, CCCP-85295 (c/n 78A295), was built in September 1978. From this aircraft onwards the Tu-154B-2 became the sole – and most numerous – production version; 311 air-

craft, including VIP examples (up to and including CCCP-85605) were built before the Kuibyshev factory switched to the radically modernised Tu-154M in 1984. Actually the last Tu-154B-2s were not completed and delivered until October 1986 because they were VIP aircraft manufactured with special care and fitted with special systems (see next entry).

For some reason the Tu-154B-2 was not represented at the 33rd Paris Air Show in 1979. Two years later, however, Tu-154B-2 CCCP-85479 (c/n 81A479) participated in the 34th Paris Air Show with the exhibit code 353.

As with the other versions, different interior layouts were available. For instance, several Tu-154B-2s were custom-built for the 235th IAD in a mixed-class 99-seat (for instance, CCCP-85575, c/n 83A575) or all-tourist 110-seat (for example, CCCP-85538, c/n 82A538) layout with a more generous seat pitch. These aircraft were intended for supporting state visits when a lot of service personnel had to be carried.

Tu-154B 'Salon', Tu-154B-1 'Salon' and Tu-154B-2 'Salon' VIP Aircraft

As a follow-on to the Tu-154K, the Tupolev OKB developed similarly configured VIP versions of the rewinged Tu-154B and its Tu-154B-1/B-2 varieties for the 235th IFD, the Soviet Ministry of Defence and foreign customers. In due course this version was made available for export and delivered to several 'friendly nations'. Several interior layouts were available.

As in the case of the Tu-154K, several versions featuring a VHF secure communications suite were produced for the Soviet government flight and the Air Force. One of these, based solely on the Tu-154B-2 variant, was equipped with the Karpaty-ST VHF comms suite (*Karpahty* is the Russian name for the Carpathian Mountains). This sub-variant was readily identifiable by the prominent dorsal fairing housing communications antennas and wiring which ran all the way from the rear edge of the 11th window to the rear edge of the 24th window (the numeration is given for the port

Above: **Kazakhstan Government Tu-154B-2 'Salon' UN-85464 featuring the Karpaty-ST suite is seen at Astana airport.** Aidan Curley

Left: **The rear cabin of a Tu-154B-2 'Salon' equipped with the Surgut suite. The starboard side is occupied by privacy compartments with curtained entrances at the front, followed by the so-called 'special bay' – an enclosure for the classified scramblers/descramblers and radios and their operators' workstations.** Tupolev PLC

Below left: **The No 2 VIP cabin of a Tu-154B-2 'Salon', with a sofa on one side. Note the cabin décor.** Tupolev PLC

Below right: **The No 1 VIP cabin of a Tu-154B-2 'Salon', with facing sofas and a table in between. Note the dual-time clock finished like a world map on the cabin bulkhead.** Tupolev PLC

side because of the asymmetric window arrangement). Additionally, two small blade aerials were mounted atop the fin and under the rear fuselage.

Known Soviet examples were registered *CCCP-85132*, -85133, -85147, -85163, -85166, -85176, -85216 (all built to Tu-154B standard), -85255, -85282 through -85284 (all built to Tu-154B-1 standard), -85335, -85353, -85359, -85360, -85380, -85426*, -85435, -85436, -85445, -85456, -85463, -85464*, -85482, -85486, -85496, -85510, -85534, -85554, -85555, -85559, -85560, -85561, -85563, -85567, -85571, -85572, -85574, -85575, -85578, -85587, -85594**, -85600, -85602**, -85603**, -85604** and -85605* (all built to Tu-154B-2 standard). The machines indicated in italics are unconfirmed, since the fact that the aircraft is operated by the 235th IAD or the Air Force does not automatically make it a VIP jet. Quite apart from the 99-/110-seaters mentioned earlier, some Air Force aircraft built as VIP jets are known to have been converted to airline configuration as personnel carriers. Aircraft marked with an asterisk are fitted with the Karpaty-ST VHF comms suite, while those marked ** featured it originally but had it removed along with the VIP interior before being sold to Orenburg Airlines.

Five VIP-configured Tu-154Bs were delivered to foreign customers – the Bulgarian Air Force (Tu-154B-1 'Salon' LZ-BTJ) and the Czechoslovak federal government flight (Tu-154B-2 'Salons' OK-BYA, -BYB, -BYC and -BYD). OK-BYD later passed to the Czech Air Force as '0601 White' and was fitted with special communications equipment identifiable by a large strake aerial on top of the centre fuselage and an extra blade aerial aft of the nose gear. Like most of the Soviet/Russian examples, they were eventually stripped of their VIP interiors and sold to airlines.

Tu-154S Freighter
(Tu-154T, Tu-164, Tu-154C)
The first project studies of a freighter version began back in 1968 when the prototype was under construction. The aircraft was to carry a 25-ton (55,115-lb) payload over 2,000-2,500km (1,240-1,550 miles), cruising at 900km/h (559mph). However, the initial problems with the Tu-154's wings caused the project to be shelved for the time being.

The OKB dusted off the idea when the Tu-154B was brought out. Originally the aircraft was known as the Tu-154T – the first to have this designation (T = *trahnsportnyy* – transport, used attributively) – and regarded as a convertible aircraft that could be operated in all-passenger, all-cargo or combi configurations.

Later the designation was changed to Tu-154S; actually some foreign publications called it Tu-154C (for 'convertible'), but the Russian designation has come to be used universally.

The OKB brought out several alternative conversion projects in the late 1970s, but Aeroflot was in no hurry to place an order. It was not until 1980 that the customer took itself off the fence. Between 29th May and 4th June 1980 MAP and MGA issued a joint decision calling for the development of the freighter version (initially referred to in official documents as the Tu-164); the MGA specifications followed on 3rd July – 5th August 1980. Eventually the idea of a convertible version was dropped and the Tu-154S evolved into a pure freighter conversion of the kind often undertaken on ageing Western jetliners and propliners. The changes to the Tu-154B's design were kept to an absolute minimum.

The most obvious change was, of course, the upward-opening cargo door measuring 2.9 x 1.8m (114¹¹⁄₆₄ x 70⁵⁵⁄₆₄in) on the port side halfway between the existing entry doors (specifically, between fuselage frames 23A-29A); the door aperture measured 2.9 x 1.87m (114¹¹⁄₆₄ x 73⅜in). The door incorporated five windows; thus the number of windows to port was reduced to 42 (door+7+5+2+door+7+exit+2+exit+15). The very conspicuous breaks in the row of windows were due to the need to rivet on a large reinforcement plate of complex shape around the cargo door to increase fatigue resistance. The door was opened through 88° or 160° by two hydraulic actuators operated by the No 2 hydraulic system or (if no hydraulic power was available) by a hand-driven pump. The door was secured by locks actuated by individual hydraulic rams at the bottom; the control panel was located at the front of the cabin. The inside of the door was heated by the aircraft's air conditioning system along with the remainder of the cabin.

The cabins were stripped of all passenger equipment and furnishings to form a common cargo cabin with a volume of 135m³ (4,767ft³) delimited by frames 15 and 62. It was big enough to accommodate nine international standard air cargo pallets measuring 2.235 x 2.743 x 0.025m (88 x 108 x 1in) – two forward of

the cargo door and seven aft. Given a maximum height of 1.82m (5ft 11²¹⁄₃₂in) from the cabin floor, the maximum volume of the palletised cargo was 72m³ (2,542ft³), leaving unobstructed passages along the cabin walls. The cargo cabin floor was fitted with a 'ball mat' near the cargo door and roller tracks, allowing the pallets to be moved manually, and was stressed to 400kg/m² (82lb/ft²). Once in position, the pallets would be tied down by nylon nets and straps secured by locks attached to the existing seat tracks. The underfloor baggage compartments were left unchanged, with an aggregate volume of 38m³ (1,342ft³) and floors stressed to 600kg/m² (123lb/ft²), and could be used for bulk cargo.

Removing the seats, overhead baggage racks, cabin partitions and galley gave a weight saving of some 3,000kg (6,610lb). On the other hand, the cargo door with its actuating and locking mechanisms, the cargo handling equipment, the protective panels on the sidewalls and protective bars on the cabin windows and the sealing of the cabin floor against possible leakage of liquids from the cargo added about 2,000kg (4,410lb).

The forward entry vestibule featured the usual jump seats for the flight attendants, which were now used by the cargo attendants. The cargo cabin was equipped with smoke sensors and door lock position sensors, with appropriate 'cabin fire' and 'cargo door unsafe' warning panels in the flightdeck; fire extinguishers were provided in the cargo cabin.

According to the project the Tu-154S had an empty operating weight of 52 tons (114,640lb) and a maximum TOW of 98 tons (216,050lb). The maximum payload was 20 tons (44,090lb), including 19 tons (41,890lb) for the cargo proper (distributed between the main cabin and the underfloor baggage compartments) and 1 ton (2,200lb) for the pallets and restraining nets/straps. The palletised payload carried in the main cabin was limited to 19.6 tons (43,210lb). With a full payload and 6,000kg (13,230lb) of fuel reserves the aircraft had an effective range of 2,900km (1,800 miles), cruising at 11,000m (36,090ft) and 850-900km/h (528-559mph). All other performance parameters were similar to those of the Tu-154B.

Tu-154S CCCP-85067 of the Central Directorate of International Services (TsUMVS)/63rd Flight with the cargo door in the intermediate position (opened 88°). Tupolev PLC

In this view the cargo door is fully open (through 160°), showing clearly the two hydraulic actuators. Tu-154S CCCP-85067 was written off in an accident at Monrovia-Roberts International airport on 13th June 1989. Tupolev PLC

The cargo cabin of a Tu-154S, looking towards the nose. The roller tracks on the floor and the safety net at the far end are clearly visible. Tupolev PLC

The original plans envisaged the conversion of 20 aircraft to Tu-154S standard at the Kuibyshev aircraft factory. Eventually, however, only nine aircraft were thus modified; these were two Tu-154s *sans suffixe* – CCCP-85019 (c/n 71A019) and CCCP-85037 (c/n 73A037) – and seven Tu-154As: CCCP-85060 (c/n 74A060), CCCP-85062 (c/n 74A062), CCCP-85063 (c/n 74A063), CCCP-85067 (c/n 74A067, conversion completed on 30th November 1982), CCCP-85081 (c/n 74A081), CCCP-85084 (c/n 74A084) and CCCP-85086 (c/n 74A086). Concurrently with the freighter conversion all nine aircraft had their structure and systems updated to Tu-154B standard.

The actual Tu-154S differed in a few minor details from the project. For instance, the aggregate weight of the Soviet PAV-3 pallets was slightly higher (1,080kg/2,380 lb). A safety net stressed for 6Gs was provided at the front of the cargo cabin to protect the crew, should the cargo become dislodged in a crash landing.

After a brief manufacturer's flight test programme the Tu-154S underwent operational trials with Aeroflot between 15th November 1982 and 31st March 1983. Two aircraft (CCCP-85067 and CCCP-85086) were used for evaluating the freighter itself and the associated ground support equipment (container loaders and such). In January-February 1983 CCCP-85067 and CCCP-85081 were operated by TsUMVS/63rd Flight under the auspices of the Tupolev OKB. A further series of checkout trials was performed with CCCP-85019 in July 1983.

It should be noted here that Aeroflot's structure closely resembled an air force's order of battle – which is hardly surprising, considering that the Soviet civil air fleet constituted an immediately available military reserve (and considering the militarisation of the Soviet economy at large). There were a number of Civil Aviation Directorates (UGA – *Oopravleniye grazhdahnskoy aviahtsii*), several of which were in the Russian Federation and one in each of the other Soviet republics. These were broadly equivalent to the numbered air forces of the USAF or the air armies of the Soviet Air Force. Each CAD consisted of several United Air Detachments (OAO – *obyedinyonnyy aviaotryad*) based in major cities; these were equivalent to an air group (USAF) or an air division (SovAF). Each UAD had several Flights (LO – *lyotnyy otryad*) similar to an air wing

The cargo cabin of a Tu-154S, looking aft. This view shows the 'ball mat' near the cargo door, the hinged door sill guard (painted in red and white stripes) and the door actuators with folding arms. The fairing at the bottom of the door encloses the locks. The cabin windows are fitted with protective grilles. Tupolev PLC

This drawing shows the cargo cabin layout of the Tu-154S, with two pallets accommodated forward of the cargo door and seven aft. The inscriptions read (top to bottom, left to right): Cargo loading mechanisation and securing of the pallets; Nylon net with restraining straps; Cargo door; 'Ball mat'; roller tracks; Upper and lower baggage compartments; Loading the pallets by means of ground loaders. Tupolev PLC

(USAF) or an air regiment (SovAF). Finally, a Flight comprised up to four, or maybe more, squadrons (yes, squadrons – *aviaeskadril'ya*!); not infrequently different squadrons of the same Flight operated different aircraft types.

The extensive trials confirmed that the aircraft met the specifications it was designed to. Finally, on 30th March 1984 Boris Pavlovich Boogayev, the then Minister of Civil Aviation (he held this office in 1970-87), signed an order reading: '...*On the basis of the positive results set forth in the Evaluation Protocol, of the results of monitored Tu-154S operations by TsUMVS and the measures taken to rectify the faults discovered during the trials, I hereby order that scheduled operations of the Tu-154S freighter be started on domestic and international civil aviation services.*'

Most of the Tu-154S freighters were operated by TsUMVS/63rd Flight on international services; CCCP-85019 and CCCP-85037 belonged to the Far Eastern CAD/1st Khabarovsk UAD/198th Flight/3rd Sqn, while CCCP-85086 reportedly went to the Tajik CAD/Dushanbe UAD/186th Flight. Most of them, except CCCP-85063, CCCP-85067 and CCCP-85086, remained in service after the break-up of the Soviet Union and gained the Russian RA- nationality prefix. By 1997 all Tu-154Ss had been retired; however, in the early 1990s the Tupolev Joint-Stock Co developed a successor – the Tu-204C freighter.

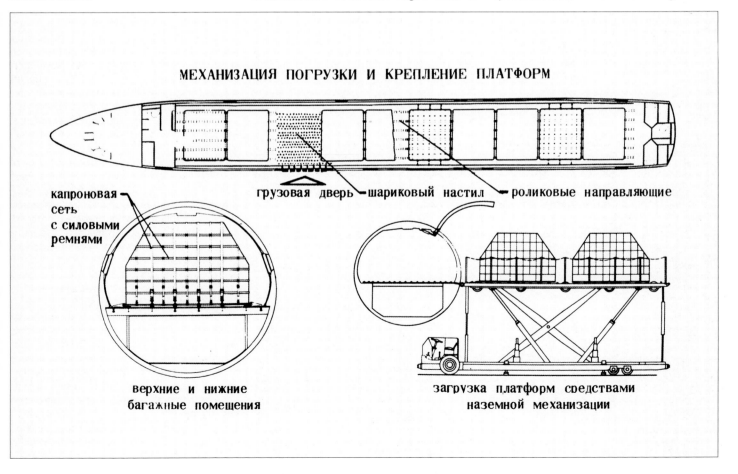

МЕХАНИЗАЦИЯ ПОГРУЗКИ И КРЕПЛЕНИЕ ПЛАТФОРМ

капроновая сеть с силовыми ремнями

грузовая дверь — шариковый настил — роликовые направляющие

верхние и нижние багажные помещения

загрузка платформ средствами наземной механизации

Tu-154M Medium-haul Airliner (Tu-154-160, Tu-160A, Tu-164)

On 30th August – 13th September 1977 MAP and MGA issued a joint decision calling for the further development of the Tu-154B. The document said:

'...Considering the need to refine the Tu-154B aircraft further with a view to reducing its fuel burn per tonne-km and increasing its range, the following decisions are hereby taken:

- *Comrade A. A. Tupolev, General Designer of MMZ 'Opyt' named after A. N. Tupolev, shall complete the drawings for the installation of D-30KU engines on the Tu-154B aircraft by April 1978; the aircraft powered by D-30KU engines shall be designated Tu-154-160;*
- *the Tu-154-160 shall have the same 144-, 160- and 180-seat cabin layouts as approved for the Tu-154B;*
- *the Tu-154-160 shall retain the systems and equipment of the Tu-154B, except that the air bleed system for the air conditioning and de-icing systems shall be patterned on that of the IL-62M aircraft;*
- *the Kuibyshev aircraft factory shall manufacture a single Tu-154-160 in the first quarter of 1979 for the purpose of holding joint checkout tests (sic); the airframe prepared for refitting with D-30KU engines shall be allocated and paid for from the 1978 delivery plan;*
- *MAP and MGA shall hold joint checkout tests of the Tu-154-160 aircraft in 1979 and, providing the results are positive, clear it for production entry in 1980 within a month after the tests.'*

The 11,000-kgp (24,250-lbst) D-30KU turbofan was originally developed by Pavel A Solov'yov's OKB-19 for the IL-62M long-haul airliner. As compared to the NK-8-2U it had a higher bypass ratio (2.43 versus 1.05) and a clamshell thrust reverser instead of the Kuznetsov engine's cascade thrust reverser. As on the NK-8-2, the thrust reverser was optional and was not envisaged for the centre engine. The documents continued the following provisional specifications (as given in the table below).

On 9th August 1978 the CofM Presidium's Commission on defence industry matters

(VPK – *Voyenno-promyshlennaya komissiya*) backed up the MAP/MGA decision with a special ruling (No 207) on the Tu-154-160. Later the aircraft was known as the Tu-160A (rather confusingly, considering that the Tu-160 *Blackjack* strategic missile strike aircraft had been under development since 1967!) and then as the Tu-164; it is not certain whether this aircraft or the future Tu-154S freighter bore this designation first.

The main objective of radically reducing the fuel burn as compared to the Tu-154B was to be attained by installing D-30KU turbofans (this was the most fuel-efficient Soviet aero engine then in production), optimising the aerodynamics of the engines' thrust reversers and some non-stressed airframe parts, and optimising the flight profile.

The Tu-154M's rear fuselage aft of the rear pressure dome was new. Since the D-30KU had a larger diameter and a higher mass flow (not to mention the totally different thrust reverser), the engine nacelles, their pylons and the centre engine's S-duct and air intake trunk had to be designed anew (the S-duct had a bigger cross-section, which gave the air intake trunk a slightly hump-backed appearance in side elevation). The pylons were repositioned so that the Nos 1 and 3 engines' thrust line was set higher.

The APU was moved from its original position at the base of the rudder to a special bay beneath the S-duct offset to starboard (between frames 72-74). Now it breathed through a single ventral intake with an aft-hinged door and exhausted through a port in line with the starboard engine's thrust reverser; the exhaust port was closed by a forward-hinged door surrounded by a heat-resistant steel liner when the APU was not running. Concurrently the Tu-154's distinctive centre engine nozzle with that strongly concave contour in side elevation was replaced by a simple circular-section nozzle with a vertically cut-off edge and a fillet between it and the rudder; the overall result was a much more elegant rear end.

The wing/fuselage fairings were reshaped; each fairing had a distinctive pointed front end ('beak') and an extended rear end, which

necessitated some changes to the No 2 baggage door design. New double-slotted flaps were fitted; measures were taken to 'seal' the flaps so as to reduce drag when retracted, and the flap track fairings were recontoured and lengthened for the same reason. The leading-edge slats were also new – the sections were all located together, with no fixed portion of the leading edge between the inboard section and the others. The area of the horizontal tail was increased thanks to the longer-chord elevators.

The new airframe components were to be manufactured, using traditional technologies and structural materials. The structural design and outline of the wings and vertical tail were to be identical to those of the Tu-154B, as were the pressurised forward/centre fuselage, the flightdeck, cabins and their equipment, the landing gear and the general systems (including the air conditioning system, except where it was mated to the engine bleed valves).

In 1978 the Tupolev OKB's branch office at the Kuibyshev aircraft factory started work on the manufacturing drawings for prototype conversion. A full-scale mock-up of the rear fuselage was built, allowing the technologists to work out the placement of the equipment and the routing of piping/wiring runs in various 'un-get-at-able' spots. Thus the OKB was able to issue the manufacturing documents to the plant without requiring any major changes of production technology.

The Tu-154M was to be manufactured with several interior layouts – a mixed-class 154-seater, an all-tourist 164-seater, an all-economy 180-seater, a 144-seat mixed-class version for TsUMVS offering greater comfort and a VIP version. An all-cargo variant equivalent to the as-yet non-existent Tu-154S was envisaged (this evolved into the Tu-154MS project – see next chapter), as was a combi version carrying two standard air freight containers or pallets in the forward cabin and 102 passengers in the rear cabin.

Meanwhile, OKB-19 developed a version of the D-30KU optimised for the Tu-154M. Known as the D-30KU-154, it was derated somewhat in order to improve reliability and fuel efficiency. The new engine had a maximum take-off rating of 10,500kgp (23,150 lbst) and a nominal take-off rating of 9,500kgp (20,940 lbst),with a reverse thrust of 3,600-3,800kgp (7,940-8,380 lbst). The cruise SFC at 11,000m (36,090ft) and Mach 0.8 was 0.71-0.74kg/kgp·hr. The bypass ratio was 2.45; still, in spite of the higher BPR (which generally means higher drag), the designers succeeded in achieving a lift/drag ratio of 14.3-15.0 with the Tu-154M – an improvement of 2-3% on the Tu-154B. This was achieved thanks to the modified flaps, new wing/fuselage fairings and flap track fairings, the relocation of the APU, the revised pylons and so on.

The first prototype Tu-154M was converted from an early-production Tu-154B-2, CCCP-85317 (c/n 78A317), which had been set aside

	Tu-154B	Tu-154-160
Powerplant	3 x NK-8-2U	3 x D-30KU
Take-off thrust, kgp (lbst)	3 x 10,500	3 x 11,000
	(3 x 23,150)	(3 x 24,250)
Maximum payload, kg (lb)	18,000	18,000-20,000
	(39,680)	(39,680-44,090)
Maximum TOW, kg (lb)	96,000	100,000-102,000
	(211,640)	(220,460-224,870)
Effective range at 11,000m (36,090ft), km (miles): *		
maximum	5,000 (3,100)	5,000 (3,100)
with max payload and 2,900-kg (6,390-lb) fuel reserves	2,900 (1,800)	3,700 (2,298)
with a 12,000-kg (26,455-lb) payload and 3,900-kg (8,600-lb) fuel reserves	4,400 (2,732)	5,200 (3,230)
Fuel burn in maximum-range flight, g/tonne-km	360	290
Required runway length, m (ft)	2,500 (8,200)	2,500 (8,200)

* with no wind, at a cruising speed of 850km/h (527mph)

CCCP-85317, the first prototype Tu-154M. Tupolev PLC

The second prototype, CCCP-85606 (seen here at Zhukovskiy in August 1993 as RA-85606), had a modified rear fuselage with a spin recovery parachute above the centre engine nozzle, which required the rudder trailing edge to be cut away at the base. This view shows the new engine nacelles with clamshell thrust reversers and the APU exhaust door above the starboard engine pylon. Author

CCCP-85640 (c/n 88A772), an early-production Tu-154M operated by TsUMVS/63rd Flight, taxies at Moscow-Sheremet'yevo. Tupolev PLC

for conversion pursuant to the above-mentioned MAP/MGA joint decision. Hence, unlike all subsequent Tu-154Ms, CCCP-85317 retained the bulged dielectric panel of the DISS-013 Doppler speed and drift sensor system immediately aft of the radome and the original high-lift devices.

The Tu-154M made its first flight from Kuibyshev-Bezymyanka in 1980, captained by Tupolev OKB test pilot Sergey T Agapov. After a series of manufacturer's flight tests, which basically confirmed the anticipated performance, the aircraft underwent joint state acceptance trials between 1st June and 14th August 1981; these were held by the Tupolev OKB in cooperation with GosNII GA, LII and TsAGI.

The first prototype underwent maximum range tests as part of the state acceptance trials programme. With a 100-ton (220,460-lb)

maximum take-off weight and 5,000kg (11,020 lb) of fuel reserves, the Tu-154M had a range of 3,700km (2,298 miles) with a 20-ton (44,090-lb) payload or 5,200km (3,230 miles) with a 12-ton (26,455-lb) payload, cruising at 10,900-11,500m (35,760-37,730ft) with a speed of Mach 0.805.

The concluding part of the state acceptance trials report said that, given a TOW of 100 tons, the effective range of the upgraded aircraft met the target stipulated by the MAP/MGA decision of 30th August 1977. With a full load of passengers (180) and a 95-ton (209,435-ton) TOW the fuel efficiency was 28.7g/seat-km. The results were deemed positive and a decision to go ahead with series production was taken.

Originally, proceeding from a Tu-154 fleet analysis (that is, a rundown of the total time since new accumulated by specific Tu-154s in Aeroflot's fleet), MAP planned to terminate Tu-154B-2 production in 1982, switching to Tu-154M production in 1983. A total of 200 new-build Tu-154Ms were to be manufactured in 1983-87; additionally, it was considered advisable to convert 200 low-time Tu-154B-2s to Tu-154M standard in 1986-1990, and a conversion technology was duly developed. The 150 or so high-time Tu-154Bs remaining operational by then were to be used as freighters, with a reduction in the cabin pressure differential to prolong their active life.

Later, however, the ministry reconsidered these plans and the *en masse* conversion idea was dropped; it was deemed more expedient to build the Tu-154M in larger numbers instead, letting the Tu-154Bs serve on. The remaining Tu-154B/B-1/B-2 fleet would be placed under close scrutiny, and a multi-stage service life extension programme (SLEP) would be developed and progressively implemented, building on research and operational experience.

It was not until 1984 that the first new-build Tu-154M – the second prototype (though some regard it as the first production example) – was built. Registered CCCP-85606 (c/n 84A701), this aircraft made its first flight at Kuibyshev-Bezymyanka on 16th July 1984, flown by a Tupolev OKB crew captained by A I Talalakin. The second prototype was used for high-alpha/low-speed tests; consequently a large fairing housing a spin recovery parachute canister was installed at the base of the fin in lieu of the trailing-edge fillet. (Later, spotting CCCP-85606 at Zhukovskiy during the MosAeroShow '92 on 11th-16th August, some Western observers mistook this fairing for a 'closed APU', although the APU outlet was clearly visible.) The second new-build Tu-154M – the first production example, CCCP-85607 (c/n 84A702) manufactured on 22nd November 1984 – was likewise retained by the Tupolev OKB and used in the trials programme, as indicated by the cruciform phototheodolite calibration markings on the fuselage.

Here, a curious fact must be mentioned. While the last three registration digits of Aeroflot's Kuznetsov-powered Tu-154 versions always matched the last three of the c/n (thus creating gaps in the registration sequence where export aircraft 'took the registrations away'), this was **not** the case with the Tu-154M. For reasons unknown the first new-build Tu-154M received the c/n 84A701 instead of its rightful 84A606, and the last digits accrued from 701 to an eventual 1020 (c/n 01A1020). Thus, to determine the sequence number of a production Tu-154M (that is, counting from the start of Tu-154 production and including earlier versions!) you need to subtract 95 from the construction number; for instance, CCCP-85733 (c/n 92A915) manufactured on 30th June 1992 is the 820th Kuibyshev-built example. On the one hand, this allowed Tu-154M registrations to be allocated in sequence (without gaps) from CCCP-85606 onwards, and the disparity between the registrations and the c/ns grew as export aircraft 'butted in'. On the other hand, unlike pre-Tu-154M times, Soviet/CIS Tu-154M registrations did not necessarily run in sequence, especially during the final years of production.

Three more aircraft were manufactured before the end of the year. Full-scale production of the Tu-154M began in January 1985; that year the new version had its international debut when CCCP-85609 (c/n 84A704) participated in the 36th Paris Air Show with the exhibit code 317. Production Tu-154Ms were powered by improved D-30KU-154 Srs 2 (D-30KU-154-II) engines. Outwardly the new-build examples differed from the first prototype in having the new 'unbroken' LE slats, a pair of runway turnoff lights buried in the nose immediately aft of the radome and a flush dielectric panel of the Doppler speed and drift sensor (not bulged as on the Tu-154B-2).

As compared to the preceding versions, the Tu-154M was much cleaner aerodynamically, but it was also much dirtier – literally. The D-30KU is a rather smoky engine; because of the clamshell thrust reverser design lacking grilles to direct the exhaust gases away from the fuselage, soot deposits formed on the rear fuselage and fin when reverse thrust was repeatedly applied on landing, making the aircraft look rather untidy. Since the late 1980s several air carriers, including Aeroflot, have addressed this issue by painting the rear fuselage (and sometimes the vertical tail) a darker colour to make the tell-tale exhaust stains less conspicuous; washing the aircraft every now and then would obviously be too troublesome. Also, unlike the Kuznetsov-engined versions, the Tu-154M leaves a smoke trail that can be seen for miles.

The story of the Tu-154 *sans suffixe* was repeated: Aeroflot's Vnukovo UAD/200th Flight was the first to take delivery of the Tu-154M, followed by the Ul'yanovsk Higher Civil Aviation Flying School, while Balkan Bulgarian Airlines became the first foreign customer. Airline-configured Tu-154Ms were built in a 176-seat all-economy version with a small galley aft of the flightdeck (instead of the 180-seat version envisaged originally) and a 164-seat all-tourist version with a regular galley. The latter version could be rapidly reconfigured as a mixed-class 154-seater (F8CY146); the number of first class seats could be increased to 24, with an accompanying reduction in overall seating capacity. The seats could be removed if necessary, allowing the Tu-154M to be used as a package freighter.

The aircraft had ICAO Cat II automatic landing approach capability. Its operating costs were significantly reduced thanks to an improved maintenance system, and the noise footprint was also smaller than the Tu-154B's. The fuel burn per seat-mile was reduced 10-20% over a range of up to 3,000km (1,863 miles) and 30-60% on longer routes; this gave a fuel saving of 1,000kg (2,204 lb) per hour as compared to the Tu-154B.

After the demise of the Soviet Union and Russia's plunge into capitalism, the former divisions of MAP turned into state-owned or private enterprises pursuing their own business. The Kuibyshev aircraft factory changed its name, becoming the AVI.S Joint-Stock Co. By 1995 the enterprise had been renamed once more, gaining its present-day name, Aviacor.

Like the previous versions, the Tu-154M was steadily refined as production progressed. For instance, late-production Tu-154Ms have improved D-30KU-154 Srs 3 (D-30KU-154-III) engines offering a 5.5% lower SFC and an 800-hour increase in designated engine life. Aircraft manufactured from the late 1980s onwards featured a new *Zhasmin* (Jasmine) navigation suite including an I-21 inertial navigation system (INS). The INS worked in concert with an upgraded ABSU-154 Srs 3 AFCS enabling ICAO Cat IIIA automatic approach.

Investigation of a fatal crash which occurred on 2nd January 1994, when the entire hydraulic system of Tu-154M RA-85656 was put out of action by an uncontained engine air starter failure, led the Tupolev ANTK to modify the hydraulic system. To preclude total hydraulics failure in this situation, the routing of the hydraulic lines was changed to place them outside the potential shrapnel damage zone; hence a characteristic piping conduit appeared low on the starboard side of the fin. All existing Tu-154Ms were progressively modified in this fashion. The rear pressure dome was also reinforced. Additionally, porous noise attenuation liners were installed in the engine nacelles.

A total of 320 Tu-154Ms was built in 1984-2001, although production was interrupted several times. Although airframe production finished in the early 1990s, the last known Tu-154M assembled from Aviacor's pool of components was not delivered until July 2006.

Two of the latest Tu-154Ms – RA-85123 No 2 and RA-85795 No 2 (c/ns unknown) – were built without the forward pair of overwing emergency exits. The window arrangement is door+18+door+10+exit+13+exit to port and 4+exit+10+door+1+10+exit+13+exit to starboard.

Top: **Tu-154M RA-85782 (c/n 93A966) was refitted as a Tu-154M 'Salon' with a plush interior by the Tupolev PLC for the president of the Alrosa diamond mining company and is operated by the company's identically named airline division. It is seen here at Zhukovskiy during the MAKS-2005 airshow. Note the additional communications aerials on top of the fuselage between the entry doors.** Author

Above left and right: **The cubicle for the 'main passenger' in the forward cabin of Tu-154M 'Salon' RA-85782.** Author

Tu-154M 'Salon' RA-85675 is one of several completed with the Karpaty-ST HF communications suite. It is seen in the early version of the Rossiya State Transport Company's livery. Martin Novak

Tu-154M 'Salon' VIP Aircraft

Like its Kuznetsov-powered precursors, the Tu-154M also had a VIP version developed for the 235th IFD and the Soviet Ministry of Defence. In due course this version was made available for export and delivered to several 'friendly nations'. Several interior layouts were available. Again, the top-of-the-range version for the Soviet government flight was equipped with a VHF secure communications suite and featured the associated dorsal fairing and extra blade aerials.

Known new-build Tu-154M 'Salons' were registered RA-85019 No 2, CCCP-85613 (?), CCCP-85614 (?), CCCP-85616 (?), CCCP-85653, CCCP-85658, CCCP-85659, CCCP-85666 (equipped with Karpaty-ST HF comms gear), CCCP-85675 (equipped with HF comms gear), CCCP-85686 (equipped with HF comms gear), EW-85815, 4K-AZ10, LZ-BTZ, YN-CBT, OK-BYO (later OM-BYO), OK-BYP, OK-BYZ (later Czech Air Force '1016 White'), Czech Air Force '1003 White', DDR-SFA (later Luftwaffe 11+01), DDR-SFB (later Luftwaffe 11+02), Polish Air Force '837 Black' and '862 Black'. Additionally, in post-Soviet times several Tu-154Ms were outfitted as VIP jets; these included EX-85718, 4K-85729 (?) and RA-85782 No 2.

Actually the latter aircraft is something of a mystery – the 'No 2' bit is unconfirmed. Fact is, the original Tu-154M RA-85782 (c/n 93A966) was sold to Kazakhstan, becoming UN-85782. When freshly painted Tu-154M 'Salon' RA-85782 was seen in the colours of the Russian carrier Alrosa at the MAKS-2005 airshow in Zhukovskiy, the data plates were illegible but the c/n was checked on the port main gear oleo as 917 (that is, 92A917). This makes it a re-export aircraft (ex-B-2627); however, there have been reports that B-2628 was sold to Aeroflot Russian Airlines as RA-85735 and that RA-85782 simply reverted to its original identity after resale to Russia.

Tu-154M Lux

This designation was applied in Poland to the Polish Air Force's two Tu-154M 'Salons' ('837 Black' and '862 Black', later reserialled '101 Red' and '102 Red' respectively).

Tu-154-100 (Tu-154M-100) Medium-haul Airliner

Development of an upgraded version of the Tu-154M designated Tu-154-100 (some sources call it Tu-154M-100) began in 1994 as a joint effort of the Tupolev ANTK and Aviacor. The aircraft was to have a maximum TOW increased to 104 tons (229,280 lb) and a maximum landing weight increased to 82.5 tons (181,880 lb). It was to be equipped with an automatic flap/LE slat control system and a system reminding the crew to extend the landing gear and high-lift devices on final approach; the main gear bogies were to feature new KT-141E wheels with riveted rims. To enhance flight safety the Tu-154-100 was to feature an AUW and CG position determination system. The aircraft was to feature a new interior with larger overhead baggage bins and an automatic oxygen system, as well as a new modular galley; the cabin layout was likewise new, accommodating 132 in the baseline version (F12C18Y102) with a seat pitch of 102cm (40⁵⁄₃₂in), 81cm (31⅞in) and 75cm (29½in) respectively. The avionics suite was to be tailored to the customer's requirements, featuring such optional items as satellite navigation and satellite communication systems, a Kontoor-10 (Contour) weather radar instead of the usual Groza-154, a colour radar display with wind shear indication, long-range radio navigation (LORAN) equipment and an *Ooniversal* navigation computer.

Development of the Tu-154-100 proceeded slowly because the airliner market was saturated and there was no demand. In 1996 Iran Air took out an option for 12 such aircraft but subsequently cancelled the order. Eventually, however, an order for three was placed by start-up Slovak Airlines in 1997. The aircraft built as Tu-154-100s – OM-AAA through OM-AAC (c/ns 98A1014, 98A1015 and 98A1018) were outwardly identical to any Tu-154M but were fitted with some Western avionics (including a Litton autopilot and a Honeywell traffic collision avoidance system) and new cabin interiors (variously reported as being of French or Hungarian origin) with an automatic oxygen system. Outwardly the Tu-154-100 could be identified by an additional small blade aerial on the centre engine's air intake trunk. The three aircraft were delivered in March, May and December 1998 respectively.

Tu-154M-LK1 Cosmonaut Trainer

In February 1976 the Soviet Union embarked on an ambitious programme to create a reusable space transport system – the indigenous counterpart of the US Space Shuttle. While the system as a whole was officially named Baikal after the world's deepest lake located in East Siberia, the Soviet space shuttle was known to the general public the world over under the name Buran (Blizzard; pronounced *boorahn*). It featured a unique custom-made control system which, among other things, enabled it to land in fully automatic mode. NPO Energiya ('Energy' Scientific & Production Association; NPO = *naoochno-proizvodstvennoye obyedineniye*) had overall responsibility for the programme, as well as for the huge space launch vehicle (SLV) of the same name that was to place the Buran into orbit; NPO Molniya (Lightning) was the 'prime contractor' for the shuttle orbiter itself.

Once the shuttle's automatic landing system and flight pattern involving a very steep descent had been verified on the three Tu-154LL avionics testbeds/control configured vehicles (see

'102 Red' is one of the Polish Air Force's two Tu-154M 'Salons' known locally as the Tu-154M Lux. Yuriy Kirsanov

below), in the late 1980s it was decided that a special version of the Tu-154M should be developed for training Buran pilots; it also served for training cosmonauts in observation and photography techniques. The aircraft was designated Tu-154M-LK1; the suffix letters denoted [*dlya podgotovki*] **lyot***chikov-kosmon-***ahv***tov* – 'for pilot-cosmonaut training'. (This **lyot***chik-kosmo***nahv***t* appellation was quite logical, since you have to qualify as a pilot before becoming an astronaut!)

The one-off Tu-154M-LK1, CCCP-85655 (c/n 89A798), was based on the Tu-154M 'Salon', featuring the VIP version's integral airstairs and even retaining a VIP cabin section. However, the cabin also featured trainee workstations, one of which emulated the Buran's flightdeck. The forward baggage compartment was converted into a camera bay; the aircraft was equipped with AFA-41/10 and AFA-41/20 cameras and an SA-1 commenting system (*sistema annoteerovaniya*) allowing relevant text information to be appended to each photo. Other cameras, such as the East German Zeiss Ikon MSK-4 multi-spectrum camera, could be fitted. The presence of the cameras was revealed by three ventral camera ports on the centreline just ahead of the rear entry door for vertical photography and a pair of camera ports for oblique photography ahead of them. Additionally, the 14th window to port and the 12th window to starboard were replaced by circular windows featuring special high-quality quartz glass, and a pair of similar windows was located in the cabin roof between the 16th and 17th window on each side, 'looking up' at 45° to port and starboard. These windows served for observation/photography training.

As in the case of the Tu-154LL, the required steep descent trajectory was obtained by means of the spoilers and in-flight application of reverse thrust. The designers considered installing large airbrakes on the rear fuselage, but these were not fitted eventually.

After a series of tests conducted under the leadership of Col Anatoliy Andronov (head of the Soviet Air Force's Flight Test Department) the Tu-154M-LK1 was taken on charge by the 70th Independent Special Test and Training Air Regiment named after Vladimir S Seryogin[5] at Chkalovskaya AB. From 11-16th August 1992 CCCP-85655 attended MosAeroShow '92.

OM-AAA, the first of three Tu-154-100s delivered to Slovak Airlines, on final approach to Moscow-Sheremet'yevo. Note the additional blade aerial on the centre engine air intake trunk. Dmitriy Petrochenko

RA-85655, the one-off Tu-154M-LK1 cosmonaut trainer, on final approach to Chkalovskaya AB. The lower port side camera port is visible halfway between the nose gear and the wing leading edge. Dmitriy Petrochenko

This view of the Tu-154M-LK1 on display at the MosAeroShow '92 (as CCCP-85655) shows the camera ports and the deployed integral airstairs at the rear entry door. Author

КОМПОНОВКА САМОЛЕТА ОТКРЫТОГО НЕБА Ту-154М-он

1 КАБИНА ЭКИПАЖА
2 ШТАБНОЙ САЛОН
3 РАБОЧИЕ МЕСТА ОПЕРАТОРОВ
4 МЕСТА СОПРОВОЖДАЮЩЕГО ПЕРСОНАЛА
5 БОРТОВАЯ АППАРАТУРА СИСТЕМЫ НАБЛЮДЕНИЯ

ЗОНЫ ЗАХВАТА ПОВЕРХНОСТИ АППАРАТУРОЙ НАБЛЮДЕНИЯ

1 ПАНОРАМНЫЙ ФОТОАППАРАТ
2 КАДРОВЫЕ АППАРАТЫ
3 ТЕЛЕВИЗИОННЫЕ КАМЕРЫ
4 РАДИОЛОКАЦИОННАЯ СТАНЦИЯ БОКОВОГО ОБЗОРА
5 ИНФРАКРАСНАЯ АППАРАТУРА

Tu-154M-ON Monitoring Aircraft (German version, Tu-154M-OS)

Not all Tu-154 variants were developed in the Soviet Union or Russia. On 24th March 1992 twenty-five states (the NATO nations, former Warsaw Pact nations which were not yet NATO members then, and the CIS republics) signed the Open Skies Treaty during an Organisation for Security and Cooperation in Europe (OSCE) summit. This document gave the signatories the right to perform up to 42 flights annually over each other's military bases and facilities in order to monitor the observance of international arms reduction treaties. The flights would be performed by specially equipped aircraft; in addition to the regular crew, these would carry representatives of the USA's On-Site Inspection Agency (OSIA) and of the country being inspected. The latter was

11+02, the Luftwaffe's ill-starred Tu-154M-ON Open Skies monitoring aircraft. Sergey and Dmitriy Komissarov collection

This drawing depicting the internal layout of the German Tu-154M-ON appeared on the Tupolev PLC stand at the MAKS-95 airshow. The figures denote: 1. Flightdeck; 2. Staff cabin ('war room'); 3. Mission equipment operators' workstations; 4. Seats for accompanying personnel; 5. Surveillance equipment. Author

Another drawing from the same stand showing the fields of view of the Tu-154M-ON's mission equipment in the projected Stage 2 configuration. The figures denote: 1. PAN panoramic camera; 2. LMK 2015 framing cameras; 3. VOS 60 video cameras; 4. Infra-red line scan system; 5. Synthetic aperture radar. Author

The flightdeck of the Tu-154M-LL FACT CCV with the captain's workstation reconfigured with experimental systems. Note the cutaway instrument panel with two CRT multi-function displays and the head-up display above it; the fighter-type control stick and one of the two side-stick controllers (on the central control pedestal) are also visible. Author

A second side-stick controller is installed on the port cockpit console of the FACT CCV; thus the captain has *three* sticks to choose from! Author

In contrast, the first officer's station is perfectly standard, acting as a back-up in case the experimental systems fail. Author

retained as a back-up. The cabins were crammed with test and recording equipment.

The aircraft communicated in real time with a ground data processing facility via a data link system functioning in two-way (uplink/downlink) mode. Its applications were as follows:

- in-flight simulation and assessment of flight dynamics of future transports in normal and abnormal situations;
- verification of different types of pilot's controllers;
- in-flight optimisation of the aircraft's handling qualities, development of handling quality criteria and certification standards;
- development of the philosophy and standard graphic formats for HUDs and head-down displays;
- pilot training;
- flightdeck ergonomics studies and flight safety research (the onboard equipment permitted analysis of the pilot workload and the pilots' psychological parameters

In this guise CCCP-85317 was first displayed at the MosAeroShow '92. Since then it was an invariable participant of all Moscow airshows, gaining the RA- prefix by August 1995. The experimental equipment changed from time to time.

At the MAKS-2001 airshow (14th-19th August 2001) RA-85317 was first shown in a new grey/blue colour scheme with LII titles and logo. By 2003 the aircraft had gained huge FACT titles; the acronym stood for Future Aircraft Control Testbed. Its equipment had been considerably altered by then (among other things, it included ambient air water content/humidity sensors). Part of the associated ground equipment was housed in a Volkswagen LT 35D van outfitted as a mobile laboratory which was displayed alongside.

In addition to the applications stated above, the aircraft now fulfilled the following missions:
- research of aircraft condensation trail (contrail) formation conditions;
- development and research of navigation system and air traffic management (ATM) concepts;
- flight test of high-accuracy inertial and inertial/satellite navigation systems;
- development of noise abatement procedures;
- elaboration of new equipment test techniques.

The overhead circuit breaker panel of the Tu-154M-LL FACT. This shot gives a better view of the HUD. Author

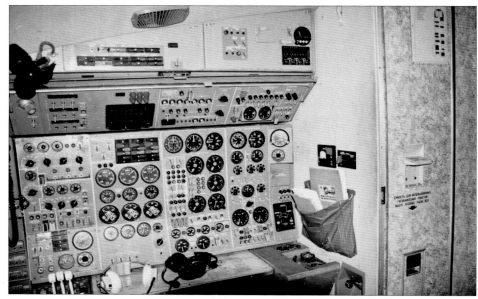

The flight engineer's station of the Tu-154M-LL FACT. Author

One of the test engineers' workstations in the forward cabin of the Tu-154M-LL. Author

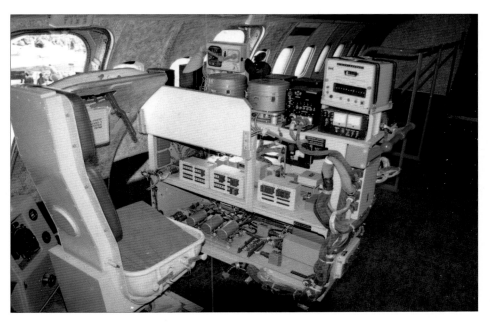

Test equipment (data recorders) installed near the port overwing emergency exits. Author

Another test engineer's workstation and test equipment rack in the forward cabin of the Tu-154M-LL. Note that the seat pans are dished to take parachutes in case the need arises to bale out. Author

As a last resort, the crew of the Tu-154M-LL can bail out through the forward cabin emergency exit. Note the emergency depressurisation valve in the window to the left and the handrails assisting bailing out. Author

Tu-155 Cryogenic Fuel Technology Demonstrator

In the mid-1970s, soaring oil prices and the global energy crisis forced scientists to step up research into alternative fuels for industrial applications and transportation. Liquefied natural gas (LNG) and liquid hydrogen (LH_2) became prime candidates for the aviation fuel of the future. LNG had a number of valuable advantages over traditional kerosene fuels. The global reserves of natural gas were more abundant than those of oil, which meant that the price of LNG fuel would go down as the oil reserves shrank and the oil prices rose; here it should be noted that the Soviet Union possessed large supplies of natural gas. Also, the calorific value of natural gas is 15% greater than that of kerosene; last but not least, the toxic emissions are much lower (for example, unlike oil, natural gas has no sulphur content and produces no corrosive sulphurous oxides).

LH_2 held even greater promise; it had a specific calorific value three times greater than fossil fuel and was ecologically 'clean', to say

nothing of the fact that, unlike fossil fuel, it was replenishable. Therefore the Soviet Academy of Sciences joined forces with a number of industry research and development establishments and design bureaux to work out a programme envisaging large-scale introduction of hydrogen fuel in the national economy. Implementation of this programme was to bring about a marked improvement of the nation's ecology and lay the foundations for the development of future hypersonic aircraft and aerospaceplanes.

In the aircraft industry the programme was codenamed **Kholod** (Cold) as a reference to cryogenic fuels (LNG and LH_2). First, in 1974 the OKB-23 design bureau led by Vladimir Mikhaïlovich Myasishchev started work on a hypersonic aerospaceplane with a cryogenic powerplant known as *tema devyatnadtsat'* – Subject (that is, project) 19. As a first step towards the aerospaceplane, OKB-23 was to create a propulsion technology testbed designated IL-76Kh (the suffix letter referring to the Kholod-2 programme) – a heavily modified

IL-76 *Candid* military transport with a single experimental cryogenic-fuel turbojet and heat-insulated LH_2 tanks housed in the freight hold. Later, the Powers That Be intervened; when development was well advanced the Myasishchev OKB was ordered to transfer its know-how to the Tupolev OKB.

Designated Tu-155, the cryogenic fuel technology demonstrator was converted from a rewinged Tu-154 *sans suffixe* (CCCP-85035, c/n 72A035). The extensive conversion involved a whole raft of major structural and external changes. The rear fuselage section between the overwing emergency exits and the rear pressure dome was remanufactured as a windowless bay housing a heavily insulated cryogenic fuel tank with a capacity of 20m³ (706.29ft³); this could hold LH_2 chilled to −253°C (−423°F) or LNG chilled to −162°C (−259°F). This installation was necessary because LH_2 has a four times lower specific gravity than kerosene and the fuel tanks need to be pressurised to stop the LH_2 or LNG from boiling out as the aircraft climbs to high altitude, which makes it impossible to house them in the wings.

The starboard NK-8-2 engine was replaced by an NK-88 turbofan rated at 10,500kgp (23,150lbst) – an experimental derivative of the NK-8-2U adapted to run on cryogenic fuels; Chief Designer V N Orlov was responsible for this engine. The basic design changes included installation of a cryogenic turbine pump (a two-stage centrifugal pump driven by

CCCP-85035, the Tu-155 cryogenic propulsion technology demonstrator. Tupolev PLC

A cutaway drawing of the Tu-155, showing the helium and nitrogen bottles aft of the extended flightdeck, the test equipment consoles further aft and the cryogenic tank at the rear. Tupolev PLC

ЭКСПЕРИМЕНТАЛЬНЫЙ САМОЛЕТ ТУ-155

Рис.1

The Tu-155's flightdeck appears to be pretty much standard – except for the red-painted throttle knob of the experimental No 3 engine and the dished seat pans designed to take parachutes. Note the nosewheel steering tiller on the captain's console. Yefim Gordon

The flight engineer's workstation of the Tu-155 (foreground). Yefim Gordon

The Tu-155's crew section is extended aft to accommodate the test engineers' workstations. Note the red-knobbed throttle of the No 3 engine. Part of the instrumentation is missing from the retired aircraft. Yefim Gordon

engine bleed air); it was housed in a special box on top of the engine casing ventilated by air under pressure to prevent accumulation of explosive fuel vapours. An annular heat exchanger was installed downstream of the low-pressure turbine (at the location formerly occupied by the thrust reverser) to convert the fuel to gaseous state before it was fed into the combustion chamber; no attempt was made to feed the hydrogen to the engine in liquid form because vaporisation in the fuel lines made it extremely difficult to maintain a stable flow and regulate combustion. Bench tests of the NK-88 began in February 1980.

The fuel system was considerably redesigned to include a cryogenic fuel delivery system, a cryogenic tank pressure monitoring system activating the safety valves if necessary, a recirculation system, a cryogenic tank pressurisation system and an emergency fuel jettison system. The delivery system featured centrifugal and jet (transfer) pumps in the cryogenic tank, heat-insulated fuel lines, a fuel flow regulator and valves.

Three additional systems were installed to operate and monitor the cryogenic fuel complex. These were: a helium system controlling the experimental powerplant units; a nitrogen system which replaced the air in the cryogenic tank bay and fuel system compartments with nitrogen and alerted the crew about any cryogenic fuel leak well before it reached an explosive concentration; and a system monitoring the vacuum in the cryogenic tank's heat insulation. The numerous helium bottles were installed ten-abreast on the floor in the centre portion of the former forward cabin, while the larger nitrogen bottles were mounted above the cabin windows in the same area (in lieu of the overhead baggage racks) and in the forward baggage compartment. Test and recording equipment racks were located fore and aft of this 'bottle bay'; the flightdeck was extended aft to accommodate three test engineers' workstations facing the starboard side, and a further workstation was located near the rear entry door, with more test equipment between it and the bulkhead separating the manned cabin from the cryogenic fuel tank bay. An extra large complement of fire extinguishers was installed in the unpressurised rear fuselage near the experimental engine.

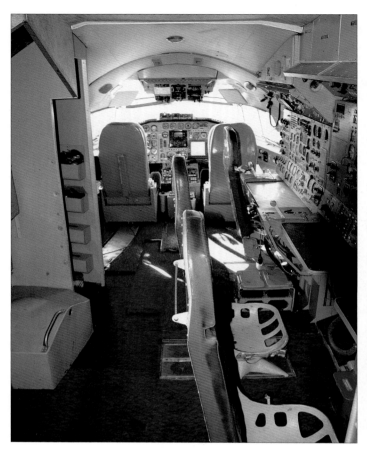

The Tu-155's window arrangement was now door+18+door+7+exit+1+exit to port and 4+exit+10+door+7+exit+1+exit to starboard; the rear pair of windows between the emergency exits was replaced by vertically paired vents. Other non-standard external features included a small fin-like excrescence atop the vertical tail near the leading edge which incorporated twin (normal and emergency) fuel vapour vents; the drains to these vents were routed along the starboard side and top of the centre engine air intake trunk and the fin leading edge. This required the usual spike housing the radio antenna to be deleted and the upper

anti-collision light to be relocated to the fuse-lage amidships.

Three large conduits enclosing pipelines (one to port and two to starboard) ran along the rear fuselage sides from the pair of windows immediately ahead of the emergency exits. The flattened upper conduits associated with the cryogenic tank bay pressurisation system were located symmetrically above the windows, terminating in line with the fin/centre engine air intake trunk junction. The starboard lower conduit, which housed the heat-insulated fuel line and was fatter than the others, ran below the windows in such a way as to obstruct the emer-

gency exits (which no one would use anyway) and then curved upwards to mate with the engine pylon. Additionally, two thinner conduits ran from the port wing/fuselage fairing and along the rear fuselage underside (offset to port) from the wing centre section to a point in line with the fin leading edge. A fuel jettison pipe curved gently from a ventral fairing offset to starboard to the starboard side of the centre engine nozzle. Finally, the starboard engine nacelle was considerably modified, with no thrust reverser and a boxy fairing with streamlined front and rear ends (offset to starboard) over the NK-88's cryogenic turbine pump housing.

A special cryogenic refuelling installation was built at the OKB's flight test facility in Zhukovskiy for servicing the Tu-155 with LH$_2$ or LNG during the tests. The installation allowed tests involving large quantities of cryogenic fuel to be performed and included the following systems:
- a cryogenic fuelling system utilising special refuelling vehicles based on the KrAZ-257 6x4 conventional lorry;

Top left: **An overall view of the Tu-155's crew section. All the seats have dished seat pans.** Yefim Gordon

Top right: **The rear end of the Tu-155, with a cryogenic fuel jettison pipe running from a ventral fairing to the starboard side.** *Flug Revue*

Left: **The Tu-155's forward cabin; the front half is occupied by helium bottles on the floor and nitrogen bottles under the ceiling, while the rear half accommodates test equipment racks.** Yefim Gordon

Top left: **The starboard side of the Tu-155's rear fuselage features two conduits, the upper one housing the fuel lines for the NK-88 cryogenic engine.** Author

Top right: **This view shows the missing cabin windows in the area where the cryogenic tank is housed, as well as the faired pipe running along the centre engine air intake trunk and the fin leading edge to a vent atop the fin. Note the position of the upper anti-collision light ahead of the emergency exits.** Author

Right: **The aircrew and the ground test personnel involved in the Tu-155 programme pose with the aircraft.** Tupolev PLC

Below: **An air-to-air of the Tu-155. The cross on the service door is a photo calibration mark.** Tupolev PLC

- a compressed nitrogen supply;
- an electrical power supply,
- a television monitoring system;
- a gas analysis system;
- a fire-precaution sprinkler system;
- a cryogenic fuel quality monitoring system;
- a vacuum pump vehicle;
- a command and control centre located in an underground bunker to ensure safety in the event of a fire or explosion on the hardstand;
- mobile communications posts.

Because the OKB was breaking new ground and a lot of research was involved, the initial part of the programme proved to be quite protracted. The Tu-155 made its first flight – the historic first-ever flight of a hydrogen-fuelled aircraft – on 15th April 1988; the aircraft was captained by Merited Test Pilot V A Sevan'kayev. This was the beginning of an extensive test programme. Initially liquid hydrogen was used as the cryogenic fuel; in January 1989 the Tu-155 began a new stage of the tests with a modified NK-88 running on liquefied natural gas. The Tu-155's performance was basically similar to that of the Tu-154B; the supply of cryogenic fuel in the 20-m³ tank was sufficient to give an endurance of two hours.

In the course of the tests the Tu-155 established 14 world records. It also made two visits abroad – to Nice (with a stopover in Bratislava) and to Hannover. At the latter location the aircraft participated in the ILA '90 airshow, becoming one of the stars of the show. As a result, Deutsche Airbus (the German division of the Airbus Industrie international consortium) made a deal with the Tupolev OKB envisaging cooperation in the development of hydrogen-fuelled aircraft, including a version of the A300B4 wide-body airliner. On 11th-16th August 1992 the aircraft was displayed statically at the MosAeroShow '92. After that, the aircraft was placed in storage and is still parked on its own hardstand in Zhukovskiy.

The advent of the Tu-155 aroused immense interest in the world's aviation community and aviation press. Inevitably, there were detractors who questioned the safety of cryogenic fuels and dismissed the idea.

The development and testing of the Tu-155 yielded invaluable practical material for further development of cryogenic-fuel aircraft, paving the way for such projects as the Tupolev C-Prop, Tu-130SPG, Tu-330SPG and Tu-206 (see also next chapter). Soviet aircraft designers gained practical experience of operating and testing such aircraft and evolved new testing techniques, as well as fire safety procedures for cryogenic-fuel aircraft.

As part of the Tu-155 programme, a special cryogenic refuelling facility with all required safety features was built at Zhukovskiy. Yefim Gordon

Two views of the heat-insulated cryogenic fuel transfer lines and hoses that were connected to the Tu-155. Yefim Gordon

These colours proved a bit controversial ('if this is a Russian airline, how come they have the Lithuanian flag all over the place?'). Therefore a more restrained version appeared, featuring a grey belly, no stripes on the forward fuselage and smaller '*авиаэнерго*' titles in heavier type ahead of the wings (c/s No 2). Finally, in 2001 RA-85809 received the current livery introduced in March of that year (white with a bit of dark grey trim and a stylised 'A' logo).

RA-85101 No 2 was one of four Tu-154Ms acquired by Aviaexpresscruise from Blagoveshchensk Airlines; it still wears the basic livery of its first owner, China Southwest Airlines. Yuriy Kirsanov

Registration	C/n	Notes
RA-85797	93A981	C/s No 1, later No 2B (grey nacelles), still later No 3. Leased or sold to Aeroflot Russian Airlines by 2006
RA-85798	93A982	C/s No 1. Sold to Tatneft'aero by 12-98
RA-85809	94A985	C/s No 2A (white nacelles), later No 3. Leased or sold to Aeroflot Russian Airlines by 2006

The charter carrier **Aviaexpresscruise [E6/BKS]**[2] based at Moscow-Vnukovo operated eight Tu-154s. All have now been disposed of.

Registration	Version	C/n	Notes
RA-85101 No 2	Tu-154M	88A783	Ex-Blagoveshchensk Air Enterprise, bought 7-02; basic China Southwest Airlines c/s, Aviaexpresscruise titles/logo
RA-85109 No 2	Tu-154M	88A790	Ex-Blagoveshchensk Air Enterprise, bought 7-02; basic China Southwest Airlines c/s, Aviaexpresscruise titles/logo; still as such
RA-85136	Tu-154M	88A791	Ex-Blagoveshchensk Air Enterprise, bought 7-02; basic China Southwest Airlines c/s, Aviaexpresscruise titles/logo. Transferred to Yakutia 12-03
RA-85149	Tu-154M	88A797	Ex-Blagoveshchensk Air Enterprise, bought 7-02; basic China Southwest Airlines c/s, Aviaexpresscruise titles/logo. Sold to Aeroflot-Don by 10-03
RA-85604	Tu-154B-2	84A604	Leased from Orenburg Airlines July-October 1998; basic Orenburg Airlines c/s, Aviaexpresscruise titles
RA-85609	Tu-154M	84A704	Leased from Ul'yanovsk Higher Flying School 2002, basic Aeroflot c/s, no titles
RA-85636	Tu-154M	87A766	Leased from Ul'yanovsk Higher Flying School 2002, basic Aeroflot c/s, no titles
RA-85660	Tu-154M	89A810	Leased from AeroBratsk 5-01 to 9-01; basic AeroBratsk c/s, no titles
RA-85712	Tu-154M	91A888	Bought from ALAK 1999, basic ALAK red/white c/s. Leased to Yakutsk Airlines 10-00 to ?-03, basic Yakutsk Airlines grey c/s with Aviaexpresscruise titles/logo after return from lease

The cargo carrier **Avial'-NV [–/RLC]** based at Moscow-Domodedovo, Moscow/Sheremet'yevo-1 and Zhukovskiy operated Tu-154B-2 RA-85312 in January-February 2002. Later the aircraft was sold to Aerofreight Airlines. Also, Avial'-NV intended to buy five Tu-154B-2s being disposed of by Malév (HA-LCN/-LCO/-LCP/-LCU/-LCV). However, HA-LCO and HA-LCP were eventually bought by Turan Air of Azerbaijan, while HA-LCN, HA-LCU and HA-LCV delivered to Moscow/Vnukovo-1 on 3rd May, 23rd April and 25th April 2001 respectively were seized by the Russian Customs and never entered service.

Avialinii Chetyresto (Airlines 400) **[–/VAZ]**, the flying division of Aircraft Overhaul Plant No 400 at Moscow-Vnukovo, operated eight Tu-154Ms. Most are flown in the basic green/white colours of Bulgarian Air Charter with red '*Авиалинии 400 Air Charter*' titles on the fuselage and '*A. C.*' tail titles. In 2005 the airline acquired three Tu-154Ms from VIA – Varna International Airways.

Registration	Version	C/n	Notes
RA-85217	Tu-154B-1	89A795	Basic Aeroflot c/s, probably A400 titles. Leased from Primeaviaexport LLC by 9-02
RA-85479	Tu-154M	91A895?	Ex-9XR-DU? Basic 2003-standard Aeroflot c/s, red 'A400' titles. Seen 3-05; sold to Atlant-Soyuz by 6-05 as RA-85740?
RA-85630	Tu-154M	87A759	Leased from Rossiya State Transport Co 6-01 to 11-01, basic Yamal Airlines c/s, red 'A400' titles
RA-85650	Tu-154M	88A788	Ex-Bulgarian Air Charter LZ-LCI, basic BAC c/s. Leased to Iran Air Tour as EP-MCF. crashed as such Mashhad 1-9-06
RA-85653	Tu-154M 'Salon'	89A795	Bought from Rossiya State Transport Co by 7-01. Opf Vostokgazprom (which see). Sold to Sibir' Airlines by 4-04
RA-85680	Tu-154M	90A847	Ex-Bulgarian Air Charter LZ-LCE, basic BAC c/s. Reregistered by 7-05 as, see next line
LZ-LCU			Still basic BAC c/s but Avialinii 400 Air Charter titles, Russian Football Team badge
RA-85847	Tu-154M	88A792	Leased from Bashkirian Airlines ?-01, BAL c/s with tail logo but red 'A400' titles
LZ-LCA	Tu-154M	89A829	Leased from/jointly operated with Bulgarian Air Charter, full BAC c/s; to become RA-85671

Aviaprima Sochi Airlines [J5/PRL] leased Tupolev airliners as required until it went bankrupt in 1998. While these were mostly Tu-134s, at least six Tu-154s were leased over the years (all from the Chelyabinsk Air Enterprise); they flew in basic Aeroflot colours with the Aviaprima titles and logo on the nose.

Registration	Version	C/n	Notes
RA-85098	Tu-154B	75A098	Y164. Leased 9-93 to ?-?? and 4-95 to ?-??
RA-85114	Tu-154A	75A114	Y164. Leased 1-95 to 3-95 and 1-97 to ?-97
RA-85180	Tu-154B	76A180	Y164. Leased 9-93 to ?-??
RA-85183	Tu-154B-1	76A183	Y164. Leased 6-93 to 1-94
RA-85467	Tu-154B-2	81A467	C26Y102. Leased 1-94 to ?-??
RA-85514	Tu-154B-2	81A514	C26Y102. Leased 8-93 to 2-94 and 1-95 to ?-95

AVL Arkhangel'sk Airlines (*Arkhangel'skiye vozdooshnyye linii*) **[5N/AUL]** had five Tu-154B-2s.

Registration	C/n	Notes
RA-85302	78A302	Y180. Retired before takeover, date unknown
RA-85365	79A365	Y164. C/s No 3

Tu-154B-2 RA-85386 in full AVL Arkhangel'sk Airlines livery takes off from runway 25R at Moscow-Sheremet'yevo in July 2004. It was the carrier's only Tu-154 to be thus painted. Sergey Sergeyev

RA-85386	79A386	Y164. C/s No 1, no pinstripe; later c/s No 2
RA-85468	81A468	Y164. Basic Aeroflot c/s, no titles. Leased to Gromov Air 11-05
RA-85551	82A551	Y164. Basic Aeroflot c/s, no titles; later c/s No 3

At first the entire AVL fleet wore Aeroflot colours, sometimes with a round *Arkhangel'skiye vozdooshnyye linïï* badge on the nose (c/s No 1). Later the airline's Tu-134As had the fins painted blue with white Cyrillic letters 'AVL' and no titles but the trijets never received this livery. A smart new livery appeared in 1997, featuring a dark blue belly and tail, 'Northern lights' tail trim and red titles (c/s No 2). RA-85386 was the only aircraft to be thus repainted before the airline was absorbed by Aeroflot Russian Airlines as the flag carrier's Arkhangel'sk subsidiary in October 2004, changing its name to **Aeroflot-Nord** (the flight codes remained the same). Accordingly the rebranded carrier adopted a version of Aeroflot's

current 'Airbus livery' with a 'Northern lights' tail flash instead of the Russian flag fin flash (c/s No 3). Again, small variations of the livery exist: RA-85551 carries '**АЭРОФЛОТ**' in red and '**НОРД**' in black, whereas RA-85365 has all-black titles.

Moscow-based **Ayaks Airlines** bought Tu-154Ms RA-85713 and RA-85714 (c/ns 91A889 and 91A890) from the defunct airline ALAK. However, the airline ceased own operations in 1998 and sold the trijets to Georgia; the former aircraft became 4L-85713 with Georgian Airlines, while RA-85714 was sold to Aviaexpresscruise (the sister company of the Russian Aviaexpresscruise) as 4L-AAF in March 1998.

Baikal Airlines (Baikalavia) [X3/BKL] was the successor of the East Siberian CAD/Irkutsk UAD based at Irkutsk-1 airport. Among other things, its fleet included 20 Tu-154s of various versions formerly operated by the 201st Flight. These were transferred to the airline on 7th February 1995 and used on domestic and international scheduled services. Two liveries were used; the early version (c/s No 1) was based on Aeroflot's 1973 colours, while c/s No 2 (introduced on the airline's first and only Western aircraft, a Boeing 757-2Q8) featured a blue top and a white belly.

The airline's financial position was shaky in the late 1990s and plans of a merger with Chita-Avia in the hope of improving things were announced in April 1998. However, the 17th August 1998 bank crisis ruined these plans and Baikal Airlines filed for bankruptcy in September. Operations were restarted on a small scale under outside management in the spring of 1999 but the company finally folded soon afterwards.

After the rebranding of AVL as Aeroflot-Nord the fleet received this stylish new livery patterned on that of the parent company. Sergey Sergeyev

Registration	Version	C/n	Notes
RA-85038	Tu-154B-1	73A038	Converted Tu-154 *sans suffixe*. Retired 1999
RA-85041	Tu-154B	73A041	Converted Tu-154 *sans suffixe*. Aeroflot c/s; retired 1995

Tu-154B-2 RA-85453 seen on short finals to runway 14L at Moscow-Domodedovo illustrates the full livery of Baikal Airlines. Yuriy Kirsanov

RA-85123	Tu-154B	75A123	Y164. Retired by 1996
RA-85145	Tu-154B-1	76A145	Y164. Converted Tu-154B. Retired Irkutsk-1 1997
RA-85146 No 1	Tu-154B	76A146	Y164. Retired Irkutsk-1 1995
RA-85172	Tu-154B-1	76A172	Y164. Retired Irkutsk-1 1999
RA-85204 No 1	Tu-154B-1	77A204	Y164. Converted Tu-154B. Retired 1996
RA-85280 No 1	Tu-154B-2	78A280	Y164. Converted Tu-154B-1
RA-85453	Tu-154B-2	80A453	Y164. C/s No 2
RA-85462	Tu-154B-2	80A462	Y164. C/s No 1. Leased to Tesis by 5-99
RA-85503	Tu-154B-2	81A503	Y164. Aeroflot c/s. Leased to Tesis 2001
RA-85512	Tu-154B-2	81A512	Y164. Leased to Tesis 28-9-01 to 1-11-05
RA-85613	Tu-154M	85A722	Y164. C/s No 1. Sold to Sibir' Airlines
RA-85652	Tu-154M	88A794	Y164. C/s No 1, later No 2. Sold to Sibir' Airlines
RA-85654	Tu-154M	88A796	Y164. Sold to Alrosa
RA-85656	Tu-154M	89A801	Y164. Aeroflot c/s. Crashed near Irkutsk 2-1-94
RA-85657	Tu-154M	89A802	Y164. C/s No 1. Sold to Airlines 400
RA-85690	Tu-154M	90A861	Y164. C/s No 1, later No 2. Leased to Sibir' Airlines 31-10-00, later sold
RA-85695	Tu-154M	91A868	Y164. C/s No 1. Sold to Pulkovo Air Enterprise by 9-99
CCCP-85735	Tu-154M	92A917	Sold to Air Great Wall 8-92 as B-2627

BAL Bashkirian Airlines (*Bashkirskiye avialinii*) **[V9/BTC]** operated 22 Tu-154s from the republic's capital, Ufa. The airline's early livery was limited to the addition of a blue tail sporting BAL's stylised bee logo (the Republic of Bashkortostan is famous for its high-quality honey, among other things), 'Bashkirskiye avialinii' titles and the relocation of the registration to the engine nacelles (c/s No 1). Later the Aeroflot fuselage colours gave way to a predominantly white fuselage with a green belly, a blue stripe wrapped around the nose and huge 'БАЛ' titles (c/s No 2).

Interestingly, many of the carrier's Tu-154Ms are re-export aircraft. For instance, the former Polish examples were procured for US$ 2.5 million apiece – half the flyaway price of a new Tu-154M.

Until now BAL's Tu-154s were operated on both domestic and foreign services. Recently, however, the airline has announced that it plans to cease operations in Russia and wet-lease all of its Tu-154s to Iran.

Registration	Version	C/n	Notes
RA-85056	Tu-154A	74A056	Y164. Aeroflot c/s. Wfu Ufa by 4-94, used as rescue trainer
RA-85112	Tu-154B	75A112	Y164. Converted Tu-154A. Retired by 1998
RA-85265	Tu-154B-1	78A265	Y164. Retired by 1998
RA-85275	Tu-154B-1	78A275	Y164. C/s No 1. Derelict Ufa by 8-99, scrapped by 11-01
RA-85283	Tu-154B-1	78A283	Y164. Wfu Ufa by 1999
RA-85318	Tu-154B-2	78A318	Y164. Leased from Nizhniy Novgorod Airlines (date unknown), returned; basic Aeroflot c/s, Bashkirskiye Avialinii titles
RA-85347	Tu-154B-2	79A347	Y164. C/s No 1. Wfu Ufa by 11-01
RA-85349	Tu-154B-2	79A349	Y164. C/s No 2. Retired by 1998
RA-85404	Tu-154B-2	80A404	Y164. C/s No 1. Wfu Ufa by 8-99, scrapped by 11-01
RA-85450	Tu-154B-2	80A450	All-white c/s with BAL titles/logo, Avialeasing Co badge on nose; was leased in July-November 2002
RA-85525	Tu-154B-2	82A525	Y164. C/s No 1. Wfu Ufa 1999
RA-85773	Tu-154M	93A955	Y166. C/s No 1, later No 2. Leased to Iran Air Tour 2005
RA-85774	Tu-154M	93A956	Y166. C/s No 1. Sold to Gazpromavia 6-98
RA-85777	Tu-154M	93A959	Y166. C/s No 1, later No 2; see Yuzhnaya Aircompany/UN 85777!
RA-85816	Tu-154M	95A1006	Y166. Was leased to Shaheen Airlines, basic Shaheen Airlines c/s. Crashed near Überlingen, Germany, 1-7-02
RA-85824*	Tu-154M	88A769	CY150. Ex LOT Polish Airlines SP-LCE, bought 4-96; c/s No 2. Sold to Continental Airways 2006
RA-85825	Tu-154M	88A776	CY150. Ex-LOT Polish Airlines SP-LCH, bought 3-96; c/s No 2
RA-85826	Tu-154M	89A812	CY150. Ex-LOT Polish Airlines SP-LCL, bought 5-96; c/s No 2
RA-85831	Tu-154M	88A774	CY150. Ex-LOT Polish Airlines SP-LCF, bought 11-97; c/s No 2
RA-85846	Tu-154M	89A807	F12C12Y102. Ex-ČSA Czech Airlines OK-UCF, bought 12-99; c/s No 2
RA-85847	Tu-154M	88A792	CY142. Ex-ČSA Czech Airlines OK-TCD, bought 1-00; c/s No 2

Tu-154M RA-85847 seen here a few minutes after arriving at Moscow-Domodedovo on 5th September 2001 still wears the livery of Bashkirian Airlines but has A400 (= Airlines 400) titles. It was later repainted in basic Bulgarian Air Charter green/white colours with Avialinii 400 Air Charter titles. Author

The fleet of Bashkirian Airlines includes a large proportion of re-export Tu-154Ms, such as RA-85846 seen here a few seconds before touching down on runway 14R at Moscow-Domodedovo. Yuriy Kirsanov

RA-85848	Tu-154M	89A804	F12C12Y102. Ex-ČSA Czech Airlines OK-UCE, bought 1-00; c/s No 2. Sold or leased to Aeroflot Russian Airlines by 11-05

* Curiously, the registration CCCP-85824 was used by the sixth prototype Sukhoi Su-27K (Su-33) shipboard fighter (T10K-6, '79 Blue', c/n 49051003301) as a callsign.

The **Barnaul Air Enterprise** formed as the successor of the West Siberian CAD/Barnaul UAD (the administrative centre of the Altai Territory), had four Tu-154s. These are sometimes reported for **Altai Airlines** (*Altaiskiye avialinii*) which separated from the Barnaul Air Enterprise.

Registration	Version	C/n	Notes
RA-85094	Tu-154B	75A094	Y164. Converted Tu-154A. Transferred to Altai Airlines 4-4-94
RA-85117	Tu-154B	75A117	Y164. Converted Tu-154A. Transferred to Altai Airlines 4-4-94. Retired 1997, derelict Barnaul
RA-85235	Tu-154B-1	71A013	Y164.
RA-85402	Tu-154B-2	80A402	Y164. Sold to Sibir' Airlines

The **Blagoveshchensk Air Enterprise**, aka **Amurtransavia**, located in the Russian Far East had six Tu-154s. Only one of these was actually operated, however – the other four were resold immediately.

Registration	Version	C/n	Notes
RA-85101 No 2	Tu-154M	88A783	Ex-B-608L, ex-China Southwest Airlines B-2615, bought by 7-01, regd 12-7-02. Sold to Aviaexpresscruise
RA-85109 No 2	Tu-154M	88A790	Ex-B-606L, ex-China Southwest Airlines B-2616, bought by 7-01, regd 17-4-02. Sold to Aviaexpresscruise
RA-85136	Tu-154M	88A791	Ex-B-607L, ex-China Southwest Airlines B-2617, bought by 7-01, regd 14-12-01. Sold to Aviaexpresscruise
RA-85149	Tu-154M	88A797	Ex-B-609L, ex-China Southwest Airlines

			B-2618, bought by 7-01. Sold to Aviaexpresscruise
CCCP-85742	Tu-154B-2	79A320	Ex-Balkan Bulgarian Airlines LZ-BTR No 2, bought 8-92. Basic Balkan c/s, later Aeroflot c/s. Transferred to Amurtransavia as, see next line
RA-85742			Sold to Jana-Arka 1999 as UN-85742
RA-85753	Tu-154M	92A935	Sold to Pulkovo Air Enterprise

Established in 1993, **Buryatia Airlines [–/UUD]** were originally known as **Motom** (a Buryat word whose meaning is unknown). From its base in the Buryatian capital of Ulan-Ude (Mookhino airport) the airline operates regional passenger and cargo services with An-24/26 turboprops and performs utility work; the three Tu-154Ms have been sold or leased off.

Registration	C/n	Notes
RA-85800	94A984	F12C18Y104. Motom Buryatia c/s. Sold to Pulkovo Air Enterprise 1995.
RA-85827	86A745	CY150. Ex-LOT Polish Airlines SP-LCC, bought 3-97. Full Buryuatia Airlines c/s. Sold to Enkor 7-01.
RA-85829	87A755	CY150. Ex-LOT Polish Airlines SP-LCD, bought 10-97. Sold to Enkor 7-01.

The fleet of the **Chelyabinsk Air Enterprise [H6/CHB]**, aka **Chelal** (Chelyabinsk Airlines), included 12 Tu-154s. Initially most of them were flown in basic Aeroflot colours with a Chelal 'bird' on the nose (c/s No 1); by 1998 the two newest Tu-154B-2s received a smart livery with a white fuselage, a 'triple bird' logo on a blue tail and Cyrillic *Chelyabinskoye aviapredpriyatiye* titles (c/s No 2). The two ex-Belorussian Tu-154Ms, on the other hand, retained the basic colours of their former owner.

In 1997 Chelal formed a charter subsidiary called **Enkor [5Z/ENK]** which started operations on a small scale – initially with two Tu-154s. In 2001 a reorganisation saw the parent company vanish, and the entire fleet was from then on operated by Enkor **[H6/ENK]**. In May 2005 Enkor suspended operations, being gobbled up by Sibir' Airlines which took over some of its Tu-154s.

Tu-154M RA-85800 was the only one to wear the festive, if rather gaudy, livery of Motom. A more restrained livery appeared when the airline was renamed Buryat Airlines. Yuriy Kirsanov

RA-85467, one of two Tu-154B-2s to wear the full colours of the Chelyabinsk Air Enterprise, is seen at Moscow-Domodedovo on 3rd November 1998. Author

Registration	Version	C/n	Notes
RA-85098	Tu-154B	75A098	Y164. Converted Tu-154A. Basic Aeroflot c/s, no titles; later c/s No 1. Retired 1998
RA-85114	Tu-154A	75A114	Y164. Converted Tu-154A. Basic Aeroflot c/s, no titles; later c/s No 1. Retired 1998
RA-85171 No 1	Tu-154B-1	76A171	Y164. Converted Tu-154B. Basic Aeroflot c/s, no titles. Retired 1995
RA-85180	Tu-154B-1	76A180	Y164. Converted Tu-154B. C/s No 1. Retired 2000
RA-85183	Tu-154B-1	76A183	Y164. C/s No 1. Retired 2000
RA-85467	Tu-154B-2	81A467	C26Y102. C/s No 2 (later with Enkor nose titles added). Leased to Eurasia 9-02
RA-85514	Tu-154B-2	81A514	C26Y102. C/s No 2. Transferred to Enkor 1997, Enkor nose titles added. Sold to Sibir' Airlines 4-05
RA-85724	Tu-154M	92A906	C26Y102. Ex-Belavia EW-85724, bought 2-10-96. Basic Belavia c/s, old Chelal nose logo. Transferred to Enkor 1997, Enkor titles on nose. Sold to Sibir' Airlines 4-05
RA-85725	Tu-154M	92A907	Y164. Ex-Belavia EW-85725, bought 2-10-96. Basic Belavia c/s, old Chelal nose logo (later Enkor titles on nose). Sold to Sibir' Airlines 4-05
RA-85747	Tu-154M	92A930	Y164. Leased from Aerokuznetsk 7-00 to 9-00, c/s No 1
RA-85754	Tu-154M	92A936	C26Y102. Ex-Korsar, bought 1998. Basic Aeroflot c/s, no titles; later grey/white fuselage, green tail and Enkor titles on nose
RA-85786	Tu-154M	93A970	Y166. Leased from Kolavia 2004; returned by 1-05
RA-85827	Tu-154M	86A745	CY150. Bought from Buryatia Airlines 7-01; all-white c/s, Enkor titles on nose. Sold to Sibir' Airlines by 2-05
RA-85829	Tu-154M	87A755	CY150. Bought from Buryatia Airlines 7-01; all-white c/s, Enkor titles on nose. Sold to Sibir' Airlines by 2-05

Chernomorskiye Avialinïï [–/CMK] (Black Sea Airlines, a Russian-Armenian joint venture based in Sochi) operated three Tu-154s. In 1998 the airline was renamed **Chernomor-Avia**.

Registration	Version	C/n	Notes
RA-85291	Tu-154B-1	78A291	Ex-East Line, bought 2000. Sold to Karat by 5-05
RA-85332	Tu-154B-2	79A332	Ex-Air Moldova ER-85332, bought 6-99. Basic Aeroflot c/s, Chernomor-Avia titles
RA-85384	Tu-154B-2	79A384	Ex-Air Moldova ER-85384, bought 6-99. Basic Aeroflot c/s, Chernomor-Avia titles

Chernomor Soyuz [–/CHZ], likewise based in Sochi, bought two Tu-154B-1s – RA-85273 (c/n 78A273) and RA-85291 – from Omskavia in mid-1998. Only the former aircraft, which was in basic Aeroflot colours. wore Chernomor Soyuz titles; the other machine had a green Omskavia cheatline but was anonymous. The airline ceased operations in 1998, selling the two airliners to Sibaviatrans and East Line respectively.

Established in 1991 as the successor of the East Siberian CAD/Chita UAD, **Chitaavia [X7/CHF]** was one of the major airlines east of the Urals Mountains in the 1990s. Its fleet included eight Tu-154s.

In April 1998 Chitaavia announced a decision to merge with Baikalavia. However, the Russian bank crisis of 1998 foiled these plans – Baikalavia vanished altogether while Chitaavia reduced its fleet to four Tu-154s. Finally, in mid-2004 the airline was forced to cease operations.

Registration	Version	C/n	Notes
RA-85167	Tu-154B	76A167	Y164. Retired 1996, derelict Chita-Kadala
RA-85235	Tu-154B-1	77A235	Y164. WFU/stored Moscow-Vnukovo (ARZ No 400)
RA-85280 No 1	Tu-154B-2	78A280	Y164. Leased to Sayany
RA-85506	Tu-154B-2	81A506	Y164. Leased to Sayany
RA-85684	Tu-154M	90A851	Y151. Sold to Alrosa by 5-00
RA-85735	Tu-154M	92A917	Y164. Sold to China Great Wall Airlines as B-2627
RA-85765	Tu-154M	92A922	Y164. Sold to China Great Wall Airlines as B-2628
RA-85766	Tu-154M	92A923	Y151. Sold to Vladivostok Air
RA-85802	Tu-154M	93A961	CY153. Sold to AeroBratsk 9-04

Chitaavia Tu-154M RA-85766 climbs away from Moscow-Domodedovo. Yuriy Kirsanov

CNG Transavia [–/CGT] based in Voronezh has a single Tu-154B-1, RA-85255 (c/n 78A255), bought from Tyumen' Airlines in June 2003.

The Moscow charter carrier **Continental Airways Joint-Stock Company** (*Kontinentahl'nyye Avialinii*) **[PC/PVV]** operated five Tu-154Ms.

Registration	C/n	Notes
RA-85140 No 2	85A721	Ex-Sayakhat UN 85835, bought 2004. White fuselage (no cheatline), dark blue tail, Continental Airways titles below windows
RA-85146 No 2	86A724	Ex-Sayakhat UN 85837, bought 6-04. Grey belly, blue cheatline without pinstripe, light blue tail, Continental Airways titles above windows

RA-85828, one of Daghestan Airlines' three Tu-154Ms, 'fires up' under sullen skies at Moscow/Vnukovo-1 on 4th October 2000 for the daily flight to Makhachkala. Author

RA-85696	91A869	Bought from Mavial Magadan Airlines 2002, all-white c/s with Continental Airways titles/logo
RA-85757	92A939	Ex-EW-85757, leased from Gomelavia 2000? Basic Belavia c/s, no titles/logo. Not confirmed as operated by Continental Airways
RA-85760	92A942	Ex-Gomelavia EW-85760. Basic Belavia c/s, no titles/logo, small tail logo by 3-03; sold to Aeroflot Russian Airlines by 12-04
RA-85824	88A769	CY150. Ex BAL Bashkirian Airlines, bought 2006; all-white c/s with Continental Airways titles/logo

Daghestan Airlines (*Avialinii̇ Daghestana*) **[–/DAG]** based at Makhachkala-Uitash is the successor of the North Caucasian CAD/Makhachkala UAD. Originally its fleet included two Tu-154Ms; this number was doubled in the 1990s, though one aircraft has been sold since. The aircraft wear two different versions of the full livery with a cheatline and tail in the Daghestani flag colours of green, blue and red; the tail logo is white (version 1) or a more elaborate version in blue (version 2).

Registration	C/n	Notes
RA-85728	92A910	Y164. Sold to Alrosa 2-02
RA-85756	92A938	Y166. Was leased to Konveyer/Touch&Go, then operated in ex-Konveyer colours; full c/s No 2 by 1999
RA-85828	97A1009	F12C18Y104. Full c/s No 1, named *Rasul Gamzatov*
RA-85840	98A1011	Y166. Full c/s No 2

Looking rather weathered, Dalavia Far East Airlines Tu-154B RA-85220 awaits the next flight at Khabarovsk-Novyy in February 2002 in company with four sister ships. Dmitriy Petrochenko

Dalavia Far East Airways (*Dal'nevostochnyye avialinii̇*) **[H8/KHB]** based at Khabarovsk-Novyy operates a mixed fleet. Over the years this included 29 Tu-154s, mostly taken over from the Far East CAD/1st Khabarovsk UAD/198th Flight.

Registration	Version	C/n	Notes
RA-85019	Tu-154S	71A019	Converted Tu-154 sans suffixe. Aeroflot c/s. Leased to Transaero 4-93. SOC 1994, scrapped Khabarovsk 5-95
RA-85031	Tu-154B-1	72A031	Converted Tu-154 sans suffixe. Aeroflot c/s. Wfu Irkutsk-1 1996
RA-85037	Tu-154S	73A037	Converted Tu-154 sans suffixe. Aeroflot c/s. Wfu 1995
RA-85043	Tu-154B-1	73A043	Converted Tu-154 sans suffixe. Aeroflot c/s. Retired 1996
RA-85060	Tu-154S	74A060	Converted Tu-154A. Aeroflot c/s. Retired 1996
RA-85069	Tu-154B-1	74A069	Converted Tu-154A. Aeroflot c/s. Retired 1995
RA-85114 No 2	Tu-154M	89A814	Ex-Aria Air Tour EP-EAC, D/D 2-04
RA-85130	Tu-154B	75A130	Y164. Retired 1995
RA-85157	Tu-154B-1	76A157	Converted Tu-154B. Aeroflot c/s. Retired 1996
RA-85164	Tu-154B	76A164	Aeroflot c/s. Crashed 193km east of Khabarovsk 6-12-95
RA-85176	Tu-154B-1	76A176	Converted Tu-154B. Aeroflot c/s. Retired 1996
RA-85178	Tu-154B-1	76A178	Converted Tu-154B. Aeroflot c/s. Retired 1997
RA-85185 No 1	Tu-154B-1	76A185	Converted Tu-154B. Aeroflot c/s. Retired 1996
RA-85187 No 1	Tu-154B	76A187	Aeroflot c/s. Retired 1996
RA-85190	Tu-154B-1	76A190	Converted Tu-154B. Retired 1999
RA-85205 No 1	Tu-154B-1	77A205	Converted Tu-154B. Aeroflot c/s. Retired 1998
RA-85206	Tu-154B-1	77A206	Converted Tu-154B. Aeroflot c/s. Retired 1998
RA-85207	Tu-154B-1	77A207	Converted Tu-154B. Aeroflot c/s. Retired 1998
RA-85216	Tu-154B-1	77A216	Converted Tu-154B. Full c/s
RA-85220	Tu-154B-1	77A220	Converted Tu-154B. Full c/s
RA-85266	Tu-154B-2	78A266	Converted Tu-154B-1. Full c/s. Retired 2001
RA-85336	Tu-154B-2	79A336	Full c/s. Scrapped Khabarovsk 2006
RA-85341	Tu-154B-2	79A341	Full c/s
RA-85443	Tu-154B-2	80A443	Full c/s
RA-85477	Tu-154B-2	81A477	Full c/s
RA-85607	Tu-154M	84A702	Y160. Bought 1999, ex-Abakan-Avia; full c/s
RA-85734	Tu-154M	86A734	Ex-China Northwest Airlines B-2608, bought 10-02; see AZAL 4K-85734!
RA-85752	Tu-154M	92A934	Leased from Omskavia 2003
RA-85802	Tu-154M	93A961	Ex-AeroBratsk, bought 12-04

For many years **Domodedovo Airlines [E3/DMO]** (*Domodedovskiye avialinii̇*, known in Soviet times and in the 1990s as the Domodedovo Civil Aviation Production Association) had operated an all-Ilyushin fleet. However, as the airline launched new services for which its long-haul

RA-85841, one of Domodedovo Airlines' two leased Tu-154Ms, wears an all-white livery. The other aircraft has the airline's full colours – that is, basic Aeroflot colours with new titles/logo. Martin Novak

IL-62Ms and IL-96-300s were ill-suited, the need arose to procure medium-haul airliners. First, two 120-seat Yak-42Ds were purchased in Lithuania; these were augmented in late 2004/early 2005 by two Tu-154Ms leased from Omskavia – RA-85745 (c/n 92A928) and RA-85841 (c/n 90A858). The former aircraft has full Domodedovo Airlines colours with an Aeroflot-style cheatline and a white belly, while the other aircraft is white overall with Domodedovo Airlines titles and logo.

In 2005 Domodedovo Airlines teamed up with Kras Air, Samara Airlines, Omskavia and Sibaviatrans to form an alliance called AiRUnion (*sic*).

Donavia (*Donskiye avialinii* – Don Airlines) **[D9/DNV]** based in Rostov-on-Don took over the Tu-154s of the former North Caucasian CAD's Rostov UAD. Some retained the standard Aeroflot cheatline combined with Donavia titles and logo (c/s No 1), while on other aircraft the cheatline curved upwards to run along the fin (c/s No 2).

In 1998 the debt-ridden airline succumbed to the 17th August bank crisis and filed for bankruptcy protection. After a period of negotiations with Aeroflot Russian Airlines it became a wholly-owned subsidiary, changing its name to **Aeroflot-Don** in 2000 (aircraft which received the new titles are marked * in the table). A total of 21 Tu-154s saw service with the airline before and after the rebranding.

After being taken over by Aeroflot, Donavia changed its name to Aeroflot-Don. Tu-154M RA-85149 No 2 acquired from Aviaexpresscruise still wears a China Southwest Airlines cheatline. Note the unusually bold tail logo. Dmitriy Petrochenko

Tu-154B-2 RA-85414 seen at Rostov-on-Don, its home base, displays the full livery of Donavia with the pre-takeover titles. Note how the cheatline curves up onto the tail. Sergey and Dmitriy Komissarov collection

Registration	Version	C/n	Notes
RA-85149	Tu-154M	88A797	Ex-Aviaexpresscruise, bought by 10-03. Basic China Northwest Airlines c/s, Aeroflot-Don titles/logo
RA-85285	Tu-154B-1	78A285	Ex-Air Moldova ER-85285, bought ?-00. Sold by 7-03
RA-85295	Tu-154B-2	78A295	C14Y119/Combi. Converted Tu-154B-1. C/s No 2; retired 2000, scrapped Rostov-on-Don
RA-85305	Tu-154B-2	78A305	C14Y119. Full c/s. Wfu Rostov-on-Don by 7-01
RA-85306	Tu-154B-2	78A306	Y180. Basic Aeroflot c/s, no titles. Retired 1996
RA-85308	Tu-154B-2	78A308	Y180. Basic Aeroflot c/s, no titles. Retired 1998
RA-85309	Tu-154B-2	78A309	C14Y119. C/s No 1. Retired 2001
RA-85400	Tu-154B-2	80A400	C14Y119. C/s No 2
RA-85409*	Tu-154B-2	80A409	Y164. C/s No 1
RA-85414	Tu-154B-2	80A414	C14Y119. C/s No 2. Retired by 2001, scrapped 6-02
RA-85425	Tu-154B-2	80A425	Y164. Basic Aeroflot c/s, no titles, later c/s No 1. Retired by 10-03
RA-85435*	Tu-154B-2	80A435	C14Y119. C/s No 1 + blue stripes on nacelles
RA-85436*	Tu-154B-2	80A436	C14Y119. C/s No 1
RA-85437	Tu-154B-2	80A437	C14Y119/Combi. C/s No 2. Sold to ARZ No 411 9-00/leased to Sibir' Airlines
RA-85452*	Tu-154B-2	80A452	Y164. Basic Aeroflot c/s, no titles, later c/s No 1
RA-85454	Tu-154B-2	80A454	Y164 or combi. C/s No 2. Wfu Rostov-on-Don by 7-01; sold Perm Airlines by 11-06
RA-85495	Tu-154B-2	81A495	Y164 or Combi. Basic Aeroflot c/s, no titles. Sold to ARZ No 411 5-99/leased to Sibir' Airlines
RA-85527	Tu-154B-2	82A527	C14Y119. Basic Aeroflot c/s, no titles, later c/s No 1
RA-85626	Tu-154M	87A753	Ex-Aeroflot Russian International Airlines, bought 2000. Basic old ARIA c/s
RA-85640	Tu-154M	88A772	Ex-Aeroflot Russian International Airlines, bought 2000. Basic old ARIA c/s No 2B, Aeroflot-Don titles
RA-85726 No 2	Tu-154M	86A725	Ex-Qeshmair EP-TQD, bought 7-02, c/s No 1

Established in 1993 as a cargo charter carrier based at Moscow-Domodedovo, **East Line [P7/ESL]** quickly grew into a major airline with both cargo and passenger services. For many years the impressive and constantly changing fleet consisted entirely of aircraft leased as required and wearing a baffling variety of liveries. These included eight Tu-154s; only one of them wore East Line's smart green/white livery as applied to some of the airline's IL-76TDs.

Registration	Version	C/n	Notes
RA-85291	Tu-154B-1	78A291	Ex-Chernomor-Soyuz, bought 1999. Sold to Chernomor-Avia 2000
RA-85365	Tu-154B-2	79A365	Y164. Leased from AVL Arkhangel'sk Airlines 1997; returned to lessor
RA-85386	Tu-154B-2	79A386	Y164. Leased from AVL Arkhangel'sk Airlines 1998, basic Aeroflot c/s; returned to lessor
RA-85468	Tu-154B-2	81A468	Y164. Leased from AVL Arkhangel'sk Airlines 1997; returned to lessor
RA-85551	Tu-154B-2	82A551	Y164. Leased from AVL Arkhangel'sk Airlines 1998; basic Aeroflot colours, small East Line titles above windows; returned to lessor 20-10-01
RA-85567	Tu-154B-2	82A567	Y164. Leased from Mavial Magadan Airlines June 2003 for one month
RA-85689	Tu-154M	90A860	Leased from AeroBratsk 2002-03; basic AeroBratsk c/s, small East Line titles above windows
RA-85788	Tu-154M	93A972	Y166. Leased from Kaliningrad-Avia, basic Aeroflot c/s with small East Line titles/logo below windows; returned to lessor
RA-85789	Tu-154M	93A973	Y166. Leased from Kaliningrad-Avia, basic Aeroflot c/s with small East Line titles/logo below windows; returned to lessor
RA-85798	Tu-154M	94A982	C26Y102. Leased from Tatarstan Airlines. Basic ex-Tatneft'aero c/s with broken cheatline, East Line titles and logo in circle (later painted out)
RA-85799	Tu-154M	94A983	C26Y102. Leased from Tatarstan Airlines. Basic ex-Tatneft'aero c/s with unbroken cheatline, East Line titles and logo in circle (later painted out)
RA-85827	Tu-154M	86A745	CY150. Leased from Buryatia Airlines 1998; basic Buryatia colours, large East Line titles. To Enkor 7-01
RA-85829	Tu-154M	87A755	CY150. Leased from Buryatia Airlines 1998; full East Line c/s, additional Buryatskiye Avialinii titles. To Enkor 7-01

Above: **East Line leased its aircraft from far and wide, and the colour schemes varied accordingly. Tu-154M RA-85827 seen at Moscow-Domodedovo on 3rd November 1998 has basic Buryatia Airlines colours.** Author

Below: **In contrast, Tu-154M RA-85829 leased from the same carrier wore East Line's smart green/white livery. Here it is seen leaving runway 14L at Moscow-Domodedovo in mid-1998; small 'Buryatskiye avialinii' subtitles had been added by November.** Yuriy Kirsanov

In December 2004 the airline division of East Line was renamed **Roosskoye Nebo/Russian Sky**, adopting a new livery but retaining the original IATA/ICAO codes. In 2005, however, the airline was purchased wholesale by another Russian charter airline, Vim Airlines [NN/MOV], which had a fleet consisting entirely of Boeing 757-200s. Apparently the new owner may keep the Ilyushin IL-86 widebodies but is certainly not going to operate the Tupolev trijets.

Eurasia Airlines operated three Tu-154s leased from different airlines, and each one was painted differently. Tu-154B-2 RA-85467 was in the basic colours of the Chelyabinsk Air Enterprise/Enkor. Dmitriy Petrochenko

Eurasia Airlines [UH/EUS] started life in 1997, operating two Yak-40s from Moscow-Bykovo. In 2001 the airline moved to Moscow/Vnukovo-1 and started operating heavier types on scheduled and charter international and domestic services, the fleet included four Tu-154s. In 2003, however, the Russian CAA unearthed two grave breaches affecting safety (advanced corrosion on one aircraft and overloading by 50% on another) and withdrew Eurasia's operating licence in October 2003.

Registration	Version	C/n	Notes
RA-85429	Tu-154B-2	80A429	Leased from AeroBratsk for one month 8-02, basic AeroBratsk c/s with Eurasia titles/logo
RA-85467	Tu-154B-2	81A467	Leased from Enkor by 9-02, basic Chelyabinsk Air Enterprise c/s with Eurasia titles/logo
RA-85788	Tu-154M	93A972	Y166. Leased from Kaliningrad-Avia, basic Aeroflot c/s with Eurasia titles
RA-85840	Tu-154M	97A1011	Leased from Daghestan Airlines 9-02 to 9-03, basic Daghestan Airlines c/s with Eurasia titles/logo

The **Federal Security Service** (FSB – *Federahl'naya sloozhba bezopahsnosti*) took delivery of a new-build Tu-154M 'Salon' on 20th December 2005. Actually the aircraft was not exactly new – it was a 'white-tail' that had been completed several years ago (c/n 0…A1019). Originally this aircraft was reportedly earmarked for the Russian government flight (Rossiya State Transport Co) as RA-85860; however, when the aircraft was delivered to the FSB it wore the registration RA-85019 No 2 – probably derived from the c/n.

The **Flight Research Institute named after Mikhail M Gromov (LII)** in Zhukovskiy operated several Tu-154s for test and research purposes, mostly in full Aeroflot colours.

In 1997 LII established its second commercial division, **Gromov Air [–/LII, later –/GAI]**, which performed support operations (such as carrying delegations to airshows) and business charters. The airline operated a mix of types, including Tu-154s leased as required; its precursor, Volare Air Transport Co, had not operated the type. In late 2005 the airline was renamed **Moskoviya** (Muscovy).

Registration	Version	C/n	Notes
RA-85307	Tu-154B-2	78A307	Leased from Kavminvodyavia 3-03 to 3-05 (?); basic Kavminvodyavia c/s, Gromov Air titles
RA-85312	Tu-154B-2	78A312	Ex-Atlant-Soyuz, bought 2005. Basic SPAir white/purple/red c/s, no titles; named *San Sanych*
RA-85429	Tu-154B-2	80A429	Leased from AeroBratsk May-June 2005; basic AeroBratsk c/s, Gromov Air titles/logo
RA-85486	Tu-154B-2	81A486	Ex-Atlant-Soyuz, bought by 7-05; basic Aeroflot c/s, Gromov Air titles, no tail logo
RA-85736	Tu-154M	92A918	Ex-Atlant-Soyuz, bought 6-06; basic full Gromov Air c/s but Moskoviya titles
RA-85743	Tu-154M	92A926	Ex-Atlant-Soyuz, received 6-5-06; basic full Gromov Air c/s but Moskoviya titles, named *Yuriy Sheffer*

Additionally, LII operated the following Tu-154s which were not used by Gromov Air/Moskoviya.

Registration	Version	C/n	Notes
CCCP-85024	Tu-154LL	72A024	Built as Tu-154 sans suffixe, converted to Tu-154B. Wfu Zhukovskiy by 8-95, scrapped
CCCP-85032	Tu-154	72A032	Avionics testbed. Wfu and preserved Zhukovskiy by 1989
CCCP-85055	Tu-154	73A055	Ex-Egyptair SU-AXI, transferred from Soviet Air Force 1983, avionics testbed. Wfu Zhukovskiy by 8-92; scrapped by 8-99
CCCP-85083	Tu-154LL	74A083	Built as Tu-154A, converted to Tu-154B. Wfu Zhukovskiy ?-95, scrapped?
CCCP-85108	Tu-154LL	75A108	Built as Tu-154A, converted to Tu-154B-1. Wfu Zhukovskiy ?-95, scrapped?
CCCP-85119	Tu-154LL?	75A119	Built as Tu-154A, converted to Tu-154B; avionics or control system testbed. Wfu Zhukovskiy ?-95, scrapped?
RA-85317	Tu-154M	78A317	First prototype Tu-154M/converted Tu-154B-2. FACT (Future Aircraft Control Testbed)
CCCP-85737	Tu-154M	92A920	Aeroflot c/s. Sold to VIA 1993 as LZ-MIV
RA-85783	Tu-154M	93A967	Sold to China United Airlines 12-93 as B-4028
RA-85801	Tu-154M	93A960	Grey/white c/s, no titles. Sold to Kolavia by 11-98

Gazpromavia Ltd [–/GZP], the flying division of the powerful Gazprom corporation controlling Russia's natural gas industry, has five Tu-154Ms. Most of them wear full colours, with Gazprom's logo on the tail (a G with a small tongue of flame, dubbed 'lighter'). The aircraft are based at Moscow-Vnukovo and Ostaf'yevo, a Naval Aviation base just south of Moscow where a business terminal was opened in 2004.

Registration	C/n	Notes
RA-85625	87A752	Y164? Ex-Aeroflot Russian International Airlines, bought 6-99. Full c/s
RA-85690	90A861	Y164? Leased from Baikal Airlines 1998-99, basic Baikal Airlines c/s
RA-85751	92A933	Y164. Ex-Tyumen'AviaTrans, bought 1996; briefly leased back 1997. Full c/s
RA-85774	93A956	Y164. Ex-BAL Bashkirian Airlines, bought 6-98. Aeroflot cheatline, no titles, BAL tail colours with Gazprom 'lighter' tail logo, later full c/s
RA-85778	93A962	Y164. Ex-Kogalymavia, bought 1997. Basic Aeroflot c/s, no titles, 'lighter' logo; later full c/s

GosNII GA (the State Civil Aviation Research Institute) **[–/ISP]** at Moscow/Sheremet'yevo-1 operated a steady succession of Tu-154s. These included RA-85333 (c/n 79A333) which was leased to IRS Aero in June 1998. GosNII GA suspended commercial flights in 1998; after the demise of IRS Aero the aircraft was withdrawn from use and ultimately flown to Vnukovo, where it was scrapped at ARZ No 400 in the summer of 2006.

Gromov Air – see Flight Research Institute.

The Tatar regional airline **Iron Dragonfly (IDF) [–/IDF]** based in Kazan' operated three Tu-154s. One of them, RA-85358, was named *S'uyumbiké* after the last empress of the Kazan' Khanate who was defeated by Czar Ivan IV the Terrible. The airline suspended operations in 2002.

Registration	Version	C/n	Notes
RA-85358	Tu-154B-2	79A358	Leased from Tatarstan Airlines 1996-99; all-white c/s, Tatarstan flag on tail, small IDF logo, named *S'uyumbiké*
RA-85782	Tu-154M	93A966	Sold to Aerovolga 10-95
RA-85842	Tu-154B-2 'Salon'	80A420	Ex-Czech Air Force '0420 White', should have been RA-85420!), bought 5-98; grey/white c/s with red/blue cheatline and 'IDF/Tatarstan' titles. Sold to Karat 2001

Established in 1997, **IRS Aero [LD/LDF, later 5R/LDF]** operated a mix of owned and leased aircraft, including Tu-154B-2 RA-85333 (c/n 79A333) leased from GosNII GA in June 1998 and Tu-154M RA-85696 (c/n 91A869) leased from Mavial Magadan Airlines in 2000. Despite the fact that the airline's registered office was in Moscow, rumours circulated that IRS Aero was in fact owned by the Chechens (with obvious negative implications).

The investigation of an incident involving one of the airline's IL-18s unearthed several grave breaches (mostly forged paperwork), which eventually led the Russian CAA to withdraw IRS Aero's operating licence later that year. The Tu-154s were thus returned to their lessors.

IRS-Aero operated two Tu-154s in 1997-2002. Here, Tu-154B-2 RA-85333 is seen on the hardstand of GosNII GA (the aircraft's owner) at Moscow/Sheremet'yevo-1, with Tu-154M RA-85696 in the background; note the different colour of the titles. Mike Kell

Kaliningrad-Avia [K8/KLN, later KD/KNI] operated two 166-seat Tu-154Ms – RA-85788 and RA-85789 (c/ns 93A972 and 93A973). Both aircraft, which (unlike the carrier's Tu-134As) retained basic Aeroflot colours without titles, have been leased out most of the time. In 2005 the airline was rebranded **KD-Avia [KD/KNI]** and started re-equipping with Boeing 737-300s, disposing of its Soviet hardware; both Tu-154Ms were sold to UTair in April 2006.

The charter carrier **Karat [2U/AKT, later V2/AKT]** based at Moscow-Vnukovo operated at least eight Tu-154s.

Registration	Version	C/n	Notes
RA-85291	Tu-154B-1	78A291	Bought from Omskavia by 5-05; all-white with Karat titles/logo
RA-85358	Tu-154B-2	79A358	Leased from Iron Dragonfly. All-white c/s with Karat titles/logo + IDF logo (later removed), named *S'uyumbiké* (name removed by 2-02; aircraft bought?)
RA-85412	*Tu-154B-2*	*80A412*	*Y164. Leased from Tatarstan Airlines 1-00 to 8-00, basic Aeroflot c/s, Karat titles/logo*
RA-85468	*Tu-154B-2*	*81A468*	*Leased from AVL Arkhangel'sk Airlines 9-00 to 7-01.Basic Aeroflot c/s, Karat titles/logo*
RA-85437	Tu-154B-2	80A437	Bought from Sibir' Airlines by 8-05. Basic Sibir' c/s No 3A with Karat titles/logo
RA-85495	Tu-154B-2	81A495	Bought from Sibir' Airlines by 4-05
RA-85630	*Tu-154M*	*87A759*	*Leased from Rossiya State Transport Co. Basic Yamal Airlines c/s, Karat titles/logo*
RA-85842	*Tu-154B-2*	*80A420*	*Bought from Iron Dragonfly 2001; red/blue cheatline below windows, Karat titles/logo. Sold to Yamal Airlines 7-01*

Kavminvodyavia or **KMV [KV/MVD]** operated 15 Tu-154s. The carrier is based in Mineral'nyye Vody, a popular health resort (KMV = *Kavkazskiye minerahl'nyye vody*, Caucasian Mineral Waters). The fairly simple but pleasant livery includes the city crest on a blue tail, a rudder painted in Russian flag colours and huge KMV titles which may be black (c/s No 1) or red (c/s No 2).

Registration	Version	C/n	Notes
RA-85226	*Tu-154B-1*	*77A226*	*Y60 and cargo. Retired 2004*
RA-85287	*Tu-154B-1*	*78A287*	*Y164. Lsf Vnukovo ARZ No 411 2-02 to 9-02*

Wearing the restrained livery of charter carrier Karat, Tu-154B-1 RA-85291 sits at Moscow/Vnukovo-1 on 20th May 2005 during a thunderstorm. Yefim Gordon

Kavminvodyavia Tu-154M RA-85715 awaits the next flight on a wet, snow-covered apron at Moscow/Vnukovo-1 on 18th February 2002, the canvas intake covers billowing in the wind. Author

RA-85303	Tu-154B-2	78A303	Y180. C/s No 2. Retired 2004
RA-85304	Tu-154B-2	78A304	Y180. C/s No 2. Retired 1996
RA-85307	Tu-154B-2	78A307	Y180. C/s No 2, cheatline broken near KMV titles, white radome
RA-85330	Tu-154B-2	79A330	Y164. C/s No 2. Retired and scrapped Mneral'nyye Vody 2005
RA-85332	Tu-154B-2	79A332	Y164. Ex-Chernomor-Avia, leased from ARZ No 411 17-3-03
RA-85340	Tu-154B-2	79A340	Y164. C/s No 2
RA-85371	Tu-154B-2	79A371	Y164. C/s No 2
RA-85373	Tu-154B-2	79A373	Y164. C/s No 2, white radome
RA-85382	Tu-154B-2	79A382	Y164. C/s No 2, white radome
RA-85393	Tu-154B-2	80A393	F12Y120. C/s No 1, black radome
RA-85457	Tu-154B-2	80A457	F12Y120. C/s No 1, grey radome
RA-85494	Tu-154B-2	81A494	Y164. C/s No 2
RA-85715	Tu-154M	91A891	F12Y120. Ex-Rossiya State Transport Co? C/s No 2, painted 23-9-95
RA-85722	Tu-154M	92A904	F12Y120. C/s No 2, painted 14-10-95
RA-85746	Tu-154M	92A929	Y166. Basic Aeroflot c/s, no titles; painted in c/s No 2 24-2-96

RA-85676	Tu-154M	90A836	CY124. Leased to Vladivostok Air 6-03
RA-85681	Tu-154M	90A848	CY124. Possibly leased to Sibaviatrans

Kogalymavia [7K/KGL], an airline operating from Kogalym and Surgut and doing business as **Kolavia**, operated 16 Tu-154s. Originally operated in basic Aeroflot colours with a small Kolavia sticker on the nose (c/s No 1), the airline's Tu-154Ms soon gained a smart three-tone blue/white livery (c/s No 2); the aircraft acquired later received this livery from the outset. The names worn by some aircraft actually indicate their home bases!

Registration	Version	C/n	Notes
RA-85110	Tu-154B-1	75A110	Retired 1997
RA-85255	Tu-154B-1	77A255	Y164. Leased from Tyumen' Airlines 1998
RA-85335	Tu-154B-2	79A335	Y164. Leased from Tyumen' Airlines 7-98
RA-85395	Tu-154B-2	80A395	Leased from Air Ukraine/Lugansk Air Enterprise. Basic 1993-standard Air Ukraine c/s, Kolavia titles/logo

The **Kemerovo Air Enterprise** operated Tu-154B-2 RA-85389 (c/n 80A389) in Aeroflot colours in 1993-2000.

Khakasia Airlines [–/BKN], the other airline based in Abakan, was strictly a passenger carrier. Its fleet consisted of six Tu-154s. The airline suspended operations in February 2003; however, in recent reports some Tu-154s are still listed as 'leased from Khakasia', suggesting that the airline is still their nominal owner.

Registration	Version	C/n	Notes
RA-85160	Tu-154B	76A160	Sold to Sibaviatrans 8-98
RA-85174	Tu-154B	76A174	Retired 1997
RA-85195	Tu-154B	77A195	No titles
RA-85223	Tu-154B-1	77A223	Received 11-93; basic Aeroflot c/s, no titles, later with titles

Khakasia Airlines Tu-154B-1 RA-85223 is depicted during one of its visits to Moscow-Domodedovo. Dmitriy Petrochenko

RA-85427	Tu-154B-2	80A427	Y164. Leased from Tyumen' Airlines since 6-6-00
RA-85450	Tu-154B-2	80A450	Y164. Leased from Tyumen' Airlines 1996-98
RA-85481	Tu-154B-2	81A481	Y164. Ex-Tyumen' Airlines, bought by 8-05
RA-85522	Tu-154B-2	82A522	Y164. Ex-Tyumen' Airlines, bought by 8-05
RA-85630	Tu-154M	87A759	Leased from Rossiya State Transport Co 2-02, full c/s
RA-85761	Tu-154M	92A944	Y166. Basic Aeroflot c/s, no titles, Kolavia sticker on nose; later full c/s, named *Kogalym*. Leased to Aria Air 12-05
RA-85778	Tu-154M	93A962	Y166. Basic Aeroflot c/s, no titles, Kolavia sticker on nose. Lsd (later sold) to Gazpromavia 1997
RA-85784	Tu-154M	93A968	F12C18Y104. Basic Aeroflot c/s, no titles, Kolavia sticker on nose; later full c/s, named *Surgut* (later *Kogalym*!)
RA-85786	Tu-154M	93A970	Y166. Ex-Aviacor factory demonstrator. Full c/s, named *Kogalym*. Leased to Aria Air 1-05
RA-85787	Tu-154M	93A971	Y166. Basic Aeroflot c/s, no titles, Kolavia sticker on nose; later full c/s, named *Surgut*
RA-85801	Tu-154M	93A960	Y166. Bought from Gromov Flight Research Institute 5-98; full c/s. Sold to Omskavia 4-03
RA-85803	Tu-154M	89A822	Leased from Vladivostok Air 12-02 to ?-??

Tu-154M RA-85801 in the full colours of Kogalymavia (Kolavia) taxies out for take-off from runway 32R at Moscow-Domodedovo on 25th November 1998 past an Antonov An-12 freighter of Atran that has just landed. Unlike most of Kolavia's Tu-154s, RA-85801 did not have a name. Author

Displaying the still-fresh colours of Konveyer (alias Touch&Go), Tu-154M RA-85756 applies reverse thrust after landing on runway 24 at Moscow-Vnukovo. The aircraft retained this livery long after the lease from Daghestan Airlines had ended. Dmitriy Petrochenko

In 1992 the airline **Konveyer [EC/TUG]** based at Moscow-Vnukovo took delivery of a single Tu-154M, RA-85756 (c/n 92A938); on 10th December 1995 the aircraft was transferred to Daghestan Airlines. Generally *konveyer* means 'conveyor belt' or 'assembly line' in Russian; when used as an aviation term, however, it means 'touch and go'. Hence the airline was also known as **Touch & Go Ltd,** and the smart blue/white livery included **КОНВЕЙЕР** titles to port and **Touch & Go** titles to starboard. Obviously whoever picked the English name wanted to hint at the carrier's efficiency, with excellent turnaround times ('we barely touch down at all', that is) and was unaware of the expression's *other* meaning. (Incidentally, the Russian name isn't the best choice either, implying the passengers are routinely whisked from A to B without the 'personal touch'.) Additionally, Tu-154M RA-85767 (c/n 93A948) was operated by Konveyer/Touch & Go in 1993 before being transferred to the Pulkovo Air Enterprise on 22nd November 1994.

The charter airline **Korsar [6K/KRS]** based at Moscow/Vnukovo-3 reportedly operated Tu-154M RA-85754 (c/n 92A936) jointly with Aeroflot Russian International Airlines in the mid-1990s, using it for inclusive tour flights and even scheduled services to Cyprus. *Korsar* is Russian for 'corsair', but the name has nothing to do with pirates; it derives from the names of the airline's founders, Korovin and Sarzhveladze. In 1998 the aircraft was sold to the Chelyabinsk Air Enterprise.

Krai-Aero [K3/KIO], another charter carrier based at Moscow-Vnukovo, operated three Tu-154s.

Registration	Version	C/n	Notes
RA-85745	Tu-154M	92A928	Y164. Leased from/jointly operated with Vnukovo Airlines 1994, basic META-Aviotransport Makedonija c/s

A picture of days gone by. Tu-154M RA-85803 of Krai-Aero is seen on final approach to Moscow-Vnukovo in 1993. Dmitriy Petrochenko

RA-85803	Tu-154M	89A822	Bought 1-5-92, ex-Alyemda 7O-ACT; full c/s. Sold to Arax Airways as EK-85803
RA-85804	Tu-154B-2	81A517	F8Y125. Bought 12-92, ex-Cargo Moravia Airlines OK-LCS; should have been RA-85517 but this registration already existed (c/n unknown)! Sold to Tatarstan Airlines 12-92

Kras Air (Krasnoyarsk Airlines/*Krasnoyarskiye avialinii*) **[7B/KJC]** based at Krasnoyarsk-Yemel'yanovo operated 29 Tu-154s. These sported a variety of colour schemes: basic Aeroflot colours with Kras Air titles and the registration and flag in the usual places (c/s No 1); ditto with a blue fin flash and white/blue/red '*KA*' logo below the flag (c/s No 2); ditto with an all-white tail and the registration/flag on the rear fuselage (c/s No 3); the early full colour scheme with a blue/green cheatline, Kras Air/Krasnoyarskiye avialinii titles and 'wing' tail logo (c/s No 4) and the current version with a brighter blue/green cheatline and a bolder tail logo (c/s No 5). Since 2005 Kras Air is a member of the AiRUnion alliance.

Registration	Version	C/n	Notes
RA-85124	Tu-154B-1	75A124	Y164. Converted Tu-154B. C/s No 2. Retired 1997
RA-85165	Tu-154B	76A165	Y164. Retired 1998
RA-85181	Tu-154B-1	76A181	Y164. Converted Tu-154B. C/s No 1. Retired 1998
RA-85184	Tu-154B	76A184	Y164. Retired 1999
RA-85201	Tu-154B-1	77A201	Y164. C/s No 1; later basic Sibaviatrans c/s, Kras Air titles/logo. Scrapped 2006
RA-85202	Tu-154B-1	77A202	Y164. C/s No 4. Retired Krasnoyarsk 2003
RA-85213	Tu-154B	77A213	Y164. C/s No 1. Retired 1996
RA-85417	Tu-154B-2	81A417	Y164. C/s No 4, Kras Air titles only
RA-85418	Tu-154B-2	81A418	Y164. C/s No 4
RA-85456	Tu-154B-2	81A456	Y164. C/s No 3. Sold to Nizhegorodskiye Avialinii
RA-85489	Tu-154B-2	81A489	F12Y120. C/s No 1, later No 5
RA-85505	Tu-154B-2	81A505	F12Y120. Initially operated as CCCP-85505.

			C/s No 1 with additional Cyrillic 'Krasnoyarskavia' titles and blue 'KA' badge on tail
RA-85529	Tu-154B-2	82A529	Y164. C/s No 1B, later No 4
RA-85660	Tu-154M	89A810	Leased from AeroBratsk; basic AeroBratsk c/s, Kras Air titles
RA-85672	Tu-154M	89A830	Y164. C/s No 4
RA-85676	Tu-154M	90A836	CY124. Leased from Khakasia Airlines 2001, basic Sibaviatrans c/s, Kras Air titles/logo. To Vladivostok Air 6-03
RA-85677	Tu-154M	90A839	Y164. Leased from Mavial Magadan Airlines 7-00 to 8-00?
RA-85678	Tu-154M	90A841	Y164. C/s No 4, Kras Air titles only.
RA-85679	Tu-154M	90A842	Y164. C/s No 4
RA-85681	Tu-154M	90A848	Leased from Khakasia Airlines 8-00 to 9-00 and 6-01 to 12-02; c/s No 1
RA-85682	Tu-154M	90A849	Y164. C/s No 1, later No 4

Kras Air's aircraft sported a variety of liveries. Here, Tu-154B-2 RA-85505 seen at Moscow-Domodedovo on 3rd November 1998 displays one of several variations on the 'Aeroflot '73 standard' theme. Note the small KA tail logo and the Cyrillic 'Krasnoyarskavia' subtitles below the forward cabin windows. Author

Recently Kras Air has adopted this livery (illustrated by Tu-154B-2 RA-85489) as the fleetwide standard. Still, subtle variations exist in the width of the cheatline and the placement of the Cyrillic 'Krasnoyarskiye avialinii' subtitles. Martin Novak

Mals-Deoghar was one of the least-known operators of the type, operating Tu-154M RA-85726 No 1 in 1996-99. Note the 'Tupolev-154M' titles on the engine nacelles applied in the same typeface as on Balkan Bulgarian Airlines' examples – which is not surprising, since this aircraft had previously been on lease in Bulgaria. Dmitriy Petrochenko

RA-85683	Tu-154M	90A850	Y164. C/s No 4
RA-85694	Tu-154M	91A867	Y164. C/s No 3, later No 5
RA-85702	Tu-154M	91A877	Y164. C/s No 3 plus 'wing' tail logo, later No 5
RA-85704	Tu-154M	91A879	Y164. Basic AJT Air International c/s, Kras Air titles; later c/s No 4. Leased to Iran Air Tour 2005 as EP-MCH
RA-85708	Tu-154M	91A883	Y164. C/s No 4. Leased to Iran Air Tour 2005 as EP-MCG
RA-85720	Tu-154M	91A902	Y164. C/s No 3 plus tail logo. Leased to Aria Air 1-06
RA-85759	Tu-154M	92A941	Y166. Ex-Murmansk Airlines, bought 2001; Russian Aviation Consortium c/s, Kras Air titles
RA-85768	Tu-154M	92A949	Bought from Orenburg Airlines by 5-04
RA-85801	Tu-154M	93A960	Y166. Leased from/jointly operated with Omskavia 2005
RA-85818	Tu-154M	85A719	Y164. Bought from Omskavia by 7-06; basic Omskavia c/s No 3 with Kras Air titles

Note: Tu-154B-2 RA-85450 (c/n 81A450) was also reported for Kras Air by some sources but this is unconfirmed.

Kuban' Airlines [GW/KIL] (alias ALK – *Avialinii Kubani*) based at Krasnodar's Pashkovskiy airport leased Tu-154B-2 RA-85456 from Nizhegorodskiye Avialinii on 24th April 2001 – probably to make up for a capacity shortage while some of its Yakovlev Yak-42 trijets were undergoing refurbishment. Another Tu-154B-2, RA-85458, was leased from the same carrier in 2001.

On 6th June 2006 the airline took delivery of its first own Tu-154 – a new-build ('white-tail') Tu-154M registered RA-85123 No 2 (c/n unknown); a second aircraft, RA-85795 No. 2 (c/n unknown), followed in August. Airliners hushkitted and equipped with an upgraded navigation suite conforming to RNP1 standards, enabling it to fly to Western Europe. Also, the aircraft have a non-standard airframe with one overwing emergency exit on each side instead of two.

Tu-154M RA-85726 No 1 (c/n 92A908) was operated by an airline called **Liana**, a Russian-Ukrainian joint venture, in 1992. The aircraft was leased to the Bulgarian airline Air Kona as LZ-MNA in 1993.

Reverting to the Russian register in 1994, RA-85726 No 1 was operated by an airline with the improbable (and certainly not Russian) name of **Mals-Deoghar** until 1999. The aircraft was based at Moscow-Vnukovo and wore a smart blue/white livery with a stylised 'MD' tail logo and large МАЛС titles. In 1999 the aircraft suffered a landing accident; after repairs it was sold to AJT Air International as RA-85832. Its original registration was later reused for a sister ship – a re-export aircraft delivered to Aeroflot-Don.

Established in 1994, **Mavial Magadan Airlines** (*Magadanskiye avialinii*) **[H5/MVL]** operated from Magadan-Sokol airport in the Far East which is also a Russian Air Force base. Operating an initially all-Tu-154 fleet to which a single IL-62M was added in early 2000, the carrier served such destinations as Khabarovsk, Krasnoyarsk-Yemel'yanovo, Moscow-Domodedovo, St Petersburg, Ust'-Ilimsk, Vladivostok and Yekaterinburg. Mavial also has a licence for scheduled services to the USA, flying to Anchorage and Seattle.

In June 2006 the carrier filed for bankruptcy, leaving lots of disgruntled passengers who had paid for their tickets in advance and now could neither fly nor get refunds. The fate of the aircraft remains to be seen.

Registration	Version	C/n	Notes
RA-85540	Tu-154B-2	82A540	Y164. Ex-Sibir' Airlines, bought 1998, c/s No 2
RA-85557	Tu-154B-2	82A557	Y164. Sold to Tyumen'AviaTrans by 6-02
RA-85562	Tu-154B-2	82A562	Y164. Leased to Vladivostok Air 2-7-97, sold 14-3-03
RA-85567	Tu-154B-2	82A567	Y164
RA-85584	Tu-154B-2	83A584	Y164
RA-85588	Tu-154B-2	83A588	Y164. Lst Vladivostok Air 1997, converted to mixed-class (F12Y120?)
RA-85596	Tu-154B-2	84A596	Y164. Lst Vladivostok Air 1997, converted to mixed-class (F12Y120?)
RA-85667	Tu-154M	89A825	Y164
RA-85671	Tu-154M	90A829	Y164. Sold to Vnukovo ARZ No 400

Seen taking off at Moscow-Vnukovo, Tu-154M RA-85667 displays the standard livery of Mavial Magadan Airlines. Yuriy Kirsanov

Moscow Airways leased two Tu-154s from the Tupolev PLC at different times. Here, Tu-154M RA-85606 is seen at Zhukovskiy in August 1997 – with the spin recovery parachute still in place. Author

RA-85677	Tu-154M	90A839	Y164. C/s No 2; had additional *Magadan shest'desyat let* (Magadan 60 years) titles
RA-85680	Tu-154M	90A843	Y164. Sold to Vnukovo ARZ No 400
CCCP-85685	Tu-154M	90A853	Y164. Aeroflot c/s. Wfu Magadan-Sokol by 7-94; sold to Vladivostok Air 2000
RA-85696	Tu-154M	91A869	Y164. C/s No 1. Sold to Continental Airlines 2002

Moscow Airways [M8/MSC] based at Sheremet'yevo-2 operated three Tu-154s leased as required.

Registration	Version	C/n	Notes
RA-85523	Tu-154B-2	82A523	Y164. Leased from Tupolev-Aerotrans 8-93 to ?-??, returned by 8-97; basic Aeroflot c/s, blue Moscow Airways titles to port
RA-85606	Tu-154M	84A701	Leased from Tupolev-Aerotrans 5-94 to ?-??, returned by 8-97; basic Aeroflot c/s, blue Moscow Airways titles
RA-85681	Tu-154M	90A848	Y164. Leased from Khakasia Airlines 6-94 to 7-95

Murmansk Airlines (*Moormanskiye avialinii*) **[–/MNK]** based at Murmansk-Murmashi, the only carrier based in the extreme North-West of Russia, had a mixed fleet including four Tu-154Ms; these were operated in the colours of the Russian Aviation Consortium (a short-lived joint venture with Vnukovo Airlines) which owned 60% of Murmansk Airlines' stock. These aircraft, one of which was leased from RAO Noril'skiy Nikel' (Noril'sk Nickel Russian Joint-Stock Company), a major stockholder, formed the mainstay of Murmansk Airlines' fleet and were the only completely serviceable aircraft in the fleet.

The Russian bank crisis of 1998 proved fatal for the airline, which was soon put up for sale. This triggered a conflict of interests. Noril'skiy Nikel', the biggest creditor, was all for selling the airline wholesale to a single new owner, while the Russian Aviation Consortium insisted on splitting the assets.

Registration	C/n	Notes
RA-85733	92A915	Y164. Sold to Tyumen'AviaTrans 2001
RA-85755	92A937	Y166. Sold to Tyumen'AviaTrans 2001
RA-85759	92A941	Y166. Leased from RAO Noril'skiy Nikel', additional Noril'skiy Nikel' titles. Sold to Kras Air 2001
RA-85799	94A983	Y166. Sold to Tatneft'aero

Nizhegorodskiye Avialinii [–/NGL] (= Nizhniy Novgorod Airlines, formerly the Gor'kiy UAD of the Volga CAD) based at Nizhniy Novgorod-Strigino had eight Tu-154s, receiving the first of the type as late as 1992. Unlike the carrier's Tu-134A/Tu-134AK twinjets, they all retained full Aeroflot colours; none of the trijets received the red 'HH' (that is, Cyrillic 'NN' for Nizhniy Novgorod) tail logo and Russian/English titles.

In the late 1990s the airline's financial position was shaky, with RUR 50 million (US$ 1.89 million) of debts as of mid-1999. Aeroflot Russian International Airlines considered taking over the ailing carrier as a way of expanding its route network, and in May 1999 a memorandum of understanding was signed with the Nizhniy Novgorod Region administration concerning the establishment of Aeroflot Nizhniy Novgorod JSC. Later, however, Aeroflot dropped these plans; and eventually Nizhegorodskiye Avialinii went bankrupt in 2002.

Registration	Version	C/n	Notes
RA-85080	Tu-154B-1	74A080	Y164. Converted Tu-154A. Wfu Nizhniy Novgorod 1995, scrapped 1997
RA-85228	Tu-154B-1	77A228	Y164. Wfu Nizhniy Novgorod 1998, scrapped 2002
RA-85253	Tu-154B-1	77A253	Y164. Wfu Nizhniy Novgorod 2000, scrapped 3-03
RA-85263	Tu-154B-1	78A263	Y164. Basic Aeroflot colours, no titles. Wfu Nizhniy Novgorod 2000
RA-85287	Tu-154B-1	78A287	Y164. Sold to Vnukovo ARZ No 411 5-01
RA-85318	Tu-154B-2	78A318	Y164. Basic Aeroflot c/s, no titles. Stored Nizhniy Novgorod 2000; scrapped 2004
RA-85456	Tu-154B-2	80A456	Y164. Ex-Kras Air, bought 2000. Sold to Mega Aero 12-03/opb Atlant-Soyuz
RA-85458	Tu-154B-2	80A458	Y164. Sold to Spetsavia/stored Nizhniy Novgorod

In October 1999 **Noril'sk Airlines** based at Noril'sk-Alykel' reportedly took delivery of Tu-154B-1 RA-85273 (c/n 78A273) which was previously operated by Sibaviatrans. However, the airline in question may actually be Severaero (which see).

Novosibirsk Airlines (*Novosibeerskiye avialinii*) **[L8/NLB]** based at Tolmachovo airport leased Tu-154B-2 RA-85470 (c/n 81A470) from the Ul'yanovsk Higher Flying School at an unknown date.

Omskavia [–/OMS] came into being on 1st February 1994 when the Omsk UAD of the former West Siberian CAD was organisationally separated from Omsk airport. Its fleet included 16 Tu-154s. These displayed a variety of liveries, starting out with basic Aeroflot colours and Cyrillic Omskavia titles (c/s No 1). The first own livery featured a green cheatline

'Burning rubber' as it touches down on runway 14L at Moscow-Domodedovo, Murmansk Airlines Tu-154M RA-85759 displays the badge of the Noril'sk Nickel company which owns it. Yuriy Kirsanov

and a stylised green 'fir tree' tail logo, plus English 'Omskavia' titles (c/s No 2). By 1998 this was superseded by a much smarter colour scheme with the green cheatline augmented by red pinstripes and 'fir trees/red skies' tail colours (c/s No 3). this livery was soon dubbed *Zmey Gorynych* (the name of dragons in Russian folklore). Another version combined similar tail colours with an all-white fuselage (c/s No 4A) or with green and red pinstripes above and below the windows but no cheatline as such (c/s No 4B). Since 2005 Omskavia is a member of the AiRUnion alliance.

Registration	Version	C/n	Notes
RA-85064	Tu-154B	74A064	Y164. Converted Tu-154A; c/s No 1. Retired 1997
RA-85133	Tu-154B	78A133	Y164. Ex-Latavio YL-LAA; c/s No 3. Leased from Alexandra Avia Leasing 8-98
RA-85273	Tu-154B-1	78A273	Y164. C/s No 1. Sold to Chernomor-Soyuz by mid-1998
RA-85291	Tu-154B-1	78A291	Y164. C/s No 2/English titles. Sold to Chernomor-Soyuz 1998

Tu-154B-1 RA-85291 exemplifies the old green/white full livery of Omskavia. Dmitriy Petrochenko

Tu-154M RA-85730 shows off the more stylish version of Omskavia's current 'Ye Dragon' colours, with cheatlines above and below. Dmitriy Petrochenko

Registration	Version	C/n	Notes
RA-85358	Tu-154B-2	79A358	Y164. Aeroflot c/s. Damaged on landing at Omsk 29-12-93 and repaired
RA-85504	Tu-154B-2	81A504	Y164. Bought from Severaero 11-98. Basic Aeroflot c/s, Cyrillic Omskavia titles/Severaero tail logo. Sold to Sibaviatrans 1999
RA-85714	Tu-154M	91A890	Ex-Aviaexpresscruise 4L-AAF, bought 2001; c/s No 4A (originally without titles)
RA-85730	Tu-154M	92A912	Y164. C/s No 1, later No 4B. Leased to Eram Air 4-06 as EP-EKA
RA-85745	Tu-154M	92A928	Y164. Ex-Vnukovo Airlines, bought 11-97; all-white c/s with green Omskavia titles. Leased to Domodedovo Airlines
RA-85750	Tu-154M	92A932	Y164. C/s No 2, later grey/white c/s with green Omskavia titles after Iranian lease
RA-85752	Tu-154M	92A934	Y164. C/s No 1. Leased to Dalavia 2003
RA-85763	Tu-154M	93A963	Y164. Bought from Sibir' Airlines 6-01. Leased to Eram
RA-85801	Tu-154M	93A960	Y166. Bought from Kolavia 4-03. Leased to/jointly operated with Kras Air 2005
RA-85818	Tu-154M	85A719	Y164. Ex-Cubana CU-T1276, bought 12-95; c/s No 2/Russian titles, later No 4A. Sold to Kras Air by 7-06
RA-85830	Tu-154M	89A821	Y164. Ex-Aeronica YN-CBT, D/D 7-97. C/s No 3, later No 4B, named *Tara*. Leased to Mahan Air 9-02 as EP-MHS; returned?
RA-85841	Tu-154M	90A858	Ex-Travel Air Service OK-VCP, D/D 17-10-99; all-white c/s with green Omskavia titles. Leased to Domodedovo Airlines

Orenburg Airlines [R2/ORB] operated five Tu-154s.

Registration	Version	C/n	Notes
RA-85595	Tu-154B-2	84A595	Sold to UTair 1-03
RA-85602	Tu-154B-2	84A602	Ex-Tu-154B-2 'Salon' with HF communications gear. Leased to UTair 7-05
RA-85603	Tu-154B-2	84A603	Ex-Tu-154B-2 'Salon' with HF comms gear

Orenburg Airlines Tu-154B-2 RA-85603 sits under threatening skies at Moscow-Domodedovo on 3rd November 1998. Like sister ships RA-85602 and RA-85604, it used to be a Tu-154B-2 'Salon' with Surgut HF communications gear. Author

Registration	Version	C/n	Notes
RA-85604	Tu-154B-2	84A604	Ex-Tu-154B-2 'Salon' with HF communications gear
RA-85768	Tu-154M	92A949	Sold to Kras Air by 5-04

Perm Airlines (Permskiye avialinii) [UP/PGP, later 9D/PGP][3] based at Perm'-Bol'shoye Savino operated 12 Tu-154s over the years. Some retained basic Aeroflot colours with Cyrillic 'Permskiye avialinii' titles (c/s No 1); others combined an Aeroflot cheatline with a blue tail adorned with the airline's bear logo (c/s No 2A) but most aircraft lacked the cheatline, having a grey/white fuselage and full tail colours (c/s No 2B).

Registration	Version	C/n	Notes
RA-85104	Tu-154B	75A104	Y164. Converted Tu-154A; basic Aeroflot c/s, no titles. Ex-Ural Airlines, bought 2-96. C/s No 2A. Retired 2002
RA-85142	Tu-154B	76A142	Y164. Converted Tu-154A; basic Aeroflot c/s, no titles. Retired 1999
RA-85212	Tu-154B-1	77A212	Y164. Converted Tu-154B; basic Aeroflot c/s, no titles. Retired 1999
RA-85217	Tu-154B-1	77A217	Y164. Converted Tu-154B; c/s No 1. Sold to Primaviaexport LLC/opb Avialinii 400 by 9-02
RA-85284	Tu-154B-1	78A284	Y164. Ex-Ural Airlines? Basic Aeroflot c/s, no titles; later c/s No 2A
RA-85287	Tu-154B-1	78A287	Y164. C/s No 2B; leased from Vnukovo ARZ No 411
RA-85312	Tu-154B-2	78A312	Y164. Sold to Avial'-NV late 2001
RA-85450	Tu-154B-2	80A450	C/s No 2B, Avialeasing Co badge on nose
RA-85454	Tu-154B-2	80A454	Y164.C/s No 2B. Ex-Aeroflot-Don
RA-85607	Tu-154M	85A702	Y160. Ex-Arax Airways EK-85607, ex-Tupolev Design Bureau RA-85607. C/s No 2A. Sold to Abakan-Avia by 8-99
RA-85615	Tu-154M	86A731	Y164. Ex-Sibir' Airlines, bought by 5-06; Russian Aviation Consortium c/s, Permskiye Avialinii titles

Polyarnyye Avialinii (Polar Airlines) based in Polyarnyy, Yakutia, leased Tu-154M RA-85794 (c/n 93A978) from Sakha-Avia in 1998-2001.

Although normally it operates only regional turboprop aircraft (An-24 airliners and An-26 freighters), **Pskovavia [–PSW]** based at Pskov-Kresty leased Tu-154M RA-85802 (c/n 93A961) from Chitaavia in mid-2001.

Based at St Petersburg-Pulkovo, the **Pulkovo Air Enterprise** (formerly **St Petersburg Air Enterprise**) **[Z8/PLK]** operated a total of 46 Tu-154s. The airline's fleet includes a sizeable number of re-export aircraft, and some of the Tu-154Ms are ex-Chinese machines while the three Tu-154-100s come from Slovakia.

For years the entire fleet wore Aeroflot colours with or without titles. Eventually some aircraft gained Cyrillic 'Pulkovo' titles (c/s No 1). It was not until 1997 that Pulkovo introduced a full livery, by which time it was too late for some of the aircraft! Tu-154B-2 CCCP-85530 was the first to be repainted; originally the Cyrillic 'Pulkovo' (ПУЛКОВО) titles used a rather unfortunate typeface and could be misread as 'Pupkovo' (ПУПКОВО; *pupok* means 'navel' in Russian)! Obviously someone pointed this out to the management and the offending titles were promptly changed (ПУЛКОВО). RA-85530 and a few others have bright blue trim (c/s No 2A), while most of the airline's aircraft use a much darker shade of blue (c/s No 2B).

After the crash of Tu-154M RA-85185 No 2 the airline was on the brink of being blacklisted by the European civil aviation authorities. However, even before that it had been decided to merge the Pulkovo Air Enterprise with the Rossiya State Transport Co, and the crash accelerated this merger; the 'unlucky' Pulkovo brand vanished in the process. The merger was completed on 26th October 2006.

Registration	Version	C/n	Notes
RA-85092	Tu-154B-1	74A092	Y164. Converted Tu-154A. Aeroflot c/s. Retired 1994
RA-85096 No 1	Tu-154B-1	75A096	Y164. Converted Tu-154A (or Tu-154K?). Aeroflot c/s. Retired 1995, scrapped Mineral'nyye Vody
RA-85101 No 1	Tu-154B-1	75A101	Y164. Converted Tu-154A. Aeroflot c/s. Retired 1994, scrapped
RA-85107	Tu-154B-1	75A107	Y164. Converted Tu-154A. Aeroflot c/s. Retired 1997, scrapped
RA-85109 No 1	Tu-154B-1	75A109	Y164. Converted Tu-154A. Aeroflot c/s. Retired 1994, scrapped
RA-85139	Tu-154B-1	76A139	Y164. Converted Tu-154B. Aeroflot c/s, no titles. Retired by 1996
RA-85153	Tu-154B-1	76A153	Y164. Converted Tu-154B. Aeroflot c/s, no titles. Retired 1997
RA-85171 No 2	Tu-154M	91A893	C4Y150. Ex-Sichuan Airlines B-2625, regd 10-12-01, D/D 12-01. C/s No 2A
RA-85185 No 2	Tu-154M	91A894	C4Y150. Ex-Sichuan Airlines B-2626, regd 10-12-01, del. by 4-02. C/s No 2A. Crashed near Donetsk 22-8-06
RA-85187 No 2	Tu-154M	92A919	C4Y150. Ex-Sichuan Airlines B-2629, regd 10-12-01, del. by 4-02. C/s No 2
RA-85204 No 2	Tu-154M	91A886	C4Y150. Ex-Sichuan Airlines B-2624, regd 10-12-01, del. by 7-02. C/s No 2A

Tu-154B-1 RA-85284, the second-oldest example operated by Perm Airlines, was unusual in combining full tail colours with an Aeroflot cheatline, which was usually eliminated. Dmitriy Petrochenko

Most of the Pulkovo Air Enterprise's Tu-154s, including Tu-154B-2 RA-85542 shown here making the daily flight from St Petersburg to Moscow/Sheremet'yevo-1, have a dark blue rear fuselage/rudder and dark blue titles; examples having the light blue version are relatively rare. Dmitriy Petrochenko

RA-85229	Tu-154B-1	77A229	Y164. Retired 1997, scrapped
RA-85236	Tu-154B-1	77A236	Y164. Retired 1996, scrapped
RA-85238	Tu-154B-1	77A238	Y164. Retired 1996, scrapped
RA-85242	Tu-154B-1	77A242	Y164. Retired 1997, scrapped
RA-85293	Tu-154B-1	78A293	Y152. Retired by 2000, scrapped
RA-85298	Tu-154B-2	78A293	Y180. Retired 1996, scrapped
RA-85300	Tu-154B-2	78A300	Y180. Retired 1996, scrapped
RA-85334	Tu-154B-2	79A334	Y164
RA-85343	Tu-154B-2	79A343	Y164. Stored St Petersburg-Pulkovo
RA-85346	Tu-154B-2	79A346	Y152. C/s No 1?
RA-85377	Tu-154B-2	79A377	Y152. Aeroflot c/s, no titles; later c/s No 1
RA-85381	Tu-154B-2	79A381	Y152
RA-85390	Tu-154B-2	79A390	Y152. Aeroflot c/s, no titles
RA-85441	Tu-154B-2	80A441	C4Y154. C/s No 2A. Stored St Petersburg-Pulkovo
RA-85530	Tu-154B-2	82A530	F12C18Y102. C/s No 2A. Stored St Petersburg-Pulkovo
RA-85542	Tu-154B-2	82A542	F12C18Y102. C/s No 2B. Stored St Petersburg-Pulkovo
RA-85551	Tu-154B-2	82A551	Y164. Leased from AVL Arkhangel'sk Airlines, returned 1996
RA-85552	Tu-154B-2	82A552	F12C18Y102. C/s No 2B. Stored St Petersburg-Pulkovo
RA-85553	Tu-154B-2	82A553	F12C18Y102. Stored St Petersburg-Pulkovo
RA-85579	Tu-154B-2	83A579	F12C18Y102. C/s No 2B. Stored St Petersburg-Pulkovo
RA-85658	Tu-154M	89A808	C4Y150. Ex-Rossiya State Transport Co, bought 9-00
RA-85695	Tu-154M	91A868	Y164. Ex-Baikal Airlines, bought 1999. C/s No 2B, named Sankt-Peterburg
RA-85739	Tu-154M	92A925	Y164. Bought from Samara Airlines 11-03. C/s No 2B
RA-85753	Tu-154M	92A935	Y166. Ex-Amuravia, bought 1998. C/s No 2
RA-85767	Tu-154M	93A948	Y166. Ex-Konveyer/Touch & Go Airlines, D/D 22-11-94. Full c/s
RA-85769	Tu-154M	93A951	Y166. C/s No 2A
RA-85770	Tu-154M	93A952	Y166. C/s No 2B
RA-85771	Tu-154M	93A953	Y166. Full c/s. Was leased to C-Air 4-93?
RA-85779	Tu-154M	93A963	F12C18Y104. C/s No 2B
RA-85785	Tu-154M	93A969	Y166. C/s No 2A
RA-85800	Tu-154M	94A984	F12C18Y104. Ex-Motom Buryatia Airlines, bought 1995. C/s No 2B
RA-85832	Tu-154M	92A908	Ex-AJT Air International, bought 11-03; c/s No 2B
RA-85834	Tu-154-100	98A1014	Ex-Slovak Airlines OM-AAA, regd 5-12-03. C/s No 2A
RA-85835	Tu-154-100	98A1015	Ex-Slovak Airlines OM-AAB, regd 5-12-03. C/s No 2B
RA-85836	Tu-154-100	98A1018	Ex-Slovak Airlines OM-AAC, regd 5-12-03. C/s No 2B

Over the years the 235th Independent Air Detachment (the Soviet Federal Government flight) based at Moscow-Vnukovo operated a steady succession of Tu-154s, not all of which were VIP-configured. On 3rd December 1993 the 235th IAD became **GTK Rossiya** (*Gosoodarstvennaya* **trahns***portnaya* *kompaniya 'Rossiya'* – **Russia State Transport Co) [R4/SDM]**. This operated 12 Tu-154s, many of which were not VIP aircraft.

Registration	Version	C/n	Notes
RA-85629	Tu-154M	87A758	C/s No 4. Sold or leased to S7 Airlines by 7-06
RA-85630	Tu-154M	87A759	C/s No 1. Leased to Kolavia 2-02
RA-85631	Tu-154M	87A760	C/s No 3, later No 4
RA-85645	Tu-154M	88A782	C/s No 4
RA-85651	Tu-154M 'Salon'	88A793	Originally operated as 85651. C/s No 1. Sold to Tajikistan Airlines by 1-00 as EY-85651
RA-85653	Tu-154M 'Salon'	88A795	Originally operated as 85653. C/s No 1. Sold to Airlines 400 by 7-01

RA-85658	Tu-154M	89A808	C4Y150. Sold to Pulkovo Air Enterprise 9-00
RA-85659	Tu-154M 'Salon'	89A809	C/s No 4
RA-85666	Tu-154M 'Salon'	89A820	Originally operated as 85666. HF comms equipped. C/s No 2, later No 4
RA-85675	Tu-154M 'Salon'	90A835	Originally operated as 85675. HF comms equipped. C/s No 2. Converted to 164-seater and sold to Alrosa 6-00
RA-85686	Tu-154M 'Salon'	90A854	HF comms equipped. C/s No 4
RA-85715?	Tu-154M	91A891	Originally operated as 85715? Ownership unconfirmed; if yes, then sold to Kavminvodyavia by 1-00
RA-85843	Tu-154M	01A991	C/s No 4; also reported as Tu-154M 'Salon'
RA-85844	Tu-154M	01A1020	C/s No 4; not delivered, to Ural Airlines

In Soviet times the 235th IAD's Tu-154s wore standard Aeroflot colours. Shortly after the demise of the USSR most of the government jets had the tails painted grey to make the white stripe of the Russian flag stand out, but Aeroflot titles were retained for the time being. (The normal practice is to highlight this stripe with a grey 'shadow'; incidentally, many aircraft operated by the 'new' Aeroflot and some other carriers sported these horrid grey tails.)

Regrettably the white livery with a blue/red cheatline, red 'Rossiya' titles in stylised ancient Slavic script and the Russian coat of arms on the fin was never applied to the Tu-154s. On most grey-tailed examples the pinstripe below the Aeroflot cheatline was broken on the extreme nose and small blue '**РОССИЯ**' (Rossiya) titles in italics applied there (c/s No 1). At least two wore large '**РОССИЯ**' titles in gold in the same typeface above the windows (c/s No 2). Still others had small titles on the nose but a white tail (c/s No 3).

A new fleetwide standard livery was finally introduced in July 1997 (No 4), and yours truly was disgusted when he saw it. The aircraft is grey overall with a white/blue/red cheatline and red 'Rossiya' titles in plain script. This livery has earned the disdainful nickname *seryy oozhas* ('abominable grey'), though Grey Ghost would sound better perhaps. By 2002 some aircraft had the doors and exits outlined in blue.

Since you cannot make much of a living carrying government officials alone, in 1998 GTK Rossiya started flying passenger charters, later launching scheduled services to several destinations, including the Black Sea resorts of Sochi and Anapa. Hence a major portion of the airline's fleet, including some Tu-154Ms, has been delivered in (or converted to) tourist class configuration.

As already noted, in 2006 GTK Rossiya absorbed the Pulkovo Air Enterprise. The 'new' aircraft are flown in Pulkovo colours with additional Rossiya Russian Airlines titles for the time being.

Originally a pure cargo carrier, the **Roos'[4] Air Transport Company [-/RUR]** based in Zhukovskiy decided to move into the passenger air transport market in 2000 and leased Tu-154M RA-85766 (c/n 92A923)

Tu-154B-2 RA-85453 shown here on finals to Moscow-Vnukovo was operated by the short-lived carrier Rusavia-Charter in 2000. Dmitriy Petrochenko

from Chita Avia. The aircraft was repainted in the carrier's full livery (predominantly white with blue 'РУСЬ' titles in stylised ancient Slavic script and a blue stylised swan tail logo), but passenger operations with this aircraft and an ex-Georgian Tu-134A-1 were never started – which was probably just as well. On 14th July 2001 one of the airline's IL-76TD freighters (RA-76588) crashed fatally on take-off from Chkalovskaya AB. The ensuing investigation turned up grave breaches of flight safety and resulted in the airline's operating licence being withdrawn. Hence the Roos' Air Transport Co cancelled the lease immediately, and on 20th July 2001 RA-85766 was returned to the lessor.

The charter carrier **Rusavia-Charter [2Q/RMK]** operated Tu-154B-2 RA-85453 leased from Baikalavia in 2000; the aircraft was in basic Baikalavia colours with white Rusavia titles in stylised Old Slavic script. However, as early as January 2001 the airline had its licence withdrawn when forged paperwork and generally poor operational standards (insufficient aircraft availability, which meant passengers were stranded if an aircraft broke down) were discovered.

Some 40 Tu-154s were delivered to the Soviet Air Force and the Soviet Naval Aviation. Today the **Russian Air Force** (VVS RF) continues to operate the Tu-154, and many of the military examples are not VIP aircraft. Known first-line units include the 8th ADON/223rd OSAP (Chkalovskaya AB), a 23rd VA unit based at Domna AB near Chita and the 978th VTAP (*voyenno-trahnsportnyy aviapolk* – military airlift regiment, ≅ Military Airlift Wing) at Klin-5 AB, Moscow Defence District.

Like most of the Russian Air Force's quasi-civil aircraft, the Tu-154s wore 1973-standard Aeroflot colours for many years. Lately, however, some examples have started to appear in various colour schemes without titles but incorporating plainly recognisable elements of other airlines' liveries.

This HF-equipped Tu-154M 'Salon' RA-85666, is the aircraft used by Russia's Prime Minister. Here it is seen departing its home base, Moscow-Vnukovo, in the old grey-tailed/Aeroflot-style livery of the Rossiya State Transport Co; the version with large 'Rossiya' titles in gold was rare. Yuriy Kirsanov

Delivered in May 2001, Tu-154M RA-85843 is the newest example in the fleet of the Rossiya State Transport Co. Seen here immediately after arriving at Moscow/Vnukovo-1 on 18th June 2002, it wears the current 'abominable grey' livery and is a 158-seater flying scheduled services and charters. Author

At the turn of the century the Russian Air Force's Tu-154s began to shed their 'quasi-Aeroflot' image. Tu-154B-2 RA-85574 depicted at Moscow/Vnukovo-1 on 4th October 2000 has a cheatline looking like a cross-breed between Gazpromavia and Belavia, a grey tail (note that the registration is carried on the fuselage) and no titles. Author

Regn/Code	Version	C/n	Notes
CCCP-85049	Tu-154	73A049	Ex-Egyptair SU-AXC, delivered 1974. Moscow DD, Chkalovskaya AB; scrapped 1999?
CCCP-85050	Tu-154	73A050	Ex-Egyptair SU-AXD, delivered 1974. Upgraded to Tu-154B; to Uzbekistan Air Force as 85050
RA-85052	Tu-154	73A052	Ex-Egyptair SU-AXF, ex-CCCP-85052, delivered 1974. Upgraded to Tu-154B; wfu 1998
CCCP-85053	Tu-154	73A053	Ex-Egyptair SU-AXG, delivered 1974
CCCP--85054	Tu-154	73A054	Ex-Egyptair SU-AXH, delivered 1974
CCCP-85055	Tu-154	73A055	Ex-Egyptair SU-AXI, delivered 1974. Transferred to MAP/LII 1983
CCCP-85353	Tu-154B-2 ('Salon'?)	79A353	978th VTAP, Klin-5 AB, Moscow DD; for sale 2006
RA-85360	Tu-154B-2	79A360	223rd Flight Unit, Chkalovskaya AB. Aeroflot c/s
RA-85380	Tu-154B-2 ('Salon'?)	79A380	978th VTAP, Klin-5 AB, Moscow DD; for sale 2006
RA-85426	Tu-154B-2 'Salon'	80A426	HF comms suite. Basic Rossiya State Transport Co 'Grey Ghost' c/s, no titles
RA-85446	Tu-154B-2	80A446	Gazpromavia-style cheatline, white tail, no titles
RA-85463	Tu-154B-2 ('Salon'?)	80A463	978th VTAP, Klin-5 AB, Moscow DD? Sold to Air Kazakstan by 9-00 as UN 85463
RA-85510	Tu-154B-2 'Salon'	81A510	Transbaikalian DD, Domna AB, Chita. Aeroflot c/s; later Gazpromavia-style cheatline, ARIA-style grey/blue tail, blue engine nacelles, no titles
RA-85534	Tu-154B-2 ('Salon'?)	82A534	223rd Flight Unit, Aeroflot c/s
RA-85554	Tu-154B-2	82A554	223rd Flight Unit, Aeroflot c/s; now basic Rossiya State Transport Co 'Grey Ghost' c/s, no titles
RA-85555	Tu-154B-2	82A555	223rd Flight Unit, Aeroflot c/s
RA-85559	Tu-154B-2	82A559	223rd Flight Unit, Aeroflot c/s
RA-85563	Tu-154B-2	82A563	223rd Flight Unit, Aeroflot c/s
RA-85565	Tu-154B-2	82A565	223rd Flight Unit, transferred from Ministry of the Interior 2005
RA-85571	Tu-154B-2	83A571	223rd Flight Unit, Aeroflot c/s, later no titles
RA-85572	Tu-154B-2	83A572	Aeroflot c/s
RA-85574	Tu-154B-2 'Salon'	83A574	Aeroflot c/s, later Gazpromavia-style cheatline, grey tail, no titles
RA-85586	Tu-154B-2	83A586	223rd Flight Unit, Aeroflot c/s
RA-85587	Tu-154B-2	83A587	Aeroflot c/s
RA-85594	Tu-154B-2 'Salon'	84A594	HF comms suite. 223rd Flight Unit, Aeroflot c/s
RA-85605	Tu-154B-2 'Salon'	84A605	HF comms suite. 223rd Flight Unit, Aeroflot c/s
RA-85655	Tu-154M-LK1	89A798	Cosmonaut trainer, 70th OITAP ON, Chkalovskaya AB. Basic Aeroflot c/s. Converted to, see next line
	Tu-154M-ON		Open Skies aircraft, white c/s with blue/black cheatline and 'Russian Federation – Open Skies' titles; later red/blue cheatline and 'Y. A. Gagarin Space Training Center' titles
32 Red	Tu-154K	71A015?	Ex-CCCP-85015? Opb GNIKI VVS (929th GLITs), Vladimirovka AB, Akhtoobinsk, blue tail flash

The Russian Air Force also has commercial divisions. The 223rd OSAP at Chkalovskaya AB was transformed into an 'airline' called **223rd Flight Unit State Airline [–/CHD]**. The aircraft it operated are marked in the table above.

In 2004 the **Russian Ministry of the Interior** purchased former Air Moldova Tu-154B-2 ER-85565, which was reregistered RA-85565. This was probably the ministerial aircraft of Boris Gryzlov. The anonymous-looking aircraft was transferred to the Russian Air Force in 2005.

The **Russian Naval Air Arm (AVMF)** also operates a few Tu-154s in the VIP role. Known examples are Tu-154Ms RA-85614 (c/n 86A723) and RA-85616 (c/n 86A732). Again, for many years they wore Aeroflot colours; RA-85614 later lost the Aeroflot titles, while RA-85616 received an AeroBratsk-style light blue cheatline with no pinstripe, 'Tu-154m' titles in black below the cheatline and the Russian Navy's St Andrew's flag aft of the forward entry door.

Tu-154K '32 Red' (c/n 71A015?) is the only known Russian Air Force example to wear full military markings. The blue 'wing' trim on the tail is noteworthy. Victor Drushlyakov

The Russian Navy also has a few Tu-154s. Originally painted in standard Aeroflot colours, Tu-154M RA-85616 (seen here on short finals to Chkalovskaya AB in 2006) now has an AeroBratsk-style cheatline with no pinstripe and carries the Navy's St Andrew's flag aft of the forward entry door. Sergey Krivchikov

Tu-154B-2 RA-85804 in the full white colours of Tatarstan Air with the winged lion logo is seen a few seconds before touching down at Sharjah. Aidan Curley

Registration	Version	C/n	Notes
RA-85804	Tu-154B-2	81A517	F8Y125. Bought 12-92, ex-Krai-Aero. Basic Aeroflot c/s, Tatarstan titles, Tatarstan flag on tail; later all-white c/s with Tatarstan titles

In 2000 a second attempt was made to unite Tatarstan's civil aviation in a single airline by merging the First Kazan' Flight Detachment, the Nizhnekamsk Air Enterprise and Begishevo airport which serves Naberezhnyye Chelny and Nizhnekamsk. The result was **Tatarstan Air** (*Aviakompaniya Tatarstan*) **[U9/KAZ, later U9/TAK]**. The new carrier's Tu-154s are listed below. Additionally, in 2007 the airline will take delivery of three former China United Airlines Tu-154Ms (B-4001, B-4003 and B-4004, c/ns 85A711, 85A713 and 85A714).

Registration	Version	C/n	Notes
RA-85412	Tu-154B-2	80A412	Y164 Full white c/s
RA-85429	Tu-154B-2	80A429	Leased from AeroBratsk 2006
RA-85488	Tu-154B-2	81A488	Y158 or F12Y120. Wfu Kazan' by 8-01
RA-85504	Tu-154B-2	81A504	Y164. Ex-Sibaviatrans, in service 2000. Sold to UTair 5-03
RA-85798	Tu-154M	94A982	C26Y102. Basic ex-Tatneft'aero c/s, TATARSTAN titles and tail logo
RA-85799	Tu-154M	94A983	C26Y102. Basic ex-Tatneft'aero c/s, TATARSTAN titles
RA-85804	Tu-154B-2	81A517	F8Y125, full c/s

RA-85798 was one of two Tu-154Ms operated by Tatneft'aero; unlike the other aircraft, it wore full titles in a gap in the cheatline. Here it is shown taking off from runway 24 at Moscow-Vnukovo with the additional titles of Tatarstan Air, which leased this aircraft. Yuriy Kirsanov

In late 1998 **Tatneft'aero [–/TNF]**, the airline of the Tatneft' corporation (Tatarstan Oil Co), bought Tu-154M RA-85798 from Aviaenergo. The aircraft received an appealing livery with a cheatline in the Tatarstan flag colours of green, white and red broken by the TAT**NEFT**AERO titles beneath the forward cabin windows. A second example, RA-85799, was bought from the defunct Murmansk Airlines in March 2001; it had a slightly different livery with an unbroken cheatline and small *ТАТНЕФТЬАЭРО* titles above the windows.

In February 2002 Tatneft'aero suspended operations and the trijets were sold to Tatarstan Air.

The Moscow airline **Tesis [UZ/TIS]** operated four Tu-154s, three of which had blue tails with the Tesis logo (a T superimposed on a white circle). By 2006 the airline had stopped passenger operations, concentrating on the freight market; the fate of the three Tu-154s, which are no longer in the fleet list, remains unknown.

Registration	Version	C/n	Notes
RA-85280 No 1	Tu-154B-2	78A280	Y164. Converted Tu-154B-1. Sub-leased from Sayany 2000, basic Aeroflot c/s with Sayany/Tesis titles
RA-85462	Tu-154B-2	80A462	Y164. Leased from Baikal Airlines by 5-99, full c/s
RA-85503	Tu-154B-2	81A503	Y164. from Baikal Airlines Leased 2001, full c/s
RA-85512	Tu-154B-2	81A512	Y164. Leased from Baikal Airlines 28-9-01 to 1-11-05, full c/s

Established in 1992 as the successor of the West Siberian CAD/Tomsk UAD based at Tomsk-Bogashevo, **Tomsk-Avia [–/TSK]** operated three Tu-154s – two 'B-2s (RA-85421 c/n 80A421 and RA-85485 c/n 81A485) and a single 'M (RA-85763, c/n 93A946); the latter was bought from Aerovolga on 13th February 1995. In 1998 the airline became an associate of Sibir' Airlines and the parent company took over all three trijets in December.

Another sight to be seen no more – Tu-154B-2 RA-85485 in the colours of Tomsk-Avia at Moscow-Domodedovo on 20th September 1998. It was sold to Sibir' Airlines shortly afterwards. Author

Transaero [4J/TSO, later UN/TSO], the Soviet Union's (and later Russia's) first passenger airline to compete with Aeroflot, operated at least eight Tu-154s on charter flights from Moscow-Sheremet'yevo where the carrier was originally based. None of them wore the airline's full white livery with blue titles in English and red/blue/white tail logo. Instead, they retained basic Aeroflot colours with red Cyrillic ТРАНСАЭРО titles. The airline's involvement with the type ended in 1993 and Transaero has since moved to Moscow-Domodedovo.

Registration	Version	C/n	Notes
RA-85019	Tu-154S	71A019	Leased from Dalavia Far East Airlines 1993
RA-85333?	Tu-154B-2	79A333	Occasionally lsf IRS-Aero in full IRS-Aero c/s? Operation unconfirmed

CCCP-85530	Tu-154B-2	82A530	F12C18Y102? Leased from 1st Pulkovo UAD 2-92
CCCP-85553	Tu-154B-2	82A553	F12C18Y102. Leased from TsUMVS/63rd Flight 7-93
CCCP-85565	Tu-154B-2	82A565	F12C18Y102. Leased from TsUMVS/63rd Flight 7-93
CCCP-85649	Tu-154M	88A787	F12C18Y102. Leased from TsUMVS/63rd Flight 7-93
CCCP-85669	Tu-154M	89A827	F12C18Y102. Leased from TsUMVS/63rd Flight 6-92
CCCP-85685	Tu-154M	90A853	Y164? Leased from Magadan UAD 1-92 to 5-92
CCCP-85699	Tu-154M	91A874	F8Y130. Leased from Sibir' Airlines 6-92

Transeuropean Airlines [–/TEP] were founded in 1996, operating passenger charters from Moscow-Sheremet'yevo with aircraft leased from other carriers as required. These included three Tu-154Ms. RA-85676 (c/n 90A836) leased from Khakasia Airlines in 1996 retained basic Aeroflot colours with blue 'TRANSEUROPEAN' titles, a tail logo consisting of a blue soaring eagle ringed with gold stars and the registration on the rear fuselage. In contrast, RA-85799 (c/n 94A983) leased from Murmansk Airlines in 1997 wore the stylish purple/white full livery with gold titles and the eagle on the tail logo in white. RA-85816 (c/n 95A1006) leased from Bashkirian Airlines in 1998-99 had basic BAL colours with Transeuropean titles and logo. In late 1999 Transeuropean Airlines went out of business.

Transeuropean Airlines operated a succession or Tu-154Ms leased as required. RA-85799 operated in 1997 was the only example to wear the full livery. Yuriy Kirsanov

Like most Russian aviation design bureaux, ANTK Tupolev established its own airline, **Tupolev-Aerotrans [–/TUP]**, in 1996. It operated three Tu-154s, which were mostly leased to other carriers. In mid-2000 the airline ceased operations.

Registration	Version	C/n	Notes
RA-85523	Tu-154B-2	81A523	Aeroflot c/s, no titles by 8-97. Wfu Zhukovskiy by 8-99
RA-85606	Tu-154M	84A701	Aeroflot c/s, later no titles. Wfu Zhukovskiy by 8-97; sold to UTair by 10-04
RA-85627	Tu-154M	87A756	Wfu Zhukovskiy by 8-95; sold to Aeroflot Russian Airlines

Additionally, ANTK Tupolev owns the unique Tu-155 cryogenic propulsion technology demonstrator (CCCP-85035, c/n 72A035). This aircraft has been sitting in storage at Zhukovskiy for many years and may be scrapped unless someone has the wisdom to preserve it.

Tyumen' Airlines/Tyumenskiye Avialinïï [7M/TYM] based at Tyumen'-Roschchino operated 17 Tu-134s. However, the airline's financial state went from bad to worse after the 1998 Russian bank crisis and eventually the carrier was declared bankrupt, ceasing operations on 1st November 2003 when no buyer could be found.

Tyumen' Airlines Tu-154B-2 RA-85255 touches down on runway 14L at Moscow-Domodedovo, whizzing past the private apron of the cargo airline Atran. Yuriy Kirsanov

Registration	Version	C/n	Notes
RA-85255	Tu-154B-1	77A255	Y164. C/s No 2. Sold to CNG Transavia 6-03
RA-85312	Tu-154B-2	78A312	Y164. Sold to Perm' Airlines by 1997
RA-85314	Tu-154B-2	78A314	Y164. Retired 1997
RA-85335	Tu-154B-2	79A335	Y164. C/s No 2. Wfu Tyumen' 2000
RA-85361	Tu-154B-2	79A361	Y164. Retired 1997
RA-85366	Tu-154B-2	79A366	Y164. C/s No 2. Derelict Tyumen' by 7-00
RA-85378	Tu-154B-2	79A378	Y164. Derelict Tyumen' by 7-00
RA-85427	Tu-154B-2	80A427	Y164. Leased to Kolavia 6-6-00, never returned due to lessor's bankruptcy?
RA-85434	Tu-154B-2	80A434	Y164. Retired 1997, derelict Tyumen'
RA-85450	Tu-154B-2	80A450	Y164. Aeroflot c/s. Derelict by 2000 but restored and sold to Avialeasing Co
RA-85451	Tu-154B-2	80A451	Y164. Sold to ARZ No 411 11-99/opb Sibir' Airlines
RA-85481	Tu-154B-2	81A481	Y164. C/s No 2. Sold to Kolavia 2005
RA-85498	Tu-154B-2	81A498	Y164. C/s No 2
RA-85502	Tu-154B-2	81A502	Y164. C/s No 2
RA-85522	Tu-154B-2	82A522	Y164. Sold to Kolavia
RA-85550	Tu-154B-2	82A550	Y164. Sold to UTair
RA-85819	Tu-154M	97A1009	Y166. Lsf Yamalo-Nenets Autonomous District Administration 6-97; c/s No 2. Sold to Yamal Airlines

Tyumen'AviaTrans [P2/TMN] based at Tyumen'-Plekhanovo was the other major airline in the Tyumen' Region of Siberia. Originally its Tu-154s retained basic Aeroflot colours with Cyrillic **ТюменьАВИАТранс** titles and a white tail (c/s No 1). Later some aircraft gained a more eyecatching livery – basically white with a bold blue side flash (c/s No 2A).

Tu-154M RA-85733 seen during a turnaround at Moscow/Vnukovo-1 on 5th September 2001 demonstrates the full livery of what was then Tyumen'AviaTrans. The aircraft was named *Antonina Grigor'yeva* after purchase from Murmansk Airlines. The badge on the tail is the crest of Yugra, as the Khanty-Mansi Autonomous District was called of old. Author

Tu-154M RA-85727, a re-export from Estonia (ex-ES-LTP), is seen at Moscow/Vnukovo-1 on 6th May 2003 shortly after delivery to UTair. Regrettably, few aircraft sport this TAT-style blue side flash; most have an all-white fuselage. Author

Additionally, some aircraft sported the ancient crest of Yugra – the 19th century name of the Tyumen' Region – on the tail (c/s No 2B).

On 1st October 2002 (some sources say May 2002!) the airline was rebranded **UTair** – partly because its activities were not limited to the Tyumen' Region, partly because foreigners had trouble pronouncing the old name. Yet it was not until May 2003 that the new titles began appearing on the actual aircraft. Some Tu-154s retained the basic Tyumen'AviaTrans livery but with large *UTair* titles in white on the side flash, smaller *ЮТэйр* titles on the nose and a tail logo consisting of the letters *UT* on a rakishly tilted blue ellipse (c/s No 3). Others, like most of the carrier's aircraft, had an even simpler livery with an all-white fuselage and blue *UTair* main titles (c/s No 4). All in all, the carrier operated 20 Tu-154s.

Registration	Version	C/n	Notes
RA-85328	Tu-154B-2	79A328	Y152. Lsf Ural Airlines 2001, returned
RA-85452	Tu-154B-2	80A452	Y164. Leased from Donavia 1997, returned
RA-85504	Tu-154B-2	81A504	Y164. Bought from Tatarstan Air 5-03. C/s No 3
RA-85550	Tu-154B-2	82A550	Y164. Bought from Tyumen' Airlines by 5-05, c/s No 4
RA-85557	Tu-154B-2	82A557	C/s No 2A, later No 3
RA-85595	Tu-154B-2	84A595	Bought from Orenburg Airlines 1-03
RA-85602	Tu-154B-2	84A602	Leased from Orenburg Airlines as Tyumen'AviaTrans by 10-01, returned by 5-03, basic Aeroflot c/s, Tyumen'AviaTrans titles. Leased again as UTair 7-03 to 3-04 (basic Aeroflot c/s, UTair titles) and again 7-05
RA-85606	Tu-154M	84A701	Ex-Tupolev-Aerotrans, bought by 10-04
RA-85727	Tu-154M	92A909	Ex-ELK Estonian ES-LTP, bought 4-03; c/s No 3
RA-85733	Tu-154M	92A915	Y164. Ex-Murmansk Airlines, bought 2001; c/s No 2B, named *Antonina Grigor'yeva*
RA-85755	Tu-154M	92A937	Y166. Ex-Murmansk Airlines, bought 2001; c/s No 2B, later No 4B; named *Vasiliy Bakhilov*
RA-85751	Tu-154M	92A933	Y164. Sold to Gazpromavia 1996; leased back 1997 to ?-??
RA-85788	Tu-154M	93A972	Ex-Kaliningrad-Avia, bought 2006; c/s No 4?
RA-85789	Tu-154M	93A973	Ex-Kaliningrad-Avia, bought 2006; c/s No 4?
RA-85796	Tu-154M	94A980	F12C18Y108. C/s No 1, later No 2A, still later No 3A
RA-85805	Tu-154M	94A986	F12C18Y108. C/s No 1, later c/s No 2A, still later c/s No 3
RA-85806	Tu-154M	94A987	F12C18Y108. C/s No 1
RA-85808	Tu-154M	94A989	F12C18Y108. C/s No 1
RA-85813	Tu-154M	95A990	F12C18Y108. C/s No 1, later No 4
RA-85820	Tu-154M	98A995	F12C18Y108. C/s No 2A, named *Roman Marchenko*; now c/s No 4

The fleet of the **Ul'yanovsk Higher Civil Aviation Flying School**[6] (UVAU GA – *Ool'yahnovskoye vyssheye aviatsionnoye oochilischche grazhdahnskoy aviahtsii*) **[–/UHS]** included 13 Tu-154s. Most are in basic 1973-standard Aeroflot colours without titles; a few carry a small UVAU GA badge on the nose.

Registration	Version	C/n	Notes
85008	Tu-154	70M006	Sold to the Ukraine ?-94
RA-85013	Tu-154B	71A013	Converted Tu-154 sans suffixe. Retired 1999
RA-85016	Tu-154B	71A016	Converted Tu-154 sans suffixe. Retired 1999
CCCP-85025	Tu-154B	72A025	Converted Tu-154 sans suffixe. Retired 1996
RA-85061	Tu-154B	74A061	Converted Tu-154A. To Civil Air Fleet Museum, Ul'yanovsk
RA-85078	Tu-154B-1	74A078	Converted Tu-154A
RA-85091	Tu-154B-1	75A091	Converted Tu-154A
RA-85315	Tu-154B-2	78A315	
RA-85388	Tu-154B-2	79A388	
RA-85470	Tu-154B-2	81A470	

Ural Airlines' long-serving Tu-154B-1 RA-85219 comes in to land on runway 32L at Moscow-Domodedovo. Yuriy Kirsanov

RA-85609	Tu-154M	84A704	UVAU GA badge on nose
CCCP-85617	Tu-154M	86A736	Retired 1990
RA-85636	Tu-154M	87A766	Basic Aeroflot c/s, no titles

Ural Airlines/Ural'skiye Avialinii [U6/SVR] based in Yekaterinburg (formerly Sverdlovsk) came into being in 1993 when the Sverdlovsk Aviation Enterprise was organisationally separated from Kol'tsovo airport. Since then Ural Airlines have established themselves as one of Russia's major air carriers. The fleet included 20 Tu-154s.

Registration	Version	C/n	Notes
RA-85104?	Tu-154B	75A104	Y164. Converted Tu-154A. Aeroflot c/s; originally no prefix. Ownership unconfirmed (see Perm Airlines); if owned by Ural Airlines, then sold to Perm Airlines 2-96
RA-85141	Tu-154B-1	76A141	Y164. Converted Tu-154B. Retired 1999
RA-85193	Tu-154B-2	77A193	Y152. Converted Tu-154B. Full c/s
RA-85219	Tu-154B-2	77A219	Y152. Converted Tu-154B. Full c/s
RA-85284?	Tu-154B-1	78A284	Y164. Aeroflot c/s. Ownership unconfirmed (see Perm Airlines); if owned by Ural Airlines, then sold to Perm Airlines 1995
RA-85310	Tu-154B-2	78A310	Y152. Aeroflot c/s. Basic Aeroflot c/s, no titles. Wfu Yekaterinburg 1995
RA-85319	Tu-154B-2	78A319	Y152. Full c/s
RA-85328	Tu-154B-2	79A328	Y152. Basic Aeroflot c/s, no titles. Was lst Tyumen'AviaTrans 2001
RA-85337	Tu-154B-2	79A337	Y152.
RA-85357	Tu-154B-2	79A357	Y152. Full c/s
RA-85374	Tu-154B-2	79A374	Y152. Full c/s
RA-85375	Tu-154B-2	79A375	Y152. Full c/s
RA-85432	Tu-154B-2	80A432	Y152. Full c/s
RA-85439	Tu-154B-2	80A439	Y152. Aeroflot c/s with Ural Airlines sticker, later full c/s
RA-85459	Tu-154B-2	80A459	Y152. Aeroflot c/s with Ural Airlines sticker, later full c/s
RA-85508	Tu-154B-2	81A508	Y152. Aeroflot c/s with Ural Airlines sticker, later full c/s
RA-85807	Tu-154M	95A988	F12C18Y104. D/D 1995, full c/s
RA-85814	Tu-154M	95A994	F12C18Y104. D/D 1995, full c/s
RA-85833	Tu-154M	01A1020	Full c/s
RA-85844	Tu-154M	03A992	Full c/s

An airline named **Vityaz'** ('knight' in Russian) briefly operated Tu-154Ms CCCP-85728 and CCCP-85729 (c/ns 92A910 and 92A911) in Aeroflot colours in 1992. The aircraft were sold to Daghestan Airlines and Azerbaijan Airlines respectively, becoming RA-85728 and 4K-85729.

Vladivostok Air [XF/VLK], aka Vladivostokavia, had 13 Tu-154s.

Registration	Version	C/n	Notes
RA-85562	Tu-154B-2	82A562	Y164. Leased from Mavial Magadan Airlines 2-7-97, bought 14-3-03, named Dal'nerechensk
RA-85588	Tu-154B-2	83A588	F12Y120? Leased from Mavial Magadan Airlines 1997. C/s No 1, named Artyom
RA-85596	Tu-154B-2	84A596	F12Y120? Leased from Mavial Magadan Airlines 1997. C/s No 1
RA-85676	Tu-154M	90A836	CY124. Leased from Khakasia Airlines, D/D 6-6-03, named Sayanogorsk
RA-85681	Tu-154M	90A848	Leased from Khakasia Airlines, D/D 5-3-03, named Abakan
RA-85685	Tu-154M	90A853	Y164. Bought from Mavial Magadan Airlines 2000; c/s No 1, named Nakhodka
RA-85689	Tu-154M	90A860	Ex-AeroBratsk, bought by 5-04; c/s No 2
RA-85710	Tu-154M	91A885	Y164. Ex-Atlant, bought 10-94; c/s No 1, named Vladivostok
RA-85766	Tu-154M	92A923	Y151. Ex-Chitaavia, bought 8-04; c/s No 1

Tu-154M RA-85849 *Arsen'yev*, a former Chinese aircraft, displays the old livery of Vladivostok Air. Dmitriy Petrochenko

Resplendent in the stylish new livery of Vladivostok Air, Tu-154M RA-85689 is pictured at Moscow/Vnukovo-1 awaiting redelivery to the owner after an overhaul. Sergey Sergeyev

RA-85803	Tu-154M	89A822	Y164. Ex-Abakan-Avia, bought 10-99. C/s No 1, named *Primor'ye* (later *Spassk-Dal'niy*)
RA-85837	Tu-154M	91A876	C8Y143 or Y161. Ex-Air Ukraine UR-85701, bought 9-04
RA-85845	Tu-154M	86A735	Ex-China Northwest Airlines B-2609, bought 30-9-00. C/s No 1, named *Ussuriysk*. Crashed Irkutsk 3-7-01
RA-85849	Tu-154M	89A815	Ex-China Northwest Airlines B-2620, bought 9-01. C/s No 1, named *Arsen'yev*

Most aircraft wear a rather 'Aeroflotish' livery with a simple blue cheatline and a red pinstripe (c/s No 1). However, the service entry of the Tu-204-300 long-haul twinjet (for which Vladivostok Air was the launch customer) in 2005 saw the introduction of a brand-new and much smarter livery with a stylised red seagull sprawling across a white/blue/grey fuselage (c/s No 2), and some of the Tu-154s have gained the new livery.

Established in 1993, **Vnukovo Airlines** (*Vnookovskiye avialinii*) **[V5/VKO]** operated a total of 36 Tu-154s from Moscow/Vnukovo-1. Thanks largely to this fleet (and also, undeniably, to its IL-86s) it was Russia's second-largest air carrier in 1997 as far as passenger numbers were concerned.

All of the Kuznetsov-powered 'first-generation' Tu-154s retained their Aeroflot colours with or without titles. Most of the Tu-154Ms, on the other hand, received the airline's full livery introduced in 1993 (basically white with grey undersurfaces and dark blue/bronze stripes); the titles were in Russian to port and in English to starboard. Two versions existed – with grey engine nacelles (c/s No 1A) and with white nacelles (c/s No 1B). This livery proved to be somewhat controversial, earning such nicknames as *okun'* (perch – because the fish is striped) and, pardon the expression, 'bandaged dick'. Some aircraft that had been leased abroad were oper-

ated without titles for extended periods (for example, RA-85620 in 1996-97). In 1997, when Vnukovo Airlines joined the Russian Aviation Consortium, a few of its aircraft received the predominantly white RAC livery with 'pinstriped' Russian flag tail colours (c/s No 2).

In the late 1990s, however, the carrier ran into trouble, with frequent changes of the top executives and labour/management conflicts over the personnel's working conditions (on a couple of occasions the carrier's operations were severely hampered by strikes). In the summer of 1998 Sibir' Airlines' General Director Vladislav Filyov stated that the carrier needed to make a strategic alliance with a major Moscow-based airline and viewed Vnukovo Airlines as the prime candidate. Eventually Sibir' in effect, absorbed the troubled carrier in 2001, taking over the flyable aircraft.

Registration	Version	C/n	Notes
RA-85007 No 1	Tu-154B	70M007	Y164. Converted Tu-154 *sans suffixe*, Aeroflot c/s. Used as trainer since 1991; wfu Moscow/Vnukovo-1 by 7-95, scrapped
RA-85028	Tu-154B	72A028	Y164. Converted Tu-154 *sans suffixe*. Used as trainer since 1991; wfu Moscow/Vnukovo-1 by 5-93, scrapped
RA-85033	Tu-154B	73A033	Y164. Converted Tu-154 *sans suffixe*. Wfu Moscow/Vnukovo-1 1996, scrapped
RA-85039?	Tu-154B	73A039	Y164. Converted Tu-154 *sans suffixe*. Used as trainer since 1991. Wfu Moscow/Vnukovo-1 by 1993, scrapped; possibly opb Pulkovo Air Enterprise!
RA-85057	Tu-154B	74A057	Y164. Converted Tu-154A, Aeroflot c/s. Used as trainer since 1991; wfu Moscow/Vnukovo-1 ?-95, scrapped
RA-85084	Tu-154S	74A084	Converted Tu-154A. Aeroflot c/s, no titles. Wfu Moscow/Vnukovo-1 1997, scrapped
RA-85099	Tu-154B	75A099	Y164. Converted Tu-154A. Aeroflot c/s, no titles
RA-85140 No 1	Tu-154B-2	76A140	Y164. Converted Tu-154B, Aeroflot c/s, no titles. Wfu Moscow/Vnukovo-1 1995, scrapped 2003
RA-85156	Tu-154B-1	76A156	Y164. Aeroflot c/s, no titles. Wfu Moscow/Vnukovo-1 by 1997, scrapped
RA-85182	Tu-154B	76A182	Y164. Aeroflot c/s. Wfu Moscow/Vnukovo-1 1998, scrapped
RA-85215	Tu-154B-1	77A215	Y164. Aeroflot c/s, titles later removed; 'Tu-154B' nose titles. Wfu Moscow/Vnukovo-1 1999, scrapped
RA-85296	Tu-154B-2	78A296	Y164. Converted Tu-154B-1, Aeroflot c/s. Crash-landed at Groznyy-Severnyy airport 25-12-93; destroyed by air raid 11-12-94
RA-85299	Tu-154B-2	78A299	Y164. Converted Tu-154B-1 Aeroflot c/s, later no titles. Wfu Moscow/Vnukovo-1 2001, scrapped?
RA-85301	Tu-154B-2	78A301	Y164. Aeroflot c/s. Retired 1998, scrapped?
RA-85304	Tu-154B-2	78A307	Y164. Aeroflot c/s. Retired 1996, scrapped
RA-85312	Tu-154B-2	78A312	Leased from Perm Airlines 2000, SPAir-style purple/red/white c/s, no titles. Returned to lessor
RA-85610	Tu-154M	85A705	Y164. Basic Aeroflot c/s, no titles. Sold to Sibir' Airlines 4-01
RA-85611	Tu-154M	85A715	Y164. Aeroflot c/s plus ARIA-style 'anti-soot' blue tail flash. WFU Vnukovo-1 maintenance base by 5-00, titles crudely painted out in blue. Sold to Sibir' Airlines by 7-04
RA-85612	Tu-154M	85A721	Y164. C/s No 1A. Sold to Sibir' Airlines 7-03
RA-85615	Tu-154M	86A731	Y164. C/s No 1A, later c/s No 2. Sold to Sibir' Airlines 7-03
RA-85618	Tu-154M	86A737	Y164. C/s No 1B. Sold to Sibir' Airlines 10-01
RA-85619	Tu-154M	86A738	Y164. Basic META-Aviotransport Makedonija c/s until 1995, later c/s No 1B. Sold to Sibir' Airlines 4-02

Tu-154M RA-85736 in Vnukovo Airlines's standard livery (with white nacelles) touches down on runway 24 at its home base. The thrust reverser doors are just beginning to open. The titles on the other side are in Russian. Yuriy Kirsanov

RA-85620	Tu-154M	87A739	Y164. C/s No 1B. Sold to Sibir' Airlines 6-01
RA-85621	Tu-154M	86A742	Y164. C/s No 1B (painted 23-12-94). Crashed into Mt Opera near Longyearbyen, Svalbard, 29-8-96
RA-85622	Tu-154M	87A746	Y164. C/s No 1A. Sold to Sibir' Airlines 2-03
RA-85623	Tu-154M	87A749	Y164. C/s No 1A. Sold to Sibir' Airlines 8-03
RA-85624	Tu-154M	87A750	Y164. C/s No 1B. Sold to Sibir' Airlines 4-01
RA-85628	Tu-154M	87A757	Y164. C/s No 1B, grey/white wings. Sold to Sibir' Airlines 2-03
RA-85632	Tu-154M	87A761	Y164. C/s No 1A. Sold to Sibir' Airlines 7-01
RA-85633	Tu-154M	87A762	Y164. C/s No 1B. Wfu Moscow/Vnukovo-1 by 6-99; sold to Sibir' Airlines 12-03
RA-85635	Tu-154M	87A764	Y164. C/s No 2. Sold to Sibir' Airlines 11-01
RA-85673	Tu-154M	90A833	Y164. C/s No 1A, no titles, later c/s No 2. Sold to Sibir' Airlines 2-02
RA-85674	Tu-154M	90A834	Y164. C/s No 1B, no titles. Sold to Sibir' Airlines 7-01

RA-85736	Tu-154M	92A918	Y164. C/s No 1B, grey/white wings. Sold to Sibir' Airlines 8-02
RA-85743	Tu-154M	92A926	Y164. Basic Aeroflot c/s, no titles, later Vnukovo Airlines titles. Sold to Sibir' Airlines 4-01
RA-85745	Tu-154M	92A928	Y164. Basic META-Aviotransport Makedonija c/s; was occasionally leased to/jointly operated with Krai-Aero. Sold to Omskavia 11-97

Yakutia Airlines [K7/SYL] were established in December 2002 as the successor of the defunct Sakha Airlines' Yakutsk division, taking over its Tu-154s and adding further examples. Operations were started in January 2003. The striking colour scheme includes aurora borealis and, inevitably, diamond motifs.

Registration	Version	C/n	Notes
RA-85007 No 2	Tu-154M	88A777	CY154. Ex-Hemus Air LZ-HMF, bought 7-04, full c/s
RA-85136	Tu-154M	88A791	Ex-Aviaexpresscruise. Transferred 12-03
RA-85354	Tu-154B-2	79A354	Y164. D/D 1-03
RA-85376	Tu-154B-2	79A376	Y164. D/D 1-03
RA-85520	Tu-154B-2	81A520	Y164. D/D 1-03
RA-85577	Tu-154B-2	83A577	Y164. D/D 1-03
RA-85597	Tu-154B-2	84A597	Y164. D/D 1-03
RA-85700	Tu-154M	91A875	CY154. Ex-Hemus Air LZ-HMY, bought 5-05, basic Hemus Air c/s, no titles/logo
RA-85790	Tu-154M	93A974	F12C18Y104. D/D 1-03; named *Valeriy Kooz'min*
RA-85791	Tu-154M	93A975	CY154. D/D 1-03
RA-85793	Tu-154M	93A977	CY154. D/D 1-03
RA-85794	Tu-154M	93A978	CY154. D/D 1-03
RA-85812	Tu-154M	94A1005	CY154. D/D 1-03, full c/s

Formerly with Sakha Avia, Tu-154M RA-85794 gained Yakutua Airlines colours in early 2003. Here it is seen on finals to Moscow-Sheremet'yevo. Yuriy Kirsanov

Tu-154M RA-85712 wore this rather drab grey/blue livery when operated by Yakutsk Airlines in 1999. Note the small flag of the Republic of Sakha (Yakutia) aft of the flightdeck. Yuriy Kirsanov

Yakutsk Airlines (*Yakootskiye avialinii*) **[–/KUT]** were established in 1999, starting operations from Yakutsk with two Tu-154Ms as the mainstay of their small fleet. RA-85712 leased from Aviaexpresscruise looked rather drab, being grey overall with a blue cheatline and red/white titles and snowflake logo. RA-85794 leased from Sakha Avia looked a bit more appealing, retaining basic Aeroflot colours – at least it had a white top. In December 2002 the airline merged into Yakutia Airlines and the two aircraft returned to their respective 'homes'.

Yamal Airlines [YL/LLM] based in Salekhard, which is located on the Yamal Peninsula in the Russian High North, operated four Tu-154s. Unlike the carrier's Tu-134s whose colour scheme varies from aircraft to aircraft, the trijets have the same livery with an unbroken cheatline widening at the front to include the radome.

Registration	Version	C/n	Notes
RA-85324	Tu-154B-2	79A324	CY144. Ex-Taraz Wings UN 85324, bought 1998; full c/s
RA-85630	Tu-154M	87A759	Leased from Rossiya State Transport Co 2000; full c/s
RA-85819	Tu-154M	97A1008	Y164. Leased from Tyumen' Airlines by 4-98, Tyumen' Airlines c/s with additional Yamal titles; bought and painted in full c/s by 5-99
RA-85842	Tu-154B-2	80A420	Y164. Ex-Slovak Air Force Tu-154B-2 'Salon' '0420 White', bought 2002, full c/s

The following Russian-registered Tu-154s were in service with **unknown operators** (the aircraft wore Aeroflot colours unless otherwise stated):

Registration	Version	C/n	Notes
RA-85018	Tu-154B-1	71A018	Possibly Tatarstan Airlines. Scrapped Kazan'-Osnovnoy 11-97
RA-85051	Tu-154A	73A051	
RA-85089	Tu-154A	75A089	Possibly Samara Airlines. Retired 1994 and scrapped Samara-Kurumoch 5-96
RA-85135 No 1	Tu-154B	76A135	Operated by either Sibir' Airlines or Baikal Airlines. Preserved Kemerovo
RA-85280 No 2	Tu-154M	?	In primer at Aviacor factory 8-97
RA-85448	Tu-154B-2	80A448	Possibly Ural Airlines; retired but date unknown
RA-85453	Tu-154B-2	80A453	Y164. Basic Baikal Airlines c/s No 2, no titles. Seen operational Irkutsk 6-01 and wfu Novosibirsk 7-03
RA-85541	Tu-154B-2	?	Not c/n 82A541 (see CU-T1227); probably mispaint
85601	Tu-154B-2	84A601	Ex-Czech Air Force '0601 White', bought 4-05, all-white c/s, no titles
RA-85744	Tu-154M	92A927	Ex-Azamat UN 85744; basic Aeroflot c/s, no titles
RA-85764	Tu-154M	93A947	Sold to Uzbekistan Airways 1994 as UK 85764
RA-85851	Tu-154B-2	82A531	Ex-Malév HA-LCU, basic Malév c/s, no titles; seen 7-03 (delivered to Russia 23-4-01 but stored without registration, registered 9-03)
RA-85775	Tu-154M	93A957	Sold to Kazakstan Airlines by 2-05 as UN 85775
RA-85780	Tu-154M	93A964	Sold to Kazakstan Airlines by 4-05 as UN 85780

In early 2000 Yamal Airlines leased Tu-154M RA-85630 from the Rossiya State Transport Co. Here the aircraft is seen parked at the south end of the apron at Moscow/Vnukovo-1 on 29th May 2000 after the end of the lease. Author

Registration	Version	C/n	Notes
RA-85811 No 2	Tu-154M	?	In primer at Aviacor factory 8-97
RA-85816 No 2	Tu-154M	?	In primer at Aviacor factory 1999-2001
RA-85817 No 2	Tu-154M	?	In primer at Aviacor factory 1997-99
RA-85819 No 2	Tu-154M	?	In primer at Aviacor factory 1997
RA-85826 No 2	Tu-154M	?	In primer at Aviacor factory 8-97

Note: The aircraft listed as seen in primer at the factory are guaranteed to be doubles because operational aircraft with the same registrations were seen elsewhere at the same time.

ARMENIA

Armenian Airlines [R3/RME], the one-time Armenian flag carrier based at Yerevan-Zvartnots, had ten Tu-154s.

Registration	Version	C/n	Notes
EK-85162	Tu-154B	76A162	Y169. C/s No 1. Aeroflot c/s, no titles. Wfu Yerevan 1996, scrapped 2000
EK-85166	Tu-154B-1	76A166	Y169. Converted Tu-154B. C/s No 2, later No 3. Wfu Yerevan by 7-01
EK-85196	Tu-154B-1	77A196	Y169. Converted Tu-154B. Aeroflot c/s, no titles. Wfu Yerevan 1997
EK-85200	Tu-154B	77A200	Y169. C/s No 1. Wfu Yerevan by 2000
EK-85210	Tu-154B	77A210	Y169. C/s No 1. Retired 1997
EK-85279	Tu-154B-1	78A279	Y169. C/s No 1, later c/s No 2. Wfu/stored Yerevan by 10-01
EK-85403	Tu-154B-2	80A403	Y169. C/s No 2. Wfu/stored Yerevan by 4-03
EK-85442	Tu-154B-2	80A442	Y169. C/s No 2
EK-85536	Tu-154B-2 'Salon'	82A536	Opf government. Later reconverted to 169-seater, c/s No 2. Sold to South Airlines 3-93
EK-85566	Tu-154B-2	82A566	Y169. C/s No 2, later No 3

Initially all aircraft retained Aeroflot colours without titles and with an Armenian flag on the tail in lieu of the Soviet flag (c/s No 1). The first livery introduced in 1993 (c/s No 2) was predominantly white, with a grey belly, an **AAL** nose badge (the letters were orange, blue and red respectively), small titles (in English and Armenian script) and a round tail logo in the same national flag colours. Soon, however, this gave way to a striking new livery with a dark blue belly and rear fuselage/tail, a yellow cheatline and an 'AA' tail logo (c/s No 3).

In 2004 Armenian Airlines shut down. Armavia, which succeeded it as the new flag carrier, adopted a more pro-Western image, flying predominantly Airbus Industrie A320-211s. While it did take over Armenian Airlines' IL-86 widebodies for inclusive tour charters, the surviving Tu-154s found themselves unwanted and their fate remains unknown.

Tu-154B-2 EK-85566 displays the new livery of Armenian Airlines as it touches down on runway 24 at Moscow-Vnukovo. Dmitriy Petrochenko

Arax Airways of Yerevan operated Tu-154M EK-85803 in 1996-98. The legend below the flag reads 'Armenia' but this is hardly the aircraft's name. Dmitriy Petrochenko

Arax Airways [Y5/RXR], also based at Yerevan-Zvartnots, had a fleet comprising two Tu-154Ms.

Registration	Version	C/n	Notes
EK-85607		84A702	Y160. Ex-Perm Airlines RA-85607, bought 6-95. Sold to Abakan-Avia 7-99
EK-85803		89A822	Y164. Ex-Avia Urartu, bought 7-96. Sold to Abakan-Avia 1998

EK-85803 was previously operated by **Avia Urartu [–/URT]** based at Yerevan's other airport, Erebuni. The airline bought the machine from Krai Aero which had operated it as RA-85803.

South Airlines [–/STH] bought Tu-154B-2 EK-85536 from Armenian Airlines in March 1993; like the airline's other aircraft, it was based at Sharjah, UAE. In September 2005 the aircraft was wet-leased to the Libyan carrier Kallat El Saker.

AZERBAIJAN

AZAL Avia [J2/AHY], alias **Azerbaijan Airlines** or **AHY – Azerbaijan Hava Yollari**, operated 19 Tu-154s from Baku-Bina airport.

Originally some of AZAL's aircraft wore basic Aeroflot colours without titles or logo and no country prefix, their ownership being indicated only by the Azeri flag on the nose or tail (c/s No 1). Later, when AZAL introduced its own livery, most aircraft featured a blue/green/orange tail (c/s No 2), but some gained a revised colour scheme with a brighter-coloured cheatline and a white tail (c/s No 3).

Registration	Version	C/n	Notes
4K-85147	Tu-154B	76A147	Originally operated as 85147. Basic Aeroflot c/s, no titles. Retired 1997
4K-85158	Tu-154B	76A158	Originally operated as 85158. Basic Aeroflot c/s, no titles. Retired by 1996
4K-85177	Tu-154B	76A177	Originally operated as 85177. C/s No 1. Retired by 1996
4K-85192	Tu-154B-1	77A192	Converted Tu-154B. Originally operated as 85192. C/s No 1. Retired by 2000
4K-85199	Tu-154B-1	77A199	Converted Tu-154B. Originally operated as 85199. C/s No 1. Derelict Baku by 1996
4K-85211	Tu-154B	77A211	Retired by 1998
4K-85214	Tu-154B-1	77A214	Converted Tu-154B. Originally operated as 85214. C/s No 1, later No 2. Derelict Baku by 1996

Azerbaijan Airlines Tu-154B-2 4K-85548 taxies in at Moscow-Domodedovo on a flight from Baku in late November 1998. Author

4K-85250	Tu-154B-1	77A250	Leased from Turkmenistan Airlines August-September 1997, ex/to EZ-85250. Basic Aeroflot c/s, no titles.
4K-85274	Tu-154B-1	78A274	Originally operated as 85274. Aeroflot c/s with Azeri flag, later c/s No 1, still later Bo. 2. Retired Baku by 2001
4K-85329	Tu-154B-2	79A329	Originally operated as 85329. C/s No 1. Retired by 12-02
4K-85362	Tu-154B-2	79A362	Ex-Air Ukraine UR-85362, bought or leased 1998; basic Aeroflot c/s, no titles
4K-85364	Tu-154B-2	79A364	Basic Aeroflot c/s, no titles; later c/s No 1. Retired by 1-02
4K-85391	Tu-154B-2	80A391	Originally operated as 85391. C/s No 1. Retired by 12-00
4K-85548	Tu-154B-2	82A548	Originally operated as 85548. C/s No 2. Retired by 11-03
4K-85698	Tu-154M	91A871	Originally operated as CCCP-85698 and 85698. Aeroflot c/s with additional 'Azerbaijan Airlines – AHY' titles and Azeri flag, later no titles. Sold to VARZ 2001 as RA-85698
4K-85729	Tu-154M 'Salon'	92A911	Ex-Vityaz' CCCP-85729, bought 5-93. Opf Azerbaijan government; basic Aeroflot c/s with AZƏRBAYCAN – AHY titles, later basic c/s No 3 with the same titles. Refitted/reregistered by 2006 as, see next line
4K-729	Tu-154M	CY145	
4K-85734	Tu-154M	92A916	Originally operated as 85734; see Dalavia/RA-85734! C/s No 1, later No 2. Reregistered by 2006 as, see next line
4K-734		CY145;	named Shusha
4K-85738	Tu-154M	92A921	C/s No 1. Reregistered by 2006 as, see next line
4K-738		CY145	
4K-AZ10	Tu-154M 'Salon'	98A1013	Opf Azerbaijan government; basic c/s No 3, AZƏRBAYCAN – AHY titles

Baku-based **Imair [IK/ITX]**, a division of the Improtex trade corporation, operated five Tu-154s.

Registration	Version	C/n	Notes
4K-85395	Tu-154B-2	80A395	Ex/to UR-85395, leased from Air Ukraine late 1993 to ?-??; basic Aeroflot c/s, no titles, Azeri flag on fuselage
4K-85538	Tu-154B-2	82A538	Ex/to EW-85538, leased from Belavia 1995, basic Belavia c/s, no titles, Azeri flag on fuselage
EW-85703	Tu-154M	91A878	Leased from Belavia 1998 (?); basic Belavia c/s, no titles, Azeri flag on fuselage
4K-85732	Tu-154M	92A914	D/D 5-95, basic Aeroflot c/s, Azeri flag, no titles (small Improtex titles added later); full c/s by 7-98

Wearing an Azeri flag and Imair titles and logo over the basic Belavia livery, Tu-154M EW-85757 touches down on runway 14L at Moscow-Domodedovo in late 1998. Yuriy Kirsanov

Looking rather weathered, Belavia Tu-154M EW-85748 departs Prague-Ruzyne. Martin Novak

EW-85757	Tu-154M	92A939	Leased from Gomelavia 1998; basic Belavia c/s, Imair titles/logo
4K-AZ17	Tu-154M	85A718	Ex-China Xinjiang Airlines B-2603, bought 4-01; basic China Xinjiang AL blue tail c/s, later full Imair c/s

Turan Air [3T/URN] operated six Tu-154s, all of which were re-export aircraft originating from Hungary, Poland and Latvia.

Registration	Version	C/n	Notes
4K-325	Tu-154B-2	79A325	Ex-Malév HA-LCM, D/D 23-9-98. Basic Malév c/s, Turan Air titles/logo. Derelict Gyandzha by 6-04
4K-473	Tu-154B-2	81A473	Ex-Malév HA-LCO, D/D 29-5-02. Basic Malév c/s, Turan Air titles/logo
4K-85474	Tu-154B-2	81A474	Ex-Malév HA-LCP, D/D 23-5-02. Basic Malév c/s, Turan Air titles/logo. Reregistered, see next line
4K-474			Reregistered by 7-02
4K-727	Tu-154M	86A727	Ex-LOT SP-LCA, bought 7-95. Basic LOT c/s, no titles; later full c/s, named Naxçivan (Nakhichevan'). Sold to VARZ/leased to Bulgarian Air Charter as LZ-LCS
4K-733	Tu-154M	86A733	Ex-LOT SP-LCB, bought 8-95. Basic LOT c/s, no titles; later full c/s, named Gäncä (Gyandzha). Sold to VARZ/ leased to Bulgarian Air Charter as LZ-LCV
4K-85524	Tu-154B-2	82A524	Ex-Latavio YL-LAG, bought 1995; named Baki (Baku). Stored Baku-Bina by 2-02

BELARUS' (BELORUSSIA)

The Belorussian flag carrier **Belavia [B2/BRU]** operated 24 Tu-154s from Minsk-2 and Gomel'.

Registration	Version	C/n	Notes
EW-85260	Tu-154B-1	78A260	Wfu Minsk-2 by 9-97
EW-85331	Tu-154B-2	79A331	Wfu Minsk-2 by 5-96
EW-85339	Tu-154B-2	79A339	Retired by 1999
EW-85352	Tu-154B-2	79A352	Retired by 1999
EW-85372	Tu-154B-2	79A372	Wfu Minsk-2 by 9-94
EW-85411	Tu-154B-2	80A411	
EW-85419	Tu-154B-2	80A419	C/s No 1, no titles
EW-85465	Tu-154B-2	80A465	
EW-85509	Tu-154B-2	81A509	C/s No 1. Leased to Shaheen Air International ?-01 to ?-05
EW-85538	Tu-154B-2	82A538	Leased to Shaheen Air International ?-01 to ?-05, stored Minsk-2 with Shaheen Air titles
EW-85545	Tu-154B-2	82A545	Leased to Shaheen Air International ?-01 to ?-05, stored Minsk-2 with Shaheen Air titles
EW-85580	Tu-154B-2	83A580	
EW-85581	Tu-154B-2	83A581	
EW-85582	Tu-154B-2	83A582	
EW-85583	Tu-154B-2	83A583	
EW-85591	Tu-154B-2	84A591	C/s No 1
EW-85593	Tu-154B-2	84A593	
EW-85703	Tu-154M	91A878	
EW-85706	Tu-154M	91A881	C/s No 1
EW-85724	Tu-154M	92A906	C/s No 1. Sold to Chelal 2-10-96 as RA-85724
EW-85725	Tu-154M	92A907	C/s No 1. Sold to Chelal 2-10-96 as RA-85725

Rather stylish-looking Tu-154M 'Salon' EW-85815 is operated by the Belorussian government flight. Yuriy Kirsanov

Tu-154B-2 4L-85430 of ORBI completes its landing run on runway 24 during one of its frequent visits to Moscow-Vnukovo. Dmitriy Petrochenko

EW-85741	Tu-154M	91A896	Ex-ELK Estonian ES-LTR, bought 1998; basic ELK Estonian c/s, Belavia titles. Was leased back to ELK Estonian 5-00 to late 2000 or early 2001 as ES-LTC
EW-85748	Tu-154M	92A924	C/s No 1
EW-85760	Tu-154M	92A942	C/s No 1. Sold to Continental Airways 3-99 as RA-85760

Originally (in 1992) the airline was incorporated under the trading name **Belarus'**. In common with some of the airline's Tu-134As, Tu-154M CCCP-85703 No 2 was painted up accordingly to feature the red/white Belorussian flag superimposed on a dark blue band on the tail, red **БЕЛАРУСЬ** (Belarus') titles in plain script above the windows and small Aeroflot titles/logo beneath the windows. (This was because the airline was not yet an ICAO member and operated under Aeroflot's SU flight code for the time being.)

Later Belavia standardised on a dark blue tail with the logo in a white ellipse, dark blue engine nacelles with a lighter stripe outlined in white and italic **BELAVIA** titles; this livery was designed in-house. Yet, variations persisted; some aircraft retained an Aeroflot cheatline (c/s No 1), while others had a cheatline with pinstripes above and below (c/s No 2). Finally, when the Russian Federation and the Republic of Belarus began preparing for integration into a new union in April 1997, the 'CIS-style' Belorussian flag on the rudder was replaced by a new red/green flag (strongly resembling the flag of the former Belorussian SSR) on the centre fuselage.

In 1996 the Gomel' division of Belavia became a separate entity called **Gomelavia [YD/GOM]**. The airline operated four Tu-154s.

Registration	Version	C/n	Notes
EW-85217	Tu-154B-1	77A217	Ex-RA-85217, leased from Sakha Avia 2000; basic Aeroflot c/s, no titles. To Perm Airlines by 9-02 as RA-85217
EW-85486	Tu-154B-2	81A486	Ex-RA-85486, leased from Sakha Avia 2000; basic Aeroflot c/s, no titles, Gomelavia tail logo. To Atlant-Soyuz by 2004 as RA-85486
EW-85757	Tu-154M	92A939	Ex-RA-85757. Sold to Alrosa 6-02 as RA-85757
EW-85760	Tu-154M	92A942	Ex-Bratsk Air Enterprise RA-85760, bought 1997. Sold to Continental Airways 3-99 as RA-85760

The **Belorussian government flight** operates Tu-154M 'Salon' EW-85815 (c/n 95A1010) delivered in 1998. This aircraft is used by President Aleksandr G Lukashenko on his visits abroad.

Tbilisi-based **ORBI [NQ/DVU]**, which used to be Georgia's flag carrier, operated 15 Tu-154s from Tbilisi-Lochini. Most of these aircraft wore a stylish blue/white livery with an eagle tail logo; at least until January 1993 they had no prefix and no flag to reveal their 'nationality'. 85496 was the VIP jet of Georgia's first president Zviad Gamsakhurdia, later passing to his successor Eduard A Shevardnadze.

However, by October 1997 all of the original aircraft had been sold or retired. By mid-1998, ORBI's fleet consisted of a single Tu-134A-1. This could not save the day and in 1999 the airline finally ceased operations.

Registration	Version	C/n	Notes
4L-85168	Tu-154B	76A168	Originally operated as 85168. Full c/s. Sold to Air Zena by 1997
4L-85188	Tu-154B	76A188	Originally operated as 85188. Basic Aeroflot c/s, no titles. Wfu Tbilisi 1996, used for spares
4L-85197	Tu-154B-1	77A197	Converted Tu-154B. Retired by 1997
4L-85359	Tu-154B-2	79A359	Originally operated as 85359. Retired by 1997
4L-85430	Tu-154B-2	80A430	Originally operated as 85430. Full c/s. Sold to Georgian International Air Lines by 9-97
4L-85496	Tu-154B-2 'Salon'	81A496	Originally operated as 85496. White c/s. Sold to Georgian International Air Lines by 9-97
4L-85518	Tu-154B-2	81A518	Originally operated as 85518. Full c/s. Sold to Georgian International Air Lines by 9-97
GR-85547	Tu-154B-2	82A547	Basic Aeroflot c/s, no titles, Georgian flag on tail. Became, see next line
4L-85547			Rereg by 12-93, same c/s. Sold to Air Georgia

Displaying the latest livery of Georgian Airlines, Tu-154M 4L-85713 languishes in the snowbound maintenance area at Moscow/Vnukovo-1 on 22nd March 2001 in company with several more or less dead sister ships belonging to the ailing Vnukovo Airlines. Author

In 1997 the newly formed **Georgian International Air Lines [3P/GEG]**, later renamed **Georgian Air Lines [6R/GEG]**, took over three of ORBI's Tu-154B-2s.[7] A fourth example bought in Russia was added later.

Registration	Version	C/n	Notes
4L-85430	Tu-154B-2	80A430	ORBI-style blue tail with logo on white circle. Wfu Tbilisi by 6-00
4L-85496	Tu-154B-2	81A496	No longer VIP aircraft; all-white c/s. Leased to Air Libya Tibesti 10-03 to ?-05; stored Tbilisi, no titles
4L-85518	Tu-154B-2	81A518	Combi (Y62+cargo). Stored Tbilisi by 2001
4L-85713	Tu-154M	91A889	Ex-Ayaks RA-85713, bought by 3-00; grey/white fuselage, blue tail. Stored Moscow/Vnukovo-1 by 10-00

Tbilisi-based **Aviaexpresscruise [–/AEQ]**, the sister company of the Russian Aviaexpresscruise, bought Tu-154M RA-85714 (c/n 91A890) from Ayaks Airlines in March 1998. Reregistered 4L-AAF, the aircraft was in service until 2001 when it was sold to Omskavia as RA-85714.

Transair Georgia was one of the first air carriers to appear in post-Soviet Georgia. Among other things it operated Tu-154B 85163 (c/n 76A163) in Aeroflot colours. Tragically, this latter aircraft was shot down at Sukhumi-Babushara on 22nd September 1993 during the Georgian/Abkhazian war. This, together with the loss of at least two Tu-134As in similar circumstances, left Transair Georgia no alternative but to lease Tu-154Ms from Russian carriers.

Air Georgia [DA/GEO] operated three Tu-154s.

Registration	Version	C/n	Notes
4L-85168	Tu-154B	76A168	Leased from Air Zena early 1999; wfu Tbilisi 2001
4L-85547	Tu-154B-2	82A547	Blue 'wraparound' cheatline and blue tail with white logo. Reregistered by 1999 as, see next line
4L-AAG			Wfu/stored Tbilisi 2001
4L-85558	Tu-154B	82A558	Ex-Latavio YL-LAH, bought 1993. All-white c/s and blue tail logo. Reregistered by 1999 as...
4L-AAH			Still had 4L-85558 on nose gear doors. Wfu/stored Tbilisi 2001

In 1997 **Air Zena [A9/TGZ]** (or Airzena Georgian Airlines) of Tbilisi bought Tu-154B 4L-85168 from ORBI, operating it in the ex-owner's basic colours. From November 1999 onwards Tu-154B-2s 4L-AAG and 4L-AAH were also listed as operated by Air Zena (the carrier has since been rebranded Georgian Airways).

Tu-154B-2 4L-85547 wearing the smarter of Air Georgia's two liveries 'cleans up' as it departs Moscow-Vnukovo. Dmitriy Petrochenko

GACo Kavkasia [–/GAK], an airline based at Sukhumi (Abkhazia), leased Tu-154B-2 ER-85285 from Air Moldova in January-September 1997.

KAZAKHSTAN (KAZAKSTAN)

Aeroservis Kazakstan Aviakompaniyasy (Aeroservice Kazakstan Airlines) **[–/AVZ]** based in Almaty had two Tu-154B-2s bought from Latavio in 1993 – UN-85516 (ex-YL-LAC, c/n 82A516) and UN-85539 (ex-YL-LAF, c/n 82A539). The airline suspended operations in 1999 and the aircraft were placed in storage; UN-85516 was eventually sold to Asia Continental Airlines.

UN-85539, one of two Tu-154B-2s operated by Aeroservice Kazakstan Aviakompaniyasy, is seen taxying at Sharjah. Peter Davison

Aerotrans [–/ATG] based based at Taraz airport, Zhambyl (formerly Dzhamboul), operates three Tu-154B-2s.

Registration	C/n	Notes
UN 85422	80A422	Ex-Balkan Bulgarian Airlines LZ-BTS, bought 1-00, basic Balkan c/s with Aerotrans titles
UN 85521	82A521	Ex-Air Kazakstan, bought 2004
UN 85569	82A569	Ex-Balkan Bulgarian Airlines LZ-BTV, bought 2002; basic Balkan c/s with Aerotrans titles

Almaty-based **Asia Continental Airlines (ACA) [–/CID]** bought Tu-154B-2 UN-85516 from Aeroservis Kazakstan. The aircraft is stored at Almaty in basic Aeroservis Kazakstan colours.

Atyrau Air Ways/Atyrau Aue Zholy [IP/JOL] based in Atyrau (formerly Goor'yev) operated three Tu-154s.

Tu-154M UN-85855 was operated by Atyrau Airways and is seen here in the airlines' standard colour scheme. Aidan Curley

Registration	Version	C/n	Notes
UN-85742	Tu-154B-2	79A320	Ex-Jana-Arka, bought 2002, white with orange diagonal band on fuselage and 'Terra Incognita' titles. Retired 2006?
UN-85781	Tu-154M	93A965	Ex-Air Kazakstan. Standard c/s
UN 85855	Tu-154M	89A823	Bought from Sayakhat by 8-03. Standard c/s

An airline called **Azamat [–/AZB]** based in Almaty operated a Tu-154M, UN 85744 (c/n 92A927), in a 164-seat or combi configuration in 1994-97. The aircraft was sold to an unidentified Russian airline as RA-85744.

Earlier, UN-85742 had belonged to **Jana-Arka [–/JAK]** based in Almaty; this airline had bought the former RA-85742 from Amurtransavia in 1998. That same year the carrier leased Tu-154B-2 EY-85385 (c/n 79A385) from Tajikistan Airlines; the aircraft was reregistered UN-85385 for the duration but it is not known when it was returned to become EY-85385 again. Jana-Arka suspended operations in 2002.

Kazakhstan Airlines/Kazakhstan Aue Zholy or **Kazair [K4/KZA]** was this Central Asian republic's first flag carrier. Its large fleet included 25 Tu-154s.

Registration	Version	C/n	Notes
UN-85066	Tu-154B	74A066	Converted Tu-154A. C/s No 1, later no titles. Wfu Almaty 1997
UN-85076	Tu-154B	74A076	Converted Tu-154A. Retired 1995
UN 85111	Tu-154B-1	75A111	Cvtd Tu-154A. C/s No 1. Retired Almaty 1997
UN 85113	Tu-154B-1	75A113	Converted Tu-154A. C/s No 1, later No 2. Wfu/stored Astana 1995
UN 85151	Tu-154B	76A151	C/s No 2, registration on tail. Wfu Almaty 1997
UN 85173	Tu-154B-1	76A173	Converted Tu-154B. Wfu/stored Mineral'nyye Vody 1996
UN 85194	Tu-154B-1	77A194	Converted Tu-154B. C/s No 1, later c/s No 2/no titles (titles added by 1996). Wfu Almaty 1999
UN 85221	Tu-154B-1	77A221	C/s No 2. Wfu Almaty by 1997
UN 85230	Tu-154B-1	77A230	Converted Tu-154B. C/s No 1, later no titles, later c/s No 1A. Retired by 2001
UN 85231	Tu-154B-1	77A231	C/s No 1. Wfu Almaty by 1997
UN 85240*	Tu-154B-1	77A240	C/s No 1, later no titles, later c/s No 2. **Retired by 2002**
UN 85271	Tu-154B-1	78A271	C/s No 2. Wfu Almaty by 1999
UN 85276*	Tu-154B-1	78A276	C/s No 2, later No 3, **later No 5. Retired by 2001**
UN 85387	Tu-154B-2	79A387	C/s No 1, later no titles. Wfu Almaty 1997
UN 85396*	Tu-154B-2	80A396	C/s No 2, **later No 4. Retired by 2001**
UN 85431*	Tu-154B-2	80A431	C/s No 1, later No 3, **later No 5. Retired by 2001**
UN 85455	Tu-154B-2	80A455	DBR Karachi 21-1-95
UN 85463	Tu-154B-2	80A463	Ex-Russian Air Force RA-85463, bought by 9-00. Transferred to Kazakstan Air Force 3-01
UN 85478	Tu-154B-2	81A478	C/s No 1, later no titles. Sold to Yuzhnaya Aircompany by 2000 but jointly operated (Yuzhnaya and Kazakstan Airlines titles)
UN-85521*	Tu-154B-2	81A521	C/s No 1, later no titles, **later UN 85521, c/s No 4**
UN-85537*	Tu-154B-2	82A537	Initially operated as 85537. C/s No 1, later no titles, later c/s No 3, **later No 5**
UN-85589	Tu-154B-2	83A589	C/s No 1, later no titles, registration on tail
UN 85719*	Tu-154M	91A901	C/s No 1, later no titles, **later c/s No 4. Sold to MVM Trading 10-00 as RA-85719**
UN 85775*	Tu-154M	93A957	Ex-RA-85775, bought by 2-95. **C/s No 4**
UN 85780*	Tu-154M	93A964	Ex-RA-85780, bought by 5-95. C/s No 2, **later No 4**
UN 85781*	Tu-154M	93A965	

Shown here on final approach to Moscow-Domodedovo, Tu-154B-2 UN 85537 was one of several to wear the definitive colours of Kazakhstan Airlines. Yuriy Kirsanov

Originally flown in Aeroflot colours with titles and a Kazakh flag on the tail (c/s No 1) or ditto with '**Kazaкhstan aiяlines**' titles (c/s No 1A), some aircraft later gained a blue tail with the sun-and-eagle motif of the national flag and '**Kazaкhstan aiяlines**' titles, the registration usually being relocated to the engine nacelles (c/s No 2). A new livery featuring a predominantly white fuselage with a blue pinstripe (c/s No 3) appeared in late 1994; incidentally, the titles now read '**Kazaкstan aiяlines**', without the 'h'.

On 20th August 1996 Kazakstan Airlines filed for bankruptcy, with debts of 19 billion tenge (more than US$ 180 million). Rather than attempt to rescue the ailing giant, the government chose to liquidate the airline and establish a new flag carrier, **Air Kazakstan [9Y/KZK]**, which inherited most of Kazair's fleet, including the surviving Tu-154s. The livery was extremely similar, with '**Air Kazakstan**' titles, a new logo (an arrow on a yellow circle) and Aeroflot fuselage colours (c/s No 4) or a white fuselage with a grey belly and no cheatline – only a pinstripe at the most (c/s No 5). (Note: As there is no point in repeating the ex-Kazair fleet list, the transferred aircraft are marked * in the above table, and post-takeover changes of status for Air Kazakstan Tu-154s are marked in bold type.) In February 2004 Air Kazakstan, too, ceased operations, Air Astana becoming the new flag carrier.

SAN Air Company [S3/SND], a Kazakh-German joint venture based in Karaganda, leased four Tu-154Ms. These aircraft were flown in a predominantly white livery with blue titles and a black/red/yellow flash near the wing roots to indicate the airline's German affiliations.

Registration	C/n	Notes
RA-85822	89A806	CY150. Leased from Samara Airlines 1-96 to 2-99
RA-85823	88A775	CY150. Leased from Samara Airlines 5-96 to 2-97
RA-85824	88A769	CY150. Leased from BAL Bashkirian Airlines 5-96 to 8-97 (?)
RA-85825	88A776	CY150. Leased from BAL Bashkirian Airlines 5-96 to 7-96

Tu-154M UN 85780 seen at Moscow-Domodedovo during a turnaround on 3rd November 1998 wears the partial livery of Air Kazakstan. Author

Sayakhat operated seven ex-Chinese Tu-154Ms, including UN 85837 which retained basic China Northwest Airlines colours. Sergey and Dmitriy Komissarov collection

Established in 1989 as a cargo carrier flying IL-76TD freighters, Almaty-based **Sayakhat [Q9/SAH, later W7/SAH]**[8] diversified in 2002, starting passenger operations with seven ex-Chinese Tu-154Ms. Three remain in service now.

Registration	C/n	Notes
UN 85835	85A716	Ex-China Northwest Airlines B-2601, bought 1-98; basic CNWA c/s, Sayakhat titles/logo. Sold to Continental Airways 10-04 as RA-85140 No 2
UN 85836	85A717	Ex-China Northwest Airlines B-2602, bought 1-98; basic CNWA c/s, Sayakhat titles/logo. Sold to Kish Air 12-99 as EP-LBN
UN 85837	85A724	Ex-China Northwest Airlines B-2604, bought 1-98; basic CNWA c/s, Sayakhat titles/logo. Sold to Continental Airways 6-04 as RA-85146 No 2
UN 85852	86A726	Ex-China Xinjiang Airlines B-2611, bought by 4-01
UN 85853	86A728	Ex-China Xinjiang Airlines B-2606, bought 6-01; basic China Xinjiang AL blue tail c/s, Sayakhat titles/logo
UN 85854	86A729	Ex-China Xinjiang Airlines B-2607, bought by 6-01; basic China Xinjiang AL blue tail c/s, Sayakhat titles/logo
UN 85855	89A823	Ex-China Xinjiang Airlines B-2621, bought 2002 sold to Atyrau Airways by 9-03

Taraz Wings (Kryl'ya Taraza) **[–/TWC]**, a regional airline which, as the name suggests, is based at Zhambyl-Taraz airport, bought Tu-154B-2 ER-85324 (c/n 79A324) from Air Moldova in 1997 or early 1998. Duly reregistered UN-85324, the aircraft was operated for a year or so before being sold to Yamal Airlines as RA-85324.

VIPAir Airlines [9V/VIP] based at Astana operated two Tu-154Ms – UN-85775 (c/n 93A957) leased from Air Kazakstan in 1995 and UN-85782 (ex-RA-85782, c/n 93A966) purchased from Aerovolga in 1997; the latter aircraft wore additional Air Kazakstan titles. In 1999 the airline ceased operations; UN-85775 returned to the lessor, while the other aircraft was eventually sold to Alrosa as RA-85782.

In June 1999 an Almaty-based airline called **Yuzhnaya Aircompany Ltd [–/UGN]** ('yuzhnaya' is Russian for 'southern' in the feminine gender) bought Tu-154B-1 YR-TPG (c/n 78A262) from TAROM Romanian Airlines. For reasons unknown (and against all rules) the aircraft was registered UN 85777, even though Tu-154M **RA**-85777 was on the Russian register at the time (see Bashkirian Airlines); probably the operator wanted the three 'lucky sevens' badly enough to steal them! In 1999-2001 the aircraft, which retained basic blue/white TAROM colours until then, was leased to the Bulgarian carrier Air Scorpio.

In 2000 Yuzhnaya Aircompany acquired Tu-154B-2 UN 85478 from Kazakstan Airlines, operating it jointly with the ex-owner for a while (the aircraft carrier both titles). In 2003 the aircraft was transferred to the Kyrgyzstan register as EX-017 for some reason; by 2005, however, it had reverted to its previous Kazakh registration.

The **Kazakstan government flight** operated Tu-154B-2 'Salon' 85464 equipped with HF communications gear. The registration was soon amended to UN-85464; originally flown in basic Aeroflot colours with bold *KAZAKHSTAN* titles and a large Kazakh flag on the tail, the aircraft subsequently received a basically white colour scheme similar to Kazakhstan Airlines' livery No 3. By 2005 the flight division of the Presidential administration had been named **Berkut State Air Company [–/BEC]**; *berkut* is Russian for 'golden eagle', which is the symbol of Kazakhstan.

In March 2001 the **Kazakstan Air Force** acquired Tu-154B-2 UN 85463 from Air Kazakstan. It is in basic Aeroflot colours without titles and with the Kazakh flag on the tail.

An unknown Kazakh airline acquired Tu-154M LZ-HMH from Hemus Air. The aircraft was reregistered UN 85570 (see Aeroflot Russian Airlines/RA-85570!).

Full steam ahead? No, Vipair' Tu-154M UN-85782 does not run on coal. This aircraft was sold to Alrosa in 2005 to become RA-85782. Dmitriy Petrochenko

Tu-154M UR-FVV was briefly operated by Donbass Airlines before being sold to Iran. The cheatline is that of ex-owner China Northwest Airlines. Dmitriy Petrochenko

UR-85132	Tu-154B	76A132	Originally Air Ukraine c/s without titles; titles added 1997. Wfu Odessa 2002, scrapped in the spring of 2005
UR-85137	Tu-154B	76A137	Air Ukraine c/s without titles. Scrapped Odessa 12-99
UR-85148	Tu-154B	76A148	Retired Odessa by 1-02, scrapped 3-05
UR-85152	Tu-154B	76A152	Air Ukraine c/s without titles. Scrapped Odessa 12-99
UR-85154	Tu-154B	76A154	Aeroflot c/s, no titles, later Odes'ki Avialinii titles/logo; derelict Odessa by 1-02, scrapped 3-05
UR-85179	Tu-154B-1	76A179	Converted Tu-154B. Retired Odessa by 1-02, scrapped 4-02
UR-85218	Tu-154B-1	77A218	Basic Aeroflot c/s, Odes'ki Avialinii titles/logo. Wfu Odessa 2002
UR-85232	Tu-154B-1	77A232	Basic Aeroflot c/s, Odes'ki Avialinii titles/logo. Retired Odessa by 5-02, scrapped 4-05
UR-85288	Tu-154B-1	78A288	Air Ukraine c/s without titles. Scrapped Odessa early 2000

Odessa Airlines Tu-154B-1 UR-85218 is seen on final approach to runway 24 at Moscow-Vnukovo. Dmitriy Petrochenko

Tavria-MAC Joint-Stock Co [BE/TVM], another airline based in Simferopol' (the 'capital' of the Crimea Region), purchased Tu-154B-2 YL-LAE (c/n 82A546) from Baltic International Airlines in 1996. Reregistered UR-85546, the airliner was in service until December 2000, whereupon it was leased to Air Somalia. In the course of the lease the aircraft moved to the Moldovan register, becoming ER-TAI.

Ukrainian Cargo Airways (UCA, or UATK – *Ookrayins'ka aviatseeyna trahnsportna kompahniya*)-[–/UKS], another commercial division of the Ukrainian Air Force based in Zaporozhye, operated Tu-154B-2 UR-85561 (c/n 82A561) in an all-white livery with titles and logos. In 2000 it was reregistered UR-UCZ in keeping with the new trend. The aircraft is used for carrying Ukrainian military personnel on overseas deployments and other military personnel during peacekeeping operations.

The **Ukrainian Air Force** (UAF, or VPS – *Viys'kovo-povitryany seely*) operated the abovementioned Tu-154B-2 'Salon' CCCP-85445 in Aeroflot colours initially; by March 1993 it had become UR-85445 and gained Air Ukraine colours to sidetrack the casual observer. After a period of service with BSL Airline the aircraft received Ukrainian Air Force insignia and Збройні Сили України (*Zbroyny Seely Ookraïny* – Ukrainian Armed Forces) titles but retained the civil registration and basic 1993-standard Air Ukraine colours. By May 2002 it had been retired at Kiev-Borispol'. Similarly, Tu-154B-2 CCCP-85561 (later 85561) was painted in Air Ukraine colours back in 1992 when still CCCP- registered. In 1994 it was transferred to BSL Airline as UR-85561.

UZBEKISTAN

Uzbekistan Airways (Uzbekiston Havo Yullari) **[HY/UZB]**, the Uzbek flag carrier based at Tashkent-International and Samarkand, had 22 Tu-154s. The airline has a penchant for changing its livery, and the airliners have worn three different colour schemes. Some had basic Aeroflot colours with УЗБЕКИСТОН ('Uzbekistan' in the native language) titles and the Uzbek flag on the tail (c/s No 1). Others wore a national flag cheatline with blue above/white across/green below the windows, grey undersurfaces, *Uzbekistan Airways* titles and a blue tail with a white stylised bird logo (c/s No 2). Still others have the livery introduced on the carrier's Boeings and Airbuses, with a blue top and tail (with a blue bird logo on a yellow disc), a white nose/cheatline and a green belly (c/s No 3). Most aircraft have the registration painted on with no hyphen after the nationality prefix.

Registration	Version	C/n	Notes
UK 85189	Tu-154B	76A189	Wfu Tashkent by 10-97
UK 85245	Tu-154B-1	77A245	Wfu Tashkent by 10-97
UK 85248	Tu-154B-1	77A248	Wfu Tashkent by 10-97
UK 85249	Tu-154B-1	77A249	Initially operated as 85249. Wfu Tashkent by 10-97, scrapped 2000-01
UK85272	Tu-154B-1	78A272	C/s No 2; no space after prefix. Wfu Tashkent 21-10-90
UK 85286	Tu-154B-1	78A286	
UK 85322	Tu-154B-2	79A322	Wfu Tashkent by 10-97
UK 85344	Tu-154B-2	79A344	C/s No 2. Stored Tashkent/for sale
UK 85356	Tu-154B-2	79A356	Stored Tashkent by 10-00
UK 85370	Tu-154B-2	79A370	Stored Tashkent by 10-00; scrapped 2004-05
UK 85397	Tu-154B-2	80A397	Initially operated as 85397. Stored Tashkent by 10-00
UK 85398	Tu-154B-2	80A398	Initially operated as 85398. C/s No 2. Stored Tashkent by 10-00
UK 85401	Tu-154B-2	80A401	Initially operated as 85401. C/s No 1. Wfu Tashkent by 10-00, scrapped 2004-05
UK 85416	Tu-154B-2	80A416	Wfu Tashkent by 10-00
UK 85423	Tu-154B-2	80A423	Wfu Tashkent by 1-01
UK 85438	Tu-154B-2	80A438	Initially operated as 85438
UK85449	Tu-154B-2	80A449	No space after prefix. C/s No 2. Stored Tashkent by 8-02
UK-85575	Tu-154B-2 'Salon'	83A575	Initially operated as 85575. C/s No 1
UK 85578	Tu-154B-2 'Salon'	83A578	Initially operated as 85578
UK 85711	Tu-154M	91A887	Was leased to Pakistan International Airways as 85711. C/s No 3. Sold to Aeroflot Russian Airlines by 5-06 as RA-85711
UK 85764	Tu-154M	93A947	Ex-RA-85764, bought 1994; stored Tashkent. C/s No 3
UK 85776	Tu-154M	93A958	C/s No 2, later No 3

Above: **Tu-154B-2 UK 85344 taxying at Moscow-Domodedovo wears the old version of Uzbekistan Airways' livery.** Dmitriy Petrochenko

Below: **Tu-154M UK 85776 in the current colours of Uzbekistan Airways as it arrives at Moscow-Vnukovo for a check-up at ARZ No 400.** Sergey Krivchikov

In 1997 UK 85764 was cannibalised for spares to keep the other Tu-154Ms flying; however, by October 2003 it had been reportedly restored to airworthy status.

The **Uzbekistan government flight** purchased Tu-154B-2 'Salon' YA-TAT (c/n 84A600) from the Afghan government in 1991. Registered 85600 (later amended to UK 85600), the aircraft wears a colour scheme patterned on Uzbekistan Airways' 'Airbus-style' livery, except that the tail is white with an Uzbek flag, not blue with the airline's logo, and the national coat of arms is carried on the nose.

The **Uzbekistan Air Force** operated Tu-154B-2 85050 (c/n 73A050), a converted Tu-154A returned from Egypt (see Soviet/Russian Air Force), from Tashkent-Toozel'. Later the operator decided to apply the Uzbek country prefix UK, but because of a painting error the aircraft ended up wearing the Colombian prefix HK instead! At the closing stage of its service career the aircraft was painted in Uzbekistan Airways colours and the registration was painted correctly as UK 85050.

Chapter Seven

The Foreign Service Non-CIS Operators

The Tu-154 may rightly be called one of the bestsellers among Soviet airliners. It was supplied to 13 nations, becoming the first jet aircraft for some of its operators; a total of 138 were exported. Additionally, the Tu-134 was leased by the airlines of seven more nations. Thus it has seen service almost all over the world!

AFGHANISTAN

In 1986 **Bakhtar Afghan Airlines** (formerly Ariana Afghan Airlines) placed an order for two Tu-154Ms. The reason for this order was that the Afghan War had led to a Western, Pakistani, and Iranian blockade and an embargo on spares supplies, rendering the airline's McDonnell Douglas DC-10s and Boeing 727-200s unserviceable. The Tu-154 alleviated this problem, since product support by 'Big Brother' was guaranteed as long as the nation followed the 'correct' course.

The first Afghan crews came to Ul'yanovsk in late December 1986 to take their training. On 20th April 1987 the Afghans accepted two brand-new Tu-154Ms, YA-TAP (ex-CCCP85747, c/n 87A747) and YA-TAR (ex-CCCP85748, c/n 87A748), at Kuibyshev-Bezymyanka and flew them to Moscow where the official handover ceremony took place. This was attended by the aircraft's project chief A S Shengardt, General Director of the Aviaexport agency V S Stoodenikin, Bakhtar's President F M Fedawi, the airline's chief pilot A S Jadran, the Afghan Deputy Minister of Civil Aviation K A Amani and other dignitaries.

Bakhtar Afghan Airlines utilised the Tu-154Ms on its traditional services to India, Iraq, Saudi Arabia (including the carriage of pilgrims during the Hadj season), as well as flights to Moscow, Prague, Berlin and other European destinations. Due to the aircraft's flexible cabin layout it could be readily refitted to combi configuration for carrying small packaged goods. Speaking at the press conference following the ceremony, A S Jadran said, *'The aircraft has an excellent power/weight ratio, a high rate of climb and powerful high-lift devices making it possible to lose altitude rapidly on final approach. All of this is extremely important when operating in Afghanistan where the airfields are surrounded by tall mountains, which means the climbout and descent trajectories are quite steep.'* Additionally, the two aircraft featured an enhanced navigation suite and new reinforced landing gear wheels which could stand the augmented loads on Afghanistan's far-from-perfect runways.

In 1988 the airline reverted to its original name, **Ariana Afghan Airlines [FG/AFG]**. Unfortunately YA-TAP was lost to enemy action, being hit by a surface-to-air missile on approach to Kabul on 29th May 1992 and being destroyed by shelling on 1st-2nd August 1992 as it sat awaiting repairs. The other aircraft was luckier, being sold to Caspian Airlines of Iran as EP-CPG in 1998.

In 1989 the **Afghan government flight** took delivery of Tu-154B-2 'Salon' CCCP-85600 (c/n 84A600). Reregistered YA-TAT and repainted in Ariana Afghan Airlines colours, the aircraft served as the presidential jet of President Najibullah for a while. However, sometime between April and December 1991 the aircraft was returned to the former Soviet Union to become 85600 with the government flight of Uzbekistan.

ALBANIA

Deciding to finally come out of self-imposed political isolation, Albania launched economic reforms. Hence **Albanian Airlines [LV/LBC]** were established in 1992 for furthering communication with the outside world. Since the impoverished country could not afford to buy aircraft, leasing them was the only option. Bulgaria became the preferred lessor. Among other things, Albanian Airlines sub-leased Tu-154M LZ-LTV (c/n 91A895) from Balkan Bulgarian Airlines at an unknown date; the aircraft was in the basic colours of its previous operator, Moldtransavia. By July 2003 it had been returned to the CIS.

BULGARIA

Air Scorpio, alias **Scorpion Air [–/SPN]**, leased Tu-154B-1 UN 85777 (c/n 78A262) from Yuzhnaya Aircompany between October 1999 and early 2001.

As had been the case with the Tu-134, **Balkan Bulgarian Airlines** (*Bolgarski vozdooshni linii*) **[LZ/LAZ]** became the first foreign customer for the Tu-154. The Bulgarians needed a medium-haul jet for their expanding tourist industry and were contemplating various Western types. The Soviet Union would not put up with this, so the 'freshly baked' (or rather

Tu-154M YA-TAP was one of two operated by Ariana Afghan Airlines. It is seen here visiting Prague. Martin Novak

Balkan Bulgarian Airlines Tu-154B LZ-BTK is pictured in its original livery at Prague-Ruzyne in the late 1970s. Martin Novak

Tu-154M LZ-BTQ displays the new colours of Balkan Bulgarian Airlines (and the perpetually soot-stained rear end) as it taxies out for take-off from runway 07L at Moscow-Sheremet'yevo on a flight to Sofia. Dmitriy Petrochenko

half-baked) Tu-154 was offered in order to safeguard the Soviet monopoly of the Bulgarian market.

The first two Tu-154s *sans suffixe* arrived in 1972; eventually the airline came to operate 47 of the type, including aircraft on short-term leases (only 25 of these aircraft were owned by the airline). The trijets were registered in the BT... block; the BT very probably stood for 'big Tu', since the TU... registration block was already in use by the 'little Tu' – the Tu-134.

Registration	Version	C/n	Notes
LZ-BTA	Tu-154	72A026	Ex-CCCP85026, D/D 5-72. Upgraded to Tu-154A by 1981, then to Tu-154B in 1982; wfu Sofia-Vrazhdebna
LZ-BTB	Tu-154	72A027	Ex-CCCP85027, D/D 5-72. C/s No 1, later No 2. Crashed Baghdad 23-3-78
LZ-BTC	Tu-154	73A036	Ex-CCCP85036, D/D 3-73; converted to Tu-154B by 1985. Wfu Sofia by 1-98
LZ-BTD	Tu-154A	74A058	Ex-CCCP85058, D/D 1974; converted to Tu-154B by 4-78. DBR Varna 5-6-92
LZ-BTE	Tu-154A	74A073	Ex-CCCP85073, D/D 1974; converted to Tu-154B by 5-79. Wfu Sofia by 1-98
LZ-BTF	Tu-154A	74A077	Ex-CCCP85077, D/D 1974; converted to Tu-154B by 7-80. Wfu Sofia by 1-98
LZ-BTG	Tu-154A	75A095	Ex-CCCP85095, D/D 1975; converted to Tu-154B by 3-80. Wfu Sofia
LZ-BTH	Tu-154M	87A754	Ex-CCCP85754, D/D 1988. Sold to Hemus Air 2001 as LZ-HMH
LZ-BTI	Tu-154M	85A706	Ex-CCCP85706, D/D 5-85. Sold to Hemus Air 2001 as LZ-HMI
LZ-BTJ	Tu-154B-1	78A270	Ex-Bulgarian Air Force Tu-154B-1 'Salon', D/D 5-89, full c/s. Was leased to Palair Macedonian, all-white/Balkan titles after lease. Wfu Varna by 6-02
LZ-BTK	Tu-154B	76A144	Ex-CCCP85144, D/D 1976. Retired 1999
LZ-BTL No 1	Tu-154	73A051	Ex/to CCCP-85051, leased from Aeroflot 5-76 to 11-76
LZ-BTL No 2	Tu-154B	77A208	Ex-CCCP85208, D/D 1977. Wfu Varna by 1997 in all-white c/s, no titles
LZ-BTM No 1	Tu-154	73A052	Ex/to CCCP-85052, leased from Aeroflot 5-76 to 11-76
LZ-BTM No 2	Tu-154B	77A209	Ex-CCCP85209, D/D 1977. Wfu Sofia by 1-98
LZ-BTN No 1	Tu-154	73A054	Ex-CCCP-85054, leased from Aeroflot 30-5-77. Sub-leased to Libyan Arab Airlines 11-77; crashed Tripoli-Benghazi 2-12-77
LZ-BTN No 2	Tu-154M	89A832	Ex-CCCP85832, D/D 1989. Was operated for UN Peace Forces in 1995 as 'UN-180', all-white c/s after lease. Sold to Hemus Air 2001 as LZ-HMN
LZ-BTO	Tu-154B-1	78A258	Ex-CCCP85258, D/D 24-2-78. Retired by 12-99
LZ-BTP	Tu-154B-1	78A278	Ex-CCCP85278, D/D 26-5-78. Stored Sofia by 6-99
LZ-BTQ	Tu-154M	86A743	Ex-CCCP85743, D/D 1986. Sold to Hemus Air 2001 as LZ-HMQ
LZ-BTR No 1	Tu-154	73A051	Ex/to CCCP-85051, leased from Aeroflot 6-77 to 4-78; sub-leased to Libyan Arab Airlines 11-77
LZ-BTR No 2	Tu-154B-2	79A320	Ex-CCCP85320, D/D 1979. Sold to Blagoveshchensk Airlines 8-92 as CCCP-85742
LZ-BTR No 3	Tu-154M	87A760	Ex/to Rossiya State Transport Co RA-85631, leased 1996; returned
LZ-BTS	Tu-154B-2	80A422	Ex-CCCP-85422; reportedly built for Aeroflot but diverted to Balkan, D/D 1980. Sold to Aerotrans 1999 as UN 85422
LZ-BTT	Tu-154B-2	81A483	Ex-CCCP85483, D/D 4-80. Stored Sofia by 6-99
LZ-BTU	Tu-154B-2	81A484	Ex-CCCP85484, D/D 4-80. C/s No 2, later basic Palair Macedonian c/s, no titles; later all-white, n/t. Last flight to Burgas 31-10-96, preserved Burgas museum
LZ-BTV	Tu-154B-2	82A569	Ex-CCCP85569, D/D 11-82. Sold to Aerotrans 2002 as UN-85569
LZ-BTW	Tu-154M	85A707	Ex-CCCP85707, D/D 5-85. Sold to Hemus Air 2001 as LZ-HMW
LZ-BTX	Tu-154M	86A744	Ex-CCCP85744, D/D 1986. Sold to Russia? See LZ-LTX
LZ-BTY	Tu-154M	89A800	Ex-CCCP85800, D/D 1989. Sold to VARZ 2001 as RA-85096 No 2
LZ-LTA	Tu-154M	92A927	Ex/to RA-85744, leased from unknown operator 6-98 to 10-98; basic Aeroflot c/s, no titles, later Balkan titles
LZ-LTB	Tu-154B-2	79A365	Ex/to RA-85365, leased from AVL Arkhangel'sk Airlines 1998

LZ-LTC	Tu-154M	93A974	Ex-RA-85790, leased from Sakha Avia 3-99 to 10-99; to Caspian Airlines as EP-CPL
LZ-LTD	Tu-154M	89A802	Ex/to RA-85657, leased from Baikal Airlines
LZ-LTE	Tu-154M	90A848	Ex/to RA-85681, leased from Khakasia Airlines
LZ-LTF	Tu-154M	88A794	Y164. Ex/to RA-85652, leased from Baikal Airlines 1999-2000, basic Aeroflot c/s
LZ-LTG	Tu-154M	92A927	Ex/to RA-85744, leased from unknown operator 8-99 to 8-00. Grey/white c/s
LZ-LTK	Tu-154M	89A810	Ex-EP-ITV, leased from AeroBratsk, D/D 5-6-00. To RA-85660 late 2000 or early 2001
LZ-LTO	Tu-154M	91A871	Y164. Ex/to 4K-85698, leased from AZAL 13-6-00 to ?-00
LZ-LTP	Tu-154M	90A860	Y164. Ex/to RA-85689, leased from Sibir' Airlines 22-6-00 to 9-00
LZ-LTR	Tu-154M	90A843	Y164. Ex/to RA-85680, leased from Airlines 400 8-00 to 9-00
LZ-LTV	Tu-154M	91A895?	Ex-Moldtransavia ER-TAG? Leased 6-01 to 10-01; to 9XR-DU?
LZ-LTX	Tu-154M	86A744	Ex-LZ-BTX, D/D 9-6-00; in service at least until 9-00. To Bulgarian Air Charter as LZ-LCX
ER-85324	Tu-154B-2	79A324	Chartered from Air Moldova 7-97, Air Moldova c/s No 2 with 'Chartered by Balkan Bulgarian Airlines' titles
ER-85332	Tu-154B-2	79A332	Chartered from Air Moldova 8-97, Air Moldova c/s No 2 with 'Chartered by Balkan Bulgarian Airlines' titles
CCCP-85591	Tu-154B-2	84A591	Chartered from TsUMVS 1-89, Aeroflot c/s with Balkan Bulgarian Airlines sticker
OM-AAB	Tu-154-100	98A1015	Leased from Slovakian Airlines 10-01 to 9-02, basic Slovakian Airlines c/s with Balkan titles

Along with the Tu-134, which was introduced in 1975, the trijets served 28 destinations abroad. Later the Tu-134s were repainted to match the fleetwide standard, with a heavier cheatline running across the windows instead of underneath. In the late 1980s Balkan introduced a new predominantly white livery matching the latest fashion, with curved stripes in the national flag colours of red, white and green.

In the early 1990s Balkan started withdrawing the thirsty Tu-154s from scheduled services, replacing them with fuel-efficient Boeing 737-53As. Yet the type continued to render valuable service in the summer charter season, and the Tu-154Ms leased in Russia for the occasion were registered in the LT… series – presumably standing for 'leased Tu'.

At the end of the 1990s Balkan started suffering serious financial troubles, with US$111 million in outstanding debt. An attempt was made to rescue the airline by selling it to the Israeli holding company Knafaïm (which owns the Israeli airline Arkia), aided by the financial company Ze'evi Group. The new owner started settling the debt and implementing a fleet renewal programme. This change of ownership had an immediate adverse effect – some Middle Eastern nations whose cities had, until then, been served by Balkan denied access to Balkan aircraft because the carrier 'had sold out to the enemy'! However, the Israeli investments came too late and in December 2002 Balkan finally ceased operations, ceding the flag carrier role to Bulgaria Air.

The Sofia-based charter airline **Hemus Air [DU/HMS]** founded in 1986 operated nine Tu-154Ms.

Registration	C/n	Notes
LZ-HMF	88A777	Ex-Cubana CU-T1275, leased in Russia 2003-04. Returned, to Yakutia as RA-85007 No 2
LZ-HMH	87A754	Ex-Balkan LZ-BTH. Basic Balkan c/s, no titles. Sold to Kazakstan 5-06 as UN 85570
LZ-HMI	85A706	Ex-Balkan LZ-BTI, bought 2001; basic Balkan c/s, later 'Balkan Holidays' c/s
LZ-HMN	89A832	Ex-Balkan LZ-BTN No 2, bought 2001. Sold to Aeroflot Russian
		Airlines 2005 as RA-85765
LZ-HMP	86A733	Ex-Turan Air 4K-733, leased by 6-00, Turan Air c/s but Hemus Air titles. To Bulgarian Air Charter by 6-02 as LZ-LCV
LZ-HMQ	86A743	Ex-Balkan LZ-BTQ, bought 2001; basic Balkan c/s, later 'Balkan Holidays' c/s
LZ-HMS	87A751	Ex-RA-85721, leased from Meton Trade LLC. To Kyrghyzstan Airlines 11-05 as EX-087?
LZ-HMW	85A707	Ex-Balkan LZ-BTW, bought 2001; basic Balkan c/s, later 'Balkan Holidays' c/s
LZ-HMY	91A875	Ex-Air Ukraine UR-85700, bought by 5-02, grey/white c/s. Sold to Russia 2005 as RA-85700

Tu-154Ms LZ-HMI, -HMN, -HMQ and -HMV were leased to another charter airline called **Balkan Holidays** or **BH Air [–/BGH]** in May 2002, gaining a rather gaudy black/red/orange/blue livery.

VIA – Varna International Airlines [VL/VIM] (sometimes called Air VIA) was a charter carrier formed in mid-1990 specifically to take over an unwanted batch of five Tu-154Ms form a cancelled Balkan order (they were originally to be delivered from August 1990 onwards). It went on to become one of Bulgaria's better inclusive-tour airlines. In a pun on the abbreviated version of the name, most aircraft eventually had the original **VIA** titles amended to **VIA est vita**. In addition to their own services, the airline leased the trijets to other carriers.

However, in late 2005 VIA decided to phase out the type because of noise restrictions and high operating costs. In March 2006 the carrier took delivery of a single Airbus Industrie A320-232, with two more on order.

Registration	C/n	Notes
LZ-MIG	90A840	Ex-CCCP85840, D/D 1990. Sold to Avialinii 400
LZ-MIK	90A844	Ex-CCCP85844, D/D 1990. Sold to Avialinii 400
LZ-MIL	90A845	Ex-CCCP85845, D/D 1990; no titles (tail logo only). Stored Varna
LZ-MIR	90A852	Ex-CCCP85852, D/D 1990. Sold to Avialinii 400
LZ-MIS	90A863	Ex-CCCP85863, D/D 1990. Stored Varna
LZ-MIV	92A920	Ex-Flight Research Institute CCCP-85737, D/D 1993. Stored Varna since 5-05

Bulgarian Air Charter [–/BUC] operated eleven Tu-154Ms in an attractive green/white livery.

Registration	C/n	Notes
LZ-LCA	89A829	Ex-RA-85671, leased to/jointly operated with Airlines 400; to become RA-85671
LZ-LCB	93A975	Ex-RA-85791, leased from Sakha Avia 6-01 to 8-01. To Iran Air Tour as EP-MBR

VIA Varna International Airlines operated six Tu-154Ms, including LZ-MIG which was the first aircraft delivered. Martin Novak

The Bulgarian government flight operates this Tu-154M 'Salon', LZ-BTZ. Note the black 'anti-soot' colouring of the rear fuselage. Dmitriy Petrochenko

Tu-154M TL-ACF of Centrafrican Airlines parked at Sharjah. Sergey Popsuyevich

LZ-LCD	?	In service 5-01 to 7-02
LZ-LCE	90A847	Ex/to RA-85680, leased from Airlines 400 by 10-01. See below
LZ-LCI	88A788	Ex/to RA-85650, leased from Airlines 400 6-02 to 4-04
LZ-LCO	91A871	Ex/to 4K-85698, leased from Azerbaijan Airlines 12-00 to 9-01
LZ-LCQ	89A802	Leased from VARZ by 6-04, ex-EP-MBK
LZ-LCS	86A727	Owned by Turan Air, sub-leased from VARZ 5-02 to 10-03
LZ-LCU	90A847	Leased from Airlines 400 by 7-05, basic BAC c/s but Avialinii 400 Air Charter titles
LZ-LCV	86A733	Ex-Hemus Air LZ-HMP, transferred (bought?) by 6-02
LZ-LCX	86A744	Ex-Balkan LZ-LTX, in service by 1-01; reported in error (?) as Balkan Air Charter. Leased to Iran Air Tour 4-05

Air Kona [–/KON] leased a single Tu-154M, RA-85726 No 1 (c/n 92A908), from Liana in 1993; the aircraft was placed on the Bulgarian register as LZ-MNA. In addition to its own services, the airline sub-leased the jet to Macedonian Air Services. However, in 1994 Air Kona suspended operations and the airliner was returned to Russia, regaining its previous identity.

In 1999 **Scorpion Air**, aka **Air Scorpio [–/SPN]**, leased Tu-154B-1 UN 85777 (c/n 78A262) from Yuzhnaya Aircompany. The aircraft was apparently returned to the lessor in mid-2001.

The 16th Airlift Regiment (16 *Transporten Aviopolk*) of the **Bulgarian Air Force** (BVVS – *Bolgarski Voyenno Vozdooshni Seeli*) based at Dobroslavtzi AB near Sofia included a government VIP flight (formerly Sqn 1) operating from Sofia-Vrazhdebna airport. Among other things it operated nine Tu-154s, which initially wore full Balkan colours to facilitate flights abroad. Since 1964 the government flight was nominally part of Bulgaria's Ministry of Transport, but its entire flight and ground personnel consisted of BVVS officers on temporary duty at the Ministry. In 1972 the unit was renamed **28th Government Flight**.

Over the years the government flight operated two Tu-154s. The first aircraft, Tu-154B-1 'Salon' LZ-BTJ (ex-CCCP85270, c/n 78A270) was delivered in 1978 and operated in Balkan colours. In May 1989 it was transferred to Balkan and converted to airline configuration. The other machine was Tu-154M 'Salon' LZ-BTZ (ex-CCCP85781, c/n 88A781) delivered in 1988. Initially it also wore standard Balkan livery but in May or June 1999 it gained a new colour scheme with a cheatline in the national flag colours of white, green and red fanning out across the tail.

CENTRAL AFRICAN REPUBLIC

Founded in 1998, **Centrafrican Airlines [GC/CET]** bought almost the entire fleet of the defunct Air Pass **(see Swaziland section)** that year – including Tu-154M 3D-RTP, which was reregistered TL-ACF. The aircraft

retained basic Air Pass colours. Interestingly, besides Bangui (the capital of the Central African Republic), the airline was also based at Sharjah, UAE – as was Air Cess, a Liberian sister company of Air Pass. The key to the puzzle is that all three airlines had a common owner and Centrafrican Airlines is simply the successor of Air Cess/Air Pass incorporated under a new name when things became too hot for comfort at the previous location. All three airlines have been connected with the name of one Victor Bout, an expatriate Russian notorious as a gun-runner.

In March 2000 the Centrafrican titles were painted out. The following month the aircraft was apparently prepared for sale; eventually it was sold to Moldtransavia by October that year.

CHINA (PEOPLE'S REPUBLIC OF CHINA)

China has the distinction of being the largest foreign operator of the Tu-154M, taking delivery of 36 new examples between 1985 and 1994; these were augmented by seven second-hand examples, giving a total of 43. 29 of these aircraft were civil-operated.

The first 13 Tu-154Ms ordered by China were delivered to the 'Chinese Aeroflot' – the **Civil Aviation Administration of China** (CAAC, or *Zhongguo Minhang*), and this is listed first 'in order of appearance'. (No kidding – not only was the CAAC a one-size-fits-all, jack-of-all-trades outfit but the organisational structure was also similar and even the livery was, in most cases, extremely similar to Aeroflot's fleetwide standard of 1973.) The aircraft saw service with the Beijing, Xian and Urumqi directorates.

Registration	C/n	Notes
B-2601	85A716	Ex-CCCP85716. Xian Directorate. Transferred to China Northwest Airlines 7-88
B-2602	85A717	Ex-CCCP85717. Xian Directorate. Transferred to China Northwest Airlines 7-88
B-2603	85A718	Ex-CCCP85718. Urumqi Directorate. Transferred to China Xinjiang Airlines 7-88
B-2604	85A724	Ex-CCCP85724. Xian Directorate. Transferred to China Northwest Airlines
B-2605	85A725	Ex-CCCP85725. Xian Directorate. Transferred to China Northwest Airlines
B-2606	86A728	Ex-CCCP85728. Urumqi Directorate. Transferred to China Xinjiang Airlines
B-2607	86A729	Ex-CCCP85729. Urumqi Directorate. Transferred to China Xinjiang Airlines
B-2608	86A734	Ex-CCCP85734. Xian Directorate. Transferred to China Northwest Airlines
B-2609	86A735	Ex-CCCP85735. Xian Directorate. Transferred to China Northwest Airlines

B-2605, the fifth Tu-154M delivered to CAAC, taxies at Beijing International airport. Peter Davison

B-2610	86A740	Ex-CCCP85740. Xian Directorate. Transferred to China Northwest Airlines
B-2611	86A726	Ex-CCCP85726. Urumqi Directorate. Transferred to China Xinjiang Airlines
B-2612	85A730	Ex-CCCP85730. Beijing Directorate. Sold to China United Airlines ?-94 as B-4050

In 1987 the CAAC disintegrated into numerous airlines large and small, and the existing further deliveries of Tu-154Ms were made to the new independent carriers listed below.

Air Great Wall [G8/CGW], a subsidiary of the former CAAC's Flying College founded in 1992 and based in Chongqing (Jiangbei airport), bought a pair of Tu-154Ms from the Russian carrier Chita-Avia that year. The aircraft were registered B-2627 (ex-CCCP-85735, c/n 92A917) and B-2628 (ex-CCCP-85765, c/n 92A922); the c/n of the latter aircraft was consistently misquoted as 92A925, which is really RA-85739.

In 1997 both aircraft were placed into flyable storage at Chongqing. Eventually they were sold to Aeroflot Russian Airlines in January 2005; B-2627 properly regained its original registration, RA-85735, but B-2628 became RA-85135 No 2 – presumably because the registration RA-85765 had already been reassigned to another re-export aircraft (incidentally, also owned by Aeroflot).

China Northwest Airlines (CNWA) [WH/CNW] based in Xi'an, Shaanxi Province, had ten Tu-154Ms.

Registration	C/n	Notes
B-2601	85A716	Transferred 7-88. Sold to Sayakhat 1-98 as UN 85835
B-2602	85A717	Transferred 7-88. Sold to Sayakhat 1-98 as UN 85836
B-2604	85A724	Transferred 7-88. Sold to Sayakhat 1-98 as UN 85837
B-2605	85A725	Transferred 7-88. Sold to Donbass Airlines as UR-FVV
B-2608	86A734	Transferred 7-88. Sold to Dalavia Far East Airways 10-02 as RA-85734
B-2609	86A735	Transferred 7-88. Stored Xi'an 1999, registration removed by 9-00; sold to Vladivostok Air 5-01 as RA-85845
B-2610	86A740	Transferred 7-88. Crashed Xi'an 6-6-94
B-2619	89A814	Ex-CCCP85814, D/D 1989. Stored Xi'an 1999; sold to Aria Air Tour as EP-EAC via Russia or Ukraine?
B-2620	89A815	Ex-CCCP85815, D/D 1989. Stored Xi'an 1999; sold to Vladivostok Air 9-01 as RA-85849
B-2623	90A855	Ex-CCCP85855, D/D 1990. Stored Xi'an 1999; sold to Middleton Group 3-02 as RA-85085

China Southwest Airlines [SZ/CXN] based in Chengdu, Sichuan Province, operated five Tu-154Ms. In 1999 the four surviving examples were grounded and, after receiving alphanumeric temporary registrations, sold to Russia.

Registration	C/n	Notes
B-2615	88A783	Ex-CCCP85783, D/D 1988. To B-608L by 7-01; sold to Blagoveshchensk Air Enterprise as RA-85101 No 2
B-2616	88A790	Ex-CCCP85790, D/D 1988. To B-606L by 7-01; sold to Blagoveshchensk Air Enterprise as RA-85109 No 2
B-2617	88A791	Ex-CCCP85791, D/D 1988. To B-607L by 7-01; sold to Blagoveshchensk Air Enterprise as RA-85136
B-2618	89A797	Ex-CCCP85797, D/D 1988. To B-609L by 7-01; sold to Blagoveshchensk Air Enterprise as RA-85149
B-2622	90A846	Crashed near Ruian 24-2-99

Starting in 1988, **China United Airlines [KN/CUA]**, the commercial division of the PLAAF, operated 16 Tu-154Ms from Nan Yuan airbase near Beijing. Their duties are not confined to carrying military top brass and high-ranking statesmen; a few aircraft have been modified for ELINT and ECM. Recent fleet lists, however, show no Tu-154s at all; they have either been disposed of or are now used for such clandestine missions that they cannot be listed for security reasons.

Registration	Version	C/n	Notes
B-2614	Tu-154M	86A741	Ex-CCCP85741, D/D 1986. Reregistered ?-94 as, see next line
B-4051			
B-4001	Tu-154M	85A711	Ex-CCCP85711, D/D 1986. Stored Nan Yuan AB. Sold to Tatarstan Air 2006
B-4002	Tu-154M	85A712	Ex-CCCP85712, D/D 1986. Converted/ reregistered 1991 or 1992 to, see next line.
B-4138	Tu-154M/D		ELINT aircraft. Stored Nan Yuan AB
B-4003	Tu-154M	85A713	Ex-CCCP85713, D/D 1986. Stored Nan Yuan AB. Sold to Tatarstan Air 2006
B-4004	Tu-154M	85A714	Ex-CCCP85714, D/D 1986. Stored Nan Yuan AB. Sold to Tatarstan Air 2006
B-4014	Tu-154M	90A847	Ex-CCCP85847, D/D 1990
B-4015	Tu-154M	90A856	Ex-CCCP85856, D/D 1990
B-4016	Tu-154M	91A872	Ex-CCCP85872, D/D 1991
B-4017	Tu-154M	91A873	Ex-CCCP85873, D/D 1991
B-4022	Tu-154M	87A765	Ex-ČSA OK-SCA, D/D 25-9-92; basic 1987-standard ČSA c/s, CUA titles/logo
B-4023	Tu-154M	88A770	Ex-ČSA OK-TCB, D/D 25-9-92; basic 1987-standard ČSA c/s, CUA titles/logo
B-4024	Tu-154M	88A789	Ex-ČSA OK-TCC, D/D 11-10-92; basic 1987-standard ČSA c/s, CUA titles/logo
B-4027	Tu-154M	92A943	Ex-RA85943? D/D 1993
B-4028	Tu-154M	93A967	Ex-LII RA-85783, bought 12-93
B-4029	Tu-154M	93A950	Ex-RA85950? D/D 1993; cvtd to ECM aircraft
B-4050	Tu-154M	85A730	Ex-CAAC/Beijing Directorate B-2612, D/D 1994

China Xinjiang Airlines [XO/CXJ] based in Urumqi, Urumqi Province, operated six Tu-154Ms. Originally the aircraft had white tails with a blue 'duck and crescent' logo (c/s No 1); by 1999 the pattern was reversed to feature a blue tail with a white logo (c/s No 2).

China United Airlines operated a total of 16 Tu-154Ms, including B-4022 whose red cheatline reveals previous ownership by ČSA Czech Airlines. Yefim Gordon archive

Registration	C/n	Notes
B-2603	85A718	Transferred 7-88. C/s No 1, later No 2. Sold to Imair 4-01 as 4K-AZ17
B-2606	86A728	Transferred 7-88. C/s No 1. Sold to Sayakhat 6-01 as UN 85853
B-2607	86A729	Transferred 7-88. C/s No 1, later No 2. Sold to Sayakhat by 6-01 as UN 85854
B-2611	86A726	Transferred 7-88. C/s No 1, later No 2. Sold to Sayakhat by 4-01 as UN 85852
B-2621	89A823	Ex-CCCP85825, D/D 3-12-89. C/s No 1. Sold to Kazakstan by 6-01 (no registration, to Sayakhat by 10-02 as UN 85855)
B-2630	93A954	Bought from Sichuan Airlines 4-97. C/s No 1. Stored Chengdu by 9-99, no titles/logo

Sichuan Airlines [3U/CSC] based in Chengdu, Sichuan Province, likewise had four Tu-154Ms.

Registration	C/n	Notes
B-2624	91A886	Ex-CCCP85886, D/D 1991. Sold to Pulkovo Air Enterprise 12-01 as RA-85204 No 2
B-2625	91A893	Ex-CCCP85893, D/D 1991. Sold to Pulkovo Air Enterprise 12-01 as RA-85171 No 2

Above: **Sichuan Airlines operated five Tu-154Ms, including B-2626, in this stylish livery.** Yefim Gordon archive

Below: **Tu-154M B-2630 taxies at Moscow/Sheremet'yevo-2, displaying the old white-tailed version of China Xinjiang Airlines' colours.** Dmitriy Petrochenko

B-2626	91A894	Ex-CCCP85894, D/D 1992. Sold to Pulkovo Air Enterprise 12-01 as RA-85185 No 2
B-2629	92A919	Ex-CCCP85919, D/D 1991. Sold to Pulkovo Air Enterprise 12-01 as RA-85187 No 2
B-2630	93A954	Ex-Surgut-Avia RA-85772, bought 12-93. Sold to China Xinjiang Airlines 4-97

CUBA

The fleet of the Cuban flag carrier **Empresa Consolidada Cubana de Aviación**, commonly known simply as **Cubana [CU/CUB]**, included nine Tu-154s based at Havana-José Marti. The trijets were used on Cubana's services to Central and South America. The original 1970s-style livery with a red cheatline and a grey belly (c/s No 1) eventually gave place to a more modern one with a white fuselage which allowed the *CUBANA* titles to be made much bolder. By 2001 Cubana had withdrawn the type.

Registration	Version	C/n	Notes
CU-T1222	Tu-154B-2	80A447	Ex-CCCP85447, D/D 8-12-80. C/s No 1. Refitted/reregistered by 10-99 as, see next line
CU-C1222 *			Freighter, Cubana Carga titles. Retired by 1-01?

Tu-154B-2 CU-T1264 illustrates the old colours of Cubana at Prague-Ruzyne. This aircraft was lost in a fatal crash at Quito on 29th August 1998. Martin Novak

Later, Cubana also adopted a new look with a predominantly white livery illustrated here by Tu-154B-2 CU-T1256 at Havana-José Marti. Scott Henderson

CU-T1224	Tu-154B-2	81A493	Ex-CCCP85493, D/D 2-7-81. C/s No 1. Scrapped Havana by 11-98
CU-T1227	Tu-154B-2	82A541	Ex-CCCP85541, D/D 17-6-82. C/s No 1. Crashed Mexico City 14-9-91
CU-T1253	Tu-154B-2	83A576	Ex-CCCP85576, D/D 27-5-83. C/s No 1. Stored by 11-98; grey c/s, no registration by 4-02
CU-T1256	Tu-154B-2	84A599	Ex-CCCP85599, D/D 7-6-84. C/s No 1, later No 2. Retired by 3-00, GIA Havana
CU-T1264	Tu-154M	85A720	Ex-CCCP85720, D/D 6-2-86. C/s No 1, later No 2. Crashed Quito 29-8-98
CU-T1265	Tu-154M	87A751	Ex-CCCP85751, D/D 5-7-87. C/s No 1. Sold to Meton Trade LLC 10-00 as RA-85721
CU-T1275	Tu-154M	88A777	Ex-CCCP85777, D/D 8-7-88, named *Ing. Fidel Sánchez*. Sold to Russia 2-01
CU-T1276	Tu-154M	85A719	Y164. Ex-Guyana Airways 8R-GGA, D/D 22-12-88. Sold to Omskavia 12-95 as RA-85818
CCCP-85223	Tu-154B	77A223	Leased from Aeroflot (TsUMVS/63rd Flight) 15-8-79 to 15-11-79

* The Cuban system of civil aircraft registrations resembles the pre-1959 Soviet system in that it features role identifier letters. Thus, passenger aircraft were registered in the CU-Txxxx series (T for *transporte*); so were freighters initially, but after a while they were reregistered in the CU-Cxxx block (C for *carga*). Similarly, agricultural aircraft are registered in the CU-Exxx series and helicopters in the CU-Hxxx series.

CYPRUS

Although the Tu-154 was never operated by Cypriot air carriers, the leasing company **ALS (Aircraft Leasing Services)** acquired several Tu-154Ms in Russia for lease to Iranian airlines.

CZECHOSLOVAKIA
CZECH REPUBLIC

The nation's flag carrier **ČSA Československé Aérolinie** (Czechoslovak Airlines) **[OK/CSA]** took delivery of seven Tu-154Ms.

Registration	C/n	Notes
OK-SCA	87A765	Ex-CCCP85765, D/D 18-2-88, named *Mesto Piešťany*. First service 5-3-88. Struck off charge 25-8-92, sold to China United Airlines 9-92 as B-4022
OK-TCB	88A770	Ex-CCCP85770, D/D 31-3-88, named *Karlovy Vary*. First service 12-4-88. SOC 5-9-92, sold to China United Airlines 9-92 as B-4023
OK-TCC	88A789	Ex-CCCP85789, D/D 11-12-88, named *Teplice*. First service 16-12-88. SOC 27-8-92, sold to China United Airlines 9-92 as B-4024
OK-TCD	88A792	Ex-CCCP85792, D/D 13-1-89, named *Trenčianske Teplice*. First service 17-1-89; last service 10-1-00 in all-white c/s. Sold to BAL Bashkirian Airlines 1-00 as RA-85847
OK-UCE	89A804	Ex-CCCP85804, D/D 2-6-89, named *Marianské Lázně*. First service 11-6-89; last service 10-1-00. Sold to BAL Bashkirian Airlines 1-00 as RA-85848
OK-UCF	89A807	Ex-CCCP85807, D/D 21-7-89, named *Vysoké Tatry*. First service 30-7-89; last service 9-12-99. Sold to BAL Bashkirian Airlines 12-99 as RA-85846
OK-VCG	90A838	Ex-CCCP85838, D/D 6-7-90, named *Luhačovice*. First service 21-7-90; last service 21-9-99. Sold to MVM Trading as RA-85089 No 2

Incidentally, the Czechs and Slovaks have a unique civil aircraft registration system. The first letter following the nationality prefix denotes the year of registration, except B (see below) and Q (which is never placed first); for example, O = 1960, Z = 1970 and so on. The second letter denotes the type (for example, A = IL-18, later reused for the Airbus A310-308) and the third letter is individual. In the case of OK-AFB, OK-CFG and OK-CFH the first letter did not match the year due to late delivery.

The first Czechoslovak crews started conversion training at the COMECON Civil Aviation centre in Ul'yanovsk in 1987, and the final ones graduated in 1990. The aircraft were delivered in ČSA's 1969-standard livery (or rather its 1987 edition) with a red cheatline running across the windows and a red tail proudly bearing a large flag and the legend **OK** *čsa*. As you see, OK is both Czechoslovakia's country prefix and the airline's flight code, but the coincidence with the universally known slang word made a good selling point – 'that's an OK airline!'

The delivery flight of ČSA's first Tu-154M was performed by captain Václav Lorenc, first officer František Bartoň, navigator Boleslav Stavovčik and flight engineer Vladimír Hrubý. On 5th March 1988 OK-SCA flew the first scheduled flight to London-Heathrow and back (flight OK754/755).

In 1989 the airline started upgrading its Tu-154Ms with American avionics; the equipment selected eventually included a UNS-1A navigation computer supplied by Universal Navigation Corp. and a Bendix/King KAD-480 air data system. The actual refitting took place in 1990-91. Prior to that the new avionics were verified on one of ČSA's IL-62Ms and certified by the Czechoslovak CAA.

A new livery introduced on OK-VCG appeared in August 1990; the basically white aircraft featured a large red ČSA logo on the fuselage, a large red 'OK' tail logo, red/white/blue pinstripes beneath the cabin windows and black 'Czechoslovak Airlines' (port)/'Československé Aérolinie' (starboard) titles. Yet another standard introduced in 1992 featured triple red/blue 'pennants' on the tail instead of the 'OK' logo; the blue pinstripe became a cheatline carrying white 'Czechoslovak Airlines'

ČSA Czechoslovak Airlines' Tu-154Ms, including OK-TCB, were delivered in this red/white livery. Martin Novak

OK-TCD seen on short finals to Moscow-Sheremet'yevo illustrates ČSA's new livery. The picture was taken prior to 1993, as indicated by the 'Czechoslovak Airlines' titles. Yuriy Kirsanov

titles. Finally, on 1st January 1993 the post-Communist Czecho-Slovak Federal Republic divided into two independent states and the airline was renamed **ČSA Czech Airlines (České Aérolinie)**.

However, the choosy passengers (especially westerners) were distrustful of the Russian hardware. Besides, the Tu-154M's operating economics left a lot to be desired in comparison to the Boeing 737-400s and 737-500s that the airline was introducing (among other things, this was due to the Tu-154's bigger crew complement). Hence the trijet was gradually relegated to charter/inclusive tour flights. Finally, on 10th January 2000 OK-UCE flew the carrier's final Tu-154M service – a charter flight from Istanbul to Prague; this flight marked the end of ČSA's involvement with Soviet/Russian aircraft. Thanks in no small part to proper maintenance, no accidents or major incidents were recorded during the type's service with the Czech flag carrier.

Air Moravia Czech Charter Airline Ltd [–/MAI] based at Prague-Ruzyne leased Tu-154s as required for carrying tourists to Mediterranean holiday resorts. At an unknown date it operated Tu-154M ES-LTP (c/n 92A909) wet-leased from ELK Estonian; the aircraft was in the full colours of its owner with 'Air Moravia' stickers on the forward fuselage and engine nacelles. Also, in April 1995 Air Moravia leased Tu-154B-2 RA-85472 (c/n 81A472) from Samara Airlines.

Cargo Moravia Airlines operated a former Czech government Tu-154B-2, OK-LCS (ex-Tu-154B-2 'Salon' OK-BYC) bought on 20th January 1990. The aircraft was sold to Krai-Aero of Russia in December 1992, becoming RA-85804.

Egretta Air Company [–/BMI] wet-leased Tu-154M RA-85696 (c/n 91A869) from Mavial Magadan Airlines in 1997. The aircraft was operated from Brno-Tuřany in full Mavial colours with an Egretta sticker on the nose; it returned to the owner on 1st October. In 1998 the airline was rebranded **CZ Airlines**, operating Tu-154-100s jointly with Slovakian Airlines.

Ensor Air [E9/ENR], likewise Prague-based, operated two former VIP examples bought from the Czech government flight. One was Tu-154B-2 OK-LCP (ex-Tu-154B-2 'Salon' OK-BYB) bought in 1992; it had a red/blue cheatline running across the windows and a large 'EA' tail logo. This machine was sold to Aeroflot in January 1993 as RA-85488.

The other aircraft was Tu-154M 'Salon' OK-BYP leased on 9th September 1992; it was subsequently bought and reregistered OK-VCP on 27th April 1993. This machine had an altogether different livery with a narrow white/red/blue cheatline below the windows, a small 'EA' tail logo and a large Czech flag on the tail. Additionally, 'Excel' titles were carried on the engine nacelles; this was probably an inclusive tour operator with which the airline was affiliated. OK-VCP was periodically leased to other operators, including the Czech government. In 1997 it was sold to Travel Service.

Georgia Air Prague leased Tu-154Ms RA-85716 and RA-85763 (c/ns 91A892 and 93A946 respectively) from Aerovolga in June-November and June-October 1995. The aircraft were in full Aerovolga colours with additional Georgia Air Prague titles.

Ensor Air operated Tu-154M OK-VCP in 1993-97. Note the titles of the Excel travel agency, the airline's partner, on the engine nacelles. Martin Novak

Mostarez Air [–/MOE] based at Brno-Tuřany leased Tu-154M RA-85696 (c/n 91A869) from Mavial Magadan Airlines for six months in 1997.

Travel Service Airlines operated Tu-154M OK-VCP in 1997-99 jointly with IT operator Canaria. The aircraft was eventually sold to Omskavia as RA-85841, departing to Russia on 17th October 1999.

The **Czech Federal Government Flight** (LOMV – *Létecký oddíl ministerstva vnitra*; also called LS FMV – *Letecká společnost federalního ministerstva vnitra*, Airline of the Federal Ministry of the Interior) and its Czech successor, the **State Flight Unit** (SLU – *Státní létecký útvar*) operated seven Tu-154s.

Registration	Version	C/n	Notes
OK-BYA	Tu-154B-2 'Salon'	80A420	Ex-CCCP85420, D/D 18-7-80. Transferred to Czechoslovak AF 28-3-89 as '0420 Black'
OK-BYB	Tu-154B-2 'Salon'	81A488	Ex-CCCP85488, D/D 4-6-81. SOC 31-3-92, sold to Ensor Air 1992 as OK-LCP
OK-BYC	Tu-154B-2 'Salon'	81A517	Ex-CCCP85517, D/D 8-12-81. SOC 31-12-89, sold to Cargo Moravia Airlines 20-1-90 as OK-LCS
OK-BYD	Tu-154B-2 'Salon'	84A601	Ex-CCCP85601, D/D 13-5-85. Transferred to Czechoslovak AF 6-2-91 as '0601 White'
OK-BYO	Tu-154M 'Salon'	89A803	Ex-CCCP85803, D/D 26-5-89. Transferred to Slovak government 1-1-93 as OK-BYO, later reregistered OM-BYO
OK-BYP	Tu-154M 'Salon'	90A858	Ex-CCCP85858, D/D 25-1-91. Sold to Ensor Air 27-4-93 as OK-VCP; see below!
OK-BYZ	Tu-154M 'Salon'	96A1016	D/D 14-12-96. Transferred to the Czech AF 31-12-98 as '1016 Black'
OK-VCP	Tu-154M 'Salon'	90A858	Ex-OK-BYP, leased from Ensor Air 1994!

As already mentioned, the letter B was never used to denote the year of registration. All LOMV fixed-wing aircraft were registered in the BYx block; the B stood for [*Veřejná*] *bezpečnost* – 'public security' (that is, police). These registrations were reused time and time again; thus, OK-BYA was previously a Li-2, OK-BYC and -BYD were LET L-200A Morava light aircraft, while the registration OK-BYO had been worn by a Li-2 and two different Avia-14 Salon (Czech-built IL-14S) VIP aircraft.

The Tu-154B-2s wore a red/white colour scheme and distinctive LOMV insignia resembling the CzAF roundels but having a quasi-triangular shape. So did Tu-154M OK-BYO.

In due course this aircraft and OK-BYP were refitted with American avionics in similar manner to âSA's Tu-154Ms; OK-BYZ received an even more up-to-date suite with a Universal Avionics Systems Corp. UNS-1D computer.

As mentioned in the previous entry, on 28th March 1989 the Federal Government Flight transferred Tu-154B-2 'Salon' OK-BYA to the **Czechoslovak Air Force** (CzAF, or ČVL – *Československé Vojenské Létectvo*) in the course of a fleet renewal programme. In CzAF service the aircraft was serialled '0420 Black' (in keeping with the current system under which the serial matches the last four digits of the c/n). The aircraft was operated by the 61st Transport Air Regiment based at Prague-Kbely AB and retained the basic red/white LOMV livery. Tu-154B-2 'Salon' OK-BYD followed suit on 6th February 1991, becoming '0601'.

On 1st January 1993 the 'velvet revolution' of 1989 which put an end to socialism in Czechoslovakia was followed by an equally gentle 'divorce'; the Czecho-Slovak Federal Republic split into the Czech Republic and Slovakia, and the CzAF assets were divided between the two in a proportion of 2:1. Since there were only two Tu-154s in military service, '0420 Black' went to Slovakia while the other machine was taken over by the 'new' **Czech Air Force** (*České Vojenské Létectvo*). The aircraft now belonged to the 3.DLP (*dopravni létecký pluk* – Transport Air Regiment) and wore a smart red/blue/white colour scheme, the serial changing to '0601 White'. The aircraft was now operated by the 6th Transport Aviation Base (6.ZDL – *Základna dopravního létectva*).

On 29th July 2000 the CzAF took delivery of a brand-new Tu-154M 'Salon', '1003 White' (c/n 00A1003); the delivery was part of Russia's foreign debt payments. Hence in April 2005 Tu-154B-2 'Salon' '0601 White' was sold to Russia as 85601. Additionally, on 31st December 1998 Tu-154M 'Salon' OK-BYZ was transferred to the CzAF, becoming '1016 Black' (it gained much the same livery but the engine nacelles were grey, not blue).

Czech Air Force Tu-154M 'Salon' '1003 White' sits at Prague-Kbely. Sister ship '1016 Black' visible in the background displays subtle differences in the colour scheme. Martin Novak

Tu-154M EY-85692 was leased by Daallo Airlines from Tajikistan Airlines in 1999. Yefim Gordon archive

DJIBOUTI

Daallo Airlines [D3/DAO] operated three Tu-154s leased as required.

Registration	Version	C/n	Notes
EY-85487	Tu-154B-2	81A487	Leased from Tajikistan Airlines 11-02, Tajikistan c/s with additional Daallo Airlines titles
RA-85690	Tu-154M	90A861	Y164. Leased from Baikal Airlines 10-00 to 11-00
CCCP-85691	Tu-154M		Leased from Tajikistan Airlines by 5-93. Basic Aeroflot c/s; became, see next line
EY-85691			Full c/s, white tail; reregistered/repainted by 5-94 during lease. Returned late 1999
EY-85692	Tu-154M		Leased from Tajikistan Airlines 12-99 to 5-02. Full c/s, blue/green tail

EGYPT

In mid-1970 Aviaexport began negotiations with **United Arab Airlines [MS/MSR]**, the Egyptian flag carrier, concerning the purchase of four Tu-134As and four Tu-154s *sans suffixe*. (The name was a leftover from the United Arab Republic, the union of Egypt and Syria which existed from February 1958 to September 1961; for some reason it persisted until 1972 when the airline was rebranded **Egyptair**, or *Misr Liltayran* in Arabic.) The aircraft were to replace UAA's IL-18Ds and Comet 4Cs on international services and An-24Vs on domestic services. Eventually Egyptair decided the Tupolev twinjets were too small and rejected the Tu-134, converting the order to eight Tu-154As; the US$ 60 million order was signed in early July 1972. The aircraft were to be delivered with a mixed-class interior having a 20-seat first-class cabin and economy-class seating for 104. The contract also provided for the training of Egyptian flight and ground crews and the setting up of a maintenance base at Cairo-International airport.

The delivery schedule envisaged delivery of the first three aircraft in July 1973, followed by another three in November and the final two in March 1974. In reality, however, the first aircraft was not handed over until 1st (some sources say 2nd) December 1973; the delay was due to the Holy Day War with Israel, or Yom Kippur War (6th-24th October 1973). The Tu-154s were delivered via London-Heathrow where, at the customer's insistence, their cabins were refitted with seats manufactured by the British company Rumbold and Western galley equipment was installed.

Despite this 'customisation', the Egyptians were dissatisfied with the Tu-154A. Egyptian CAA Chairman Gamal Erfan said that the Tu-154 suffered from 15 design flaws, three of which (in the electric, fuel and fire suppression systems) were quite dangerous. He went on to say that the delivery contract had been signed without a thorough prior study of the aircraft's performance and operating economics; as a result, the Egyptian aircrews and ground crews discovered the defects after the aircraft entered service, he said. *Air International* stated in May 1975 that *'the direct operating costs of the Tu-154 in Egyptian service were reported to be as high as £E 1,050 per hour, compared with £E 825 per hour for the Boeing 707 and £E 430 per hour for the Comet 4C. With 124 seats [...]*

SU-AXH, the last-but-one Tu-154A delivered to Egyptair, shows off its smart livery at Prague-Ruzyne as a visiting Handley Page Dart Herald taxies in. Martin Novak

the Egyptair Tu-154s had a seat-mile cost of about 5 US cents per mile, some 25-30 per cent higher than those of the Boeing 707'. Other grievances, according to *Aviation Week & Space Technology*, included a too-far-aft CG when flying with no passengers or lightly loaded, an overly complex autopilot, and a lack of spares.

A special panel was formed to look into the pilots' complaints and decide on the aircraft's fate. On 7th June the panel ruled that, unless the Soviet Union agreed to rectify the defects, in 60 days (on 6th August 1974) Egyptair's Tu-154s would be grounded as unsafe. However, on 9th July 1974, just when a Soviet technical delegation headed by the Vice-Minister of Civil Aviation was in Egypt to discuss the matter, Tu-154A SU-AXB crashed fatally during a training flight under mysterious circumstances. Gamal Erfan immediately issued a grounding order and broke off negotiations. These were resumed ten days later; the Soviet delegation acknowledged that the aircraft had design flaws which needed to be rectified. However, when asked about the time schedule, the head of the Soviet delegation said that about a year would be needed and the Tu-154s would have to log 3,000 flight hours each before being sent to the Soviet Union for modification. Erfan refused, stating flatly none of the Tu-154s would make a single flight until the modifications had been made. From then on there was nothing more to discuss; the Egyptian Prime Minister ordered the purchase deal to be cancelled and initiated a legal inquiry into the circumstances of the deal. Eventually on 19th March 1975 the surviving Tu-154As were returned to the Soviet Union, which had to refund the monies already received and pay liquidated damages. To make up for the resulting shortfall in capacity, Egyptair purchased a number of Boeing 737-266s.

Registration	C/n	Notes
SU-AXB	73A048	D/D 1-12-73, named *Nefertiti*. Crashed Cairo 9-7-74
SU-AXC	73A049	D/D 4-12-73, named *Hatshepsut*. Returned 19-3-75, to Soviet Air Force as CCCP-85049
SU-AXD	73A050	D/D 15-12-73, named *Ti*. Returned 19-3-75, to Soviet Air Force as CCCP-85050
SU-AXE	73A051	D/D 20-12-73, named *Nefertari*. Returned 19-3-75, to Aeroflot as CCCP-85051
SU-AXF	73A052	D/D 1-74. Returned 19-3-75, to Aeroflot as CCCP-85052
SU-AXG	73A053	D/D 21-1-74, named *Howait-Hur*. Returned 19-3-75, to Soviet Air Force as CCCP-85053
SU-AXH	73A054	D/D 24-2-74 (22-2-74?), named *Ptah-Howait*. Returned 19-3-75, to Soviet Air Force as CCCP-85054
SU-AXI	73A055	D/D 3-74. Returned 19-3-75, to Soviet Air Force as CCCP-85055

In 1992 **Cairo Charter & Cargo** bought two brand-new Tu-154Ms registered SU-OAC (ex-CCCP85898, c/n 91A898) and SU-OAD (ex-CCCP85899, c/n 91A899). Like the airline's two Ilyushin IL-76TD freighters (SU-OAA/SU-OAB), they wore a smart white/green/yellow colour scheme with an eagle and crescent tail logo. In March 1993, however, the airline sold its entire fleet to Mahan Air (Iran) and the airliners were reregistered EP-JAZ and EP-ARG respectively.

ESTONIA

ELK Eesti Lennukompanii (Estonian Airways), aka **ELK Airways [S8/ELK]**, took over the three Tu-154Ms of the former Estonian CAD/Tallinn UAD. The aircraft received an attractive livery in the national flag colours of white, black and blue with huge 'Estonian' titles. Originally the airliners retained their Soviet registrations because placing them on the Estonian register was delayed by the lack of certification data; they were reregistered twice during their career with ELK Airways.

On 31st December 2001 the airline suspended operations and the fleet was sold off.

ELK Estonian Tu-154M ES-LTP lines up for take-off at London-Gatwick. This aircraft is now RA-85727 with UTair. Peter Davison

Registration	C/n	Notes
CCCP-85727	92A909	Reregistered ES-AAB after 8-93, to ES-LTP by 11-93. Sold to UTair 4-03 as RA-85727
CCCP-85740	91A895	Reregistered ES-AAC 10-93, to ES-LAI immediately afterwards. Sold to Baltic Express Line immediately afterwards as YL-LAI
CCCP-85741	91A896	Reregistered ES-AAD after 10-93, to ES-LTR early 1994. Sold to Belavia 1998 as EW-85741 but see next line!
ES-LTC	91A896	Ex/to EW-85741, lsf Belavia 5-00 to late 2000 or early 2001

ETHIOPIA

A single Tu-154B-2, CCCP-85598 (c/n 84A598), was wet-leased from Aeroflot (Belorussian CAD/2nd Minsk UAD/437th Flight) to Ethiopia – presumably **Ethiopian Airlines [ET/ETH]** – in the late 1980s. After briefly coming to Russia in 1993 for overhaul the aircraft returned to Ethiopia to continue the lease. It never came back; its ultimate fate remains unknown but possibly CCCP-85598 was withdrawn from use or damaged beyond repair in the civil war that led to the secession of Eritrea.

GERMANY (EAST GERMANY & POST-REUNIFICATION GERMANY)

In 1989 the **East German Air Force** (LSK/LV – *Luftstreitkräfte und Luftverteidigung der Deutschen Demokratischen Republik*, Air Force and Air Defence Force of the German Democratic Republic) took delivery of two Tu-154M 'Salons'. Like most of the EGAF's VIP transports, they wore the livery of the national airline **Interflug [IF/IFL]**[1] to facilitate flying abroad and were registered DDR-SFA and DDR-SFB (c/ns 89A799 and 89A813 respectively). However, they did have the serials '144' and '121', which were not worn visibly.

Still in basic Interflug red/white colours, Luftwaffe Tu-154M 'Salon' 11+01 awaits the next mission at Köln-Bonn. Note the FBS badge aft of the forward entry door. Yefim Gordon archive

The aircraft belonged to **TFG-44 'Arthur Pieck'**[2] (*Transport-fliegergeschwader* – airlift wing) tasked with government VIP flights. The unit was home-based at Marxwalde AB, Brandenburg District, Vorpommern;[3] however, for the sake of convenience the Tu-154s (and the long-haul IL-62M 'Salons') permanently resided at Berlin-Schönefeld where a strictly guarded VIP hardstand was set aside for them. The jets were unofficially known as *Honecker-Maschine*, since they were used by the East German leader Erich Honecker on his trips abroad.

After German reunification both Tu-154s were taken over by the unified **German Air Force** (Luftwaffe) and reserialled 11+01 and 11+02 respectively. Initially operated by the newly formed **65th Air Transport Wing** (Lufttransportgeschwader 65) at Neuhardenberg (ex-Marxwalde), they later passed to the government flight of the **5th Air Division** (*Luftwaffendivision* 5 or LwDiv 5) known as **FBS** (*Flugbereitschaftstaffel* – lit. 'duty squadron') and based at Köln-Wahn. For a while the trijets flew in basic Interflug colours, but in due course they were repainted in the FBS's predominantly white livery with a blue/black cheatline. The FBS was so happy with the type that it contemplated buying a third Tu-154M.

As described in Chapter 3, in 1994 Tu-154M 11+02 was converted for Open Skies monitoring duties as the Tu-154M-ON while retaining its VIP role to a certain extent. Unfortunately, on 13th September 1997 the aircraft was lost in a mid-air collision with a USAF Lockheed C-141B Starlifter over the Atlantic Ocean. The other aircraft remained in service until 2000, whereupon it was sold to the Vnukovo aircraft repair plant as RA-85092 No 2 (this registration was immediately cancelled, though, because the aircraft was leased to Iran straight away).

For the sake of completeness it may be mentioned that the **Stuttgart Airport fire brigade** has a Tu-154B-2 used as a fire trainer and bearing the phoney registration D-AFSG; this is the former HA-LCB (c/n 73A046) donated by Malév in 1995.

GUYANA

Guyana Airways operated three Tu-154s on services all over the Caribbean, including the USA (Miami). For starters, the carrier leased two Tu-154B-2s from TAROM. The initial experience proved to be positive and the airline ordered and received a brand-new Tu-154M from the Soviet Union. However, two years later the aircraft was sold to Cuba.

Registration	Version	C/n	Notes
8R-GGA	Tu-154M	85A719	Y164. D/D 3-86, full c/s with green/yellow cheatline. Sold to Cubana 12-88 as CU-T1276
YR-TPJ	Tu-154B-2	80A408	Leased from TAROM 4-85 to 1-86; red TAROM cheatline, Guyana Airways titles/logo
YR-TPK	Tu-154B-2	80A415	Leased from TAROM 1-85 to 6-85; red TAROM cheatline, Guyana Airways titles/logo

Guyana Airways Tu-154M 8R-GGA is pictured on a snowbound hardstand at the factory airfield, Kuibyshev-Bezymyanka, prior to delivery. Yefim Gordon archive

HUNGARY

Over the years **Malév Hungarian Airlines [MA/MAH]** (that is, *Magyar Légiközlekedesi Vallalat* – Hungarian Air Transport Co) operated 18 Tu-154s.

Registration	Version	C/n	Notes
HA-LCA	Tu-154	73A045	Ex-CCCP85045, D/D 5-9-73; converted to Tu-154B-2 in 1979. Selcal DE-BS. Last flight 8-7-93; used as anti-terrorist trainer Budapest
HA-LCB	Tu-154	73A046	Ex-CCCP85046, D/D 23-9-73; converted to Tu-154B-2 in 1979. Selcal CS-MP. Last flight 20-1-95 (delivered to Stuttgart airport as fire trainer 'D-AFSG')
HA-LCE	Tu-154	73A047	Ex-CCCP85047, D/D 2-10-73; converted to Tu-154B-2 in 1979. Selcal DE-CR. Last flight 17-11-95; to Malév Educational Centre 25-2-97
HA-LCF	Tu-154B	75A126	Ex-CCCP85126, D/D 30-11-75. Crashed Prague-Ruzyne 21-10-81; nose section preserved Transport Museum, Budapest
HA-LCG	Tu-154B	75A127	Ex-CCCP85127, D/D 1-12-75; converted to Tu-154B-2 in 1981. Selcal CS-MQ. Last flight 31-7-92, preserved Transport Museum, Budapest
HA-LCH	Tu-154B	75A128	Ex-CCCP85128, D/D 1-12-75; converted to Tu-154B-2 in 1980. Selcal CS-MR. Last flight 13-10-94, wfu Budapest, used for spares
HA-LCI	Tu-154A	73A053	Ex-CCCP-85053, leased from Aeroflot 6-75. Crashed near Beirut 30-9-75
HA-LCK	Tu-154A	73A054	Ex-/to CCCP-85054, leased from Aeroflot 6-75 to 12-75
HA-LCL	Tu-154A	73A051	Ex-/to CCCP-85051, leased from Aeroflot 5-5-78 to 12-12-80
HA-LCM	Tu-154B-2	79A325	Ex-CCCP85325, D/D 24-2-79. Selcal DE-CS. Last service 7-4-97 and wfu; sold to Turan Air 9-98 as 4K-325
HA-LCN	Tu-154B-2	79A326	Ex-CCCP85326, D/D 3-3-79. Selcal CS-PQ. Last service 29-4-01 and wfu; sold to Russia (D/D 3-5-01), no registration
HA-LCO	Tu-154B-2	81A473	Ex-CCCP85473, D/D 28-2-81. Selcal CS-PR. Last service 16-2-01; sold to Turan Air 5-02 as 4K-473
HA-LCP	Tu-154B-2	81A474	Ex-CCCP85474, D/D 6-3-81. Selcal CS-QR. Last service 26-10-00; sold to Turan Air 5-02 as 4K-85474

Tu-154B HA-LCH in the old colours of Malév Hungarian Airlines is seen visiting Prague-Ruzyne in the late 1970s. Martin Novak

Tu-154B-2 HA-LCV shows off Malév's new livery and 'Alitalia partner' titles as it taxies at Moscow/Sheremet'yevo-2. Dmitriy Petrochenko

HA-LCR	Tu-154B-2	82A543	Ex-CCCP85543, D/D 23-6-82. Selcal DE-AR. Crash-landed Thessaloniki 4-7-00, dbr
HA-LCS	Tu-154B-2	82A530	Ex/to CCCP-85530, leased from Aeroflot/ TsUMVS 6-86 to 12-12-88; used as cargo aircraft
HA-LCT	Tu-154B-2	82A542	Ex/to CCCP-85542, leased from Aeroflot/ TsUMVS 17-6-86 to 28-11-88
HA-LCU	Tu-154B-2	82A531	Ex-CCCP-85531, transferred as debt payments, D/D 22-7-88. Selcal DE-AS. Last service 28-3-01 and wfu; sold to Russia (D/D 23-4-01), to RA-85851
HA-LCV	Tu-154B-2	82A544	Ex-CCCP-85544, transferred as debt payments, D/D 1-9-88. Selcal DE-BR. Last service 28-3-01; sold to Russia (D/D 25-4-01), no registration

The first aircraft arrived at Budapest-Férihegy on 5th September 1973, performing the inaugural service to Moscow on 13th September.
When the design flaws of the Tu-154 *sans suffixe* came to light and the aircraft had to be rewinged, Malév had to dry-lease three Tu-154As from Aeroflot to make up for the shortfall in capacity while HA-LCA, -LCB and -LCE were undergoing conversion.

HA-LCL was the last Tu-154A operated by Malev. When it was returned to the lessor in 1980, Malev switched completely to the B model.

Tu-154B HA-LCH was used for ICAO Cat II minima landing trials held in cooperation with the Tupolev OKB in 1977; hence the aircraft featured a revised avionics suite and was known as the 'Tu-154B modified'. The programme was completed successfully on 20th March 1978 and paved the way for the Tu-154B-2.

In 1988 the airline introduced its current livery with a basically white fuselage and a dark blue tail on which three stripes in the Hungarian flag colours of red, white and green form a stylised M. Later, when Malév signed a code-sharing agreement with Alitalia, some of the aircraft (including HA-LCN, -LCR, -LCU and -LCV) were adorned with 'Alitalia

partner' titles. In due course Malév's Tu-154B-2s were equipped with the Selcal HF communications system, receiving individual four-letter call-signs; also, their interiors were refurbished by Diamonite Aircraft Furnishings to add passenger appeal. HA-LCP was retrofitted with a Collins ILS enabling ICAO Cat III automatic approach.

In the mid-1980s the older, high-time Tu-154s were relegated to the package freighter role, their interiors being stripped out for carrying items of cargo small enough to go through the standard entry doors. After the introduction of the 1988-standard livery such aircraft, including HA-LCA, gained large additional 'Cargo' titles under the forward cabin windows.

Still, that same year of 1988 Malév had begun re-equipping with Western hardware, supplementing the Tu-154s with leased Boeing 737-200s and -300s. In July 1997 the airline's General Director Sandor Száthmary was quoted as saying that Malév had decided to definitely shed the socialist touch and would not operate Russian-built aircraft any more as a matter of principle. The Tu-154 was progressively replaced on the airline's routes by Boeing 737-200 and -300 twinjets, starting in December 1995. The final revenue flight from Prague-Ruzyne to Budapest was performed by HA-LCN on 29th March 2001. The following day HA-LCV made a farewell flight over Budapest.

In December 2000 Budapest/Ferihegy-based **Atlant Hungary Airlines [–/ATU]**, probably a sister company of the Ukrainian Atlant-SV and the Russian Atlant-Soyuz, leased Tu-154M RA-85823 (c/n 88A775) from Samara Airlines. The aircraft was reregistered HA-LGA and delivered in the owner's colours on 21st December, receiving Atlant Hungary Airlines titles after it had been cleared by the Hungarian customs. The first service took place on 28th March 2001 and the last one on 26th June; after that the airline ceased operations and the aircraft was returned, regaining its former identity. Thus, the plans to lease Tu-154Ms RA-85723, RA-85822 and RA-85739 (c/ns 91A905, 89A806 and 92A925 respectively) from the same carrier never materialised – the registrations HA-LGB, HA-LGC and HA-LGD were allocated but not taken up.

In May 1993 **Pannon Airlines [–/PHP]** leased Tu-154M RA-85650 (c/n (88A788) from the Vnukovo aircraft repair plant. The aircraft was reregistered HA-LCX, continuing the Malév series, and wore an overall deep blue livery with huge 'Pannon Airlines' titles/logo, as well as the titles of the travel agency Jorgos Travel. The carrier intended to lease a second Tu-154M as HA-LCY but went bankrupt before it could do so; in May 2002 HA-LCX was returned to the lessor, subsequently becoming LZ-LCI.

An airline called, with singular modesty, **The Best** (!) planned to operate a fleet of Tu-154s leased in the CIS on charter flights. Aircraft earmarked for this carrier were Tu-154Bs CCCP-85132 (c/n 76A132), CCCP-85145 (c/n 76A145).

The registrations HA-LIB and HA-LIC respectively were reserved for these aircraft; incidentally, they had previously been worn by Lisunov Li-2P *Cab* airliners with which Malév's precursor Maszovlet had started operations after the Second World War. Eventually, however, the airline never launched operations and the registrations were cancelled.

Similarly, **Napkelet Airlines** intended to lease Tu-154B-2 ER-85384 (c/n 79A384) from Air Moldova in 1993. The aircraft was allocated the registration HA-LCZ, but this was not taken up and operations never started.

INDIA

Air India [AI/AIC] wet-leased six Tu-154B-2s from Uzbekistan Airways when Air India's own pilots went on strike over a labour dispute (actually a sympathy strike to support the ground staff's demands for higher wages), leaving the airline short of capacity. Thus the Uzbek crews and their aircraft acted in the unwelcome capacity of strikebreakers.

The aircraft in question included CCCP-85592 (c/n 83A592) from TsUMVS/63rd Flight from 1st May 1989 to 30th April 1990. Later, in 1992, Tu-154B-2 85533 (c/n 82A533) was wet-leased Tragically, this aircraft crashed on landing at New Delhi on 9th January 1993.

IRAN

Aria Air [–/IRX] based at Lar and Bandar Abbas operated eight Tu-154Ms.

Registration	C/n	Notes
EP-EAA	91A897	Ex-EP-CPH, leased from Tajikistan Airlines 3-01 to 11-02; to EY-85717
EP-EAB	90A864	Ex/to EY-85691, leased from Tajikistan Airlines 12-00 to 10-01? *
EP-EAC	89A814	Ex-China Northwest Airlines B-2619, bought by 10-01? basic CNWA c/s, Aria Air titles. Sold to Dalavia Far East Airways 2-04 as RA-85114 No 2
EP-EAD	92A930	Ex/to RA-85747, leased from Aerokuznetsk 6-02 to 6-04; Aeroflot cheatline + tail colours
EP-EAG	90A864	Ex-EY-85691, leased from Tajikistan Airlines 12-02; Aeroflot cheatline, blue tail, Aria Air titles/logo
RA-85720	91A902	C8Y141. Leased from Kras Air 1-06; basic Kras Air c/s, Aria Air titles
RA-85761	92A944	Y166. Leased from Kolavia 12-05, full Kolavia c/s with additional Aria Air titles
RA-85786	93A970	Y166. Leased from Kolavia 1-05, full Kolavia c/s with additional Aria Air titles

* Tu-154M EY-85691 was reported seen as such in April 2001 when it was supposed to be still on lease as EP-EAB!

Bon Air (Bonyad Airlines) **[–/IRJ]** based at Tehran operated three Tu-154Ms. The airline suspended operations in 2000, when it was no longer operating the type.

Registration	C/n	Notes
EP-BOJ	92A904	F12Y120. Ex-RA-85722, leased from Kavminvodyavia 1996; to Iran Air Tour as EP-MAU
EP-BOM	91A891	F12Y120. Ex-Iran Air Tour EP-MAF, leased from Kavminvodyavia (RA-85715), dates unknown; to EP-MAX
EP-BON	92A929	Y166. Ex/to RA-85746, leased from Kavminvodyavia 1996

Caspian Airlines [RV/CPN] based in Tehran operated six Tu-154Ms.

Registration	C/n	Notes
EP-CPG	87A748	Y164. Ex-Ariana Afghan Airlines YA-TAR, regd 15-3-98 (see end of table)
EP-CPH	91A897?	Ex-EY-85717? Leased from Tajikistan Airlines (EY-85717) 4-99 to 3-00. To Aria Air as EP-EAA
EP-CPM	87A763	Y164. Ex/to RA-85634, leased from VARZ 3-00 to 12-00
EP-CPN	92A898	Ex-Mahan Air EP-JAZ, bought 2000; full c/s
EP-CPO	92A899	Ex-Mahan Air EP-ARG, bought 2000
EP-CPS	?	Leased 2005
YA-TAR	87A748	Leased from Ariana Afghan Airlines 3-98, later bought and reregistered EP-CPG

Eco Air operated Tu-154Ms EP-MAF, EP-MAG, EP-MAU and EP-MAV in basic Kavminvodyavia colours. These aircraft were apparently subleased from Iran Air Tour (see below).

Founded in 2005 and based in Tabriz, **Eram Air [–/IRY]** operates two Tu-154Ms leased from Omskavia – EP-EKA (ex-RA-85730, c/n 92A912) and EP-EKB (ex-RA-85763, c/n 93A946).

Iran Air Tours [B9/IRB] (sometimes called **Iran Air Tour**, without the S at the end) operates a steady succession of Tu-154Ms leased from Russian airlines as required. These usually wear the lessor's basic livery with 'Iran Air Tour' titles.

Registration	C/n	Notes
EP-ITA	91A902	Y164. Ex/to RA-85720, leased from Kras Air 2-93 to 12-93
EP-ITB	91A880	F8Y130. Ex/to RA-85705, leased from Sibir' Airlines 3-94 to 8-94
EP-ITC	91A874	F8Y130. Ex/to RA-85699, leased from Sibir' Airlines 10-92 to 4-93 (?)
EP-ITD	91A903	Ex-CCCP-85721, leased from Aerovolga. Crashed near Tehran 8-2-93
EP-ITF	90A860	Y164. Ex-CCCP-85689, leased from Bratsk Air Enterprise 1993-94?; to RA-85689

Iran Air Tour Tu-154M EP-MBB takes off from runway 07R at Moscow-Sheremet'yevo. The basic Omskavia colour scheme identifies it as ex-RA-85830. Yuriy Kirsanov

EP-ITG	90A866	Y164. Ex/to RA-85693, leased from Sibir' Airlines 10-93 to 6-94
EP-ITI	92A939	Ex/to RA-85757, leased 10-93 to 8-94
EP-ITJ	91A883	Y164. Ex/to RA-85708, leased from Kras Air 12-93 to 4-95
EP-ITK	91A877	Y164. Ex/to RA-85702, leased from Kras Air 1994-95
EP-ITL	89A810	Ex-RA-85660, leased from Bratsk Air Enterprise 1993-94?
EP-ITM	91A884	Y164. Ex/to RA-85709, leased from Kras Air 4-95 to ?-96
EP-ITN	92A942	Ex/to RA-85760, leased from Bratsk Air Enterprise 8-94 to ?-97
EP-ITS	90A859	F12Y120. Ex/to RA-85688, leased from Sibir' Airlines 1996, basic Aeroflot c/s
EP-ITS No 2?	93A972	Y166. Ex/to RA-85788, Reported Isf Kaliningrad Avia ?-?? to 4-97
EP-ITU	91A867	Y164. Ex/to RA-85694, leased from Kras Air 1995; reported in error as EP-ITS No 2
EP-ITV	89A810	Ex-EP-ITL, leased from Bratsk Air Enterprise 1996-99; basic Aeroflot c/s, white tail
EP-MAB	91A870	F8Y130. Ex/to RA-85697, leased from Sibir' Airlines (dates unknown); basic Aeroflot c/s
EP-MAC	90A857	Y164. Ex/to RA-85687, leased from Sibir' Airlines (dates unknown)
EP-MAE	91A867	Y164. Ex/to RA-85694, leased from Kras Air 1996-97; basic Aeroflot c/s
EP-MAF	91A891	F12Y120. Ex/to RA-85715, leased from Kavminvodyavia 1996. Basic KMV c/s
EP-MAG	92A929	Ex-Bon Air EP-BON, leased from Kavminvodyavia (RA-85746) 1997. To EP-MAV
EP-MAI	91A880	F8Y130. Ex/to RA-85705, leased from Sibir' Airlines 3-97 to mid-1998; basic Sibir' c/s
EP-MAJ	85A719	Y164. Ex/to RA-85818, leased from Omskavia 1998
EP-MAK	91A884	Y164. Ex/to RA-85709, leased from Kras Air 3-97 to 12-00
EP-MAM	90A836	Y164. Ex/to RA-85676, leased from Khakasia Airlines 1997
EP-MAN	93A961	Ex/to RA-85802, leased from Chitaavia
EP-MAP	92A923	Y164. Ex/to RA-85766, leased from Chitaavia 3-97 to 8-00
EP-MAQ	91A870	F8Y130. Ex/to RA-85697, leased from Sibir' Airlines 3-98 to ?-??
EP-MAR	92A932	Y164. Ex/to RA-85750, leased from Omskavia 3-97 to 3-99
EP-MAS	90A866	Y164. Ex/to RA-85693, leased from Sibir' Airlines mid-1998 to 10-98, basic Sibir' c/s No 3A
EP-MAT	92A928	Y164. Ex-RA-85745, leased from Omskavia 10-2-98 to 4-03; to Mahan Air as EP-MHR
EP-MAU	91A904	Y164. Ex-Bon Air EP-BOJ, leased from Kavminvodyavia 9-99 to 3-00, basic KMV c/s; returned as RA-85722
EP-MAV	92A929	Ex-EP-MAG, leased from Kavminvodyavia 1998, basic KMV c/s. Returned as RA-85746
EP-MAX	91A891	F12Y120. Ex/to RA-85715, Isf Kavminvodyavia 22-8-98 to 21-8-01
EP-MAZ	90A857	Y164. Ex/to RA-85687, leased from Sibir' Airlines 20-9-98 to 19-9-01, basic Sibir' c/s No 3B
EP-MBA	90A860	Y164. Ex/to RA-85689, leased from Bratsk Air Enterprise
EP-MBB	89A821	Y164. Ex/to RA-85830, leased from Omskavia 5-10-98 to 5-10-02, basic Omskavia c/s No 3B, Iran Air Tour titles
EP-MBC	90A841	Y164. Ex/to RA-85678, leased from Kras Air 9-99 to 7-00
EP-MBE	92A932	Y164. Ex/to RA-85750, leased from Omskavia 6-3-00 to 5-3-01; grey/white c/s
EP-MBF	92A934	Y164. Ex/to RA-85752, leased from Omskavia 6-3-00 to 5-3-01; grey/white c/s
EP-MBH	91A880	F8Y130. Ex/to RA-85705, leased from Sibir' Airlines 6-3-00 to 5-3-02
EP-MBJ	93A960	Ex-RA-85801, leased from Omskavia 14-5-00 to 13-5-02; basic Kolavia c/s. To Mahan Air as EP-MHT
EP-MBK,	89A802	Ex-RA-85657, leased from VARZ 27-6-00, grey/white c/s. Returned by 6-04
EP-MBL	89A799	Ex-RA-85092 No 2, leased from VARZ 19-9-00, all-white c/s. Reregistered EP-MCE by 6-05
EP-MBM	92A931	Ex/to RA-85749, leased from Aerokuznetsk 12-2-01 to 17-2-03
EP-MBN	92A940	Y166. Ex-RA-85758, leased from Aerokuzbass 1-01
EP-MBO	93A982	Ex/to RA-85798, leased from Tatneft'aero 9-6-01 to 8-6-02
EP-MBP	89A800	Ex-RA-85096 No 2, leased from VARZ 20-7-02
EP-MBQ	92A931	Y166. Ex-RA-85749, leased from Aerokuzbass 1-01
EP-MBR	93A975	Ex-Bulgarian Air Charter LZ-LCB, leased 16-10-01 to 16-10-02. To Yakutia as RA-85791
EP-MBS	91A871	Ex-RA-85698, leased from VARZ 21-1-02. Crashed near Khorramabad 12-2-02
EP-MBT	92A930	Y164. Ex-RA-85747, leased from Aerokuzbass 2-04
EP MBU	90A855	Y166. Ex-RA-85085, leased from VARZ 3-02; all-white c/s, registration painted on with no hyphen!
EP-MBV	91A877	Y164. Ex/to RA-85702, leased from Kras Air 12-02 to ?-04, returned by 7-04
EP-MBZ	91A902	Y164. Ex/to RA-85720, leased from Kras Air 2-03 to 8-04
EP-MCE	89A799	Ex-EP-MBL, leased from VARZ
EP-MCF	88A788	Y164. Ex-RA-85650, leased from Airlines 400 9-05. Crashed Mashhad 1-9-06
EP-MCG	91A883	Y164. Ex-RA-85708, leased from Kras Air 2005
EP-MCH	91A879	Y164. Ex-RA-85704, leased from Kras Air 2005
EP-MCL	91A880	Y164. Ex-RA-85705, leased from Aerokuzbass 2005; basic Sibir' Airlines c/s with small Iran Air Tours titles
LZ-LCX	86A744	Leased from Bulgarian Air Charter 4-05
RA-85773	93A955	Y166. Leased from BAL Bashkirian Airlines 2005

Unconfirmed reports state that Iran Air Tours also operated Tu-154B-1 RA-85291 on lease from Omskavia in basic green/white Omskavia colours in 1994.

Iran Asseman Airlines [EP/IRC] (now called **Iran Aseman Airlines**, with a single S) operated three Tu-154Ms.

Registration	C/n	Notes
EP-TUA	93A959	Y166. Ex/to RA-85777, leased from BAL Bashkirian Airlines ?-?? to 3-97
EP-TUB	93A955	Y166. Ex/to RA-85773, leased from BAL Bashkirian Airlines ?-?? to 3-97
EP-TUE	90A865	Y166. Ex/to EY-85692, leased from Tajikistan Airlines, dates unknown

The charter carrier **Kish Air [Y9/IRK]**, a subsidiary of the Kish Development Organisation (a free zone enterprise on Kish Island), leases Tu-154Ms from Russian ar carriers as required. Unlike many Iranian operators of the type, which simply apply their titles and logo to the lessor's livery, Kish Air went so far as to design a striking livery with a golden sun on the tail, although not all aircraft wore it.

Registration	C/n	Notes
RA-85746	92A929	Y166. Leased from Kavminvodyavia 4-93, reregistered by 8-94 as, see next line
EP-LAD		Returned by 9-95 as RA-85746
EP-LAI	91A891	F12Y120. Ex/to RA-85715, leased from KMV 8-94 to 5-95
EP-LAO	90A841	Y164. Ex/to RA-85678, leased from Kras Air 1-95 to 12-95
EP-LAP	90A842	Y164. Ex/to RA-85679, leased from Kras Air 4-95 to 12-95
EP-LAQ	90A850	Y164. Ex/to RA-85683, leased from Sibir' 8-95 to 3-97
EP-LAS	90A841	Y164. Ex/to RA-85678, leased from Kras Air 1-96 to 10-96
EP-LAT	90A842	Y164. Ex/to RA-85679, leased from Kras Air 3-96 to ?-??
EP-LAU	90A848	Y164. Ex/to RA-85681, leased from Khakasia Airways 8-96 to 4-97
EP-LAV	91A879	Y164. Ex/to RA-85704, leased from Kras Air 1997 to ?-98; basic AJT Air International c/s
EP-LAX	92A913	Y164. Ex/to RA-85731, leased from Samara Airlines 5-97 to 8-97 (?)
RA-85792	93A976	Y164. Leased from Samara Airlines 3-97; reregistered 8-97 as, see next line
EP-LAZ	93A976	Y164. Ex/to RA-85792, leased from Samara Airlines 3-97 to 7-00. Basic Samara Airlines c/s
EP-LBC	86A744	Ex/to LZ-BTX, leased from Balkan 2-98 to 12-98; basic Balkan c/s
EP-LBD	86A743	Ex/to LZ-BTQ, leased from Balkan 1-98 to 7-98; basic Balkan c/s
EP-LBE	85A706	Y164. Ex/to LZ-BTI, leased from Balkan 2-98 to 6-98; basic Balkan c/s
EP-LBF	?	In service at least 11-97 to 1-98
EP-LBG	85A706	Y164. Ex/to LZ-BTI, leased from Balkan 2-99 to 6-99; basic Balkan c/s

Kish Air Tu-154M EP-LBR displays its flamboyant colour scheme. Yuriy Kirsanov

EP-LBH	92A913	Y164. Ex/to RA-85731, leased from Samara Airlines 7-99 to ?-00 or ?-01	EP-JAZ	92A898	Ex-Cairo Charter & Cargo SU-OAC. Sold to Caspian Airlines 2000 as EP-CPN	
EP-LBI	85A707	Y164. Ex/to LZ-BTW, leased from Balkan 12-98 to 4-99 and possibly again 3-00 (or another aircraft)	EP-MHB	92A907	Ex/to RA-85725, leased from Chelal 11-00 to 1-02, basic Belavia c/s	
EP-LBL	87A754	Ex/to LZ-BTH, leased from Balkan 3-99 to 5-99; basic Balkan c/s	EP-MHD	92A936	Ex/to RA-85754, leased from Chelal 2001	
EP-LBM	95A1007	Ex/to RA-85817, leased from Samara Airlines 5-99 to 6-02; basic Samara Airlines c/s	EP-MHR	92A928	Ex-Iran Air Tour EP-MAT, leased from Omskavia 4-03 to 12-03; returned as RA-85745	
EP-LBN	85A717	Ex-Sayakhat UN 85836, D/D 16-12-99. Full c/s with white tail, titles in Britannic Bold typeface. Sold to Middleton Group as RA-85081 No 2	EP-MHS	89A821	Ex-Omskavia RA-85830, leased 9-02, basic Omskavia c/s	
			EP-MHT	93A960	Ex-Iran Air Tour EP-MBJ, leased from Kolavia 8-02 to 1-03; returned as RA-85801	
EP-LBR	90A838	Ex-RA-85089 No 2, bought from MVM Trading 1-00. Full c/s with white tail, titles in Slipstream typeface	EP-MHV	92A932	Ex/to RA-85750, leased from Omskavia 1-02 to 2-03	
EP-LBS	91A901	Ex-RA-85719, leased from MVM Trading 2000. Full c/s with blue tail	EP-MHX	92A939?	Ex/to RA-85757? Leased from VARZ or Continental Airways 9-01 to 12-01	
EP-LBX	87A763	Ex-RA-85634, leased from VARZ 2002; full c/s with blue tail. Damaged on landing Mashhad 20-2-02 and returned to VARZ for repairs	EP-MHZ	91A890	Ex/to RA-85714, leased from Omskavia 10-01 to 7-04	
EP-LCD	89A825	Ex/to RA-85667,				
RA-85722	92A904	F12Y120. Leased from Kavminvodyavia 4-93 to ?-??				

Qeshm Airlines [–/IRQ], also rendered as **Qeshm Air** or **Qeshmair**, operated four Tu-154s; all have been disposed of since.

As noted earlier, **Mahan Air [W5/IRM]** based in Kerman bought the entire fleet of the defunct airline Cairo Charter & Cargo in March 1993, including both Tu-154Ms. The new owner retained the basic colours of Cairo Charter & Cargo, replacing only the titles and tail logo (an extremely stylised bird). Ten further examples were leased later.

Mahan Air Tu-154M EP-ARG uses reverse thrust on runway 24 at Moscow-Vnukovo as it arrives for maintenance at ARZ No 400. Dmitriy Petrochenko

Registration	C/n	Notes
EP-ARG	92A899	Ex-Cairo Charter & Cargo SU-OAD. Sold to Caspian Airlines 2000 as EP-CPO
EP-ARH	92A904	F12Y120. Ex/to RA-85722, leased from Kavminvodyavia
EP-ARI	?	Basic Aeroflot c/s, in service at least 12-98 to 4-99

Registration	Version	C/n	Notes
EP-TQD	Tu-154M	86A725	Ex-Donbas Airlines UR-FVV, bought by 11-98. Sold to Aeroflot-Don 7-02 as RA-85726 No 2
EP-TQE	Tu-154M	92A940	Ex/to RA-85758, leased from Aerokuznetsk 11-98 to 12-99
EP-TQM	Tu-154M	92A906	Ex/to RA-85724, leased from Chelal 3-00 to 3-01, basic Belavia c/s and Chelal logo
RA-85804	Tu-154B-2	81A517	F8Y125. Leased from Tatarstan Airlines early/mid-1999

Incidentally, Qeshmair has been dubbed *aviakompahniya Koshmar* (Nightmare Airlines, or 'Nightmair') by Russian spotters – for purely phonetic reasons. As you see, etymology is fun!

Zagros Airlines based in Abadan operate Tu-154M RA-85831 (c/n 88A774) leased from BAL Bashkirian Airlines in December 2005. The aircraft is in the owner's full colours with additional 'Zagros Airlines' titles.

LAOS

Lao Aviation [QV/LAO], the nation's flag carrier, wet-leased Tu-154M LZ-BTN No 2 (c/n 89A832) from Balkan Bulgarian Airlines in the autumn of 1991. The aircraft sported a colour scheme similar to Balkan's then-current livery, but the green colour of the cheatline was substituted by dark blue and the tail was adorned by Lao Aviation's very stylised 'sun n' bird' logo, not to mention appropriate titles.

LATVIA

The original national flag carrier, **Latavio Latvian Airlines** (Latvijas Aviolinijas) **[PV/LTL]**, operated seven Tu-154s inherited from the Latvian CAD/Riga UAD/280th Flight based at Riga-Skul'te.

Registration	Version	C/n	Notes
YL-LAA	Tu-154B	78A133	Ex-CCCP-85133, late manufacture date! Wfu/stored
YL-LAB	Tu-154B-2	81A515	Ex-CCCP-85515. Sold to Latpass Airlines 1996
YL-LAC	Tu-154B-2	81A516	Ex-CCCP-85516 and initially operated as such. Sold to Aeroservis Kazakstan Aviakompaniyasy 1993 as UN-85516
YL-LAD	Tu-154B-2	82A556	Ex-CCCP-85556. Probably never operated; sold to Aeroflot 1993 as RA-85556
YL-LAF	Tu-154B-2	82A539	Ex-CCCP-85539. Sold to Aeroservis Kazakstan Aviakompaniyasy 1993 as UN-85539
YL-LAG	Tu-154B-2	82A524	Ex-CCCP-85524. Sold to Azerbaijan Airlines 1995 as 4K-85524
YL-LAH	Tu-154B-2	82A558	Ex-CCCP-85558. Basic Aeroflot c/s with blue/white tail, later full c/s. Sold to Air Georgia 1993 as 4L-85558

Initially Latavio's Tu-154s operated in basic Aeroflot colours with the titles, flag and Soviet registration crudely painted out; the Latvian registration was carried beneath the windows just aft of the wings. YL-LBH was an exception, wearing a large Latvian flag on the tail and '*LATAVIO LATVIAN AIRLINES*' titles. In due course part of the fleet was repainted at ARZ No 400 (Moscow-Vnukovo), receiving a smart red/white livery with black-painted wings; curiously, the last three digits of the former Soviet registration were carried on the nose gear doors. The tips of the main gear fairings were Dayglo orange to minimise the risk of damage by airport vehicles.

Still wearing an experimental version of Aeroflot's livery with a blue/white tail, Latavio Latvian Airlines Tu-154B-2 YL-LAH taxies out from Moscow/Sheremet'yevo-1 past the characteristic 'mushroom' concourse. As a rule, Latavio used Tu-134Bs on the Riga to Moscow service. *Sergey Sergeyev*

Baltic Express Line [S8/LTB] purchased Tu-154M ES-LAI from ELK Estonian in October 1993. Reregistered YL-LAI, the aircraft remained in service until January 1997 when the registration was cancelled and the aircraft placed in storage with no registration on. Subsequently it regained the registration YL-LAI for the ferry flight to Swaziland in November 1997, when the airliner was sold to Air Pass (eventually becoming 3D-RTP).

Additionally, in July-September 1997 Baltic Express Line leased Tu-154B-2 UK 85398 (c/n 80A398) from Uzbekistan Airways.

Baltic International Airlines [TI/BIA], a Latvian-US joint venture, operated the eighth example inherited from Aeroflot – Tu-154B-2 YL-LAE (c/n 82A546). The aircraft wore basic Latavio colours with Baltic International titles.

In 1996 the airline underwent a major reorganisation, changing its name to **airBaltic [BT/BTI]** and becoming Latvia's new flag carrier instead of the deceased Latavio. The rebranding involved a complete fleet renewal; hence YL-LAE was sold to Tavria-MAK, becoming UR-85546.

The charter carrier **Latpass Airlines [QJ/LTP]**, a Latvian-US joint venture, took over Tu-154B-2 YL-LAB from Latavio in 1996. The aircraft wore the same basic Latavio livery with new titles and logo; upon retirement in 2004 it became an exhibit of the aviation museum at Riga-Spilve airport. This left Latpass with no aircraft at all and the carrier was forced to cease operations.

LIECHTENSTEIN

The short-lived airline **Aerolikht**, a Soviet/Liechtenstein joint venture (hence the name, which is a contraction of 'Aeroflot' and 'Liechtenstein'), was established specifically for flying Jewish emigrant charters to Israel in 1991. Its small fleet included Tu-154B-2 CCCP-85565 (c/n 82A565) operated jointly with Transaero.

LIBYA

Air Libya Tibesti [7Q/TLR] based at Tripoli-Mitiga and Benghazi wet-leased Tu-154B-2 4L-85496 (c/n 81A496) from Georgian Air Lines in October 2003. The aircraft wore a striking white/green/black livery. By May 2005 it had been returned to Georgia and placed in storage.

In November 1977 **Libyan Arab Airlines [LN/LAA]**, the national flag carrier, wet-leased Tu-154 *sans suffixe* LZ-BTB (c/n 72A027), Tu-154As LZ-BTE (c/n 74A073), LZ-BTF (c/n 74A077), LZ-BTK (c/n 76A144), LZ-BTN No 1 (c/n 73A054) and LZ-BTR No 1 (c/n 73A051) – from Balkan

Bulgarian Airlines for carrying pilgrims to Medina during the Hadj season. The aircraft received the beige/white/black LAA livery but no titles; LZ-BTK was an exception in that it did wear the titles. In 1978 the airliners were returned – except LZ-BTN, which crashed on approach to Tripoli-Benghazi airport on 2nd December 1977.

Kallat El Saker [–/KES], based at Tripoli-Ben Gashir International, wet-leased Tu-154B-2 EK-85536 (c/n 82A536) from South Airlines in September 2005.

LITHUANIA

Although the Tu-154 was never operated by Aeroflot's Lithuanian CAD and, accordingly, none were 'inherited' by the local airlines, Kaunas-based **Lietuva [TT/KLA]** (pronounced *Letoova* – the native name of Lithuania; also known as **Air Lithuania**) leased Tu-154M RA-85712 (c/n 91A888) from ALAK for a short while in 1993.

MACEDONIA

Avioimpex [M4/AXX] wet-leased Tu-154Ms CCCP-85630 and CCCP-85631 (c/ns 87A759 and 87A760) from the 235th Independent Flight Detachment in 1992-93. The latter aircraft was reregistered RA-85631 during the lease. Later, in late 1995/early 1996, the carrier leased Tu-154M LZ-MIS from VIA (Varna International Airlines).

Macedonian Air Services [M2/MDO] – sometimes reported in error as Macedonian Airlines – wet-leased five Tu-154Ms.

Registration	C/n	Notes
LZ-MIG	90A840	Leased from Varna International Airlines 7-92 to ?-??, basic VIA c/s, 'Macedonia AS' titles
LZ-MIL	90A845	Leased from Varna International Airlines 10-92 to 4-93, basic VIA c/s, 'M.A.S.' titles
LZ-MIR	90A852	Leased from Varna International Airlines 5-92 to 8-93, basic VIA c/s, 'M.A.S.' titles
LZ-MIS	90A863	Leased from Varna International Airlines 7-92 to ?-94?, basic VIA c/s, 'M.A.S.' titles
LZ-MNA	92A908	Leased from Air Kona 1993

MAT Macedonian Airlines (*Makedonski Aviotransport*) **[IN/MAK]** reportedly wet-leased Tu-154M LZ-BTQ (c/n 86A743) from Balkan in 1995.

Meta Aviotransport Makedonija [M5/MAM] wet-leased Tu-154M RA-85745 (c/n 92A928) from Vnukovo Airlines in 1992; the aircraft wore the airline's attractive red/black/yellow/white livery and was named

META Aviotransport Makedonija had few competitors for the 'Most Striking Livery' title. Here, one of the two Tu-154Ms leased from Vnukovo Airlines (RA-85745 *Ohrid I*) is pictured at Moscow-Vnukovo. Dmitriy Petrochenko

A simple but nevertheless appealing livery was worn by the Tu-154s leased by Palair Macedonian from Balkan, including LZ-BTJ seen here on approach to Moscow-Sheremet'yevo. Dmitriy Petrochenko

Ohrid. Shortly afterwards it was joined by an identically painted second aircraft, RA-85619 *Ohrid II* (c/n 86A738) leased from the same carrier and the name of the first aircraft was amended to *Ohrid I*. In August 1995 both aircraft were returned to the lessor but still wore Meta Aviotransport Makedonija colours for a while.

Palair Macedonian [3D/PMK] wet-leased Tu-154B-1 LZ-BTJ, Tu-154B LZ-BTL No 2 and Tu-154B-2 LZ-BTU No 2 from Balkan Bulgarian Airlines in 1991-95, 1991-92 and 1992-94 respectively. The aircraft did not receive the overall red livery later worn by the airline's Fokker 100, featuring a white fuselage and a red tail with the airline's logo; even so, the result was quite impressive.
Additionally, in September 1992 Palair Macedonian wet-leased a single Tu-154 (identity unknown) from the Pulkovo Aviation Enterprise. The aircraft operated a once-weekly service betweem Skopje and Moscow, flying to various destinations in Western Europe during the rest of the week.

In May 1992 the Skopje-based airline **Vardar Air [V7/BAA]** leased Tu-154Ms CCCP-85621 (c/n 86A742) and 85624 (c/n 87A750) from the Moscow Territorial CAD/Vnukovo UAD. The former aircraft, which was named *Ohrid* after a Bosnian city, was reregistered RA-85621 in the course of the lease, which ended in November 1992.

MALI

Transair Mali [–/TSM] wet-leased Tu-154M CCCP-85694 (c/n 91A867) from the Aeroflot's 1st Krasnoyarsk UAD in the summer of 1991.

Transair Mali leased Tu-154M CCCP-85694 from Aeroflot in basic Aeroflot colours. Sergey and Dmitriy Komissarov collection

MIAT Mongolian Airlines Tu-154M MPR-85644 shares the apron at Prague-Ruzyne with a ČSA sister ship. Martin Novak

Tu-154B P-553 of Chosonminhang (CAAK) seen visiting Prague-Ruzyne. Martin Novak

MONGOLIA

The Mongolian flag carrier **MIAT** (originally *Mongolyn Irgeniy Agaaryn Te'ever* – Mongolian Air Transport Directorate; now **Mongolian International Air Transport**) **[OM/MGL]** operated two Tu-154s wet-leased from Aeroflot's TsUMVS/63rd Flight. The first of these was Tu-154B-2 БНМАУ-85564 leased in 1988 (c/n 82A564; the then-current prefix, which is a Mongolian acronym, reads BNMAU); it was returned to the lessor on 25th May 1990, regaining the original registration CCCP-85564. The other machine was Tu-154M with the non-standard registration MPR-85644 (ex-CCCP-85644, c/n 88A780) leased in May 1990; when it returned to Aeroflot in July 1944 it became RA-85644.

NICARAGUA

The fleet of **Aeronica** (Aérolineas de Nicaragua), the country's one-time flag carrier, included a single Tu-154M delivered on 20th December 1989. Registered YN-CBT (c/n 89A821) and named *Momotombo*, this was reportedly a Tu-154M 'Salon' – the presidential aircraft of Daniel Ortega Saavedra, the leader of the Sandinista party which was running the country then.

In 1992, when the civil war in Nicaragua ended, the Sandinistas lost the elections and the opposition (known as the Contras) took over, with Violetta Bárrios de Chamorro as President. A wave of change swept the country; one of the results was the demise of Aeronica, and the Tu-154M was grounded at Managua International airport. For five years the aircraft sat there, gradually falling into disrepair, which led some observers to conclude mistakenly that it had been written off in an accident. Luckily in 1997 the aircraft was sold to Russia before it could reach the point of no return; after an overhaul it joined the fleet of Omskavia as RA-85830.

NORTH KOREA

In 1975- North Korea's sole airline, **Chosonminhang** (or Civil Aviation Administration of Korea – CAAK), took delivery of four Tu-154s.

Registration	Version	C/n	Notes
551	Tu-154B	75A129	Ex-CCCP85129, D/D 1975. Reregistered P-551 by 1979; callsign P5-CVA. Damaged Budapest 30-6-79 but repaired
552	Tu-154B	76A143	Ex-CCCP85143, D/D 1975. Reregistered P-552 by 1978; callsign P5-CVB.
553	Tu-154B	77A191	Ex-CCCP85191, D/D 1977. Reregistered P-553 in 1978
P-561	Tu-154B-2	83A573	Ex-CCCP85573, D/D 1983

By 1994 the airline was renamed **Air Koryo [JS/KOR]** – and it's just as well, because the old name was a real tongue-twister. ('Koryo' is apparently how 'Korea' is pronounced in the native language.) Unlike some of the airline's aircraft, the Tu-154s retained the large North Korean flag on the tail, carrying a small Air Koryo logo on the fuselage; usually it's vice versa.

PAKISTAN

A most unlikely operator of the type was **Pakistan International Airlines [PK/PIA]**, which wet-leased Tu-154s from Uzbekistan. These aircraft wore full PIA colours and were used, among other things, for carrying pilgrims to Mecca during the Hadj season.

Registration	Version	C/n	Notes
UK 85416	Tu-154B-2	80A416	Leased late 1996 until early 2001 but returned mid-1997
UK 85438	Tu-154B-2	80A438	Leased late 1996 until early 2001 but returned mid-1997
UK 85711	Tu-154M	91A887	Leased late 1996 until early 2001 but returned mid-1997; prefix removed by 5-97

Shaheen Air International [NL/SAI] based at Karachi operates a mixed bag of airliners leased from East and West alike. These included seven Tu-154s, mostly leased in Belorussia.

Still wearing Shaheen Air International titles and logo over basic Belavia colours, Tu-154B-2 EW-85538 is seen at Minsk-2 on 20th May 2005 after return from the Pakistani lease. via Peter Davison

Registration	Version	C/n	Notes
EW-85509	Tu-154B-2	81A509	Leased from Belavia ?-01 to ?-05, basic Belavia c/s, Shaheen Air Int'l titles/logo
EW-85538	Tu-154B-2	82A538	Leased from Belavia ?-01 to ?-05, basic Belavia c/s, Shaheen Air Int'l titles/logo
EW-85545	Tu-154B-2	82A545	Leased from Belavia ?-01 to ?-05, basic Belavia c/s, Shaheen Air Int'l titles/logo
EW-85741	Tu-154M	91A896	Leased from Belavia 2-04 to ?-??, basic ELK Estonian c/s
RA-85773	Tu-154M	93A955	Y166. Leased from Bashkirian Airlines 8-97 to 3-99
RA-85816	Tu-154M	95A1006	Y166. Leased from Bashkirian Airlines 9-99 to 7-01, full black/white c/s
RA-85826	Tu-154M	89A812	Leased from Bashkirian Airlines 3-00 to 4-00

POLAND

As the IL-18s operated by **LOT Polish Airlines [LO/LOT]** (*Polskie Linie Lotnicze LOT*; 'lot' is Polish for 'flight') were getting long in the tooth, a replacement was urgently sought. The carrier's Tu-134s were too small for the higher-density routes, while the IL-62M was required for transcontinental and intercontinental services. Hence LOT selected the Tu-154 – the only Soviet offering in the same class as the IL-18 (it *was* conceived as an IL-18 replacement, after all).

For starters, three Tu-154B-2s were leased from Aeroflot in 1985 in order to gain some experience with the type. However, the B model was out of production by then, leaving the Tu-154M as the only option. Thus between May 1986 and January 1991 LOT took delivery of 14 Tu-154Ms in a 150-seat all-tourist layout.

Registration	Version	C/n	Notes
SP-LCA	Tu-154M	86A727	Regd 28-5-86. Last service 6-12-92; sold to Turan Air 7-95 as 4K-727
SP-LCB	Tu-154M	86A733	Regd 28-8-86. Last service 2-12-92; sold to Turan Air 8-95 as 4K-733
SP-LCC	Tu-154M	86A745	Regd 3-3-87. Last service 24-1-92; sold to Buryatia Airlines 3-97* as RA-85827
SP-LCD	Tu-154M	86A755	Regd 26-8-87. Last service 13-8-93; sold to Buryatia Airlines 10-97 as RA-85829
SP-LCE	Tu-154M	86A769	Regd 17-3-88. Last service 26-10-93; sold to BAL Bashkirian Airlines 4-96 as RA-85824
SP-LCF	Tu-154M	88A774	Regd 24-5-88. Last service 30-10-93; sold to BAL Bashkirian Airlines 11-97 as RA-85831
SP-LCG	Tu-154M	88A775	Regd 14-6-88. Last service 1-12-91; sold to Samara Airlines 11-95 as RA-85823

LOT Polish Airlines Tu-154M SP-LCC is seen on final approach to London-Heathrow. Peter Davison

Registration	Version	C/n	Notes
SP-LCH	Tu-154M	88A776	Regd 21-6-88. Last service 2-12-91; sold to BAL Bashkirian Airlines 3-96 as RA-85825
SP-LCI	Tu-154M	89A805	Regd 8-6-89. Last service 28-10-94; sold to Samara Airlines 9-95 as RA-85821
SP-LCK	Tu-154M	89A806	Regd 20-6-89. Last service 14-10-93; sold to Samara Airlines 10-95 as RA-85822
SP-LCL	Tu-154M	89A812	Regd 8-8-89. Last service 14-10-93; sold to BAL Bashkirian Airlines 5-96 as RA-85826
SP-LCM	Tu-154M	89A824	Regd 5-1-90. Last service 1-8-94; sold to Aeroflot Russian International Airlines 9-97 as RA-85810
SP-LCN	Tu-154M	90A831	Regd 6-3-90. Last service 15-8-94; sold to Aeroflot Russian International Airlines 9-97 as RA-85811
SP-LCO	Tu-154M	90A862	D/D 1-91. Transferred to Polish Air Force 28-9-94 as '862 Black'
CCCP-85331	Tu-154B-2	79A331	Full Aeroflot c/s with additional 'Chartered by LOT Polish Airlines' titles; lsf 1st Leningrad UAD 9-5-85 to 27-9-88
CCCP-85334	Tu-154B-2	79A334	Full Aeroflot c/s with additional 'Chartered by LOT Polish Airlines' titles; lsf 1st Leningrad UAD 2-5-86 to 16-6-86
CCCP-85455	Tu-154B-2	80A455	LOT c/s but grey belly and additional 'Chartered by LOT Polish Airlines from Aeroflot' titles

* Some sources say SP-LCC had been sold by November 1996.

The aircraft wore LOT's current livery introduced in 1977 (which was then the height of fashion and still does not look dated today); for some reason the Tu-154Ms were delivered in an all-white finish and resprayed on site. The reader may be interested to learn that a contest was announced via the *Skrzydlata Polska* (Winged Poland) magazine and the winner was selected from half a dozen liveries suggested by the readers.

Soon the Tu-154 had ousted the IL-18V/IL-18E from LOT's international services; the IL-18s were 'demoted' to cargo aircraft. To ensure observance of flight schedules LOT established so-called general maintenance facilities (SWOT – *Stacja Wspólnej Obsługi Technicznej*) in the remotest cities served by its aircraft; these could rapidly fix a minor malfunction, such as replacing a blown tyre.

In 1989 LOT started re-equipping with Western hardware when two Boeing 767-25D(ER)s and a Boeing 767-35D(ER) were acquired to replace the IL-62M fleet. (Poland had never been on really good terms with the Soviet Union; the smouldering anti-Russian sentiment goes back for centuries, and the reasons are outside the scope of this book. However, operating economics were the decisive factor in the decision to re-equip.) By July 1995 all of LOT's Tu-154Ms had been grounded and offered for sale; along with the airline's Tu-134As and 'AKs, they were gradually replaced by Boeing 737-45Ds and Boeing 737-55Ds. Poland's entire civil Tu-154 fleet was eventually sold to the CIS – except for one aircraft, which was transferred to the Air Force.

A pair of Tu-154M 'Salons' saw service with the **Polish Air Force** (originally known as PWL – *Polskie Wojsko Lotnicze*; later renamed WLiOP – *Wojska Lotnicze i Obrona Powietrzna*, Air Force & Air Defence Force; now called SPRP – *Siły Powietrzne Rzeczypospolitej Polski*). In Poland the VIP version was called Tu-154M Lux. '837 Black' (c/n 90A837) was delivered new in June 1990, while '862 Black' was a former LOT aircraft (ex-SP-LCO, c/n 90A862) transferred on 28th September 1994. The aircraft were operated by the 36. SPLT (*Specjalny Pułk Lotnictwa Transportowego* – special transport air regiment) at Warsaw-Okęcie tasked with government VIP transport duties.

Rather unusually for the 36. SPLT, the Tu-154s wore basic 1977-standard LOT colours, except that the cheatline continued all the way to the nose across the place where the huge **LOT** titles should have been and the white circle on the blue tail contained the Polish Air Force's *szachownica* (checkerboard) insignia instead of the airline's stylised flying

Still in its original basic LOT colours, Polish Air Force Tu-154M 'Salon' '862 Black' departs from Moscow-Vnukovo. Note the badge of the 36.SPLT on the centre engine air intake. Yuriy Kirsanov

crane logo. The '**LOT** POLISH AIRLINES' titles gave way to the more appropriate 'Rzeczpospolita Polska' (port side) and 'Republic of Poland' (starboard side).

By March 1995 the aircraft had been reserialled '01' and '02' respectively. In early 1996 the trijets received a smart livery in the Polish national colours of red and white, which is worn by most of the unit's aircraft and helicopters. Concurrently they changed their identities again – this time to '101 Red' and '102 Red'; these serials have been traditionally used by a steady succession of 36. SPLT aircraft (IL-18s and Tu-134AKs). Both aircraft were retrofitted with a UNS-1A navigation computer and a KAD-480 air data system. At present the Polish Air Force is considering replacing the Tu-154s with Boeing BBJs (Boeing 737-700s built as business jets).

ROMANIA

In 1976-80 the Romanian flag carrier **TAROM [RO/ROT]** (*Transporturile Aeriene Române* – Romanian Air Transport) took delivery of 12 Tu-154s.

Registration	Version	C/n	Notes
YR-TPA	Tu-154B	76A159	Ex-CCCP85159, D/D 6-76. C/s No 1. Wfu 1991, scrapped
YR-TPB	Tu-154B	76A161	Ex-CCCP85161, D/D 7-76. Converted to Tu-154B-1 by 1995. C/s No 1, later No 3. Wfu 1997, scrapped
YR-TPC	Tu-154B	76A175	Ex-CCCP85175, D/D 1976. C/s No 1. Wfu 1997, scrapped
YR-TPD	Tu-154B	77A224	Ex-CCCP85224, D/D 1977. C/s No 1, later No. 2. Wfu 1994, scrapped
YR-TPE	Tu-154B	77A225	Ex-CCCP85225, D/D 1977. C/s No 1. Wfu 1995, scrapped
YR-TPF	Tu-154B-1	77A239	Ex-CCCP85239, D/D 1977. C/s No 1. Wfu 1995, scrapped
YR-TPG	Tu-154B-1	78A262	Ex-CCCP85262, D/D 1978. C/s No 1, later No 3. Sold to Yuzhnaya Aircompany 6-99 as UN 85777
YR-TPH	Tu-154B-1	78A277	Ex-CCCP85277, D/D 1978. C/s No 1. Crashed Nouadhibou 7-8-80
YR-TPI	Tu-154B-2	79A342	Ex-CCCP85342, D/D 1979. Retired and scrapped by 1996
YR-TPJ	Tu-154B-2	80A408	Ex-CCCP85408, D/D 1980. C/s No 1. Crashed Bucharest-Otopeni 9-2-89
YR-TPK	Tu-154B-2	80A415	Ex-CCCP85415, D/D 1980. C/s No 1. Retired and scrapped by 1996
YR-TPL	Tu-154B-2	80A428	Ex-CCCP85428, D/D 8-80. C/s No 1. Retired and scrapped by 1996

The aircraft were operated in a 164-seat all-tourist configuration or a mixed-class configuration (F10CY135). Some sources, however, list YR-TPJ as a government VIP example (a Tu-154B-2 'Salon'). Originally the trijets had a red cheatline, a grey belly and a white tail with the airline's logo in red (c/s No 1). In the late 1980s the carrier introduced a new livery with a white fuselage and huge red *TAROM* titles and tail logo (c/s

Tu-154B-1 YR-TPF seen at Kuibyshev-Bezymyanka before delivery to TAROM illustrates the livery originally worn by the type. Yefim Gordon archive

Later, TAROM's Tu-154s received a white livery with red trim exemplified by Tu-154B-1 YR-TPG. George Ditchfield

No 2); this was later superseded by the current livery with dark blue titles and a dark blue tail on which the logo is superimposed on a white circle (c/s No 3).

However, when the socialist bloc collapsed in the early 1990s, TAROM terminally switched allegiance to Western manufacturers. Starting in October 1993 the airline bought five 132-seat Boeing 737-38Js and leased a further pair of 737-300s. By 1995 the surviving Tu-154s had been grounded at Bucharest-Otopeni; with the exception of one Tu-154B-1, which found a new owner in Kazakhstan, all were eventually broken up.

RWANDA

In 2004 an unmarked Tu-154M (c/n 91A895) formerly operated by Moldtransavia as ER-TAG was delivered to **an unknown Rwandan airline** and registered 9XR-DU. Curiously, in so doing the aircraft regained the basic Centrafrican Airlines livery which it had lost after being sold to Moldova.

In early 2005 the aircraft was sold to Russia (apparently to the Vnukovo aircraft repair plant). Its new identity immediately afterwards is not clear (some sources suggest it became RA-85479), but it *is* known that eventually the aircraft was registered RA-85740; thus it had run full circle, reverting to its original registration.

SLOVAKIA

Air Terrex leased Tu-154B-2 ER-85332 from Air Moldova in the summer of 1994, returning it to the lessor in September.

Air Transport Europe [–/EAT], originally a rotary-wing operator based in Poprad, leased Tu-154s as required for the summer charter season. Among other things, they flew charters to holiday destinations in Greece and Turkey.

Registration	Version	C/n	Notes
OM-VEA No 1	Tu-154M	91A866	Ex/to RA-85693, leased from Sibir' Airlines 1997 for five months, returned 6-10-97; basic Sibir' c/s No 3A with Air Transport Europe titles and ATE tail logo
OM-VEA No 2	Tu-154M	90A859	Ex/to RA-85688, leased from Sibir' Airlines 15-5-99 to 1-10-99; basic Sibir' c/s No 3A with Air Transport Europe titles and ATE tail logo
ER-85332	Tu-154B-2	79A332	Leased from Air Moldova 6-99 to 15-10-96, basic Air Moldova c/s

Slovakian Airlines/Slovenské Aérolinie [6Q/SLL] became the sole customer for the Tu-154-100. Three such aircraft were delivered in 1998 as part payment of Russia's state debt to Slovakia. They were equipped with American avionics and were configured as 157-seaters with quite modern cabins outfitted by a French company; the cabins featured an in-flight entertainment system with several TV screens under the ceiling.

Slovak Airlines Tu-154-100 OM-AAB taxies out at Moscow/Sheremet'yevo-2, showing the additional titles to the effect that Bratislava was a candidate to host the 2006 Winter Olympic Games (it lost the bid to Turin). Dmitriy Petrochenko

The Slovak Government makes use of this Tu-154M 'Salon', OM-BYR. Martin Novak

Slovak Air Force Tu-154B-2 'Salon' '0420 White' makes a flypast at an airshow, escorted by two Mikoyan MiG-29 fighters. Peter Davison

The jets wore a stylish blue/white livery with Slovak titles to port and English titles to starboard.

In addition to using the trijets on its own services to Europe and to popular holiday destinations such as Hurghada, Slovakian Airlines occasionally leased them abroad (thus, OM-AAB was operated by Balkan Bulgarian Airlines for a full year in 2001-02). Yet in 2003 the carrier decided that it would be better served with western jets, and the Tu-154-100s were sold to Russia at the end of the year.

Registration	C/n	Notes
OM-AAA	98A1014	D/D 16-1-98, named *Puchov*. Sold to Pulkovo Air Enterprise 12-03 as RA-85834
OM-AAB	98A1015	D/D 8-5-98, named *Gerlach*. Sold to Pulkovo Air Enterprise 12-03 as RA-85835
OM-AAC	98A1018	D/D 12-9-98, named *Detva* 21-9-98. Sold to Pulkovo Air Enterprise 12-03 as RA-85836

As mentioned earlier, the **Slovak Air Force** (*Slovenské Vojenské Letectvo*) received one of the ex-Czechoslovak Air Force's Tu-154B-2 'Salons' when Slovakia gained independence. '0420 Black' was repainted in a red/white/blue colour scheme and the serial was amended to '0420 White'. In a similar way to the Czech examples, the machine received a UNS-1A navigation computer and a KAD-480 air data system. The aircraft remained in service until May 1998 when it was sold to Iron Dragonfly as RA-85842.

The **Slovak government flight** owns two Tu-154M 'Salons' – OM-BYO (ex-OK-BYO, c/n 89A803) received on 1st January 1993 and OM-BYR (c/n 98A1012) delivered on 19th March 1998 as part payment of Russia's

state debt to Slovakia. The former aircraft retained the OK- prefix after being painted with the Slovak flag on the tail; for some reason it was not until 1st April 1994 that the machine was reregistered OM-BYO.

SOMALIA

Air Somalia wet-leased a single Tu-154B-2, UR-85546 (c/n 82A546), from Tavria-MAK in December 2000. During the one-year lease the aircraft, which was based at Sharjah (UAE) for the duration, changed its identity mysteriously several times. Originally retaining its Ukrainian registration and sporting the name *Tavrey*, it was transferred to the Moldovan register in September 2001 as ER-TAI; then the machine was seen again as UR-85546 in November 2001 *and then again as ER-TAI* in December! In January 2002 Air Somalia suspended operations and the aircraft went to Air Service International (see end of chapter).

SWAZILAND

The fleet of **Air Pass**, a sister company of Air Cess (Liberia),[4] included a single Tu-154M registered 3D-RTP (ex-YL-LAI, c/n 91A895) bought from Baltic Express Line in November 1997. 'Pass' is an acronym for Pietersburg Aviation Services & Systems; this was because, though nominally a Swazi company, the airline was based at Pietersburg-Gateway International airport, South Africa.

In 1998 Air Pass suspended operations, transferring almost its entire fleet to Centrafrican Airlines; Tu-154M 3D-RTP changed its identity to TL-ACF in so doing.

SYRIA

Syrianair (Syrian Arab Airlines) **[RB/SYR]**, the sole national airline, was the second export customer for the Tu-154M. Three early-production aircraft (YK-AIA through YK-AIC, ex-CCCP85708 through CCCP85710, c/ns 85A708 through 85A710) were delivered in the spring of 1985, one aircraft per month. They were used on the Damascus-Moscow service and flew to various other destinations in Europe (including Athens) and the Middle East.

In 1998 Syrianair began a large-scale fleet renewal programme. The Tu-154Ms and the airline's six Tu-134B-3s were replaced by six Airbus Industrie A320-232s; by March 2001 the trijets had been placed in storage at Damascus-International.

TURKEY

Air Moldova's Tu-154B-2 85332 (*sic*; c/n 79A332) was briefly leased by **Bosporus Airways** in April 1993.

The Tu-154M has seen service with several Turkish inclusive-tour operators. In 1990 Istanbul-based charter carrier **Greenair [–/GRN]** wet-leased three 164-seat Tu-154Ms – CCCP-85620, CCCP-85673 and

YK-AIC, the last of three Tu-154Ms delivered to Syrianair, taxies out at Prague-Ruzyne past three ČSA Tu-134As. Martin Novak

Pushback time for TC-GRA *Cappadocia*, one of three Tu-154Ms operated by Greenair. RART

CCCP-85674 (c/ns 87A739, 90A833 and 90A834 respectively) – from the Vnukovo UAD/200th Flight. Reregistered TC-GRA, TC-GRB and TC-GRC respectively, the aircraft were delivered on 20th February, 11th April and 18th April. The aircraft were painted in the airline's inevitably green/white livery, receiving the names *Cappadocia*, *Perestroika* and *Fenerbahce* respectively. TC-GRB and TC-GRC were returned to the lessor in December 1993, while TC-GRA stayed until 1st April 1995; after that, all three machines regained their original registrations, albeit with the RA- prefix.

Later in 1995 the same three aircraft (RA-85620, RA-85673 and RA-85674) were leased to **Active Air**. This time they were reregistered/named TC.ACT *Prizren*, TC.ACV *Fenerbahce* and TC.ACI *Senler* respectively; TC.ACV was delivered in May while the other two followed in June. Active Air did not bother to develop a livery of its own, retaining basic Vnukovo Airlines colours with new titles and registrations applied as stickers (!); unusually, the registrations were printed with a dot instead of the usual hyphen. RA-85673 and RA-85674 actually gained Active Air titles a couple of days before being reregistered. Like many Turkish IT operators, Active Air proved shortlived, going out of business in November 1995, whereupon two of the three aircraft were returned (see below).

The charter carrier **Holiday Air** briefly wet-leased Tu-154M RA-85714 (c/n 91A890) from ALAK as TC-RAD in July 1995. Originally it retained basic blue/white ALAK colours but received the airline's full colours by August. In late 1996 or 1997 the airliner was returned to the lessor and reverted to its Russian registration. Additionally, sister ship TC.ACI was operated by Active Air on behalf of Holiday Air in 1995.

Tu-154M TC.ACI was also operated by **Air Alfa [H7/LFA]** on sub-lease from Active Air in 1995.

One more carrier sub-leasing Tu-154M TC.ACI from Active Air in 1995 was **Pegasus Airlines [–/PGT]**.

When Active Air became passive, Tu-154M TC.ACI was leased by the Turkish-Cypriot airline **Kibris Türk Hava Yollari** (KTHY – Cyprus Turkish Airlines) **[YK/YVK, later –/KYV]** in November 1995. It, too, was soon returned.

Sultan Air leased Tu-154B-2s CCCP-85542 and CCCP-85579 (c/ns 82A542 and 83A579) from TsUMVS/63rd Flight in 1992.

UNITED KINGDOM

The **Overseas Development Agency** (ODA), an arm of the British government tasked with overseas aid and development, leased Tu-154M RA-85713 (c/n 91A889) from ALAK in September 1993.

According to press reports, on 15th February 1994 the British leasing company **TTJ** (some publications called it TTG) signed an order for ten Tu-154Ms with the Aviacor plant; the contract price was US$ 5 million per aircraft. Deliveries were to commence in February 1995 at a rate of one aircraft per month, being completed by the end of the year. According to unofficial reports, TTJ intended to offer the aircraft to African air carriers at a price of £1 million per year in leasing payments. Vladimir Ryzhkov, the acting comptroller at Aviacor, was quoted as say that TTJ controlled 15% of the world'a airliner leasing market and 'a contract with this company would restore the reputation of the Russian aircraft industry which had been rather damaged by a series of accidents [involving Russian airliners]'. Apparently, however, the deal fell through, as nothing has been heard of it since.

SOUTH YEMEN (PEOPLE'S DEMOCRATIC REPUBLIC OF YEMEN)

Founded in 1970 and based in Aden, the South Yemeni airline **Alyemda [DY/DYA][5]** purchased its first Tu-154 – a Tu-154B-2 registered 7O-ACN (c/n 81A501) – in 1981. A second aircraft, Tu-154M 7O ACT (*sic* – the registration was applied with no hyphen; c/n 89A822), followed in 1989. The aircraft were used on the airline's services around the Middle East and to Europe.

Both aircraft were returned to Russia in early 1992. The Vnukovo aircraft repair plant intended to refurbish and resell them, but upon careful examination 7O-ACN turned out to be in such poor condition that it was simply written off and stripped of usable parts. The Tu-154M was more fortunate – it was sold to Krai Aero as RA-85803 on 1st May 1992.

OPERATORS FROM UNKNOWN NATIONS

In mid-2001 Tu-154M LZ-LCX (c/n 86A744) was briefly operated by **Adriatic Air Charter**.

Air Service International operated Tu-154B-2 ER-TAI (ex-UR-85546, c/n 82A546) in 2002 from its Sharjah base. By 2004 the aircraft had been placed in storage.

An airline reported as **Blue Line** wet-leased Tu-154Ms LZ-MIL and LZ-MIR from Air VIA (Varna International Airlines) in March-April 1992. This is hardly Blue Line Charters, Inc. of Blantyre, Malawi, as this airline operated only light aircraft.

Sibir' Airlines Tu-154M RA-85697 (c/n 91A870) was leased to an airline called **Globetrotters** in September 1992.

An African carrier called **Oriental Airlines** operated Tu-154Ms LZ-MIK and LZ-MIL leased from Air VIA (Varna International Airlines) between December 1990 and March 1991.

Raji Airlines leased Tu-154M LZ-MIR from Air VIA (Varna International Airlines) in the spring of 1994.

Safe Air leased Tu-154B-2 RA-85842 (c/n 80A420) from Iron Dragonfly in 2000.

Tu-154M TC-RAD saw service with short-lived IT operator Holiday Air in 1995. Dmitriy Petrochenko

Chapter Eight

In Detail

The following structural description applies to the basic Tu-154 *sans suffixe*. Details of other versions are indicated as appropriate.

Type

Three-engined short/medium-haul airliner designed for routes 500-3,000km (310-1,860 miles) long. The airframe is of riveted all-metal construction and is largely made of D16T and D16AT duralumin and V95 aluminium alloy (although the use of the latter was discontinued from the Tu-154B onwards). Some structural elements are made of AK6 and AL19-T4 aluminium alloys, ML5-T magnesium alloy, OT4-0 titanium alloy, 30KhGSA and 30KhGSL grade steel and other materials. The materials were carefully chosen so as to ensure the highest possible strength-to-weight ratio.

Large-scale use is made of stamped parts and riveted wing and tail unit panels. To ensure corrosion protection the skin panels and internal structural members are electrochemically coated; additionally, the insides of the fuselage are coated with FL-086 primer, while parts especially susceptible to corrosion are given an additional coat of sealant.

Fuselage

Semi-monocoque stressed-skin structure of beam-and-stringer construction with 72 stringers and 83 frames which are mostly set at 0.5m (1ft 7⅝in) intervals. Flush riveting is used throughout. The cross-section is circular, with a maximum diameter of 3.8m (12ft 5³⁹⁄₆₄in), a maximum cross-section area of 11.3m² (121.5ft²) and a fineness ratio of 11.15.

Structurally the fuselage is divided into three sections: the forward fuselage, the centre fuselage and the rear fuselage. The forward and centre fuselage form a single pressure cabin including the flightdeck, passenger cabins, underfloor baggage compartments and avionics/equipment bays. To ensure adequate pressurisation the structure is sealed during manufacturing. The inside of the pressure cabin is covered with heat- and soundproofing material.

The forward fuselage of Tu-154 *sans suffixe* CCCP-85005. Note the window of the forward toilet located high up on the cabin roof; this window was deleted after only a few aircraft had been built. Author

Close-up of the radome and the dielectric panel of the DISS-3P Doppler speed/drift sensor system immediately aft of it. Author

The *forward fuselage* (frames 0-19) includes the flightdeck and the front end of the forward cabin. Unlike many aircraft, it is not a separate subassembly and is manufactured integrally with the centre fuselage, being mated to the latter along frames 17 (at the top) and 19 (at the bottom). It is built up of several components and features 18 frames, including five mainframes.

The flightdeck is delimited by the forward pressure dome (frames 4-5) and a bulkhead located halfway between frames 10-11. The forward pressure dome mounts the radar dish covered by an upward-hinged glassfibre radome (frames 0-3) featuring four lightning protection strips and Camloc fasteners. The flightdeck glazing frame is located between frames 4-7, resting on lateral beams. It consists

Top left: **The forward fuselage of Tu-154M RA-85733. Note the auxiliary light buried in the nose just aft of the radome and the ground power receptacle ahead of the nose gear unit.** Author

Above: **The forward entry door. The fixture for a padlock near the trailing edge is non-standard and has been added after preservation.** Author

Left: **This view shows how the Tu-154's entry doors open, swinging on parallel arms – just like on a typical modern coach.** Author

Below left: **The Tu-154 *sans suffixe* and Tu-154A had unequally sized overwing emergency exits. The forward pair was enlarged to the same size as the rear one from the Tu-154B onwards.** Author

Below: **VIP examples were built with electrically actuated integral airstairs near the rear entry door.** Author

of seven individual window frames bolted together. There are three optically-flat birdproof windshield panes at the front made of PO-24 boron-silicate triplex glass, plus four trapezoidal side windows with double glazing and four trapezoidal eyebrow windows; the side and upper panes are made of SO-120 Plexiglas. The foremost side windows are sliding direct vision windows which can be used as emergency exits on the ground. The port and starboard windshield panes are equipped with wipers.

A bulged dielectric panel enclosing the antennas of the Doppler speed/drift sensor is located ventrally between frames 3-4 (immediately aft of the radome); on the Tu-154M this panel is flush with the fuselage skin (not bulged). An avionics bay is provided under the flightdeck floor; it is accessible via a rectangular ventral access door between frames 9-11. The nosewheel well is located between frames 14-19 and is delimited by two longitudinal beams (which carry the nose gear fulcrum and actuating mechanism), two pressure bulkheads and a pressure floor.

The space aft of the flightdeck accommodates the forward entry vestibule. A 1.75 x 0.8m (68⁵/₆₄ x 31³¹/₆₄in; ICAO Type II) rectangular entry door incorporating a rectangular window with rounded corners is located on the port side between frames 12-14; it opens outwards, swinging forward on L-shaped arms while remaining parallel to the fuselage side. The

forward toilet and a wardrobe are located opposite. The vestibule is separated from the forward passenger cabin by a bulkhead at frame 14; the forward fuselage section includes the first two cabin windows on each side (up to frame 17).

The *centre fuselage* (frames 17/19-66) is cylindrical up to frame 56, tapering gently aft of it. Most of the frames feature transverse beams to which the cabin floor and the seat tracks are attached. The seat tracks can withstand a longitudinal load of 9Gs in a crash landing. The floor is made of PVC foam plastic reinforced with two layers of plywood.

To facilitate manufacturing the centre fuselage is broken down into the following subassemblies: the upper (roof) section, port and starboard window sections, the lower forward section, the lower rear section and the wing torsion box fairing section. The latter is unpressurised and closes from below a cutout for the wing torsion box between frames 41-49 delimited by pressure bulkheads; mainframes 41, 46 and 49 are mated with the wing spars. The roof section spans from the upper centreline stringer (stringer 0) to stringers 10L and 10R; frames 62-65 are reinforced on this subassembly. The window sections include stringers 10-20 on each side and incorporate numerous rectangular windows with rounded corners measuring approximately 35 x 25cm (13⁴⁹/₆₄ x 9²⁷/₃₂in); frames 19-62 are reinforced on these

subassemblies. Each window has triple glazing made of AO-120 oriented Plexiglas, with a 10-mm (0²⁵/₆₄in) outer pane absorbing the pressure differential at high altitude, a 4-mm (0⁵/₃₂in) middle pane and a 2-mm (0⁵/₆₄in) inner pane; all panes are fitted as a single module sealed with UT-32 sealant. The lower forward section delimited by frames 19-40 spans from the lower centreline stringer (stringer 36) to stringers 20L and 20R, while the lower rear section (frames 49-66) includes stringers 19L through 19R.

The wing/fuselage fairings are manufactured as separate subassemblies. Each fairing consists of forward, centre and rear sections; these are made of duralumin sheet and affixed to webs attached to the fuselage sides. The Tu-154M features revised wing/fuselage fairings with pointed and downturned front ends and extended rear ends.

The forward passenger cabin occupies the space between frames 14-29, followed by the galley between frames 31-33 and the rear (or rather midships) entry vestibule between frames 34-36. The rear passenger cabin occupies the space between frames 36-64, with three toilets arranged between frames 64-66; the rear pressure dome is located aft of these. The forward cabin features a 1.28 x 0.61m (50²⁵/₆₄ x 24¹/₆₄in; ICAO Type II) rectangular emergency exit on the starboard side between frames 19-21. Further aft are a rectangular service door of identical size to starboard between

The forward cabin emergency exit to starboard. Author

The service door has a differently positioned handle and a rain gutter. Author

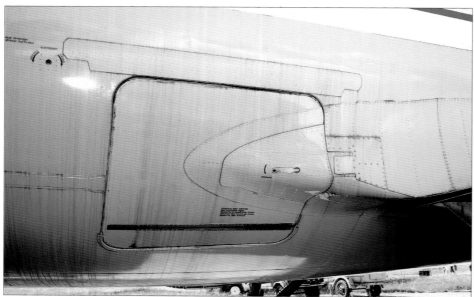

frames 31-33 and the rear entry door measuring 1.75x0.8m to port between frames 34-36. These doors are of identical design to the forward one. On the Tu-154K and later new-build VIP versions (Tu-154B/B-1/B-2 'Salon' and Tu-154M 'Salon') the rear entry door is equipped with three-section airstairs mounted on frame 37; these are turned manually through 90° towards the doorway before deploying electrically by means of linkages and cables. All three doors are provided with rain gutters.

Two pairs of rectangular overwing emergency exits on each side between frames 44-45 and 47-48. On the Tu-154 *sans suffixe* and Tu-154A the forward pair measures 0.9 x 0.48m (35⁷⁄₁₆ x 18⁵⁷⁄₆₄in) and the rear pair 1.07 x 0.48m (42⅛ x 18⁵⁷⁄₆₄in; ICAO Type III); the Tu-154B *et seq.* feature equal-sized 1.07 x 0.48m overwing emergency exits. Additionally, late-production Tu-154As manufactured from the spring of 1975 onwards and subsequent aircraft have a pair of 1.33 x 0.61m (52²³⁄₆₄ x 24¹⁄₆₄in; ICAO Type II) rectangular emergency exits located between frames 61-62; these are surrounded by reinforcement plates.

Two pressurised baggage compartments are located under the cabin floor between frames 23-40 and 50-64; they are outfitted for carrying containerised baggage. Their capacity is 21.5m³ (759.2ft³) and 16.5m³ (582.6ft³) respectively. The compartments are loaded and unloaded through doors on the starboard side between frames 25-28 and 57-60 respectively opened by pushing inwards and sliding forwards. The rear baggage door is partially obstructed by the starboard wing/fuselage fairing whose rear end swings out of the way through 90° before the door is opened. The baggage doors measure 0.8 x 1.35m (31½ x 53¾in); depending on the oleo compression, the sill height is 2.175-1.8m (7ft 1⅝ in to 5ft 10⅞in) for the forward door and 2.0 to 1.9m (6ft 6¾in to 6ft 2¹³⁄₁₆in) for the rear door. Additionally, the baggage compartments are accessible from within via hatches in the cabin floor.

Two avionics/equipment bays are provided ahead of the wings between frames 19-23 (with a ventral access hatch between frames 20-21) and 40-41 (accessed from the cabin). A further two avionics/equipment bays accessed from the cabin are located aft of the wings between frames 49-50 and 64-66.

The upper rear part of the centre fuselage carries the centre engine's air intake and the front end of its S-shaped inlet duct and air

intake trunk; the latter blends smoothly into the fin, featuring formers and skin panels.

The unpressurised *rear fuselage* (frames 66-83) carries the powerplant and the tail unit; it is attached to the centre fuselage by bolts around the perimeter of frame 66. There are 20 frames and 66 stringers; frames 67, 67A, 71, 72, 75, 77 and 78 are mainframes, while the others are ordinary extruded frames. The skin consists of large panel subassemblies riveted to the stringers.

The rear fuselage accommodates the centre engine and its S-duct; an APU bay featuring lateral air intake doors is provided above the engine bay between frames 78-83. A cutout closed by clamshell cowling doors is located between frames 74A-83 for centre engine maintenance and removal. A tailcone featuring orifices for the centre engine nozzle and the APU jetpipe is attached to frame 83; its trailing-edge portions are made of heat-resistant steel, while the lower half is detachable to facilitate engine removal. An equipment bay housing hydraulic system components is located below the engine bay. So is a bulk cargo compartment (frames 68-73) with a rectangular door on the starboard side between frames 68-71 (under the starboard engine pylon); it has a capacity of 5m³ 176.5ft³) and is normally used for carrying air intake covers, wheel chocks and the like. The engine bay is separated from these and from the pressure cabin by a titanium firewall at frame 74A.

The S-duct begins at frame 61 and terminates at frame 75 where it mates with the centre engine; its cross-section changes gradually from oval to circular at the compressor face. The duct is attached to the fuselage structure at frames 62, 68 and 71; it comprises the skin and a set of annular stiffeners riveted together. Structurally it consists of the leading edge/de-icer (consisting of an outer skin and a corrugated inner liner forming air channels), front, centre and rear portions; the front and rear portions are curved. There is an inspection hatch at frame 70.

Frames 67 and 71 incorporate attachment points for the engine pylons; the fin spars are attached to mainframes 72, 75 and 78 via a longitudinal beam. The pylons are forward-swept and carry cigar-shaped engine nacelles (see Powerplant); the latter can be detached together with the engines to facilitate engine change, significantly reducing downtime associated with heavy maintenance.

The Tu-154M has a new rear fuselage incorporating a new centre engine S-duct of larger cross-section and an accordingly revised air intake trunk, new engine pylons (set higher up) and new nacelles. The APU bay is located beneath the S-duct on the starboard side between frames 72-74, featuring a single ven-

tral air intake door on the centreline and an exhaust port to starboard with a forward-hinged door surrounded by a heat-resistant steel liner. The upper half of the tailcone is blended with a fin trailing-edge fillet.

Wings

Cantilever low-wing monoplane of modified trapezoidal planform, with small leading edge root extensions (leading-edge sweep 41° from root to rib 14 and 37° outboard); trailing edge broken by main landing gear fairings, with zero sweepback inboard of these. Sweepback at quarter-chord 35°, anhedral 1°10', incidence +3° at root and –1° at tip, camber –4°, aspect ratio 7.85, taper 3.5. Mean aerodynamic chord (MAC) 5.285m (17ft 4⅝in).

The wings utilise TsAGI high-speed airfoils – P-56M$_2$-12 at the roots, P-35M$_3$-11 at mid-span and P-35M$_3$-10 at the tips. Thickness/chord ratio decreases from root to tip; the mean ratio is 10.3%. The airfoils are chosen in such a way as to concentrate the main lift at the roots, offloading the tips and easing the bending loads. The cruise lift/drag ratio exceeds 14.

The wings are a three-spar, stressed-skin structure with 91 ribs. Structurally they are built in three pieces: the monobloc centre section/inner wing assembly and the detachable outer wings. The manufacturing joints are at ribs 14L and 14R; the sections are joined by flanges. Ribs 3, 14 and 45 on each side are sealed. The ribs are at right angles to the rear spar, except for the ribs located inside the fuselage (centre-line rib 0 and ribs 1L-3L and 1R-3R) and the tip ribs (45L and 45R), which are parallel to the fuselage axis.

The *centre section/inner wing assembly* is attached to fuselage mainframes 41, 46 and 49 whose lower portions are built integrally with

The port wing of Tu-154 *sans suffixe* CCCP-85005. Note the leading-edge kink and the air outlet of the air conditioning system heat exchanger. Author

This view shows the Tu-154's flaps, leading-edge slats, spoilers and airbrakes deployed. Tupolev PLC

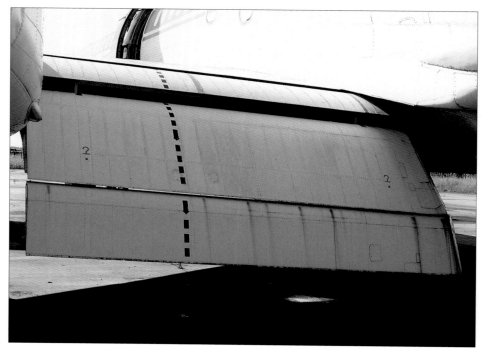

The port inboard flap of a Tu-154 *sans suffixe*. Yefim Gordon

the centre section spars; they are joined to the upper portions of the said frames by fittings during final assembly. The wing/fuselage joint is covered by fairings located between frames 36-59.

The centre section/inner wing assembly consists of the torsion box (formed by the spars, 29 ribs up to 14L/14R and skin panels), leading-edge and trailing-edge sections. There are nine upper skin panels, two of which are detachable for maintenance and repair, and six lower skin panels. The skin is supported by riveted stringers; stringers 12 and 25 on the upper side are reinforced. Eight of the ribs are reinforced, serving as attachment points for the inboard flaps and main gear units/fairings. The portions of the torsion box between ribs 3L-14L and 3R-14R are sealed to form integral fuel tanks; the middle spar features holes allowing fuel to flow within the tanks. On the Tu-154A *et seq.* the section delimited by ribs 3L/3R is sealed to form an additional integral tank (see Fuel system for details).

The detachable LE sections built in two pieces (between ribs 3-7 and 7-14) accommodate piping, electric cables and LE slat drive shafts. The TE sections are located between the fuselage sides and the main gear fairings; each TE section consists of a beam placed at right angles to the fuselage side (it carries the inboard flap/cove lip door and ground spoiler mounting brackets, as well as drive shaft supports), upper and lower skins, and webs.

Large pointed main landing gear fairings are attached to the centre section/inner wing assembly aft of the front spar near the tips by means of angle fittings. The fairings have a basically rectangular cross-section with rounded corners changing to circular at the tips. They are of beam-and-stringer construction with 19 frames; each fairing has a manufacturing break and the front ends are split to fit around the wing torsion box. The wheel wells are located between frames 1-16.

The *outer wings* each have 31 ribs (14A-45) and feature a torsion box with multiple upper and lower skin panels, detachable LE sections and a tip fairing. The outer wing torsion boxes incorporate integral fuel tanks.

Each outer wing has two prominent boundary layer fences designed to delay tip stall; they are built in several portions to avoid deformation as the wings flex. The fences are attached in line with the inboard ends of the No 2 LE slat sections and the outer ends of the outboard flaps. The LE sections are built in five pieces

The port outboard flap of a Tu-154 *sans suffixe*.
Yefim Gordon

The starboard inner flap of a Tu-154M.
Igor' Sitchikhin

The starboard outer flap of a Tu-154M.
Igor' Sitchikhin

and house piping, electric cables and LE slat drive shafts.

The wings are equipped with five-section leading-edge slats deflected 18° 30' and two-section area-increasing triple-slotted flaps (inner sections, ribs 3-11; outer sections, ribs 14-32). The LE slats are attached to the front spar and actuated by an EPV-8P electric drive via shafts and angle drives/screw jacks (two per section). The innermost sections are located on the centre section/inner wing assembly between ribs 7-13 and set apart from the others, moving on tracks located at ribs 8 and 12. Each section has outer and inner skins, upper and lower stringers, ribs and end profiles. The four slat sections on each outer wing are mechanically connected into pairs; again, each section moves on two tracks.

The flaps are actuated by an RP-60-1 twin-chamber hydraulic actuator (*roolevoy privod*) via drive shafts and angle drives/screw jacks (two for each section); the actuator is powered by two hydraulic systems. The flaps move on external tracks attached to the middle and rear spars and enclosed by fairings (two for each inboard flap and three for each outboard flap). They have cove lip doors which are mechanically linked to the flaps, deflecting 23° when the flaps deploy. Flap settings on Kuznetsov-powered versions are 15° or 28° for take-off and 45° for landing and are indicated by a UP-32-05 two-needle indicator. The middle and rear slots are active in take-off mode; the foremost segments separate from the middle portions only when the flaps are fully deployed, opening the third slot.

The Tu-154M features new double-slotted flaps with longer flap track fairings and redesigned LE slats deflected 22° with no gap between the inner/outer wing sections. Flap settings are 36° for take-off and 45° for landing.

One-piece ailerons (see Control system) are located outboard of the flaps. On the Tu-154 *sans suffixe* and the Tu-154A they occupy the entire trailing edge between the flaps and the tip fairings, being suspended on four brackets each; the Tu-154B *et seq*. have abbreviated ailerons with two brackets each, the outermost portions of the trailing edge being fixed. Thin pointed fairings are located between the flaps and the ailerons' inboard ends.

Four-section spoilers are fitted ahead of the flaps – one section each side on the centre section/inner wing assembly and three sections on each outer wing. The innermost spoilers hinged on two brackets each are ground spoilers, being armed before landing to deploy automatically 50° on touchdown. They are riveted struc-

tures with 24 ribs, upper and lower skins, a sloping forward web and a trailing-edge section; the
hinge line coincides with the leading edge. The
outer wing spoilers are flight spoilers; the
inboard and centre sections moving together
act as airbrakes/lift dumpers during normal and
emergency descent, with a maximum deflection
of 45°, while the outermost sections assist the
ailerons for roll control at high speeds (see Control system). The outer wing airbrakes also
deploy automatically on touchdown and are
used together with the ground spoilers in the
event of an aborted take-off.

The outer wing spoilers' hinge line is located
ahead of the leading edge so that a gap
appears when the spoilers are deployed; this
gap optimises the airflow, preventing pressure
fluctuations and high-speed buffeting. The air-
brakes/lift dumpers are hinged on two brackets
per section, while the roll control spoilers have
three brackets each. The spoilers are hydraulically actuated; the airbrakes/lift dumpers have
RP-59 actuators on each section, while the roll
control spoilers are powered by RP-57 and
RP-58 actuators. The Tu-154B *et seq.* have
increased-area spoilers.

Tail Unit

Cantilever swept T-tail featuring symmetrical
airfoils. The *vertical tail* consists of a fin and a
one-piece rudder (see Control system).
Sweepback at quarter-chord 45°, aspect ratio
1.0, taper 1.88, thickness/chord ratio 11%. The
fin is 5.65m (18ft 6⅞in) tall.

The fin is bolted to fuselage mainframes
72-78. It is a three-spar stressed-skin structure
with 18 ribs (including the top and bottom ribs,
three reinforced ribs and 13 regular ones) and
two skin panels; all but the top and bottom ribs
are at right angles to the rear spar. The two-piece
leading edge is detachable, doubling as a de-
icer; the centre engine's air intake trunk blends
smoothly into the lower part of the fin. A cigar-
shaped fairing is located at the top; its front end
was thinner than the remainder of the fairing on
the Tu-154 *sans suffixe*. There are four rudder
mounting brackets. The rudder is of single-spar
construction with a leading-edge section, regular
and reinforced ribs (the latter carry the attachment fittings), honeycomb-core panels, a trailing-
edge profile and a bendable balancing tab.

The variable-incidence *horizontal tail* is
hinged to the fin's rear spar, comprising two
stabilisers and one-piece elevators *(see Con-*

trol system). Sweepback at quarter-chord 40°, thickness/chord ratio 11% at root and 10% at tip, aspect ratio 4.41. Each stabiliser is of similar three-spar construction with regular and reinforced ribs, upper and lower skin panels, a trailing-edge section, a tip fairing and eight elevator mounting brackets. The Tu-154M has longer-chord elevators.

The stabilisers are attached to a narrow horizontal tail centre section and are manufactured as one subassembly. The latter is attached to the fin by two hinges side by side at the centre section's middle spar and by a support at the front where the stabiliser trim screw jack is. The centre section is enclosed by an area-ruled fairing which is a continuation of that on the fin. The elevators are single-spar structures of similar design to the rudder, with mass balancing.

Landing Gear

Electrohydraulically retractable tricycle type; all three units retract aft. Maximum landing gear transition speed during normal operations is 400km/h (248mph); no limit is imposed during emergency descent. Wheel track 11.5m (37ft 8¾in), wheelbase in no-load condition 18.92m (62ft 0⅞in).

The nose unit attached to fuselage frame 14 has jury struts and an aft-mounted drag/breaker strut. It is vertical when extended. Originally it was fitted with twin 800 x 225mm (31.49 x 8.85in) KN-10 non-braking wheels (*koleso netormoznoye*); later aircraft were equipped with KT-183 wheels of identical size featuring disc brakes (*koleso tormoznoye – brake wheel*). The nose unit features a steering mechanism/shimmy damper and is controlled by a tiller on the captain's console for taxying or by the rudder pedals to allow evasive action during the take-off/landing run; the steering mode is selected by a switch on the overhead circuit breaker panel. Steering angles for taxying are ±55° up to and including Tu-154B-2 c/n 80A459 and ±65° from Tu-154B-2 c/n 80A460 onwards. Steering angles for take-off/landing are ±8°30' up to and including Tu-154B c/n 77A225 and on Tu-154B-2s from c/n 80A460 to c/n 84A605; on aircraft from Tu-154B c/n 77A226 up to and including Tu-154B-2 c/n 80A459 it is ±7°, while the Tu-154M and some upgraded Tu-154B-2s have a limit of ±10°. In no-load condition the nosewheel steering is disabled and the nose unit is castoring.

The semi-levered-suspension main units are attached to inner wing ribs 13 (the fulcrums are located there); each unit has a forward-mounted telescopic retraction/drag strut attached to rib 11 and a six-wheel bogie. The bogies initially had 930x305mm (36.61x12.0in) KT-141 wheels equipped with multi-disc brakes (*koleso tormoznoye – brake wheel*); later aircraft have KT-141A wheels of identical size. UA51A anti-skid units are provided.

When extended, the main gear struts are inclined 6° aft in no-load condition (the angle increases during oleo compression). In no-load condition the bogies assume a slightly nose-down attitude. During retraction they are rotated aft through 180° by separate hydraulic rams/rocking dampers to lie inverted in the abovesaid fairings.

All three units have oleo-pneumatic shock absorbers and scissor links; the Tu-154 *sans suffixe* had single-chamber shock absorbers on the main units which were replaced by twin-chamber shock absorbers from the Tu-154A onwards. Maximum oleo compression is 251mm (9.88in) for the nose gear and 362mm (14.25in) for the main gear; the bogies move aft by virtue of oleo compression in the event of

The nose gear unit of Tu-154 *sans suffixe* CCCP-85005 with KN-10 wheels. Note the retracted forward pair of landing/taxi lights ahead of it. Author

From the Tu-154B-2 onwards, separate taxi lights were added to the nose gear unit; this is a Tu-154M (RA-85782) with KT-183 wheels. Author

hard braking or jolts. Tyre pressure is 8 bars (114.3psi) for the nosewheels and 9 bars (128.5psi) for the mainwheels.

The nosewheel well is closed by two pairs of doors; the small forward doors are mechanically linked to the nose gear strut. Each main unit has two large main doors, two small clamshell doors in line with the gear fulcrum (mechanically linked to the strut) and a narrow curved strip attached to the retraction strut. The main doors are hydraulically actuated, opening only when the gear is in transit.

All three units have uplocks, downlocks (built into the retraction struts for the main units) and door locks. Landing gear position is indicated by pilot lights on the captain's instrument panel. A warning horn sounds if the throttles are retarded to flight idle when the gear is up; it is silenced automatically by gear extension.

Powerplant

The Tu-154 *sans suffixe* is powered by three Kuznetsov NK-8-2 turbofans rated at 9,580kgp (21,120 lbst) at ISA for take-off, with a nominal rating of 8,000kgp (17,640 lbst) and a cruise rating of 1,800kgp (3,970 lbst) at 11,000m (36,090ft) and Mach 0.8. The engine was produced by the Kazan' Engine Production Association (KMPO).

The NK-8-2 is a two-spool turbofan with a fixed-area subsonic air intake, a two-stage fan, a two-stage axial low-pressure (LP) compressor (the two have a common shaft), an intermediate casing with accessory drive shaft and bevel gears, a six-stage axial high-pressure (HP) compressor, an annular combustion chamber with 139 burners, a single-stage axia

HP turbine, a two-stage axial LP turbine, a fixed-area subsonic jetpipe featuring a multi-chute core/bypass flow mixer, and an optional cascade-type thrust reverser.

Construction is mostly of titanium alloy. The air intake assembly has a fixed hemispherical spinner, 12 radial struts and 12 part-span inlet guide vanes (IGVs). The fan blades are scimitar-shaped and feature part-span shrouds to reduce vibration. The LP spool rotates in three shock-absorbing bearings (in the air intake assembly, in the centre casing and in the rear support frame); the HP spool has two such bearings (in the centre casing and aft of the turbine), and labyrinth and graphite seals are used to prevent gas leakage. The fifth HP compressor stage features bleed valves. The centre casing carries a PPO-62M constant-speed drive (*privod postoyannykh oborotov* – CSD) driving the accessories – generators, fuel, oil and hydraulic pumps, and starter. The turbines have shrouded blades in both rotor and stator; air-cooled disks and hollow stator blades.

Thrust reversers are fitted to the outer engines only; maximum reverse thrust 3,000kgp (6,610 lbst). The thrust reverser grids are inclined 45° forward and 15° outward to direct the jet blast away from the main gear wheels. Reverse thrust is normally cancelled

Above: **The port engine nacelle and centre engine air intake of a Tu-154 with NK-8-2U engines (note the auxiliary blow-in doors on the nacelle's air intake section).** Author

Below left: **On Tu-154s** *sans suffixe* **with the original NK-8-2 engines (note the lack of blow-in doors) the hot air outlets of the intake de-icers were grouped together. Note the forward sweep of the pylon and the S-shaped manufacturing break between it and the fuselage.** Author

Below right: **On aircraft with NK-8-2U engines the de-icers' hot air outlets were widely spaced.** Author

when the aircraft decelerates to 100km/h (62mph) to avoid exhaust gas ingestion and engine surge but may be used right down to zero speed in an emergency.

The engine has a recirculation-type pressure lubrication system using MK-8 or MK-8P mineral oil, VNII NP-50-1-4F synthetic oil[1] or equivalents (DERD.2490 or MIL-O-6081B specifications).

Starting is by means of an STV air turbine starter (*startyor vozdooshnyy*) developed and manufactured by the Aviamotor Design & Production Enterprise in Kazan'. The STV delivers 110shp and uses compressed air from the APU, ground supply or cross-feed from another engine. The starting sequence proceeds automatically and is controlled from the PDA-154 control panel. In-flight starting by windmilling is possible.

Bypass ratio (BPR) 1.05. Maximum turbine speed 5,180rpm (LP)/6,835rpm (HP); overall engine pressure ratio (EPR) at take-off power 9.6 at sea level. Turbine temperature 1,200°K. Specific fuel consumption (SFC) at take-off power 0.59kg/kgp·hr (lb/lbst·hr), cruise SFC 0.79kg/kgp·hr. Length overall 4.762m (15ft 7³¹⁄₃₂in) without thrust reverser and 5.288m (17ft 4³⁄₁₆in) with thrust reverser; inlet diameter 1.355m (4ft 5¹¹⁄₃₂in), maximum diameter 1.442m (4ft 8⁴⁹⁄₆₄in). Dry weight 2,150kg (4,720 lb) without thrust reverser and 2,350kg (5,180 lb) with thrust reverser.

The Tu-154A, Tu-154B, Tu-154B-1 and Tu-154B-2 are powered by Kuznetsov NK-8-2U engines uprated to 10,500kgp (23,150 lbst) for take-off, with a 2,200-kgp (4,850-lbst) cruise rating and a maximum reverse thrust of 3,600kgp (7,940 lbst). Overall EPR 10.8 at take-off power and 11.14 in cruise mode; mass flow at take-off power 228kg/sec (502 lb/sec). Turbine temperature 1,156°K at take-off power and 1,007°K in cruise mode; maximum turbine temperature 1,230°K. SFC at take-off power

0.58kg/kgp·hr, cruise SFC 0.79kg/kgp·hr. Dry weight 2,170kg (4,780 lb) without thrust reverser and 2,350kg with thrust reverser.

The Nos 1 and 3 engines are mounted in individual cigar-shaped nacelles on large horizontal pylons flanking the rear fuselage. The nacelles are positioned so that the outer engines' turbine rotation planes are located aft of the rear pressure dome, making sure that flying debris does not puncture the pressure cabin and cause a decompression in the event of an uncontained engine failure. The No 2 engine is buried in the rear fuselage and positioned further aft, breathing through a dorsal air intake with an S-duct. The intake is raised above the rear fuselage surface to prevent ingestion of the turbulent boundary layer which may cause engine surge. Each engine is attached to the airframe by six struts.

To reduce the drag caused by harmful interference with the rear fuselage, the nacelles are mounted with a toe-out angle of 5° (that is, the engine shafts are at 5° to the fuselage centreline). To ensure optimum working conditions for the engines the nacelles are mounted with an incidence of 1°30' because of the wing upwash and the inlets are angled 3° towards the fuselage with respect to the engine axis to compensate for the toe-out angle; the engine nozzles are angled 6°30' outward to prevent the engine efflux from impinging on the fuselage skin.

Each nacelle is built in three sections. The annular forward fairing (frames 1-5A) incorporates the inlet duct, air intake de-icer and pylon leading edge; the de-icer consists of an outer skin and a corrugated inner liner forming air channels. On NK-8-2U powered versions (the Tu-154A/B/B-1/B-2) the forward fairing features 12 spring-loaded blow-in doors around the circumference just aft of the de-icer. The inlet duct attached to frames 1 and 5A comprises the skin and a set of annular stiffeners riveted together.

The pylon leading edge has an airfoil section and features a skin, webs and a titanium sheet firewall at the junction with the nacelle.

The centre portion (frames 6-22) is attached to the pylon by four fittings and bolts at frames 12 and 22 which also carry the engine attachment fittings. It features 17 frames and formers, three beams and incorporates the centre part of the pylon; the inboard portion is separated from the pylon by a titanium sheet firewall. The large ventral cutout for engine installation/removal is closed by three pairs of clamshell cowling doors with Camloc fasteners; the centre portion features dorsal access hatches. The rear portion includes the thrust reverser cowl (frames 22-27), the detachable annular fairing fitting around the jetpipe, and the pylon trailing edge.

Early Tu-154Ms are powered by Solov'yov (Aviadvigatel') D-30KU-154 Srs 2 turbofans rated at 10,500kgp (23,150 lbst) for take-off, with a 2,750-kgp (6,060-lbst) cruise rating at 11,0000 m and Mach 0.8. The engine is produced by the Rybinsk engine plant (Rybinsk Motors Joint-Stock Co).

The D-30KU-154 Srs 2 is a two-shaft turbofan with a three-stage LP compressor, 11-stage HP compressor, cannular combustion chamber, two-stage HP turbine, four-stage LP turbine, fixed-area jetpipe with 16-chute core/bypass flow mixer, and an optional clamshell thrust reverser (outer engines only). Construction is mostly of titanium alloy, with steel used for some HP compressor parts. The LP spool rotates in three bearings: a roller bearing in the air intake assembly, a ball bearing in the division casing and a roller bearing in the rear support frame. The HP spool likewise has three bearings: a roller bearing in the division casing, a ball thrust bearing at the rear of the compressor and a roller bearing ahead of the turbine.

The air intake assembly has a fixed hemispherical spinner and 26 cambered IGVs de-iced by hot air bled from the 6th or 11th compressor stage; variable IGVs are used on the HP compressor to minimise blade vibration. The division casing is made of magnesium alloy. The combustion chamber has 12 flame tubes, two of which feature igniters; the outer casing and duct shroud are split horizontally for access to the flame tubes. The HP turbine blades are cooled by engine bleed air, while the LP turbine blades are uncooled.

Two ventral accessory gearboxes (front and rear) are provided, one of which has a CSD for the AC generator and starter. The lubrication system incorporates a fuel/oil heat exchanger and uses VNII NP-50-1-4F synthetic oil or equivalent. The engine is started by an STV-4 air turbine starter fed by the APU, ground supply or cross-bleed from other engines; time from start to idle is 40-80 sec, depending on outside air temperature; operational limits are

–60°/+50°C (–76°/+122°F). In-flight starting by windmilling is possible at up to 9,000m (29,530ft).

BPR 2.3; overall EPR 20 at sea level, mass flow at take-off power 263kg/sec (580 lb/sec). Turbine temperature 1,336°K. SFC at take-off power 0.498kg/kgp·hr, cruise SFC 0.71kg/kgp·hr. Length overall with thrust reverser 5.7m (18ft 8½in), inlet diameter 1.455m (4ft 9½in); dry weight with thrust reverser 2,305kg (5,081 lb).

Late-production Tu-154Ms have D-30KU-154 Srs 3 engines featuring a 12-chute core/bypass flow mixer, improved gas seals and reduced blade-to-casing gaps, a revised thrust reverser control system and other changes. Mass flow at take-off power 265kg/sec (584 lb/sec), turbine temperature 1,316°K; SFC at take-off power 0.482kg/kgp·hr, cruise SFC 0.69kg/ kgp·hr. Dry weight with thrust reverser 2,307kg (5,086 lb).

The Tu-154M's engine nacelles have a different design, being manufactured in two sections – the annular forward fairing (air intake assembly) and the centre section, which features two pairs of ventral cowling doors with Camloc fasteners and removable dorsal access panels; the rear end of the nacelle is formed by the engine's thrust reverser doors. The inlet duct may feature a porous noise suppression liner.

The engines are controlled by a system of cables. The throttles and reverse thrust control levers are positioned on the central control pedestal; a second set of throttles (but no reverse thrust control levers) are located at the flight engineer's station. An autothrottle with a go-around function maintaining constant speed during landing approach is provided.

A Stoopino Machinery Design Bureau TA-6A auxiliary power unit is installed in the rear fuselage for self-contained engine starting, AC/DC ground power supply and air conditioning. It has a three-stage axial compressor, a three-

stage axial turbine, a GT40PCh6 AC generator and a GS-12TO DC generator/starter. Length overall 1,585mm (5ft 2¹³⁄₃₂in), width 620mm (2ft 0¹³⁄₃₂in), height 735mm (2ft 4¹⁵⁄₁₆in); dry weight (less generator) 245kg (540 lb). The TA-6A can operate at ambient temperatures of –60°/+60°C (–76°/+140°F) and altitudes up to 3,000m (9,840ft); APU start-up is controlled by means of the APD-30A and PSG-6 control panels. Fuel consumption is 225kg/hr (496 lb/hr); the air supply rate is 1.35kg/sec (2.97 lb/sec) in normal mode or 1.8kg/sec (3.96 lb/sec) in emergency mode for accelerated engine starting, bleed air pressure 4.5kg/cm² (64.28psi).

On Kuznetsov-engined versions the APU is housed in a bay above the centre engine (frames 78-83), breathing via two lateral air intakes; the intake doors rotated on horizontal axles on early aircraft and were later replaced with aft-hinged doors acting as air scoops. The exhaust is located in the fuselage tailcone above the centre engine nozzle. On the Tu-154M the APU is located on the starboard side between frames 72-74, breathing via a ventral intake with an aft-hinged door/air scoop and exhausting through a door in line with the starboard pylon trailing edge.

Control System

Powered dual controls with irreversible hydraulic actuators and artificial-feel mechanisms in all three channels. For maximum reliability the control surface actuators are each connected to three independent hydraulic systems. There is no manual emergency backup. An ABSU-154 automatic flight control system (advanced autopilot) is fitted, providing automatic control in all flight modes. It features electrohydraulic trim mechanisms (servos) thus obviating the need for trim tabs.

Control inputs are transmitted from the control columns and rudder pedals to the actuators

by single push-pull rods, cranks and levers. The control rods are provided with pressure seals where they exit the pressure cabin. Gust locks are provided to prevent damage to the system by high winds while the aircraft is parked.

Directional control is provided by a one-piece rudder powered by an RP-56 three-chamber hydraulic actuator (*roolevoy privod*) located near the No 2 hinge and attached to rudder rib 6. Maximum deflection is ±25° with the flaps deployed and ±7°30' in cruise mode. The rudder has aerodynamic and mass balancing.

Pitch control is provided by one-piece elevators with aerodynamic and mass balancing which are connected by a shaft with a universal joint. These are likewise powered by RP-56 actuators located between the Nos. 3 and 4 hinges; maximum deflection is +29°/–16° on Kuznetsov-powered versions and +25°/–20° on the Tu-154M. The elevator control circuit incorporates spring-loaded push-pull rods ensuring that one elevator remains operational in emergency mode if the other one jams (for whatever reason).

To enhance pitch control at low speed and provide longitudinal trim the Tu-154 features variable-incidence stabilisers adjusted by an MUS-3PTV electric drive (*mekhanizm oopravleniya stabilizahtorom*) with twin D-600TV motors located on the fin's front spar. The stabiliser setting is slaved to the flap setting and additionally determined by a selector in accordance with the actual CG position (forward, middle or aft); the setting is indicated by a UP21-02 indicator as shown in the following tables.

Tu-154 to Tu-154B-2

Flap Setting	'CG Position' Switch Setting		
	Forward CG	Middle CG	Aft CG
0°	–1°30' (0°)	–1°30' (0°)	–1°30' (0°)
15°	–4°30' (–3°)	–3° (–1°30°)	–1°30' (0°)
28°	–4°30' (–3°)	–3° (–1°30°)	–1°30' (0°)
45°	–7 (–5°30')	–4°30' (–3°)	–1°30' (0°)

Below right: **The centre engine nozzle of a Tu-154 *sans suffixe*; note the flush APU exhaust above it, the shape of the surrounding structure and the tail navigation light.** Author

Below: **The centre engine nozzle and port engine nacelle of a Tu-154M with the thrust reverser deployed; note the arms on which the thrust reverser doors move.** Author

The flightdeck of Tu-154 *sans suffixe* CCCP-85005. Author

Close-up of the instrument panels and centre control pedestal of CCCP-85005; the instrumentation is a bit sparse because this is a pre-production machine. Note the weather radar display in the upper centre, the navigation system keypad below it, and the flap selector lever and the twin emergency wheel braking levers to the left of the throttles. Author

Total fuel load is 33,150kg (73,080 lb) for the Tu-154 *sans suffixe* and 39,750kg (87,630 lb) for subsequent versions. On the Tu-154A the No 4 centre section tank serves as a trim tank maintaining the correct CG position (the fuel from it can be transferred to the No 1 tank on the ground); from the Tu-154B onwards the No 4 tank is included into the fuel system (the fuel is usable in flight).

The No 1 tank is the service tank for all three engines and the APU, featuring four ETsN-325 delivery pumps (*elektricheskiy tsentrobezhnyy nasos* – electric centrifugal pump). These feed the fuel along separate pipelines to the engines' DTsN-44T feed pumps and to the APU's ETsN-319 pump. The main tanks feature ETsN-323 transfer pumps (two in each centre section/inner wing assembly tank and three in each outer wing tank).

Separate vent systems are provided for the port and starboard tanks, with ram air intakes in the wing/fuselage fairings.

The ATsT6-1AT fuel management system (FMS) automatically sequences the fuel tank usage to maintain the CG position and equalises the fuel amount in the port and starboard halves of the fuel system to prevent lateral imbalance. Manual fuel sequencing is possible if the automatic system fails. A special shut-off valve stops the fuel transfer to the service tank when it is full, opening again when the fuel level drops below a certain mark.

The Tu-154 has single-point pressure refuelling at 4.5kg/cm² (64psi); two standard refuelling connectors are located under the starboard wing leading edge. Refuelling at a delivery rate of 2,500 litres (550 Imp gal) per minute takes no more than 20 minutes. The FMS automatically closes the shut-off cocks as the tanks fill; should the FMS fail, special overflow pipes are provided at the top of the tanks to spill the excess fuel outside, stopping the tanks from overpressurising and bursting. Refuelling by gravity is also possible via filler caps on each wing. Defuelling is done via two valves under the wing centre section; there is no provision for fuel jettisoning in flight. Fuel grades used are Russian T-1, TS-1 or RT, Western JP-1, Jet A-1, Avtur or equivalent.

To prevent the water content in the fuel from crystallising and clogging the fuel filters as the fuel cools down at high altitude (or during winter operations) a pressure sensor activates a special ETsN-19A pump when the pressure differential upstream and downstream of the filter reaches a certain limit. The pump injects a spe-

Tu-154M

Flap Setting	'CG Position' Switch Setting		
	Forward CG	Middle CG	Aft CG
0°	–3° (0°)	–3° (0°)	–3° (0°)
15°	–6° (–3°)	–4°30' (–1°30')	–3° (0°)
36°	–8°30' (–5°30')	–6° (–3°)	–3° (0°)
45°	–8°30' (–5°30')	–6° (–3°)	–3° (0°)

The figures in parentheses denote the setting as per the UP21-02 stabiliser incidence indicator. Stabiliser trim change is possible up to 425km/h (264mph); the transition time is 15 seconds form 0° to –3°, 12.5 seconds from –3° to –5°30' and 27.5 seconds from –5°30' to 0° (as per indicator).

Roll control is provided by one-piece ailerons and the outermost flight spoiler sections; the latter come into play when the respective aileron is deflected more than 1°30' up and are actuated via a differential mecha-

nism. The ailerons have both aerodynamic and mass balancing and are powered by RP-55 three-chamber actuators. Each roll control spoiler has three RP-57 and RP-58 single-chamber actuators, one per hydraulic system. Maximum aileron deflection is ±20° in manual mode and ±10° in automatic control mode (as controlled by the ABSU-154); the roll control spoilers have a maximum deflection of 45°.

Fuel System

On the Tu-154 *sans suffixe* the wing torsion box houses five integral fuel tanks – three in the centre section/inner wing assembly (No 1 between the middle and rear spars/ribs 3L-3R; No 2, ribs 3L-14L and No 3, ribs 3R-14R) and one in each outer wing. They are sealed during manufacture by applying compounds over the joints. An additional integral tank (No 4) between the front and middle spars/ribs 3L-3R was introduced on the Tu-154A *et seq.*

The captain's control console of CCCP-85005. Author

The first officer's control console of CCCP-85005. Author

The overhead circuit breaker panel/systems control panel of CCCP-85005. Author

cial fluid (grade 'I' anti-gelling agent) which melts the ice deposit and is switched off when the pressure differential normalises. This avoids the need to add the anti-gelling agent to the fuel in advance; the supply of the grade 'I' fluid is 23-25 litres (5.06-5.5 Imp gal), which is enough for at least two flights lasting up to four hours.

Oil System

Each engine has its own self-contained lubrication system; so does the APU. The NK-8-2 features a 38-litre (8.36 Imp gal) oil tank installed at the front of the engine casing, a fuel/oil heat exchanger, a delivery pump and a scavenging pump. The TA-6A has an 8-litre (1.76 Imp gal) oil tank. The engine and APU oil tanks have a common refilling system.

Hydraulics

Three separate hydraulic systems, each with its own reservoir, hydraulic accumulator and controls. Primary hydraulic power is supplied by four NP-89 or NP-74 variable-delivery plunger pumps (*nasos ploonzhernyy*) – one on each outer engine and two on the centre engine, with two NS-46 electric pumps (*nasosnaya stahntsiya*) as a backup. All systems use AMG-10 oil-type hydraulic fluid (*aviatsionnoye mahslo ghidravlicheskoye*); nominal pressure 210kg/cm² (3,000psi).

The *No 1 system* uses the two pumps driven by the outer engines. It caters for normal landing gear retraction/extension, normal and emergency wheel brake operation. It also operates the No 1 channels of the rudder, elevator, aileron and roll control spoiler actuators, the No 1 channels of the autopilot servos, the primary channel of the flap drive actuator, the flight and ground spoilers/airbrakes; finally, it charges the emergency brake system's hydraulic accumulator.

The *No 2 system* uses one of the pumps driven by the centre engine plus an NS-46 electric pump (which comes into action if the normal pump or the engine which drives it fails). It operates the No 2 channels of the control surface actuators, the No 2 channels of the autopilot servos, the nosewheel steering mechanism and provides for emergency gear extension. The NS-46 also enables ground testing of the Nos. 1 and 2 hydraulic systems with the engines inoperative.

The *No 3 system* uses the other pump driven by the centre engine plus an NS-46 electric pump. It operates the No 3 channels of the control surface actuators, the No 3 channels of the autopilot servos and also provides for emergency gear extension.

Main 27V DC power is supplied by two VU-6A transformer-rectifiers (*vypryamitel'noye oostroystvo*), with a third VU-6A as a back-up (it kicks in when one of the two main rectifiers fails). Backup DC power is also provided by the APU's 12-kilowatt GS-12TO generator/starter and two 12SAM-28 lead-acid batteries (28 A·h) or, on later aircraft, 20NKBN-25 nickel-cadmium batteries (25 A·h).

The galley equipment uses 27V/400Hz single-phase AC supplied by a TS375SO4A step-down transformer. There are no back-up power sources.

Two ground power receptacles (ShRA-400-3F for AC power and ShRAP-500K for DC power) are provided low on the starboard side of the forward fuselage just ahead of the nose gear unit.

De-icing System

The fixed root portions of the wing leading edge inboard of the slats, as well as the tail unit leading edges, engine air intake leading edges and inlet guide vanes/spinners, are de-iced by hot air bled from the 5th HP compressor stage (or the NK-8-2/-2U). The air exits through louvres on the wing upper surface near the slats' inboard ends, at the stabiliser tips and in the fin top fairing, as well as triple orifices near the air intake leading edges. The engines' intake de-icers function independently from the wing and tail unit de-icers. The hot-air part of the system remains operational even if two engines fail.

Electric de-icing on the leading edge slats, pitot heads, static ports (27V DC) and flightdeck windshield (115V AC); the heated panes are provided with an AOS-81 automatic temperature regulator (*avtomaht obogreva styokol*) to prevent cracking caused by overheating. From the inside the windshield is demisted by warm air. The port and starboard windshield panes are provided with electrically actuated wipers. The LE slat de-icers have sections operating full-time (the so-called 'thermal knives') and part-time (with heating/cooling phases).

An RIO-3 radioactive isotope icing detector (*rahdioizotopnyy indikahtor obledeneniya*) is installed on the starboard side of the nose; on the ground it is closed by a lead cover to protect ground personnel against radiation. Separate icing detectors are installed in the engines.

Fire Suppression System

Nine UBSh-2-1 fire extinguisher bottles charged with $114V_2$ grade chlorofluorocarbon in the rear fuselage equipment bay for fighting fires in the engine nacelles and in the APU bay with associated electromagnetic cocks and

Electrics

The electric system uses a single-wire layout (the airframe acts as the 'neutral' wire) with wires having heat-resistant insulation to improve fire safety. There are four subsystems. Main 200/115V/400Hz three-phase alternating current for the primary subsystem is supplied by three 40-kilowatt GT40PCh6 engine-driven AC generators with constant-speed drives. Back-up 200V AC power is provided by an identical generator driven by the APU; back-up 115V AC power for the VHF radio is provided by an MA-100 transformer. The secondary subsystems powered by the main one utilise 36V/400Hz three-phase AC, 27V DC and 27V single-phase AC respectively.

Aircraft up to and including Tu-154A CCCP-85055 had a primary AC system with three generators operating in parallel. On later aircraft the primary AC system comprised three separate circuits, each with its own generator. Normally the circuits operate independently; circuit 2 powered by the centre engine's generator serves the wing LE slat de-icers, while the other electric equipment is distributed approximately 50/50 between circuits 1 and 3. If a generator fails, the affected circuit switches automatically to an alternative generator.

The 36V/400Hz AC subsystem is powered by two TS330ChO4A three-phase step-down transformers (main and back-up). The latter are connected to the flight/navigation suite's distribution buses which, in turn, are connected to the No 1 or No 2 AC circuit. Emergency 36V AC power is supplied by a PT-200Ts-3S AC converter (*preobrazovahtel' tryokhfahznyy*) which is fed by the DC batteries.

distribution manifolds. The system has a three-stage operating algorithm; the first shot is triggered automatically by flame sensors, the second and third shots are fired manually at the discretion of the crew. Impact sensors are installed under the wingtips, on the main gear retraction struts and immediately ahead of the nosewheel well to trigger all fire extinguishers automatically in a belly landing.

A separate subsystem was originally installed on the Tu-154 *sans suffixe* for fighting fires inside the engines proper (two shots per engine); however, it proved inefficient and was deleted.

Additionally, portable fire extinguishers are provided in the cabin and flightdeck. As a fire precaution, the cabin trim and the insulation of the electric wiring are made of non-combustible materials.

An SSP-2A fire warning system (*sistema signalizahtsiï pozhahra*) with DPS-1AG flame sensors provides audio and visual warnings; the engines feature a separate 2S7K fire warning system. Smoke sensors are installed in the baggage compartments.

To prevent an explosion of the centre section fuel tanks (Nos. 1 and 4) in a belly landing, they are pressurised with inert gas (carbon dioxide) from bottles installed in the lower fuselage at frame 19. The inert gas pressurisation system is activated manually by the flight engineer 2-8 minutes before touchdown if a belly landing becomes imminent.

Air Conditioning & Pressurisation System

The entire fuselage between frames 4-66 is a ventilation-type pressure cabin. The Tu-154 has an integrated air conditioning and pressurisation system using air bled from the 5th HP compressor stages, the APU or supplied by a ground air handling unit hooked up to a ventral connector. At low altitudes, outside air may be used for ventilation. All three engines supply bleed air, but the system remains fully operational with one engine out. The air delivery rate is 5,100-6,600kg/hr (11,240-14,550 lb/hr), except during descent when the engines run at low power; this equals 30-40kg/hr (66-88 lb/hr) per person.

At 350°C (662°F) the engine bleed air is fed first into Model 4487 and Model 4458 air/air heat exchangers (located in the rear fuselage and the wing roots) and then into a Model 1621 cooling turbine. It is then humidified before being fed into the pressure cabin. Heating and ventilation air is processed separately. Ventilation air having a temperature of 10°C (50°F) is distributed by ducts running along the ceiling;

additionally, there are individual ventilation nozzles for every seat. For heating, air with a temperature of 70°C (158°F) is distributed near the floor, passing between the cabin wall lining and the fuselage structure so that the walls act as 'radiators'. In the flightdeck, air is directed at the glazing to stop it from misting up.

The ART-56-1 and ART-56-2 temperature regulators (*avtomaticheskiy regoolyator temperatoory*) automatically maintain a cabin temperature of 18-22°C (64-72°F), regardless of the altitude. On a hot day the temperature does not rise above 25°C (77°F). The flight engineer may set the temperature manually if the automatic control system goes down.

The Tu-154's pressurisation system maintains a pressure differential of 0.63kg/cm^2 (9.0psi) by means of a Model 2077AT regulator. At 12,000m (39,370ft) the cabin pressure equals that at 1,800m (5,900ft) above sea level. Excess air is spilled to the atmosphere by two Model 1766B solenoid valves low on the port side ahead of the wings; the outlets were provided with fairings on the Tu-154 *sans suffixe* and Tu-154A but these vanished on later versions. A horn sounds and a warning light illuminates to alert the crew in the event of decompression.

Oxygen System

A 92-litre (20.24 Imp gal) oxygen bottle charged to 30kg/cm^2 (428psi) feeds oxygen to six KP-24M masks (*kislorodnyy pribor*) in the flightdeck and at the flight attendants' jump seats, serving the crew to fight fatigue or in the event of decompression. The charging panel features a connector, a manometer and reduction gear reducing the pressure from 150kg/cm^2 (2,140psi) to 30kg/cm^2.

The flightdeck of Tu-154M 'Salon' RA-85782 with an upgraded flight instrumentation suite featuring two multi-function liquid-crystal displays on the centre instrument panel. Author

The captain's control console of RA-85782. Note the nosewheel steering tiller and the open direct vision window. Author

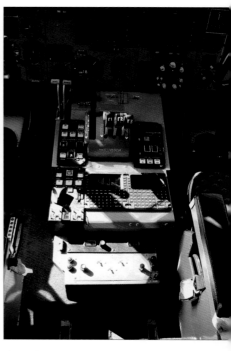

Above: **The first officer's control console of RA-85782.** Author

Right: **The centre control pedestal of RA-85782 carrying two I/O units.** Author

One KP-19M portable breathing apparatus with a 7.8-litre (1.7 Imp gal) oxygen bottle charged to 30kg/cm² is provided for the flight crew, along with nine KP-21 breathing apparatus with 1.7-litre (0.37 Imp gal) bottles charged to 30kg/cm² for the cabin crew and passengers. The portable apparatus are charged from the main bottle by means of a hose.

The VIP versions were completed with an automatic oxygen system having pop-out oxygen masks. Starting in 1993, some Tu-154B-2s and Tu-154Ms have been upgraded with automatic oxygen systems featuring chemical oxygen generators.

Avionics and Equipment

The Tu-154 is fully equipped for poor-weather day/night operation, including automatic flight assisted by an autopilot.

Navigation and piloting equipment: The Tu-154 *sans suffixe* has an NPK-154 navigation/flight director suite enabling automatic flight along designated airways and automatic blind landing with a decision altitude of 100m (330ft) and horizontal visibility of at least 1,200m (3,940ft). The NPK-154 includes the following:

- an NVU-B3 navigation computer working with a PA-3 moving-map display (MMD) indicating the aircraft's current position;
- an SVS-PN-15-4 air data system (*sistema vozdooshnykh signahlov*);
- a DISS-3P Doppler speed/drift sensor system (*doplerovskiy izmeritel' skorosti i snosa*) with antennas enclosed by a dielectric cover aft of the radome;
- a TKS-P2 precision compass system (*tochnaya koorsovaya sistema*);
- a Koors-MP1 (Heading) approach system (early aircraft only) replaced by the Koors-MP2 on later aircraft. The on-board part of the system includes a KRP-F localiser receiver (*koorsovoy*

rahdiopriyomnik), a GRP-2 glideslope beacon receiver (*glissahdnyy rahdiopriyomnik*) – both with antennas inside the radome, – an MRP-56P marker beacon receiver (*markernyy rahdiopriyomnik*) with an antenna buried in the underside of the nose and a module for working with Western ILS beacons;
- an ABSU-154 Srs 1 automatic flight control system (advanced autopilot) comprising the SAU-4 automatic control system (*sistema avtomaticheskovo oopravleniya*), the STU-154 flight director system (*sistema trayektornovo oopravleniya*), the AT-2 autothrottle (*avtomaht tyagi*) and the SVK-154 go-around system (*sistema [ukhoda na] vtoroy kroog*);
- an ARK-11 automatic direction finder (replaced by the ARK-15 on late aircraft) with a buried loop aerial in the forward fuselage roof and a ventral strake aerial in line with the wing leading edge; a backup ARK-15 ADF was fitted later;
- an RV-4 (RV-UM) radio altimeter (or an RV-5 on late aircraft) working in the 0-750m (0-2,460ft) altitude range with dipole aerials buried in the fuselage ahead of the rear pair of doors; a backup RV-5 was fitted later. The radio altimeter works with the Vektor ground proximity warning system;
- an RSBN-2SA Svod (Dome) short-range radio navigation system (*rahdiotekhnicheskaya sistema blizhney navigahtsii* – SHORAN) with flush antennas built into the fin (late aircraft only);
- SD-67 distance measuring equipment (*samolyotnyy dahl'nomer*) with rod aerials aft of the wing trailing edge; a backup set was fitted later;
- an AUASP-12KR automatic AoA/speed/G load limiter (*avtomaht ooglov atahki, skorosti i peregroozki*);
- a Groza-154 weather radar with a dish-type antenna (except the prototype Tu-154 *sans suffixe*, which had an ROZ-1 Lotsiya panoramic weather/navigation radar featuring an LTs-1 revolving antenna).

Early Tu-154As had the ABSU-154 Srs 1; on later aircraft it was replaced by an updated ABSU-154 Srs 1-1 AFCS allowing automatic blind landing in ICAO Cat I weather minima (decision altitude 60m/200ft, horizontal visibility 800m/2,600ft). The Tu-154B introduced the ABSU-154 Srs 2 giving the aircraft ICAO Cat II blind landing capability (decision altitude 30m/100ft, horizontal visibility 400m/1,310ft). The Tu-154A *et seq.* have the DISS-013 Trassa-A (Route-A) Doppler speed/drift sensor system.

The flight instrumentation is arranged on three instrument panels. The captain's instrument panel features a PKP-1 flight director (*pilotazhnyy komanhdnyy pribor*), a PNP-1 artificial horizon (*plahnovyy navigatsionnyy pribor*) – both part of the ABSU-154 AFCS, an AGR-144 backup artificial horizon (*aviagorizont rezervnyy*; later replaced by the AGR-72 model), a KUS-730/1100K combined airspeed indicator (*kombineerovannyy ookazahtel' skorosti*), a UAP-12KR AoA/G load indicator, VAR-30M and VAR-75M vertical speed indicators (the latter is used during emergency descent only; VAR = *variometr*), a VM-15 altimeter (*vysotomer*), a VMF-50 altimeter calibrated in feet (*vysotomer footovyy*), the indicator of the RV-5 radio altimeter, a UM-1K-0.82 Mach meter, a UVO-15K altitude indicator – both part of the SVS-PN-15-4 air data system, – and an IKU-1A course angle indicator (*indikahtor koorsovovo oogla*) which is part of the Koors-MP2 approach system. The first officer's instrument panel features a PKP-1 flight director, a PNP-1 artificial horizon, a KUS-730/1100K ASI, a VAR-30M VSI, a UM-1K-0.82 Mach meter, a UVO-15K altitude indicator, a USVP-K speed indicator – also part of the SVS-PN-15-4 air data system, an RV-5 radio altimeter indicator, an IKU-1A course angle indicator, the PPDA-Sh1 range and bearing indicator (*pryamopokazy-*

The front half of the forward cabin on RA-85782, looking aft; an enclosed privacy compartment for the 'main passenger' is on the left, with two armchairs and a table opposite. Author

The VIP's privacy compartment of RA-85782, looking towards the nose; note the LCD screen of the IFE system. Author

The rear half of the forward cabin on RA-85782, looking aft, with comfortable seats in a 'club-four' arrangement. Author

*ayushchiy pri**bor dahl**'nosti i ah*zimuta) of he SHORAN, the KM-5 correction mechanism of the TKS-P2 compass system, a BDK-1 emote correction module, TS-1 and TS-2 lights of the AUASP-12KR system (indicating critical AoA and critical G load respectively) and an AChS-1 clock (*aviatsi**onn**yye cha**sy** stre-* *ochnyye*). The pitot heads and static ports for he barometric instruments are located aft of he flightdeck.

The centre panel features three ITE-1T engine speed indicators, an IP-21-02 stabiliser rim indicator, a PPS-2MK flap and landing gear position indicator, seven TS-2 banks of caution/warning lights, the radar screen, an IP-3 MMD and various controls; other controls are located on the overhead circuit breaker panel. The central control pedestal carrying the throttles also mounts the controls of the NVU-B3 navigation computer, SHORAN and the Koors-MP2 approach system

The flight engineer's station features the engine instruments, the fuel, electrics and air conditioning/pressurisation system controls, the engine and APU starting control panels and more. Among other things, there are a KUS-730/1100K ASI, a VAR-30M VSI, a VM-15 altimeter, an SSN-4 dynamic pressure indicator *signali**zah**tor skoros**novo** napo**ra*) and a UVPD-5K cabin altitude and pressure indicator *ooka**zah**tel' vyso**ty** i pere**pah**da dav**len**iya*).

Communications equipment: For long-range air/ground communications (up to 3,000km/ 1,860 miles), the Tu-154 *sans suffixe* had an R-847 HF communications/command link radio with a antennas built into the fairing at the fin/tailplane junction (front and rear). Later aircraft have a Mikron HF radio with larger antennas in a recontoured fin top fairing. Short-range air/air and air/ground communications (up to 350km/217 miles) are catered for by two Lotos UHF radios with AShS aerials above the flightdeck and below the forward fuselage (replaced by Landysh-20 UHF radios with AShS-UD blade aerials on later versions). The Tu-154K, Tu-154A 'Salon', Tu-154B/B-1/B-2 'Salon' and Tu-154M 'Salon' may be fitted with additional secure HF communications equipment.

Communications equipment further includes an SPU-7 intercom (*samolyotnoye pere**govornoye** oo**stroy**stvo*) and an SGU-15 *samolyotnoye **grom**kogovorya**shcheye** oost-* *oystvo*) or SGS-25 (*samol**yot**naya **grom**ko-* *govorya**shchaya** sis**tema*) public address

This page:

Left: **The No 2 cabin of RA-85782, looking aft; note how the tabletops fold to facilitate access to the seats.** Author

Centre: **The rearmost cabin of RA-85782, looking aft; note how the tabletops fold to facilitate access to the seats.** Author

Bottom: **The rear cabin of Vnukovo Airlines Tu-154M RA-85619.** Igor' Sitchikhin

Opposite page:

Top left: **The bar located in the forward cabin just aft of the VIP's cubicle.** Author

Top centre: **The galley of Tu-154M 'Salon' RA-85782, looking aft.** Author

Top right: **The forward galley fitted to the Tu-154M in 176-seat configuration; the table folds up, enclosing the galley completely when not in use.** Igor' Sitchikhin

system featuring 35 Model 1GD18 loudspeakers in the two cabins and a Vesna-2 tape recorder for playing back music (replaced by an Arfa-MB tape recorder on later aircraft).

IFF system: SRO-2M Khrom IFF transponder (*izdeliye* 023) on civil aircraft, with characteristic triple rod aerials ahead of the flightdeck glazing and under the rear fuselage.

The aircraft also features an SO-70 ATC transponder (*samolyotnyy otvetchik* – aircraft-mounted responder), later augmented by SOM-64 (*samolyotnyy otvetchik mezhdunarodnyy* – aircraft-mounted international responder) and SO-72M transponders. These transmit the aircraft's registration, speed and altitude for presentation on ATC radar displays and may operate in 'Mayday' mode.

The antennas of the RSBN-2SA SHORAN, the Koors-MP2 approach system and the SOM-64 transponder are combined into a Pion-NP-154 (Peony; pronounced '*pee on*') integrated antenna/feeder system.

Data recording equipment: MSRP-12-96 flight data recorder (on the Tu-154 *sans suffixe* and most Tu-154As) and MS-61B cockpit voice recorder on a rack in the forward baggage compartment (frame 9). The FDR captures 12 parameters, including barometric altitude, indicated airspeed, roll rates, vertical and lateral G forces, control surface deflection and throttle settings, as well as gear/flap transition and so on.

Aircraft from Tu-154A CCCP-85088 onwards have an MSRP-64-2 or MSRP-64M-2 FDR and a Mars-BM CVR. All recorders have armoured shells to ensure survival in a crash.

Lighting equipment: Port (red) and starboard (green) BANO-57 navigation lights at the wingtips, KhS-62 white tail navigation light below the centre engine nozzle. Retractable PRF-4M landing/taxi lights (*posahdochno-*

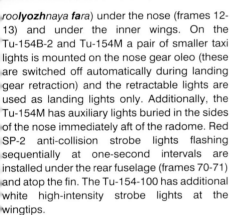

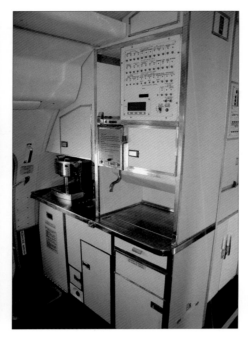

roolyozhnaya fara) under the nose (frames 12-13) and under the inner wings. On the Tu-154B-2 and Tu-154M a pair of smaller taxi lights is mounted on the nose gear oleo (these are switched off automatically during landing gear retraction) and the retractable lights are used as landing lights only. Additionally, the Tu-154M has auxiliary lights buried in the sides of the nose immediately aft of the radome. Red SP-2 anti-collision strobe lights flashing sequentially at one-second intervals are installed under the rear fuselage (frames 70-71) and atop the fin. The Tu-154-100 has additional white high-intensity strobe lights at the wingtips.

The flightdeck and baggage compartments feature PS-45 overhead lights and SBK side lights. On Kuznetsov-powered versions the cabin has combined overhead lights with LTB-15 luminescent lamps for high-intensity lighting and SM-28-5.1 light bulbs for low-intensity lighting, as well as cabin wall lighting; the Tu-154M has indirect overhead lighting. The passenger service units over the seats feature individual reading lights. Illuminated 'No smoking/Fasten seat belts' signs, seat row indicator lights and exit signs are provided.

Accommodation

The flightdeck is configured for a crew of three, with the flight engineer facing right. Provisions are made for a navigator and a radio operator or an inspector sitting on fold-down seats behind the pilots. The cabin crew comprises six flight attendants, including a purser.

The Tu-154 can be configured with first class (F), business class (C), tourist class (CY) and economy class (Y) seating.

Possible layouts for the Tu-154 *sans suffixe* as of 1973 were:
- a 158-seat all-economy layout (54+104 seats) with six-abreast seating at 75cm (29½in) pitch;

- a 164-seat all-economy layout for short high-density routes (60+104 seats) with a reduced galley to make room for an extra row of seats (only cold refreshments are served);
- a 128-seat layout (F24+Y104) featuring four-abreast seating at 102cm (40⁵⁄₃₂in) pitch in the forward cabin and six-abreast seating at 75cm pitch in the rear one. The seats in the first class cabin are sleeperette seats with backs reclining up to 45°.

The Tu-154A had the following interior layouts:
- a basic 152-seat all-tourist layout (54+98 seats at 75cm pitch);
- a winterised 144-seat all-tourist layout (54+90 seats);
- a 158-seat all-tourist layout with a smaller galley for short routes (60+98 seats);
- a 126-seat version (F12CY18+CY96) for TsUMVS with four-abreast seating at 105-cm (41²¹⁄₆₄in) pitch in the forward cabin and six-abreast seating at 75 or 96cm (29½ or 37⁵¹⁄₆₄in) in the rear one, depending on whether a rear wardrobe was fitted or not;
- a winterised 144-seat all-tourist configuration for TsUMVS (48+96 seats with a removable wardrobe aft);
- a 158-seat all-tourist basic version for Balkan Bulgarian Airlines (54+104 seats);
- a 164-seat all-tourist configuration with a smaller galley (60+104 seats) for Balkan Bulgarian Airlines;
- a 128-seat version (F24+CY104) for Balkan Bulgarian Airlines;
- a 134-seat version (F12CY18+CY104) for Malév;
- a 124-seat mixed-class basic version (F20+CY104) for Egyptair;
- a 120-seat mixed-class version (F16+CY104) for Egyptair;
- a 145-seat all-tourist version (41+104 seats) for Egyptair;
- a 151-seat all-tourist version (47+104 seats) for Egyptair.

The Tu-154B was produced in the following main versions:
- a basic 152-seat all-tourist layout (54+98 seats at 75cm pitch);
- a winterised 144-seat all-tourist layout (54+90 seats);
- a 124-seat mixed-class version for TsUMVS;
- a 136-seat all-tourist version for TsUMVS;
- a 132-seat mixed-class version for Pulkovo Airlines (C30+CY102) with four-abreast seating in the forward cabin;
138-, 140- and 146-seat versions of the Tu-154B were also available.

The Tu-154B-1 was produced in the following main versions:
- a 160-seat all-tourist version for Aeroflot's domestic routes;
- a 144-seat mixed-class version for TsUMVS.

The Tu-154B-2 was produced in the following main versions:
- a 160-seat all-tourist version for Aeroflot's domestic routes;
- a 180-seat all-economy version with no galley for high-density routes;
- a 99-seat mixed-class version for Aeroflot's 235th IAD;
- a 100-seat all-tourist version for the 235th IAD.

The Tu-154M was manufactured in the following main versions:
- a 154-seat mixed-class version;
- a 164-seat all-tourist version;
- a 166-seat all-tourist version (62+104 seats);
- a 176-seat all-economy version with no galley (the final production aircraft had 175 seats);
- a 144-seat mixed-class version for TsUMVS.
VIP versions were also built.

The lightweight seats were designed in-house for the Tu-154. They have folding backs and armrests and tip-up cushions to facilitate getting in/out; the seat backs recline at the push of a

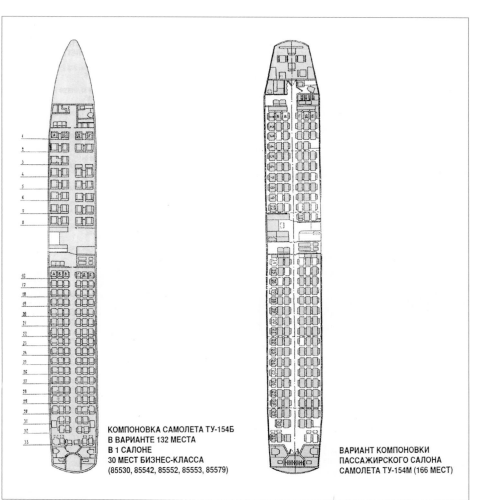

КОМПОНОВКА САМОЛЕТА ТУ-154Б
В ВАРИАНТЕ 132 МЕСТА
В 1 САЛОНЕ
30 МЕСТ БИЗНЕС-КЛАССА
(85530, 85542, 85552, 85553, 85579)

ВАРИАНТ КОМПОНОВКИ
ПАССАЖИРСКОГО САЛОНА
САМОЛЕТА ТУ-154М (166 МЕСТ)

installing additional wardrobes, increasing the total capacity to 150 overcoats.

The cabin walls are upholstered in easily washable non-combustible synthetic materials and the floor is covered with a carpet having a foam rubber base. The overhead luggage racks incorporate passenger service units with reading lams, individual ventilation nozzles and stewardess call buttons.

As standard the galley features a water boiler, an electric food heater, a sink with hot and cold water and storage lockers for tableware, food and drinks; aircraft with high-density seating lack the boiler and heater.

One toilet is located ahead of the forward cabin on the starboard side and three more at the rear of the rear cabin, so that the passengers are able to use them without passing through the galley. Each toilet features a metal toilet bowl, a water heater tank and a wash basin with a pedal-driven pump and mixing faucet. There is a circulation-type flushing system with electric pumps and filters which is charged with deodorant fluid. Water for the wash basins is stored in a 55-litre (12.1 Imp gal) tank.

Passenger evacuation in an emergency takes place via the emergency exits (forward starboard, overwing and rear) and the entry and service doors. The doors and exits (except the overwing exits) feature inflatable escape slides. Additionally, pieces of fuselage skin between frames 26-28 and 58-60 on each side can be chopped out in an emergency if the regular exits are unusable and is clearly marked in colour. For overwater flights the aircraft is equipped with inflatable life rafts, as well as life vests for all occupants.

button and incorporate meal trays (folding meal tables on the cabin bulkhead are provided for the first row of seats in each cabin). The seats feature seat belts and are stressed for longitudinal loads of 9Gs. The seat frame is shaped so as to provide adequate legroom even at the smallest seat pitch of 75cm. The seats and cabin partitions are provided with quick-release fittings,

allowing the aircraft to be easily reconfigured.

Three jump seats are installed near each entry door for the flight attendants; they are provided with seat belts and used for take-off and landing only. Wardrobes are provided near both entry doors for a total of 60 overcoats. In the winter season the two rearmost rows of seats in the rear cabin may be removed for

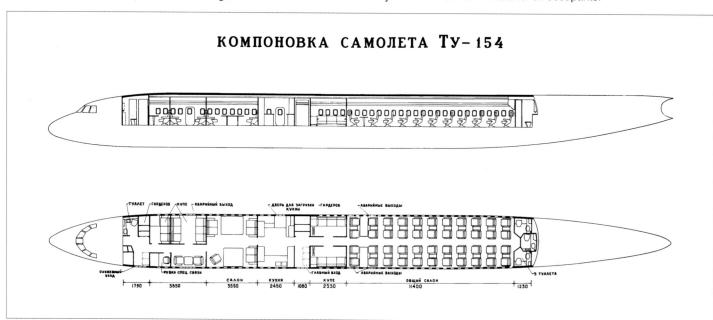

КОМПОНОВКА САМОЛЕТА Ту-154

Tu-154 Family Specifications

	Tu-154	Tu-154A	Tu-154B	Tu-154S	Tu-154M
Powerplant	3 x NK-8-2	3 x NK-8-2U	3 x NK-8-2U	3 x NK-8-2U	3 x D-30KP-154 II
Take-off rating, kgp (lbst)	3 x 9,580 (3 x 21,120)	2 x 10,500 (2 x 23,150)	2 x 10,500 (2 x 23,150)	2 x 10,500 (2 x 23,150)	2 x 10,500 (2 x 23,150)
Length overall	47.9m (157' 1⁵⁄₆₄")	47.9m (157' 1⁵⁄₆₄")	47.9m (157' 1⁵⁄₆₄")	47.9m (157' 1⁵⁄₆₄")	48.0m (157' 5⁹⁄₆₄")
Fuselage length	42.33m (138' 10¹⁷⁄₃₂")	42.33m (138' 10¹⁷⁄₃₂")	42.33m (138' 10¹⁷⁄₃₂")	42.33m (138' 10¹⁷⁄₃₂")	42.33m (138' 10¹⁷⁄₃₂")
Wing span	37.55m (123' 2¹⁄₂")	37.55m (123' 2¹⁄₂")	37.55m (123' 2¹⁄₂")	37.55m (123' 2¹⁄₂")	37.55m (123' 2¹⁄₂")
Stabiliser span	13.4m (43' 11⅜")	13.4m (43' 11⅜")	13.4m (43' 11⅜")	13.4m (43' 11⅜")	13.4m (43' 11⅜")
Height on ground	11.4m (37' 4¹³⁄₁₆")	11.4m (37' 4¹³⁄₁₆")	11.4m (37' 4¹³⁄₁₆")	11.4m (37' 4¹³⁄₁₆")	11.4m (37' 4¹³⁄₁₆")
Turning radius (measured by wingtip)	22m (72' 0")	22m (72' 0")	22m (72' 0")	22m (72' 0")	22m (72' 0")
Wing area, m² (ft²)	201.45 (2,166.12)	201.45 (2,166.12)	201.45 (2,166.12)	201.45 (2,166.12)	201.45 (2,166.12)
Flap area, m² (ft²):					
inboard	2 x 7.5 (2 x 80.64)	2 x 7.5 (2 x 80.64)	2 x 7.5 (2 x 80.64)	2 x 7.5 (2 x 80.64)	2 x 7.5 (2 x 80.64)
outboard	2 x 11.0 (2 x 118.27)	2 x 11.0 (2 x 118.27)	2 x 11.0 (2 x 118.27)	2 x 11.0 (2 x 118.27)	2 x 11.0 (2 x 118.27)
Ground spoiler area, m² (ft²)	2 x 2.78 (2 x 29.89)	2 x 2.78 (2 x 29.89)	n/a	n/a	n/a
Flight spoiler area, m² (ft²)	2 x 2.0 (2 x 21.5)	2 x 2.0 (2 x 21.5)	n/a	n/a	n/a
Roll control spoiler area, m² (ft²)	2 x 1.45 (2 x 15.59)	2 x 1.45 (2 x 15.59)	n/a	n/a	n/a
Aileron area, m² (ft²)	2 x 1.73 (2 x 18.6)	2 x 1.73 (2 x 18.6)	n/a	n/a	n/a
Vertical tail area, m² (ft²)	31.725 (341.12)	31.725 (341.12)	31.725 (341.12)	31.725 (341.12)	31.725 (341.12)
Fin area, m² (ft²)	24.255 (260.8)	24.255 (260.8)	24.255 (260.8)	24.255 (260.8)	24.255 (260.8)
Rudder area, m² (ft²)	7.535 (81.02)	7.535 (81.02)	7.535 (81.02)	7.535 (81.02)	7.535 (81.02)
Horizontal tail area, m² (ft²)	40.55 (436.02)	40.55 (436.02)	40.55 (436.02)	40.55 (436.02)	42.0 (451.61)
Stabiliser area, m² (ft²)	32.09 (345.05)	32.09 (345.05)	32.09 (345.05)	32.09 (345.05)	32.09 (345.05)
Elevator area, m² (ft²)	2 x 4.23 (2 x 45.48)	2 x 4.23 (2 x 45.48)	2 x 4.23 (2 x 45.48)	2 x 4.23 (2 x 45.48)	2 x 4.9 (2 x 52.68)
Dry weight, kg (lb)	45,700 (100,750)	n/a	50,650 (111,660)	n/a	
Operating empty weight, kg (lb):					
bulk baggage	47,200 (104,060)	49,500 (109,130)	52,000 (114,640)	52,000 (114,640)	53,500 (117,950) [1]
containerised baggage	48,700 (107,360)	50,600 (111,550)	54,000 (119,050)		
MTOW, kg (lb)	90,000 (198,410)	94,000 (207,230)	96,000 (211,640)	98,000 (216,050)	100,000 (220,460)
Max landing weight, kg (lb)	75,000 (165,340)	78,000 (171,960)	80,000 (176,370)	80,000 (176,370)	80,000/82,000 (176,370/180,780)
Max taxi weight, kg (lb)	90,500 (199,510)	94,500 (208,330)	98,500/100,500 (217,150/221,560)	98,500 (217,150)	100,500/102,500 (221,560/225,970)
Max payload, kg (lb)	16,500-18,000 (36,375-39,680)	18,000 (39,680)	18,000 (39,680)	20,000 (44,090)	18,000 (39,680)
Max fuel load, kg (lb)	33,150 (73,080)	39,750 (87,630)	39,750 (87,630)	39,750 (87,630)	39,750 (87,630)
Wing loading at MTOW, kg/m² (lb/ft²)	500 (102.5)	n/a	n/a	n/a	n/a
Maximum cruising speed, km/h (mph)	945 (587) [2]	950 (590)	950 (590)	950 (590)	935 (587)
Economic cruising speed at 10,000-11,000m (32,820-36,090ft), km/h (mph)	900/850 (559/528) [3]	900 (559)	900 (559)	900 (559)	850 (528)
Service ceiling, m (ft)	11,700 (38,385) [4]	n/a	12,300 (40,350)	12,300 (40,350)	12,000 (39,370)
Range, km (miles): [5]					
with a 18,000-kg payload/bulk baggage	2,500 (1,550)	3,000 (1,860)	2,650 (1,550)	2,900 (1,800) [9]	3,500-3,800 (2,170-2,360)
with a 16,000-kg payload/bulk baggage	2,850 (1,770)	3,300 (2,050)	3,250 (2,020) [7]		4,050 (2,515) [10]
with max fuel and a 10,100-kg payload/bulk baggage	3,850 (2,390)	4,000 (2,480) [6]	4,980 (3,090) [8]		6,500 (4,040) [11]
with a 16,500-kg max payload/containers	2,500 (1,550)	n/a	n/a		
with a 16,000-kg payload/containers	2,600 (1,615)	n/a	n/a		
with max fuel and a 8,600-kg payload/containers	3,850 (2,390)	n/a	n/a		
Take-off run (MTOW, ISA), m (ft)	1,200-1,250 (3,940-4,100)	n/a	1,290 (4,230)	1,290 (4,230)	n/a
Runway length (MTOW, ISA), m (ft)	2,000-2,080 (6,560-6,820)	2,000 (6,560)	2,030 (6,660)	2,030 (6,660)	2,500 (8,200)
Landing run, m (ft)	1,000-1,060 (3,280-3,480)	n/a	1,000 (3,280)	1,000 (3,280)	n/a
Runway length, m (ft)	2,190-2,300 (7,185-7,545)	n/a	2,250 (7,380)	2,250 (7,380)	n/a
Fuel efficiency, g/seat-km	n/a	n/a	46.5 [12]	–	31.0-32.9

1. Also reported as 55,500kg (122,350 lb). Late-production Tu-154Ms have an operating empty weight of 59,000kg (122,350 lb); 2. At 10,300m (33,790ft), all-up weight 80,000kg (lb), nominal power; 3. At 11,000m (36,090ft), range up to/over 2,450km (1,520 miles); 4. TOW 90,000kg; 5. At 11,000m, no wind, cruising speed 900km/h, MTOW, 6,000-kg (13,120-lb) fuel reserves. The figures stated for the Tu-154M are for a cruise altitude of 11,400m (37,400ft) and 5,000kg (11,020 lb) fuel reserves. 6. With a 12,500-kg (26,455-lb) payload; 7. With a 14,500-kg (31,970-lb) payload; 8. With a 4,750-kg (10,470-lb) payload, the figures stated for the Tu-154B show effective range. Maximum range at 850km/h with the same TOW and payloads is 2,760km (1,710 miles), 3,400km (2,110 miles) and 5,230km (3,250 miles); 9. With a 20,000-kg (44,090-lb) payload; 10. With a 16,600-kg (36,600-lb) payload; 11. With a 5,450-kg (12,015-lb) payload; 12. 44.5g/seat-km for the Tu-154B-1 and 40.5g/seat-km for the Tu-154B-2

Production List

Tu-154 production is presented in construction number order, with all identities worn consecutively by each aircraft. 'Deceased' examples (that is, crashed or destroyed in accidents) are marked with † (RIP crosses) followed by the date of the accident. Registrations followed by * indicate quasi-civil aircraft, while ‡ indicates the aircraft was military at first but was later sold or transferred to a civil operator. Registrations given in bold italics and with no hyphen are test registrations worn temporarily by export aircraft. Registrations given in square brackets were allocated but not taken up; those given in parentheses are ATC callsigns (not worn visibly) of aircraft in overt military markings – or military serials allocated to quasi-civil aircraft. The sign § after a name given to an individual aircraft means that the aircraft received this name after a change of operator, having previously flown nameless with the same registration. In the 'Version' column, 'Salon' ** indicates aircraft with an HF secure communications system, while 'Salon' ‡ means the aircraft was later converted to airline configuration.

Construction number	Version	Registration/ tactical code/serial	Manufacture date
KKh1	Tu-154	CCCP-85000	
no c/n?	Tu-154	static test airframe	
no c/n?	Tu-154	fatigue test airframe	
69M001	Tu-154	CCCP-85701 No 1 (see c/n 91A876!), CCCP-85001	
70M002?	Tu-154	CCCP-85702 No 1 (see c/n 91A877!), CCCP-85002	
70M003?	Tu-154	CCCP-85703 No 1 (see c/n 91A878!), CCCP-85003	
70M004?	Tu-154	CCCP-85704 No 1 (see c/n 91A879!), CCCP-85004	
70M005?	Tu-154	CCCP-85005	
70M006	Tu-154	CCCP-85006	
70M007	Tu-154, Tu-154B	CCCP-85007, RA-85007 No 1 (see c/n 88A777!)	17-8-1970
70M008	Tu-154	CCCP-85008, 85008	
70M009	Tu-154	CCCP-85009, UR-85009	
70M010	Tu-154	CCCP-85010	
71A011	Tu-154	CCCP-85011	
71A012	Tu-154	CCCP-85012	
71A013	Tu-154, Tu-154B	CCCP-85013, RA-85013	
71A014	Tu-154	CCCP-85014	
71A015	Tu-154	CCCP-85015; Soviet/Russian Air Force '32 Red'?	
71A016	Tu-154, Tu-154B	CCCP-85016, RA-85016	
71A017	Tu-154	CCCP-85017	
71A018	Tu-154, Tu-154B-1	CCCP-85018, RA-85018	
71A019	Tu-154, Tu-154S	CCCP-85019, RA-85019 No 1 (see c/n 01A1019!)	
71A020	Tu-154	CCCP-85020 † ?-?-1975	
71A021	Tu-154	CCCP-85021, EX-85021	
71A022	Tu-154	CCCP-85022	
72A023	Tu-154	CCCP-85023 † 19-2-1973	
72A024	Tu-154, Tu-154B, Tu-154LL	CCCP-85024	
72A025	Tu-154	CCCP-85025	
72A026	Tu-154, Tu-154A, Tu-154B	CCCP85026, LZ-BTA	
72A027	Tu-154	CCCP85027, LZ-BTB † 23-3-1978	
72A028	Tu-154, Tu-154B	CCCP-85028, RA-85028	
72A029	Tu-154	CCCP-85029 † 13-6-1981	
72A030	Tu-154	CCCP-85030 † 7-5-1973	
72A031	Tu-154, Tu-154B-1	CCCP-85031, RA-85031	24-11-1972
72A032	Tu-154	CCCP-85032	12-6-1973
72A033	Tu-154, Tu-154B	CCCP-85033, RA-85033	
72A034	Tu-154, Tu-154B-1	CCCP-85034, RA-85034	
72A035	Tu-154, Tu-155	CCCP-85035	
73A036	Tu-154, Tu-154B	CCCP85036, LZ-BTC	
73A037	Tu-154, Tu-154S	CCCP-85037, RA-85037	
73A038	Tu-154	CCCP-85038, RA-85038	
73A039	Tu-154, Tu-154B	CCCP-85039, RA-85039	19-4-1973
73A040	Tu-154, Tu-154B	CCCP-85040	
73A041	Tu-154, Tu-154B	CCCP-85041, RA-85041	
73A042	Tu-154, Tu-154B	CCCP-85042, RA-85042	7-6-1973
73A043	Tu-154A, Tu-154B	CCCP-85043, RA-85043	
73A044	Tu-154A, Tu-154B	CCCP-85044, ER-85044	20-10-1973
73A045	Tu-154A, Tu-154B-2	CCCP85045, HA-LCA	9-8-1973
73A046	Tu-154A, Tu-154B-2	CCCP85046, HA-LCB, 'D-AFSG'	9-8-1973
73A047	Tu-154A, Tu-154B-2	CCCP85047, HA-LCE	16-9-1973
73A048	Tu-154A	CCCP85048, SU-AXB Nefertiti † 9-7-1964	
73A049	Tu-154A	CCCP85049, SU-AXC Hatshepsut, CCCP-85049*	
73A050	Tu-154A	CCCP85050, SU-AXD Ti, CCCP-85050*, 85050*, 'HK-85050', UK-85050*	
73A051	Tu-154A	CCCP85051, SU-AXE Nefertari, CCCP-85051, LZ-BTL No 1 (see c/n 77A208!), CCCP-85051, LZ-BTR No 1 (see c/n 79A320!), CCCP-85051, HA-LCL, CCCP-85051, RA-85051	
73A052	Tu-154A, Tu-154B	CCCP85052, SU-AXF, CCCP-85052, LZ-BTM No 1 (see c/n 77A209!), CCCP-85052*, RA-85052*	

Construction number	Version	Registration/ tactical code/serial	Manufacture date
74A053	Tu-154A	CCCP85053, SU-AXG Howait-Hur, CCCP-85053*, HA-LCI † 30-9-1975	
74A054	Tu-154A	CCCP85054, SU-AXH Ptah-Howait, CCCP-85054*, HA-LCK, CCCP-85054 ‡, LZ-BTN No 1 (see c/n 90A832!) † 2-12-1977	
74A055	Tu-154A	CCCP85055, SU-AXI, CCCP-85055 ‡	
74A056	Tu-154A	CCCP-85056, RA-85056	17-4-1974
74A057	Tu-154A	CCCP-85057, RA-85057	17-4-1974
74A058	Tu-154A, Tu-154B	CCCP85058, LZ-BTD † 5-6-1992	
74A059	Tu-154A, Tu-154B-1	CCCP-85059	19-3-1974
74A060	Tu-154A, Tu-154S	CCCP-85060, RA-85060	
74A061	Tu-154A, Tu-154B	CCCP-85061, RA-85061	24-4-1974
74A062	Tu-154A, Tu-154S	CCCP-85062, RA-85062	
74A063	Tu-154A, Tu-154S	CCCP-85063	
74A064	Tu-154A, Tu-154B-1	CCCP-85064, RA-85064	
74A065	Tu-154A	CCCP-85065	
74A066	Tu-154A, Tu-154B	CCCP-85066, UN-85066	25-6-1974
74A067	Tu-154A, Tu-154S	CCCP-85067 † 13-1-1989	10-7-1974
74A068	Tu-154A, Tu-154B	CCCP-85068, UR-85068	
74A069	Tu-154A, Tu-154B-1	CCCP-85069, RA-85069	
74A070	Tu-154A, Tu-154B, Tu-154B-1	CCCP-85070, RA-85070	12-7-1974
74A071	Tu-154A	CCCP-85071	
74A072	Tu-154A	CCCP-85072	
74A073	Tu-154A, Tu-154B	CCCP85073, LZ-BTE	
74A074	Tu-154A	CCCP-85074, UR-85074	
74A075	Tu-154A, Tu-154B	CCCP-85075, UR-85075, RA-85075	24-10-1974
74A076	Tu-154A, Tu-154B	CCCP-85076, UN-85076	
74A077	Tu-154A, Tu-154B	CCCP85077, LZ-BTF	
74A078	Tu-154A, Tu-154B-1	CCCP-85078, RA-85078	
74A079	Tu-154A	CCCP-85079	
74A080	Tu-154A, Tu-154B	CCCP-85080, RA-85080	
74A081	Tu-154A, Tu-154S	CCCP-85081, RA-85081 No 1 (see c/n 85A717!)	
74A082	Tu-154A	CCCP-85082	
74A083	Tu-154A, Tu-154LL	CCCP-85083	
74A084	Tu-154A, Tu-154S	CCCP-85084, RA-85084	5-11-1974
74A085	Tu-154A	CCCP-85085 (see c/n 90A855!)	
74A086	Tu-154A, Tu-154S	CCCP-85086	
74A087	Tu-154A	CCCP-85087	
74A088	Tu-154A	CCCP-85088	
74A089	Tu-154A, Tu-154B-1	CCCP-85089, RA-85089 No 1 (see c/n 90A838!)	17-12-1974
75A090	Tu-154A, Tu-154B	CCCP-85090, ER-85090	29-1-1975
75A091	Tu-154A, Tu-154B-1	CCCP-85091, 85091	
75A092	Tu-154A	CCCP-85092, RA-85092 No 1 (see c/n 89A799!)	17-1-1975
75A093	Tu-154A	CCCP-85093, UR-85093	
75A094	Tu-154A	CCCP-85094, RA-85094	4-2-1975
75A095	Tu-154A	CCCP85095, LZ-BTG	
75A096	Tu-154K, Tu-154A, Tu-154B-1	CCCP-85096, RA-85096 No 1 (see c/n 89A800!)	22-2-1975
75A097	Tu-154K, Tu-154A, Tu-154B-1	CCCP-85097 † 23-5-1991	
75A098	Tu-154A, Tu-154B	CCCP-85098, RA-85098	
75A099	Tu-154A, Tu-154B	CCCP-85099, RA-85099	
75A100	Tu-154A	CCCP-85100	
75A101	Tu-154A, Tu-154B-1	CCCP-85101, RA-85101 No 1 (see c/n 88A783!)	20-4-1975
75A102	Tu-154A	CCCP-85102 † 1-6-1976	9-4-1975
75A103	Tu-154A	CCCP-85103 † 1-3-1980	12-5-1975
75A104	Tu-154A, Tu-154B	CCCP-85104, 85104, RA-85104	
75A105	Tu-154A	CCCP-85105 † 5-12-1992	26-4-1975
75A106	Tu-154A, Tu-154B-2	CCCP-85106, RA-85106	24-9-1975
75A107	Tu-154A, Tu-154B-1	CCCP-85107, RA-85107	
75A108	Tu-154A, Tu-154B, Tu-154LL	CCCP-85108	
75A109	Tu-154A, Tu-154B-1	CCCP-85109, RA-85109 No 1 (see c/n 88A790!)	27-6-1975
75A110	Tu-154A, Tu-154B-1	CCCP-85110, RA-85110	

Construction number	Version	Registration/ tactical code/serial	Manufacture date[1]
5A111	Tu-154A, Tu-154B-1	CCCP-85111, UN 85111	15-2-1975
5A112	Tu-154A, Tu-154B-1	CCCP-85112, RA-85112	
5A113	Tu-154A, Tu-154B-1	CCCP-85113, UN 85113	
5A114	Tu-154A	CCCP-85114, RA-85114 No 1 (see c/n 89A814!)	1-8-1975
5A115	Tu-154A, Tu-154B	CCCP-85115, RA-85115	15-7-1975
5A116	Tu-154A	CCCP-85116, UR-85116	
5A117	Tu-154A, Tu-154B-1	CCCP-85117, RA-85117	1-8-1975
5A118	Tu-154A, Tu-154B	CCCP-85118, UR-85118	
5A119	Tu-154A, Tu-154B-1, Tu-154LL	CCCP-85119	
5A120	Tu-154B	CCCP-85120	
5A121	Tu-154B	CCCP-85121, UN 85121	
5A122	Tu-154A, Tu-154B	CCCP-85122, 'EW-85122'	
5A123	Tu-154B	CCCP-85123, RA-85123 No 1	16-12-1975
5A124	Tu-154B, Tu-154B-1	CCCP-85124, RA-85124	
5A125	Tu-154B	CCCP-85125	
5A126	Tu-154B	***CCCP85126***, HA-LCF † ***21-10-1981***	*10-1975*
5A127	Tu-154B, Tu-154B-2	***CCCP85127***, HA-LCG	*1-11-1975*
5A128	Tu-154B, Tu-154B-2	***CCCP85128***, HA-LCH	*12-11-1975*
5A129	Tu-154B	***CCCP85129***, 551, P-551 (P5-CVA)	
5A130	Tu-154B	CCCP-85130, RA-85130	24-12-1975
5A131	Tu-154B	CCCP-85131	
6A132	Tu-154B ('Salon'? ‡)	CCCP-85132, [HA-LIB], UR-85132	
6A133	Tu-154B 'Salon' ‡	CCCP-85133, YL-LAA, RA-85133	
5A134	Tu-154B	CCCP-85134	
6A135	Tu-154B	CCCP-85135, RA-85135 No 1 (see c/n 92A922!)	15-6-1976
6A136	Tu-154B	**CCCP-8**5136 (see c/n 88A791!)	26-1-1976
6A137	Tu-154B	CCCP-85137, UR-85137	
6A138	Tu-154B	CCCP-85138	
6A139	Tu-154B	CCCP-85139, RA-85139	
6A140	Tu-154B	CCCP-85140, RA-85140 No 1 (see c/n 85A716!)	
6A141	Tu-154B, Tu-154B-1	CCCP-85141, RA-85141	
6A142	Tu-154B	CCCP-85142, RA-85142	28-2-1976
6A143	Tu-154B	***CCCP85143***, 552, P-552 (P5-CVB)	
6A144	Tu-154B	***CCCP85144***, LZ-BTK	
6A145	Tu-154B	CCCP-85145, [HA-LIC], RA-85145	
6A146	Tu-154B	CCCP-85146, RA-85146 No 1 (see c/n 86A724!)	31-3-1976
6A147	Tu-154B ('Salon'? ‡)	CCCP-85147, 85147, 4K-85147	19-3-1976
6A148	Tu-154B	CCCP-85148, UR-85148	
6A149	Tu-154B	**CCCP-8**5149 (see c/n 89A797!)	
6A150	Tu-154B	CCCP-85150, RA-85150	5-4-1976
6A151	Tu-154B	CCCP-85151, UN 85151	19-4-1976
6A152	Tu-154B	CCCP-85152, UR-85152	
6A153	Tu-154B	CCCP-85153, RA-85153	31-5-1976
6A154	Tu-154B	CCCP-85154, UR-85154	31-5-1976
6A155	Tu-154B	CCCP-85155, RA-85155	
6A156	Tu-154B	CCCP-85156, RA-85156	14-6-1976
6A157	Tu-154B	CCCP-85157, RA-85157	10-8-1976?
6A158	Tu-154B	CCCP-85158, 85158, 4K-85158	
6A159	Tu-154B	***CCCP85159***, YR-TPA	
6A160	Tu-154B	CCCP-85160, RA-85160	30-6-1976
6A161	Tu-154B	***CCCP85161***, YR-TPB	
6A162	Tu-154B	CCCP-85162, EK-85162	
6A163	Tu-154B ('Salon'? ‡)	CCCP-85163, 85163 † ***22-9-1993***	
6A164	Tu-154B	CCCP-85164, RA-85164 † ***6-12-1995***	
6A165	Tu-154B	CCCP-85165, RA-85165	4-8-1976
6A166	Tu-154B ('Salon'? ‡), Tu-154B-1	CCCP-85166, EK-85166	
6A167	Tu-154B	CCCP-85167, RA-85167	20-8-1976
6A168	Tu-154B	CCCP-85168, 85168, 4L-85168	
6A169	Tu-154B	CCCP-85169 † ***19-5-1978***	
6A170	Tu-154B, Tu-154B-1	CCCP-85170	
6A171	Tu-154B	CCCP-85171, RA-85171 No 1 (see c/n 91A893!)	
6A172	Tu-154B	CCCP-85172, RA-85172	
6A173	Tu-154B, Tu-154B-1	CCCP-85173, UN 85173	
6A174	Tu-154B	CCCP-85174, RA-85174	
6A175	Tu-154B	***CCCP85175***, YR-TPC	
6A176	Tu-154B ('Salon'? ‡), Tu-154B-1	CCCP-85176, RA-85176	20-10-1976
6A177	Tu-154B	CCCP-85177, 85177, 4K-85177	23-10-1976
6A178	Tu-154B, Tu-154B-1	CCCP-85178, RA-85178	
6A179	Tu-154B, Tu-154B-1	CCCP-85179, UR-85179	29-11-1976
6A180	Tu-154B, Tu-154B-1	CCCP-85180, RA-85180	***29-11-1976***
6A181	Tu-154B, Tu-154B-1	CCCP-85181, RA-85181	
6A182	Tu-154B	CCCP-85182, RA-85182	29-11-1976
6A183	Tu-154B, Tu-154B-1	CCCP-85183, RA-85183	
6A184	Tu-154B	CCCP-85184, RA-85184	
6A185	Tu-154B, Tu-154B-1	CCCP-85185, RA-85185 No 1 (see c/n 91A894!)	14-12-1976
6A186	Tu-154B	CCCP-85186	15-12-1976
6A187	Tu-154B	CCCP-85187, RA-85187 No 1 (see c/n 92A919!)	30-12-1976
6A188	Tu-154B	CCCP-85188, 85188, 4L-85188	30-12-1976
6A189	Tu-154B	CCCP-85189, UK 85189	8-6-1977
6A190	Tu-154B, Tu-154B-1	CCCP-85190, RA-85190	8-6-1977
7A191	Tu-154B	***CCCP85191***, 553, P-553	
7A192	Tu-154B, Tu-154B-1	CCCP-85192, 85192, 4K-85192	
7A193	Tu-154B	CCCP-85193, RA-85193	31-1-1977
7A194	Tu-154B, Tu-154B-1	CCCP-85194, UN 85194	
7A195	Tu-154B	CCCP-85195, RA-85195	
7A196	Tu-154B, Tu-154B-1	CCCP-85196, EK-85196	

Construction number	Version	Registration/ tactical code/serial	Manufacture date[1]
77A197	Tu-154B, Tu-154B-1	CCCP-85197, 4L-85197	
77A198	Tu-154B, Tu-154B-1	CCCP-85198	28-2-1977
77A199	Tu-154B, Tu-154B-1	CCCP-85199, 85199, 4K-85199	
77A200	Tu-154B	CCCP-85200, EK-85200	
77A201	Tu-154B, Tu-154B-1	CCCP-85201, RA-85201	18-3-1977
77A202	Tu-154B	CCCP-85202, RA-85202	
77A203	Tu-154B	CCCP-85203	18-3-1977
77A204	Tu-154B, Tu-154B-1	CCCP-85204, RA-85204 No 1 (see c/n 91A886!)	
77A205	Tu-154B, Tu-154B-1	CCCP-85205, RA-85205	
77A206	Tu-154B, Tu-154B-1	CCCP-85206, RA-85206	
77A207	Tu-154B, Tu-154B-1	CCCP-85207, RA-85207	
77A208	Tu-154B	***CCCP85208***, LZ-BTL No 2 (see c/n 73A051!)	
77A209	Tu-154B	***CCCP85209***, LZ-BTM No 2 (see c/n 73A052!)	
77A210	Tu-154B, Tu-154B-1	CCCP-85210, EK-85210	
77A211	Tu-154B	CCCP-85211, 4K-85211	
77A212	Tu-154B, Tu-154B-1	CCCP-85212, RA-85212	
77A213	Tu-154B	CCCP-85213, RA-85213	31-5-1977
77A214	Tu-154B, Tu-154B-1	CCCP-85214, 85214, 4K-85214	
77A215	Tu-154B, Tu-154B-1	CCCP-85215, RA-85215	?-6-1977
77A216	Tu-154B ('Salon'? ‡), Tu-154B-1	CCCP-85216, RA-85216	11-6-1977
77A217	Tu-154B, Tu-154B-1	CCCP-85217, RA-85217, EW-85217, RA-85217	30-6-1977
77A218	Tu-154B, Tu-154B-1	CCCP-85218, UR-85218	
77A219	Tu-154B	CCCP-85219, RA-85219	30-6-1977
77A220	Tu-154B, Tu-154B-1	CCCP-85220, RA-85220	***16-6-1977***
77A221	Tu-154B, Tu-154B-1, Tu-154B-2	CCCP-85221, UN 85221	1-7-1977
77A222	Tu-154B	CCCP-85222 † ***20-7-1992***	
77A223	Tu-154B, Tu-154B-1	CCCP-85223, RA-85223	28-7-1977
77A224	Tu-154B	***CCCP85224***, YR-TPD	
77A225	Tu-154B	***CCCP85225***, YR-TPE	
77A226	Tu-154B, Tu-154B-1	CCCP-85226, RA-85226	
77A227	Tu-154B	CCCP-85227	
77A228	Tu-154B, Tu-154B-1	CCCP-85228, RA-85228	30-8-1977
77A229	Tu-154B, Tu-154B-1	CCCP-85229	
77A230	Tu-154B, Tu-154B-1	CCCP-85230, UN 85230	31-8-1977
77A231	Tu-154B-1	CCCP-85231, UN 85231	***1-9-1977***
77A232	Tu-154B-1	CCCP-85232, UR-85232	
77A233	Tu-154B-1	CCCP-85233	
77A234	Tu-154B-1	CCCP-85234 † ***7-1992***	11-9-1977
77A235	Tu-154B-1	CCCP-85235, RA-85235	18-9-1977
77A236	Tu-154B-1	CCCP-85236, RA-85236	
77A237	Tu-154B-1	CCCP-85237, RA-85237	
77A238	Tu-154B-1	CCCP-85238, RA-85238	24-10-1977
77A239	Tu-154B-1	***CCCP85239***, YR-TPF	
77A240	Tu-154B-1	CCCP-85240, UN 85240	
77A241	Tu-154B-1	CCCP-85241, EZ-85241	
77A242	Tu-154B-1	CCCP-85242, RA-85242	4-11-1977
77A243	Tu-154B-1	CCCP-85243 † ***11-11-1984***	
77A244	Tu-154B-1	CCCP-85244	
77A245	Tu-154B-1	CCCP-85245, UK 85245	
77A246	Tu-154B-1	CCCP-85246, EZ-85246	30-11-1977
77A247	Tu-154B-1	CCCP-85247, EY-85247	
77A248	Tu-154B-1	CCCP-85248, UK 85248	
77A249	Tu-154B-1	CCCP-85249, 85249, UK 85249	6-12-1977
77A250	Tu-154B-1	CCCP-85250, EZ-85250, 4K-85250, EZ-85250	22-12-1977
77A251	Tu-154B-1	CCCP-85251, EY-85251	
77A252	Tu-154B-1	CCCP-85252, EX-85252	
78A253	Tu-154B-1	CCCP-85253, RA-85253	24-1-1978
78A254	Tu-154B-1	CCCP-85254 † ***18-1-1988***	24-1-1978
78A255	Tu-154B-1 ('Salon'? ‡)	CCCP-85255, RA-85255	
78A256	Tu-154B-1	CCCP-85256, RA-85256	
78A257	Tu-154B-1	CCCP-85257, EX-85257	31-1-1978
78A258	Tu-154B-1	***CCCP85258***, LZ-BTO	
78A259	Tu-154B-1	CCCP-85259, EX-85259	21-2-1978
78A260	Tu-154B-1	CCCP-85260, EW-85260	21-2-1978
78A261	Tu-154B-1	CCCP-85261, RA-85261	19-2-1978
78A262	Tu-154B-1, Tu-154B-2	***CCCP85262***, YR-TPG, **UN** 85777 (see c/n 93A959!)	
78A263	Tu-154B-1	CCCP-85263, RA-85263	
78A264	Tu-154B-1, Tu-154B-2	CCCP-85264, RA-85264	22-3-1978
78A265	Tu-154B-1	CCCP-85265, RA-85265	22-3-1978
78A266	Tu-154B-1	CCCP-85266, RA-85266	
78A267	Tu-154B-1	CCCP-85267, RA-85267	14-3-1978
78A268	Tu-154B-1	CCCP-85268 † ***20-11-1990***	31-5-1978
78A269	Tu-154B-1	CCCP-85269	21-4-1978
78A270	Tu-154B-1 'Salon' ‡	***CCCP85270***, LZ-BTJ ‡	
78A271	Tu-154B-1	CCCP-85271, UN 85271	***21-4-1978***
78A272	Tu-154B-1	CCCP-85272, UK85272	21-4-1978
78A273	Tu-154B-1	CCCP-85273, RA-85273	
78A274	Tu-154B-1	CCCP-85274, 85274, 4K-85274	28-4-1978
78A275	Tu-154B-1	CCCP-85275, RA-85275	28-4-1978
78A276	Tu-154B-1	CCCP-85276, UN 85276	
78A277	Tu-154B-1	***CCCP85277***, YR-TPH † ***7-8-1980***	
78A278	Tu-154B-1	***CCCP85278***, LZ-BTP	
78A279	Tu-154B-1	CCCP-85279, EK-85279	
78A280	Tu-154B-1	CCCP-85280, RA-85280 No 1 (see c/n ??A1000!)	*6-1978*
78A281	Tu-154B-1	CCCP-85281, EY-85281 † ***17-12-1997***	22-6-1978
78A282	Tu-154B-1 ('Salon'? ‡)	CCCP-85282 † ***7-1992***	23-6-1978
78A283	Tu-154B-1	CCCP-85283, RA-85283	30-6-1978
78A284	Tu-154B-1	CCCP-85284, RA-85284	
78A285	Tu-154B-1	CCCP-85285, 85285, ER-85285, RA-85285	
78A286	Tu-154B-1	CCCP-85286, UK 85286	25-7-1978

Construction number	Version	Registration/tactical code/serial	Manufacture date[1]
78A287	Tu-154B-1	CCCP-85287, RA-85287	31-7-1978
78A288	Tu-154B-1	CCCP-85288, UR-85288	31-7-1978
78A289	Tu-154B-1	CCCP-85289, RA-85289	
78A290	Tu-154B-1	CCCP-85290	
78A291	Tu-154B-1	CCCP-85291, RA-85291	*2-8-1978?*
78A292	Tu-154B-1	CCCP-85292, RA-85292	
78A293	Tu-154B-1	CCCP-85293, RA-85293	31-8-1978
78A294	Tu-154B-1	CCCP-85294, 85294, EX-85294	1-9-1978
78A295	Tu-154B-2	CCCP-85295, RA-85295	
78A296	Tu-154B-2	CCCP-85296, RA-85296 † *25-12-1993/11-12-1994*	
78A297	Tu-154B-2	CCCP-85297	
78A298	Tu-154B-2	CCCP-85298, RA-85298	
78A299	Tu-154B-2	CCCP-85299, RA-85299	30-9-1978
78A300	Tu-154B-2	CCCP-85300, RA-85300	20-10-1978
78A301	Tu-154B-2	CCCP-85301, RA-85301	
78A302	Tu-154B-2	CCCP-85302, RA-85302	20-10-1978
78A303	Tu-154B-2	CCCP-85303, RA-85303	
78A304	Tu-154B-2	CCCP-85304, RA-85304	
78A305	Tu-154B-2	CCCP-85305, RA-85305	
78A306	Tu-154B-2	CCCP-85306, RA-85306	
78A307	Tu-154B-2	CCCP-85307, RA-85307	
78A308	Tu-154B-2	CCCP-85308, RA-85308	15-11-1978
78A309	Tu-154B-2	CCCP-85309, RA-85309	
78A310	Tu-154B-2	CCCP-85310, RA-85310	
78A311	Tu-154B-2	CCCP-85311 † *10-6-1985*	
78A312	Tu-154B-2	CCCP-85312, RA-85312 *San Sanych* §	14-12-1978
78A313	Tu-154B-2	CCCP-85313, 85313, EX-85313	
78A314	Tu-154B-2	CCCP-85314, RA-85314	
78A315	Tu-154B-2	CCCP-85315, RA-85315	
78A316	Tu-154B-2	CCCP-85316, UR-85316	
78A317	Tu-154B-2, Tu-154M, Tu-154M-LL	CCCP-85317, RA-85317	
79A318	Tu-154B-2	CCCP-85318, RA-85318	7-3-1979
79A319	Tu-154B-2	CCCP-85319, RA-85319	22-1-1979
79A320	Tu-154B-2	*CCCP85320*, LZ-BTR No 2 (see c/n 73A051!), CCCP-85742, RA-85742, UN-85742	
79A321	Tu-154B-2	CCCP-85321 † *8-8-1980*	
79A322	Tu-154B-2	CCCP-85322, UK 85322	
79A323	Tu-154B-2	CCCP-85323	
79A324	Tu-154B-2	CCCP-85324, ER-85324, UN-85324, RA-85324	
79A325	Tu-154B-2	*CCCP85325*, HA-LCM, 4K-325	*27-2-1979*
79A326	Tu-154B-2	*CCCP85326*, HA-LCN, no registration	9-2-1979
79A327	Tu-154B-2	CCCP-85327 † *21-5-1986*	
79A328	Tu-154B-2	CCCP-85328, RA-85328	28-2-1979
79A329	Tu-154B-2	CCCP-85329, 85329, 4K-85329	28-2-1979
79A330	Tu-154B-2	CCCP-85330, RA-85330	20-3-1979
79A331	Tu-154B-2	CCCP-85331, EW-85331	
79A332	Tu-154B-2	CCCP-85332, 85332, ER-85332, RA-85332	
79A333	Tu-154B-2	CCCP-85333, RA-85333	26-3-1979
79A334	Tu-154B-2	CCCP-85334, RA-85334	9-4-1979
79A335	Tu-154B-2 ('Salon'? ‡)	CCCP-85335 ‡, RA-85335	
79A336	Tu-154B-2	CCCP-85336, RA-85336	13-4-1979
79A337	Tu-154B-2	CCCP-85337, RA-85337	17-4-1979
79A338	Tu-154B-2	CCCP-85338 † *23-12-1984*	
79A339	Tu-154B-2	CCCP-85339, EW-85339	
79A340	Tu-154B-2	CCCP-85340, RA-85340	26-4-1979
79A341	Tu-154B-2	CCCP-85341, RA-85341	18-5-1979
79A342	Tu-154B-2	*CCCP85342*, YR-TPI	
79A343	Tu-154B-2	CCCP-85343, RA-85343	18-5-1979
79A344	Tu-154B-2	CCCP-85344, UK 85344	24-5-1979
79A345	Tu-154B-2	CCCP-85345, 85345, EZ-85345	13-5-1979
79A346	Tu-154B-2	CCCP-85346, RA-85346	28-5-1979
79A347	Tu-154B-2	CCCP-85347, RA-85347	
79A348	Tu-154B-2	CCCP-85348, RA-85348	
79A349	Tu-154B-2	CCCP-85349, RA-85349	19-6-1979
79A350	Tu-154B-2	CCCP-85350, UR-85350	*29-6-1979*
79A351	Tu-154B-2	CCCP-85351, RA-85351	29-6-1979
79A352	Tu-154B-2	CCCP-85352, EW-85352	4-7-1979
79A353	Tu-154B-2 ('Salon'?)	CCCP-85353*	
79A354	Tu-154B-2	CCCP-85354, RA-85354	7-1979
79A355	Tu-154B-2	CCCP-85355 † *7-7-1980*	
79A356	Tu-154B-2	CCCP-85356, UK 85356	23-7-1979
79A357	Tu-154B-2	CCCP-85357, RA-85357	31-7-1979
79A358	Tu-154B-2	CCCP-85358, RA-85358 *S'uyumbiké* §	31-7-1979
79A359	Tu-154B-2 ('Salon'? ‡)	CCCP-85359, 85359, 4L-85359	
79A360	Tu-154B-2	CCCP-85360*, RA-85360*	22-8-1979
79A361	Tu-154B-2	CCCP-85361, RA-85361	
79A362	Tu-154B-2	CCCP-85362, UR-85362, 4K-85362	
79A363	Tu-154B-2	CCCP-85363, RA-85363	30-8-1979
79A364	Tu-154B-2	CCCP-85364, 4K-85364	
79A365	Tu-154B-2	CCCP-85365, RA-85365, LZ-LTB, RA-85365	17-9-1979
79A366	Tu-154B-2	CCCP-85366, RA-85366	
79A367	Tu-154B-2	CCCP-85367, RA-85367	20-9-1979
79A368	Tu-154B-2	CCCP-85368, UR-85368	
79A369	Tu-154B-2	CCCP-85369, EX-85369	27-9-1979
79A370	Tu-154B-2	CCCP-85370, UK 85370	
79A371	Tu-154B-2	CCCP-85371, RA-85371	
79A372	Tu-154B-2	CCCP-85372, EW-85372	
79A373	Tu-154B-2	CCCP-85373, RA-85373	23-10-1979
79A374	Tu-154B-2	CCCP-85374, RA-85374	
79A375	Tu-154B-2	CCCP-85375, RA-85375	31-10-1979
79A376	Tu-154B-2	CCCP-85376, RA-85376	9-1979
79A377	Tu-154B-2	CCCP-85377, RA-85377	
79A378	Tu-154B-2	CCCP-85378, RA-85378	
79A379	Tu-154B-2	CCCP-85379, UR-85379	19-11-197
79A380	Tu-154B-2 ('Salon'?)	CCCP-85380*, RA-85380*	
79A381	Tu-154B-2	CCCP-85381, RA-85381	30-11-1979
79A382	Tu-154B-2	CCCP-85382, RA-85382	30-11-197
79A383	Tu-154B-2	CCCP-85383, EZ-85383	7-12-197
79A384	Tu-154B-2	CCCP-85384, [HA-LCZ], ER-85384, RA-85384	
79A385	Tu-154B-2	CCCP-85385, EY-85385, UN-85385, EY-85385	20-12-1979
79A386	Tu-154B-2	CCCP-85386, RA-85386	25-12-197
79A387	Tu-154B-2	CCCP-85387, UN 85387	
79A388	Tu-154B-2	CCCP-85388, RA-85388	
80A389	Tu-154B-2	CCCP-85389, RA-85389	
80A390	Tu-154B-2	CCCP-85390, RA-85390	23-1-198
80A391	Tu-154B-2	CCCP-85391, 85391, 4K-85391	25-1-1980
80A392	Tu-154B-2	CCCP-85392, RA-85392	
80A393	Tu-154B-2	CCCP-85393, RA-85393	
80A394	Tu-154B-2	CCCP-85394, 85394, EZ-85394	30-1-198
80A395	Tu-154B-2	CCCP-85395, UR-85395, 4K-85395, UR-85395, RA-85395	31-1-1980
80A396	Tu-154B-2	CCCP-85396, UN 85396	
80A397	Tu-154B-2	CCCP-85397, 85397, UK 85397	14-2-198
80A398	Tu-154B-2	CCCP-85398, 85398, UK 85398	21-2-1980
80A399	Tu-154B-2	CCCP-85399, UR-85399	21-2-1980
80A400	Tu-154B-2	CCCP-85400, RA-85400	28-2-198
80A401	Tu-154B-2	CCCP-85401, 85401, UK 85401	29-2-198
80A402	Tu-154B-2	CCCP-85402, RA-85402	14-3-1980
80A403	Tu-154B-2	CCCP-85403, EK-85403	
80A404	Tu-154B-2	CCCP-85404, RA-85404	
80A405	Tu-154B-2	CCCP-85405, ER-85405	24-4-198
80A406	Tu-154B-2	CCCP-85406, EY-85406	
80A407	Tu-154B-2	CCCP-85407, UR-85407	
80A408	Tu-154B-2 ('Salon'?)	*CCCP85408*, YR-TPJ † *9-2-1989*	
80A409	Tu-154B-2	CCCP-85409, RA-85409	26-4-1980
80A410	Tu-154B-2	CCCP-85410, EZ-85410	26-4-1980
80A411	Tu-154B-2	CCCP-85411, EW-85411	26-4-1980
80A412	Tu-154B-2	CCCP-85412, RA-85412	30-4-1980
80A413	Tu-154B-2	CCCP-85413 † *8-3-1988*	26-4-1980
80A414	Tu-154B-2	CCCP-85414, RA-85414	*21-4-1980*
80A415	Tu-154B-2	*CCCP85415*, YR-TPK	
80A416	Tu-154B-2	CCCP-85416, UK 85416	
80A417	Tu-154B-2	CCCP-85417, RA-85417	24-5-1980
80A418	Tu-154B-2	CCCP-85418, RA-85418	24-5-1980
80A419	Tu-154B-2	CCCP-85419, EW-85419	30-5-1980
80A420	Tu-154B-2 'Salon' ‡	*CCCP85420*, OK-BYA, Czechoslovak Air Force '0420 Black', Slovak Air Force '0420 White', RA-85842	7-1980
80A421	Tu-154B-2	CCCP-85421, RA-85421	
80A422	Tu-154B-2	CCCP-85422, LZ-BTS, UN 85422	6-1980
80A423	Tu-154B-2	CCCP-85423, UK 85423	20-6-1980
80A424	Tu-154B-2	CCCP-85424, RA-85424	25-7-1980
80A425	Tu-154B-2	CCCP-85425, RA-85425	25-6-1980
80A426	Tu-154B-2 'Salon' **	CCCP-85426*, RA-85426*	17-4-1981
80A427	Tu-154B-2	CCCP-85427, RA-85427	
80A428	Tu-154B-2	*CCCP85428*, YR-TPL	
80A429	Tu-154B-2	CCCP-85429, RA-85429	18-7-1980
80A430	Tu-154B-2	CCCP-85430, 85430, 4L-85430	10-7-1980
80A431	Tu-154B-2	CCCP-85431, UN 85431	8-7-1980
80A432	Tu-154B-2	CCCP-85432, RA-85432	
80A433	Tu-154B-2	CCCP-85433	
80A434	Tu-154B-2	CCCP-85434, RA-85434	
80A435	Tu-154B-2 ('Salon'? ‡)	CCCP-85435, RA-85435	22-8-1980
80A436	Tu-154B-2 ('Salon'? ‡)	CCCP-85436, RA-85436	*5-8-1980*
80A437	Tu-154B-2	CCCP-85437, RA-85437	25-8-1980
80A438	Tu-154B-2	CCCP-85438, 85438, UK 85438	30-8-1980
80A439	Tu-154B-2	CCCP-85439, RA-85439	29-8-1980
80A440	Tu-154B-2	CCCP-85440, EY-85440	
80A441	Tu-154B-2	CCCP-85441, RA-85441	12-9-1980
80A442	Tu-154B-2	CCCP-85442, EK-85442	
80A443	Tu-154B-2	CCCP-85443, RA-85443	24-9-1980
80A444	Tu-154B-2	CCCP-85444, EX-85444	10-9-1980
80A445	Tu-154B-2	CCCP-85445*, UR-85445*	
80A446	Tu-154B-2	CCCP-85446*, RA-85446*	
80A447	Tu-154B-2	*CCCP85447*, CU-T1222, CU-C1222, no registration	
80A448	Tu-154B-2	CCCP-85448, RA-85448	
80A449	Tu-154B-2	CCCP-85449, UK85449	
80A450	Tu-154B-2	CCCP-85450, RA-85450	23-10-1980
80A451	Tu-154B-2	CCCP-85451, RA-85451	28-10-1980
80A452	Tu-154B-2	CCCP-85452, RA-85452	20-10-1980
80A453	Tu-154B-2	CCCP-85453, RA-85453	21-11-1980
80A454	Tu-154B-2	CCCP-85454, RA-85454	15-11-1980
80A455	Tu-154B-2	CCCP-85455, UN 85455 † *21-1-1995*	
80A456	Tu-154B-2	CCCP-85456, RA-85456	16-3-1981
80A457	Tu-154B-2	CCCP-85457, RA-85457	
80A458	Tu-154B-2	CCCP-85458, RA-85458	29-11-1980
80A459	Tu-154B-2	CCCP-85459, RA-85459	*29-11-1980*
80A460	Tu-154B-2	CCCP-85460, UR-85460	
80A461	Tu-154B-2	CCCP-85461, RA-85461	*3-12-1980*
80A462	Tu-154B-2	CCCP-85462, RA-85462	
80A463	Tu-154B-2 ('Salon'? ‡)	CCCP-85463*, RA-85463 ‡, UN 85463 (*)	
80A464	Tu-154B-2 'Salon' **	CCCP-85464*, 85464, UN-85464	
80A465	Tu-154B-2	CCCP-85465, EW-85465	22-8-1981?
80A466	Tu-154B-2	CCCP-85466, EY-85466	

On 30th June 1979 Tu-154B **P-551** (c/n 75A129) of the North Korean airline Choson-minhang suffered serious damage during a messed-up landing at Budapest-Ferihegy; the aircraft used the ATC callsign P5-CVA that day. Luckily the damage was deemed to be repairable after all.

On 1st March 1980 Tu-154A **CCCP-85103** (c/n 75A103) belonging to TsUMVS/63rd Flight was making a flight from Karaukel'dy to Orenburg. On approach to Orenburg-Tsentral'nyy the crew made a series of errors, causing the aircraft to drop below glide path. As a result, the airliner undershot 50m (164ft) and landed with a vertical acceleration of 3G; a crack developed in the rear fuselage structure and the aircraft was declared a total loss. None of the crew or passengers suffered any harm.

On 7th July 1980 Tu-154B-2 **CCCP-85355** (c/n 79A355) of the Kazakh CAD/Alma-Ata UAD/218th Flight crashed immediately after take-off from Alma-Ata on a flight to Simferopol', killing all 163 occupants. The crash was caused by wind shear. Two minutes after take-off, having barely climbed to 120-150m (400-500ft), the aircraft entered a zone of high air temperature (30-40°C; 86-104°F) where the airspeed dropped because of the wind. Then the machine was caught in a downdraught and stalled, plunging nose down into a farm and a wheat field adjacent to the airport. The Tu-154 was totally destroyed by the impact and the post-crash fire.

On 7th August 1980 TAROM Romanian Airlines Tu-154B-1 **YR-TPH** (c/n 78A277) crashed into the sea on final approach to Nouadhibou, Mauretania.

The following day, on 8th August, Tu-154B-2 **CCCP-85321** (c/n 79A321) of the Far East CAD/1st Khabarovsk UAD/198th Flight was damaged beyond repair in a hard landing at Chita-Kadala. Luckily there were no casualties.

13th June 1981 turned out to be a fateful day for Tu-154 *sans suffixe* **CCCP-85029** (c/n 72A029) of the Moscow Transport CAD. When landing on a wet runway at Bratsk the aircraft was unable to stop in time and overran, suffering irreparable damage. Again, there were no fatalities this time.

On 21st October 1981 Malév Hungarian Airlines Tu-154B **HA-LCF** (c/n 75A126) was performing a scheduled flight from Amsterdam-Schiphol to Prague. When the aircraft was on short finals to Ruzyne airport, pilot error caused the machine to 'balloon', rising above the glide path. Without thinking the pilots deployed the lift dumpers, causing the aircraft to descend with an excessively high sink rate. As a result, the airliner impacted with a vertical acceleration of 4Gs which overstressed the airframe, the rear fuselage and tail unit breaking away. The crashed aircraft's forward fuselage was subsequently transported to Budapest and used as a teaching aid at the Flight Educational Centre at Ferihegy airport, eventually becoming an exhibit of the co-located Transport Museum in August 1997.

On 16th November 1981 Tu-154B-2 **CCCP-85480** (c/n 81A480) of the Krasnoyarsk CAD/1st Krasnoyarsk UAD/400th Flight was making a scheduled flight from Krasnoyarsk to Noril'sk. The aircraft was loaded incorrectly, with a too-far-forward CG. Additionally, on final approach to Noril'sk-Alykel' the airliner was above glideslope and the pilots retarded the throttles to lose the excessive altitude. As they did so, a glitch in the autothrottle caused the latter to throttle the engines all the way back to ground idle and the machine started descending with an excessive sink rate. Realising this, the pilots cancelled autothrottle and applied full power but because of the CG position the elevator authority proved insufficient to kill the sink rate. The machine impacted in an open field about 470m (1,540ft) from the runway threshold, sliding across the frozen ground for about 300m (990ft). Four of the seven crew and 95 of the 167 passengers were killed in the crash.

On the night of 15th October 1984 ATC incompetence ended in disaster. The landing controller at Omsk-Severnyy cleared the crew of Tu-154 **CCCP-85243** (c/n 77A243), a West Siberian CAD/Omsk UAD aircraft, to land on a runway on which ice/snow clearing was in progress; quite simply this was a case of poor interaction between the tower and the ground services. When the pilots discovered a string of vehicles on the runway ahead, it was too late to make a go-around. The ensuing collision with a snow blower led to an explosion and a massive fire in which all of the airliner's 174 occupants died.

On 23rd December 1984 Tu-154B-2 **CCCP-85338** (c/n 79A338) of the Krasnoyarsk CAD/1st Krasnoyarsk UAD/400th Flight took off from Krasnoyarsk-Yemel'yanovo, heading for Irkutsk. Two minutes after take-off, just as the airliner climbed through 2040m (6,690ft), the No 3 engine suffered an uncontained failure and a fire erupted. However, the flight engineer shut down the good No 2 engine in error. As the stricken airliner attempted to return to the airport, the fire spread around the tail, causing the Tu-154 to lose control just prior to landing. The aircraft crashed and exploded, killing all 110 occupants.

On 10th July 1985 Tu-154B-2 **CCCP-85311** (c/n 78A311) of the Uzbek CAD/Tashkent UAD/219th Flight stalled at 9,100m (about 30,000ft) and spun into the ground near Uchkuduk, Uzbekistan, shortly after departing from Tashkent; all 200 occupants lost their lives. The crash – the worst that ever occurred with the type – was caused by pilot error. However, crew fatigue caused by overwork was a major contributing factor, which means the air enterprise's management was to blame.

On 21st May 1986 Tu-154B-2 **CCCP-85327** (c/n 79A327) of the Krasnoyarsk CAD/1st Krasnoyarsk UAD/400th Flight landed hard at Moscow-Sheremet'yevo when the electric de-icing of the windscreen and the pitot tubes failed, causing the pilots to make an error in judgement. The airliner suffered permanent structural damage and was written off, becom-

ing an instructional airframe at the local tech school.

On 22nd September 1987 the port main gear unit of an Aeroflot Tu-154 operated by the West Siberian CAD/Omsk UAD jammed halfway through retraction at 11:53 Moscow time as the aircraft took off from Moscow-Domodedovo on flight 227, bound from Omsk. After repeatedly but unsuccessfully trying to extend the landing gear the crew captained by Andrey V. Safonov opted for an emergency landing. After circling for two and a half hours the aircraft touched down at 14:20, veering off the runway when the starboard wing touched the ground and collapsing the nose gear unit into the bargain. The crew and the 161 passengers were unhurt; in fact, most of the passengers continued their journey to Omsk in another aircraft two hours later, although a few said no.

On 18th January 1988 Tu-154B-1 **CCCP-85254** (c/n 78A254) of the Turkmen CAD/Ashkhabad UAD/369th Flight crashed during a night landing at Krasnovodsk, Turkmenistan, where it was to make a scheduled stop en route from Moscow to Ashkhabad on flight 699. In a grave breach of the rules the captain had let the first officer make the final approach, although the first officer lacked the necessary qualification to land the aircraft on his own. When the aircraft had descended to 50m (160ft), the pilot in command inadvertently increased the sink rate to an excessively high value. Realising this, the captain belatedly took over but did not manage to kill the sink rate before the touchdown. At 04:20 Moscow time the airliner landed hard and broke up, rolling inverted and coming to rest on the runway verge. 11 of the 137 passengers lost their lives; a further 16 occupants were injured.

On 9th February 1988 the No 1 hydraulic system of a Tu-154 operated by the Tajik CAD/Dushanbe UAD/186th Flight failed immediately after take-off from Dushanbe at 20:49 Moscow time as the aircraft headed for Moscow on flight 630. The landing gear would not retract fully; nor could it be extended fully, using the No 2 system – the starboard main gear unit jammed. There was no choice but to make an emergency landing. After circling for four hours, at 0:30 on 10th February the aircraft made a perfect landing on a runway covered with a foam carpet; the Tu-154 came to rest 2,600m (8,530ft) from the point of touchdown and 87m (285ft) from the runway's edge. Inevitably the airliner suffered further damage in the process but none of the eight crew captained by V. Giro and 166 passengers suffered any harm.

As recounted in Chapter 4, on 8th March 1988 Tu-154B-2 **CCCP-85413** (c/n 80A413) of the East Siberian CAD/1st Irkutsk UAD/201st Flight/2nd Sqn was destroyed by fire at Veshchevo AB near Leningrad in the course of a failed hijack attempt.

Five days later, on 13th March, a Tu-154 of the Uzbek CAD/Tashkent UAD/219th Flight suffered a lightning strike while on approach to

Donetsk, the Ukraine, where it was to make a scheduled stop en route from Tashkent to L'vov on flight 5045. The powerful electric discharge knocked out the port and centre engines and put the automatic approach system out of action, added to which, the high-lift devices would not extend fully. To top it all, the weather was beastly, with driving snow. A go-around on one engine in these conditions was impossible. Luckily the crew captained by Stanislav F. Khar'kov managed a safe landing with no further damage to the aircraft or the occupants. For their high level of professionalism the airmen later received government awards.

On 24th September 1988 Tu-154B-2 **CCCP-85479** (c/n 81A479) of the Armenian CAD/Yerevan UAD/279th Flight crashed on approach to Aleppo, Syria,

That same day Tu-154M **CCCP-85617** (c/n 86A736) of the Moscow Territorial CAD/Vnukovo CAPA/200th Flight suffered damage during a heavy landing at Noril'sk-Alykel'. Luckily the damage turned out to be minor and the aircraft soon returned to service.

On 13th June 1989 the 'unlucky number' trick worked again. Tu-154S **CCCP-85067** (c/n 74A067) belonging to TsUMVS/63rd Flight failed to lift off at Monrovia-Roberts International when taking off on a flight to Moscow. The take-off was aborted but too late – the aircraft overran and was damaged beyond repair. Fortuitously, the crew was again unhurt. It turned out that the aircraft had been overloaded by 6,604kg (14,560 lb) and loaded incorrectly, with a too-far-forward CG.

On 20th November 1990 Tu-154B-1 **CCCP-85268** (c/n 78A268) of the Georgian CAD/Tbilisi UAD/112th Flight failed to rotate when taking off from Kutaisi-Osnovnoy on a flight to Tbilisi. The captain aborted the take-off but could not stop the aircraft in time; the airliner overran, collapsing the nose gear and coming to rest 781m (2,562ft) beyond the runway threshold. Investigation showed that the aircraft had been overloaded and the CG was too far forward. Apart from the nose gear, the aircraft had suffered permanent structural deformation with skin wrinkling ahead of the wings and was declared a write-off.

On 18th November 1990 Tu-154M **CCCP-85664** (c/n 89A818) operated by TsUMVS/63rd Flight was making a cargo flight from Basel to Moscow, laden with 15 tons (33,070 lb) of Winston cigarettes. At 10,000m (32,810ft) a fire broke out in the cabin and dense smoke started pouring into the flightdeck. The crew captained by Viktor Stolyarov had no choice but to make an off-field emergency landing near Trutnov, Czech Republic, and executed it perfectly. At 17:20 Moscow time, narrowly missing the rooftops of Velichovky village, the aircraft whizzed through the gap between two power line pylons and came to rest in a ploughed field 200-300m (660-990ft) from the village of Dubenec. The crew of six managed to leave the aircraft before it was consumed by the flames. Despite the efforts of

local volunteers and the fire brigade from Dvůr Králové, the aircraft burned out completely, only the rear fuselage and tail unit remaining intact. Part of the cargo was scattered all over the field, and the locals were quick to take advantage of this windfall of cigarettes, defying the police who tried to restore law and order.

On 6th March 1991 a Tu-154 of the Azerbaijan CAD/Baku UAD/107th Flight made a hard landing in L'vov due to pilot error. Luckily there were no fatalities.

On 23rd May 1991 Tu-154B-1 **CCCP-85097** (c/n 75A097) of the Leningrad CAD/1st Leningrad UAD was approaching Leningrad-Pulkovo, inbound from Sukhumi. Due to pilot error (the first officer was the pilot in command at the time of the accident) the airliner dropped below glide path on final approach and undershot, impacting at 13:14 hours Moscow time. The aircraft broke into three sections – the rear fuselage was severed in line with the wing trailing edge and the flightdeck section was torn off. Veering off the runway, the aircraft came to rest on the grass between Pulkovo's two runways. Eleven of the passengers were killed on the spot and two more died in hospital; another 36 passengers and the captain suffered injuries. Luckily there was no fire, otherwise the death toll would have been much higher.

On 14th September 1991 Cubana Tu-154B-2 **CU-T1227** (c/n 82A541) landed long at Mexico City-Juárez International airport, overrunning the runway and suffering damage so extensive that it was declared a total loss.

On 29th May 1992 Ariana Afghan Airlines Tu-154M **YA-TAP** (c/n 87A747) was hit by a shoulder-launched surface-to-air missile launched by Mujahideen guerrillas as it approached Kabul International airport. The crew managed a safe landing, but on 1st-2nd August 1992 the damaged aircraft was destroyed by mortar fire along with two Yakovlev Yak-40 feederliners (YA-KAB and YA-KAF) as it sat awaiting repairs.

On 5th June 1992 Balkan Bulgarian Airlines Tu-154 sans suffixe **LZ-BTD** (c/n 74A058) was damaged beyond repair when it overran the runway on landing at Varna, Bulgaria, in heavy rain, collapsing the landing gear. Nobody was hurt

On 20th July 1992 Tu-154B **CCCP-85222** (c/n 77A222) of the Georgian CAD/Tbilisi UAD/112th Flight was to make a non-scheduled cargo flight from Tbilisi-Lochini to Mineral'nyye Vody with a cargo of tea. It was later established that the aircraft was overloaded – the weight of the cargo amounted to 20 tons (44,090 lb), which is 2 tons (4,410 lb) above the limit set by the manufacturer – and was carrying fuel for the return journey; also, the CG was too far forward. The trijet did manage to become airborne but was unable to climb; seconds later it struck the localiser at the far end of the runway, then crashed through the perimeter fence and ploughed into Alekseyevka settlement which was located just outside the airport boundary. The aircraft and several resi-

dential buildings went up in flames; it took several hours to put out the blaze. The crew of six and the two cargo attendants died on the spot as did five people on the ground; another 40 persons were injured.

On 13th October 1992 Tu-154B-2 **CCCP-85528** (c/n 82A528) of the Belorussian CAD/2nd Minsk UAD/437th Flight failed to become airborne due to overloading when taking off at Vladivostok-Knevichi. The take-off was aborted but the aircraft overran, sustaining irreparable damage.

On 5th December 1992, while Tu-154A **CCCP-85105** (c/n 75A105) of the Armenian CAD/1st Yerevan UAD/279th Flight was approaching Yerevan-Zvartnots in poor visibility, the pilot in command mistook the runway edge lights for the centreline lighting. As a result, the aircraft landed with the starboard main gear unit on the runway shoulder and veered to the right, the nose gear unit striking a concrete wall and collapsing. None of the eight crew and 146 passengers suffered any harm but the aircraft was declared a write-off.

On 9th January 1993 Uzbekistan Airways Tu-154B-2 **85533** (c/n 82A533) leased by Air India was performing a flight to New Delhi. While landing at Indira Gandhi International airport in poor weather the aircraft strayed from the desired track, dropped below the glide path and landed 700m (2,300ft) beyond the threshold and 400m (1,310ft) to the right of the centreline, breaking up, rolling inverted and bursting into flames. It turned out that the Uzbek crew had ignored the approach controller's commands not to land. Incredibly there were no fatalities – all 13 crew and 152 passengers managed to escape from the burning aircraft.

On 8th February 1993 Iran Air Tours Tu-154M **EP-ITD** (c/n 91A903) took off from Mehrabad International airport, bound for Mashhad. Unbeknownst to its crew, two pairs of Sukhoi Su-24MK Fencer-D tactical bombers of the Islamic Republic of Iran Air Force (IRIAF) were flying over the mountains nearby, practising for an air display on Republic Day, which was only a few days away. Due to lack of interaction between the civil and military authorities the bombers found themselves on a collision course with the airliner; the leader of one pair had a near-miss but his wingman went smack into the Tu-154 and took the tail off the jet. Both aircraft immediately became uncontrollable and crashed; all 119 passengers and 13 crew of the Tu-154 were killed, as were the pilot and the navigator/weapons systems operator of the Su-24.

Sadly, the demise of the USSR sparked civil wars and ethnic strife in the former Soviet republics, including the Georgian-Abkhazi war. On 22nd September 1993 an atrocious act of war demonstrated that airliners are no armoured assault aircraft designed to withstand enemy fire. Tu-154B **85163** (c/n 76A163) operated by Transair Georgia was hit by a 9K32M Strela-2M surface-to-air missile (NATO code

name SA-7 *Grail*) launched from an Abkhazi separatist gunboat when on final approach to Sukhumi-Babushara. The burning airliner managed to reach the airport but crashed on the runway, with a large loss of life. Incidentally, the day before Tu-134A 65893 belonging to the same airline was similarly shot down into the Black Sea with a Strela-2M on finals to Sukhumi-Babushara, killing all on board; and on 23rd September another Transair Georgia Tu-134A, CCCP-65001 (and possibly Tu-134A CCCP-65809 as well), was destroyed on the ground when the separatists shelled the airport. No fight for independence can justify the wanton destruction of civil airliners that do not obviously carry enemy personnel.

On 25th December 1993 Vnukovo Airlines Tu-154B-2 **RA-85296** (c/n 78A296) crash-landed at Groznyy-Severnyy airport on a flight from Moscow, breaking its back aft of the wings, when the crew misjudged the altitude on final approach in thick fog. There were no fatalities but the aircraft was a write-off. Though technically repairable, the aircraft could not be repaired because of the political unrest and growing crime in the Chechen Republic, which was now run by General Djokhar Dudayev. After sitting at the airport for almost a year the mapless aircraft was eventually destroyed during a Russian air raid on 11th December 1994, the day when the First Chechen War broke out.

On 29th December 1993 the starboard main gear unit of Aeroflot/Kazan' Air Enterprise Tu-154B-2 **RA-85358** (c/n 79A358) failed to extend on landing at Omsk-Severnyy. After repeated but fruitless attempts to extend it the aircraft made an emergency landing, suffering serious damage – but not so serious as to preclude repairs and subsequent return to service.

On 3rd January 1994 Baikal Airlines Tu-154M **RA-85656** (c/n 89A801) suffered a fire in the No 2 engine and loss of hydraulic power within minutes after take-off from Irkutsk-1 airport on a flight to Moscow. Despite the pilots' attempts to bring the stricken airliner back, the aircraft lost control and crashed into the brick building of an animal farm in Mamony village 1km (6.8 miles) from the airport. All nine crew and 111 passengers lost their lives. Investigation showed that the affected engine's air turbine starter had failed to disengage after engine start-up. When the engine was spooled up to take-off power, the starter overspeeded and disintegrated, the fragments rupturing fuel and hydraulic lines, which eventually led to loss of longitudinal control. To prevent a repetition of this scenario all Tu-154Ms were progressively modified; this included rerouting the hydraulic lines in the area of the No 2 engine to take them out of harm's way in the event of an uncontained starter failure.

On 6th June 1994 China Northwest Airlines Tu-154M **B-2610** (c/n 86A740) disintegrated in mid-air a few minutes after departing from Xi'an-Xiguan airport, killing all on board. Investigation revealed that the autopilot's roll and yaw channels had been cross-wired to the wrong connectors during a sloppily performed maintenance check at Xi'an. When the pilots engaged the autopilot after take-off, this caused abnormal oscillations of the aircraft with increasing amplitude which ultimately overstressed the airframe. The CVR readout indicated that the pilots had realised what had happened and intended to disengage the autopilot but did not manage to do so before the aircraft broke up.

On 21st January 1995 Kazakhstan Airlines Tu-154B-2 **UN 85455** (c/n 80A455) failed to become airborne at Karachi International airport. The take-off was aborted at 270-280km/h (167-173mph), but the aircraft overran by some 500m (1,640ft) and was damaged beyond repair.

On 7th December 1995 Dalavia Far Eastern Airways Tu-154B **RA-85164** (c/n 76A164) crashed in mountainous country 193km (120 miles) east of Khabarovsk on flight 3949 from Yuzhno-Sakhalinsk; the aircraft was to make a stopover at its home base before continuing the journey to Ulan-Ude and Novosibirsk. Investigation of the accident showed that the airliner had 'suddenly and inexplicably' entered a downward spiral to the right with increasing right bank. The aircraft impacted in an inverted position, killing all 90 passengers and eight crew. The official explanation was that fuel transfer from the port wing to the starboard one, coupled with pilot error, had caused the aircraft to bank and then enter a spin. However, this theory causes strong doubts – both because such loss of control was highly improbable and because large pieces of wreckage were not found at the crash site. There are reasons to believe that the official story was a cover-up for criminal negligence and that RA-85164 was mistakenly shot down by a surface-to-air missile.

On 29th August 1996 Vnukovo Airlines Tu-154M **RA-85621** (c/n 86A742) approached the Spitsbergen Archipelago on charter flight VKO2801 from Moscow, carrying a planeload of mine workers to the Russian coal mines at Piramida township. As the aircraft commenced an instrument approach to runway 28 at Longyearbyen airport in low cloud and fog, the crew let the aircraft sink below the designated glide path. As a result, the Tu-154 smacked into the almost vertical rock face of Mount Opera in the Adventdalen glacial valley at 823m (2,700ft) above sea level and exploded, killing all 128 passengers and 12 crew instantly. The wreckage tumbled down the cliff, causing numerous avalanches which seriously complicated the ensuing search and rescue effort. The Russian accident investigation team succeeded in finding the aircraft's 'black boxes', sending them to Moscow for analysis. This caused loud objections from the Norwegian authorities who claimed the Russians had no authority to undertake SAR operations on their own on Spitsbergen, which is under Norwegian jurisdiction.

Soviet aircraft have a reputation for being tough, but there's a limit for everything. Sometime between September 1996 and June 1999 Tu-154M **RA-85795 No 1** (c/n 93A979), which had been sold to China, landed so hard at Chengdu that a wing spar broke and the aircraft was declared a write-off.

On 13th September 1997 the German Air Force's unique Tu-154M-ON 'Open Skies' monitoring aircraft, **11+02** (c/n 89A813), was heading from Bonn to Cape Town. For once the flight was not an inspection mission; apart from the crew of ten, the aircraft was carrying 14 German marines, yacht fanciers all, who were to participate in a regatta around the Cape of Good Hope on occasion of the South African Navy's 75th anniversary. The reason why the Tu-154M-ON had been selected for the mission was probably so that the Luftwaffe could take the opportunity to show the aircraft off in South Africa.

At 12.34 Central European Time the Tu-154 departed Niamey, Niger, on the penultimate leg of the journey, bound for Windhoek, Namibia. 24 minutes later the aircraft passed a waypoint named BATIA (the points marking the turns and crossings of airways have such silly-sounding five-letter names), cruising at flight level 350 – that is, 35,000ft (10,670m). Instead of proceeding to the nearest waypoint EMTAL, where it was to climb to FL 390 (39,000ft or 11,890m), with the consent of the ATC Centre in Accra the Tu-154 took a short cut to the next point in its flight plan (called GAPEL). When the aircraft passed the latter waypoint at 15.22 and reported doing so, it was still at 35,000ft.

Meanwhile, a US Air Force/305th Air Mobility Wing Lockheed C-141B StarLifter serialled 65-9405 (c/n 300-6142) took off from Windhoek at 16.11, bound for Ascension Island with a load of materiel; the aircraft was using the same airway as the Tu-154M-ON but on a reciprocal heading. Now, apparently the ATC authorities had never received the Tu-154's flight plan or been advised of the aircraft's actual departure from Niamey; communication between ATC authorities and the ATC infrastructure generally in Africa is notoriously poor.

Unaware of the Tu-154's flight, the tower in Windhoek authorised the C-141 to climb to FL 350, which the transport did at 17.01. Nine minutes later the two jets collided in clouds over the Atlantic Ocean, the wreckage plummeting to lie 3,300m (10,830ft) below the surface (the flash of the explosion was recorded by a US surveillance satellite); all 24 occupants of the Tu-154 and the nine crew of the C-141 were killed. Neither aircraft was equipped with a traffic collision avoidance system; worse, the C-141 did not even have a radar transponder, which means it would have been 'invisible' to a TCAS-equipped aircraft. Poor flight planning from beginning to end was cited as the cause of the accident.

On 15th December 1997 at 17.30 Moscow time Tajikistan Airlines Tu-154B-1 **EY-85281** (c/n 78A281) crashed 13km (8 miles) from Sharjah, UAE, inbound from Dushanbe on charter flight 3183. Eyewitnesses (the workers

of a natural gas prospecting team) said the aircraft had begun losing altitude unexpectedly on final approach, impacting in the desert and exploding. All 77 passengers and eight out of nine crewmembers were killed; only the navigator survived. Pilot error was cited as the cause – the pilot in command had exceeded the sink rate, letting the aircraft drop far below the glide path.

On 29th August 1998 Cubana Tu-154M **CU-T1264** (c/n 85A720) was due to depart Quito-Mariscal Sucre International airport, bound for Havana via Guayaquil on flight CU409 with 14 crew and 76 passengers. The aircraft taxied out for take-off from runway 07 some twenty minutes behind schedule. The first two attempts to take off were aborted by the crew; the third ended in disaster. Different sources give different accounts of what happened; some say the take-off was aborted again due to an engine failure – too late, while others claim the aircraft became airborne but then brushed the perimeter fence and sank back. Anyway, the Tu-154 demolished a garage, then ploughed through a football ground where children were playing and burst into flames. 71 persons on board the aircraft and ten on the ground were killed outright; a further two of the 15 rescuees from the aircraft later died in hospital. 25 persons were injured.

Quito-Mariscal Sucre International is a mountain airfield located 2,880m (9,446ft) above sea level, and operating into and out of it requires maximum engine thrust even with a light load. However, the Cuban jet had trouble starting the engines because of the rarefied air, even though technically it was fully serviceable (the 20-minute delay occurred because one of the engines wouldn't start). Incidentally, a similar crash had occurred at the same location on 18th September 1984 when a DC-8-55F freighter (HC-BKN) owned by the local airline AECA failed to become airborne and overran, killing 30 on the ground.

On 24th February 1999 China Southwest Airlines Tu-154M **B-2622** (c/n 90A846) crashed at Tangtou village near the town of Ruian about 30km (18.6 miles) out on approach to Wenzhou airport, south-western China. All 50 passengers and 11 crew died on the spot; three farmers on the ground suffered severe burns. The crash occurred in broad daylight as the aircraft was descending from 1,000 to 700m (from 3,280 to 2,300ft). Careful examination of the wreckage revealed that the elevator control linkage had become disconnected (a bolt connecting a push-pull rod with a bellcrank had fallen out), causing the aircraft to dive into the ground.

On 31st May 1999 Vnukovo Airlines Tu-154M **RA-85622** (c/n 87A746) overran the runway when landing at Nizhnevartovsk on a flight from Moscow. Luckily the damage was minor and the aircraft returned to service after repairs.

On 4th July 2000 the pilots of Malév Hungarian Airlines Tu-154B-2 **HA-LCR** (c/n 82A543) forgot to lower the landing gear on approach to Thessaloniki, Greece, inbound from Budapest. Noticing at the last moment that the aircraft was not in landing configuration (apparently after being so informed by the tower), the pilots belatedly initiated a go-around; however, the airliner continued sinking and scraped the runway in a shower of sparks before finally lifting clear and climbing away. After extending the landing gear the crew executed a normal landing; none of the 94 occupants suffered any harm but the aircraft sustained considerable damage to the wings (especially the flaps) and lower fuselage. Since Malév was phasing out the type anyway, the 18-year-old airliner was struck off charge and donated to Thessaloniki-Makedonía airport as a rescue trainer.

Investigation showed that the aircraft had been fully serviceable; however, the CVR readouts indicated that the pilots had not completed the cockpit check during the landing approach and missed the gear extension. A possible reason is that Thessaloniki-Makedonía is jointly operated with the Hellenic Air Force and has two runways – 16/34 (used for commercial operations) and 10/28 (normally used by the resident 113th Fighter Wing, then flying Northrop F-5A/Bs). On the day of the accident runway 34 was closed and incoming commercial aircraft were forced to change heading from 340° to 280° at the final approach stage. Possibly it was this non-standard approach procedure, coupled with the fact that a Boeing 757-230 of the German airline Condor was vacating the runway just as the Tu-154 approached the runway threshold, that had distracted the Hungarian pilots.

On 3rd July 2001 Vladivostok Air Tu-154M **RA-85845** *Ussuriysk* (c/n 86A735) crashed 20.9km (13 miles) from Irkutsk-1 airport at 2:10 AM local time, killing all nine crew and 136 passengers. The aircraft was on final approach for an intermediate stop en route from Yekaterinburg to Vladivostok on flight XF352.[2] Immediately before the crash the aircraft was leaving the downwind leg of the landing pattern and descending from 950m (3,100ft) to 850m (2,800ft); captain Valentin Goncharuk had radioed that he had the runway in sight.

The 'tin kickers' established that the pilots had accidentally exceeded the aircraft's angle of attack limits. As a result, the aircraft stalled at 800m (2,625ft) and spun in, impacting in a wings-level attitude with very little forward speed – the altitude was just too low to make a recovery. The wreckage was confined to an area measuring 60 x 90m (200 x 300ft); only the tail unit remained relatively intact.

On 4th October 2001 at 13:44 Moscow time Sibir' Airlines Tu-154M **RA-85693** (c/n 91A866) exploded in mid-air and plummeted into the Black Sea at 43°10' North and 34°46' East 180km (111 miles) from the Russian resort city of Sochi, while en route from Tel Aviv to Novosibirsk on flight S7 1812. There were no survivors among the 64 passengers and 12 crew.

Initially a terrorist attack was suspected as the cause; since the aircraft was outbound from Tel Aviv and there were Israelis aboard, there was speculation that these may have been targeted. Soon, however, bits and pieces of information began to fit together into a totally different picture. Firstly, the Crimea Peninsula which is part of the Ukraine, was close at hand and the Ukraine's military assets there included the Opuk practice range near Feodosiya on the peninsula's south coast, quite close to the airway which the Tu-154 was using. On that fateful day the Ukrainian Air Defence Force was holding an exercise at this very range; the exercise involved firing live S-200 surface-to-air missiles at low-flying Tupolev M-143 target drones. Secondly, the search and rescue effort mounted after the airliner's disappearance quickly turned up the place of the crash; the crew of a Mil' Mi-8 helicopter spotted floating debris on the sea – and a huge red stain looking almost like blood next to it. This, together with the close proximity of the Opuk range immediately aroused suspicion of a shoot down; the propellant of the S-200 SAM is known to enter a chemical reaction with salt water, colouring it red. Thirdly, imagery gener-

ated by a US surveillance satellite and supplied by the USA at the Russian government's request showed the Tu-154 cruising over the sea on its designated route and *an unidentified object* – probably a missile – approaching it.

Next thing, the Russian Navy was called upon for assistance. Soon enough the airliner's wreckage was located on the seabed and as much of it as possible was salvaged. Analysis of the wreckage quickly confirmed the shoot-down theory: fragments of aircraft skin, passenger seats and some of the bodies recovered from the wreckage had shrapnel damage. The holes were too large to be created by bullets during a shoot-out in the cabin; moreover, the holes in the aircraft skin had inward-curving edges clearly indicating an explosion outside the aircraft, not within – that is, a missile hit. The final piece of evidence came when steel pellets of the type used as penetrators in the S-200's fragmentation warhead were discovered among the wreckage.

The Ukrainian government was defiant at first, denying all charges against the Ukrainian military. However, faced with hard evidence and an avalanche of lawsuits and not wishing to become involved in a major international scandal, Kiev eventually admitted its fault and agreed to pay damages to the victims' families. Even though Russia and the Ukraine have had a rather rocky relationship at times, this tragic accident was certainly not a wilful and wanton destruction of a civil aircraft but an honest error; the missile must have locked onto the airliner instead of the target drone after being launched.

On 5th September 2001 Tu-154M Uzbekistan Airways **UK 85776** (c/n 93A958) suffered a landing gear collapse when landing at Ufa. Despite sustaining serious damage, the aircraft was repaired and returned to service.

On 12th February 2002 Tu-154M **EP-MBS** (c/n 91A871) operated by Iran Air Tour hit the Kuh-e Sefid Mountain near Sarab-e Do Rah at 9,100ft (2,770m) ASL as it descended for landing approach to Khorramabad, Iran, inbound from Tehran on flight B9 956. Needless to say, all 118 occupants – 12 crew and 107 passengers – were killed outright. Again this was a case of CFIT in poor weather – the aircraft had been serviceable right up to the point of impact.

Eight days later another Iranian Tu-154M – this time **EP-LBX** (c/n 87A763) of Kish Air – was substantially damaged in a hard landing at Mashad. There were no fatalities and the aircraft was ferried to Moscow for damage assessment at ARZ No 400, from which it had been leased. However, the ground crews there were clumsy enough to break off the nose gear unit when towing the aircraft; the extent of the damage was such that the airliner was written off and used for spares.

Sibir' Airlines Tu-154B-2 RA-85556 taxying at Moscow-Domodedovo. Tragically, this aircraft was destroyed in a terrorist attack after departing this location on 24th August 2004.
Dmitriy Petrochenko

On 1st July 2002 BAL Bashkirian Airlines Tu-154M **RA-85816** (c/n 95A1006) flew from Ufa to Moscow-Domodedovo, picked up a load of passengers there and took off with nine crew and 60 passengers, bound for Barcelona on charter flight BTC2927. Most of the passengers were gifted children from various Russian cities who had been granted holidays in Spain as a reward for excellent academic results. Meanwhile, a Boeing 757-23APF package freighter owned by DHL International Cargo Services but registered in Bahrain as A9C-DHL (c/n 24635, fuselage number 258) was winging its way northwards from Bergamo-Orio al Serio to Brussels-Zaventem on flight DHL611. The respective routes of both aircraft took them across Germany; the Tu-154 was using Flight Level 360 (36,000ft, or 10,970m).

Radio communications with the Russian jet were handed over by Munich to the Skyguide ATC Centre in Zürich at 23:30:11 local time. At that moment the ATC room was manned by only one controller, Peter Nielsen, who was responsible for the entire traffic in the Zürich airspace. He was monitoring two frequencies and two radarscopes. On one frequency (119.925MHz) he was guiding an aircraft landing at Friedrichshafen, on the German side of the border; and on the other frequency (128.050MHz) he had to control four aircraft.

That night, from 23:00 the configuration of the radar data processing of Skyguide was modified while maintenance work was in progress. This required, among other facts, that radar separation values be increased from 5nm to 7nm. Also, the Short-Term Conflict Alert (STCA) feature in Zürich was not available at that time. The STCA at Karlsruhe Upper Area Control Center (UAC), however, did work. Realising the danger of a mid-air collision, from 23:33:36 to 23:35:34 the controller in Karlsruhe tried in vain to contact the Zürich ATC; all he got was the 'line busy' signal.

Meanwhile, at 23:34.42 the Tu-154's Honeywell 2000 TCAS gave a Traffic Advisory; simultaneously a TA was issued by the other aircraft's TCAS. Seven seconds later the radar controller issued the following instructions to flight BTC2927: 'descend Flight Level 350 [that

is, 35,000ft or 10,668m], expedite, I have crossing traffic'. This was necessary for continuation of the flight to Barcelona and to achieve a vertical separation with respect to the approaching DHL Boeing 757.

At 23:42.56 the crews of both aircraft received a Resolution Advisory command from their TCAS; the 757 was to descend and the Tu-154 was to climb in order to achieve vertical separation. The DHL crew complied and initiated a descent; the Russian crew, however, was then trying to deal with the conflicting descent (by ATC) and climb (TCAS) instructions.

Seven seconds after the Resolution Advisory-command, the ATC controller repeated the instruction to descend. The Bashkirian crew then decided to follow Nielsen's instructions. A little later the TCAS aboard the Boeing 757 gave the crew a new Resolution Advisory – 'increase descent'. They then contacted ATC, telling the controller that they were doing a TCAS descent.

Since both aircraft were now descending, the TCAS of the Russian jet warned the crew to 'increase climb' to avoid a collision. This was eight seconds before the collision. Just prior to the collision, both crews detected the other aircraft, and reacted to avoid the collision by attempting appropriate flight manoeuvres. Nevertheless, at 23:35.32 the two aircraft collided at approximately FL354 (1,790m, or 35,400ft) over Lake Bodensee near the German town of Überlingen. The fin of the Boeing struck the left side of the Tu-154's fuselage; the trijet immediately broke up and fell in flaming fragments, while the tailless Boeing 757 dived into the ground 8km (5 miles) north. All occupants of the Tu-154 and both pilots of the 757 lost their lives.

The crash produced a huge public outcry, and Skyguide came under close scrutiny. Try as they would to shift the blame to the Russian crew, eventually the Swiss authorities had to plead guilty to negligence and agree to pay damages.

On 24th August 2004 Sibir' Airlines Tu-154B-2 **RA-85556** (c/n 82A556) took off from Moscow-Domodedovo, bound for Sochi on flight S7 1043. At 23:02 Moscow time the air-

craft suddenly vanished from ATC radarscopes and all radio contact was lost. Three minutes earlier, Volga-Aviaexpress Tu-134A RA-65080, which had also departed from Moscow-Domodedovo on a flight to Volgograd, had vanished just as suddenly. All hell was let loose and massive search and rescue efforts began. Within a few hours, the worst fears were confirmed: the wreckage of the Tu-154 was found 9km (5.6 miles) from Gloobokiy settlement in the Kamensk-Shakhtinskiy District of the Rostov Region; there were no survivors among the 43 passengers and nine crew. The remains of the other aircraft were located near Buchalki village in the Tula Region; again, all 43 occupants had lost their lives.

The almost simultaneous crashes, coupled with the distribution of the wreckage over a wide area (suggesting that the aircraft had broken up in mid-air), ominously pointed toward a carefully planned terrorist attack. Examination of the wreckage confirmed this theory – in both aircraft a powerful explosive charge had been detonated in the cabin, causing catastrophic structural failure. A careful study of the manifests and a check with the passengers' families turned up the suspects – two Chechen women acting as *shaheed* suicide bombers.

On 7th October 2004 Polish Air Force Tu-154M 'Salon' '**102 Red**' (c/n 90A862) suffered a fire in the No 2 engine as it was about to depart from Kunming, China, heading for Chengdu (that was the original destination but the aircraft had diverted because of bad weather). The fire was caused by a failure of the engine's air starter. Once the investigation had been completed, spares and tech staff arrived from Poland and the aircraft was repaired on site, departing for Warsaw on 16th October.

On 15th August 2006 Air Koryo Tu-154B-2 **P-551** (c/n 75A129) veered off the runway when landing at Pyongyang-Cheju airport on a flight from Beijing, collapsing the nose gear unit. Other reports say the aircraft in question was **P-561** (c/n 83A573). None of the occupants was hurt.

On 22nd August 2006 Pulkovo Air Enterprise Tu-154M **RA-85185 No 2** (c/n 91A894) departed from Anapa, a Black Sea resort, heading for St Petersburg on flight Z8 612. At 15:37 Moscow time, as it passed through Ukrainian airspace, the aircraft sent a Mayday signal; two minutes later it vanished from ATC radarscopes and all radio contact with it was lost. The airliner crashed and burned between the villages Sukhaya Balka and Novgorodskoye 45km (28 miles) north of Donetsk; there were no survivors among the 160 passengers (including 49 children) and ten crew.

At the time of the crash a storm front was passing through the area, and the crew

attempted to pass over it. Passing to the left or to the right of it was impossible (this involved leaving the designated airway, and the ATC did not authorise this), and returning to Anapa was undesirable because then the aircraft would have to be refuelled and the fuel at Anapa-Vityazevo was expensive. As it attempted to 'jump over the storm', the aircraft exceeded its service ceiling, stalled and entered a flat spin from which it could not recover.

At about 13:45 local time on 1st September 2006 Iran Air Tour Tu-154M **EP-MCF** (c/n 88A788) burst a nosewheel tyre and veered off runway 14L at Mashhad when arriving on flight B9 945 from Bandar Abbas, collapsing the landing gear and breaking up into three sections. The ensuing fire gutted the airliner completely; 28 of the 137 passengers (including 11 children) died and 56 more suffered burns and/or carbon monoxide poisoning. The Iranian crew of eleven was unhurt.

Finally, on 26th September 2006 an accident occurred at Manas airport, Bishkek, Kyrghyzstan, which had been turned into a US Air Force base during Operation Enduring Freedom (the

operation against the Taliban militia and the al-Qaeda terrorist network in Afghanistan). At about 20:10 local time Altyn Air Tu-154M **EX-85718** (c/n 91A900) departing from runway 08 on a scheduled flight to Moscow via Osh struck a resident USAF Boeing KC-135R Stratotanker that had just landed and had stopped, partially blocking the runway as it waited for the pilot vehicle. The accident was caused by a combination of poor visibility and ATC error (the ground controller had directed the Tu-154 to the wrong taxiway). When the airliner's crew discovered the tanker ahead of them, it was too late. The Tu-154 lost a 2.4m (8ft) chunk of the starboard wing, including the aileron; since it was too late to abort the take-off, the crew, keeping their heads cool, continued the take-off and made a safe emergency landing. None of the nine crew and 52 passengers suffered any harm. The aircraft appears to be repairable, though the starboard outer wing panel clearly will need to be replaced. The Stratotanker also suffered serious damage; a fire broke out but was extinguished by the airport fire service.

Flight Hours and Cycles of Tu-154s Written Off in Accidents (where known)

Aircraft	Registration	(c/n)	Total time since new	Total cycles since new	Overhauls
Tu-154 *sans suffixe*	LZ-BTB	(72A027)	7,800 hrs		
Tu-154A	HA-LCI	(74A053)	1,186 hrs		
Tu-154A	LZ-BTN No 1	(74A054)	3,700 hrs		
Tu-154S	CCCP-85067	(74A067)	13,266 hrs 40 min	5,949	
Tu-154A	CCCP-85102	(75A102)	2,119 hrs 44 min	1,069	
Tu-154A	CCCP-85103	(75A103)	6,922 hrs 47 min	3,075	1
Tu-154B	HA-LCF	(75A126)	8,983 hrs	5,642	
Tu-154B-1	CCCP-85234	(77A234)	31,565 hrs	13,180	
Tu-154B-1	CCCP-85268	(78A268)	23,472 hrs	10,227	3
Tu-154B-1	CCCP-85282	(78A282)	23,926 hrs	10,392	
Tu-154B-2	CCCP-85413	(80A413)	11,411 hrs	4,669	
Tu-154B-2	HA-LCR	(82A543)	22,409 hrs	13,583	
Tu-154B-2	RA-85556	(82A556)	30,751 hrs		
Tu-154M	RA-85845	(86A735)	20,953 hrs 17 min	11,387	3
Tu-154M	B-2610	(86A740)	12,507 hrs	6,651	
Tu-154M	B-2622	(90A846)	14,135 hrs	7,748	
Tu-154M	RA-85693	(91A866)	16,705 hrs	7,281	
Tu-154M	EP-MBS	(91A871)	12,701 hrs 24 min	5,516	
Tu-154M	RA-85185 No. 2	(91A894)	24,215 hrs		

The starboard wing of Kyrghyzstan Airlines Tu-154M EX-85718 damaged by a collision with a KC-135R at Bishkek-Manas on 26th September 2006. Kyrghyzstan Airlines/via Internet

End Notes

Introduction

1 OKB = *opytno-konstrooktorskoye byuro* – experimental design bureau (there were no companies as such in the USSR); the number is a code allocated for security reasons. In 1991 it became the Tupolev Aviation Scientific & Technical Complex (ANTK *imeni Tupoleva – aviatsionnyy naoochno-tekhnicheskiy kompleks*). Since 1991 the company is known as the Tupolev Joint-Stock Company (OAO Tupolev – *otkrytoye aktsionehrnoye obshchestvo*).
2 Now called the Aviadvigatel' (= Aero Engine) Production Association.
3 D = *dvigatel'* – engine. The P stands for *passazheerskiy samolyot* (passenger aircraft), implying this is a non-afterburning commercial version. The original D-20 was equipped with an afterburner and intended to power the '113' (Tu-113) unmanned aerial vehicle, which in the event never materialised.

Chapter One

1 RBP = *rahdiolokatsionnyy bombardirovochnyy pritsel* – bomb-aiming radar. The RBP-4 had been borrowed from the Tu-16 bomber, hence the primary mission and the designation.
2 OKB-276 is now called SNTK *imeni Kuznetsova Samarskiy naoochno-tekhnicheskiy kompleks* – the Samara Scientific & Technical Complex named after Nikolay D. Kuznetsov.
3 ROZ = *rahdiolokahtor obzora zemlee* – ground mapping radar. The radar had been borrowed from the An-12 *Cub-A* transport, hence the primary mission and the designation.
4 Now NPP Aerosila (= Aeropower Scientific & Production Enterprise)
5 Now part of the Moscow Aviation Production Association (MAPO – *Moskovskoye aviatsionnoye proizvodstvennoye obyedineniye*) named after Pyotr V. Demen'tyev, ex-Minister of Aircraft Industry.
6 Also known as P/O Box V-2776. Later renamed Avia Joint-Stock Co; now called Aviacor JSC. The city itself has been renamed back to Samara.
7 Also known as P/O Box V-2437.

Chapter Two

1 There are also several registration blocks reserved for Aeroflot's Polar division (04xxx), the Ministry of Aircraft Industry (29xxx, 48xxx, 69xxx, 93xxx, 98xxx and so on), the Ministry of Defence and so on. They do not correspond to any specific type and are a mixed bag of assorted aircraft.
2 *Izdeliye* (product) such-and-such is a term often used for coding Soviet military hardware items. Previously, other Tupolev aircraft built in Kuibyshev had also received alphabetical product codes. For instance, the Tu-95 *Bear-A* bomber was *izdeliye* V, and its derivatives received appropriately amended codes (*izdeliye* VK for the Tu-95K missile carrier, *izdeliye* VR for the Tu-95MR reconnaissance aircraft, *izdeliye* VTs for the Tu-95RTs over-the-horizon target designator aircraft and so on).

Chapter Three

1 Aka '1971-model MiG-23'; this 'limited edition' was an intermediate version between the original MiG-23S *Flogger-A* and the MiG-23M *Flogger-B*.
2 The radar was originally developed for the An-24 *Coke* twin-turboprop airliner. Various versions of this radar are fitted to the An-24 (the Groza-24), An-26 *Curl* (the Groza-26), An-32 *Cline*, An-30A/B/D *Clank* (the Groza-30), some versions of the Ilyushin IL-14 *Crate*, Tu-134 *Crusty* (the Groza-M134) and Yakovlev Yak-40 *Codling* (the Groza-40).

3 The 'I' is a capital letter, not a Roman numeral.
4 Still, Boeing-type doors did find use on Soviet/Russian airliners – the Ilyushin IL-86, IL-96 and IL-114, as well as the Tu-204/Tu-214, Tu-334 and Yakovlev Yak-42.
5 An instructor pilot who was killed together with the world's first spaceman Yuriy A. Gagarin in the crash of an Aero CS-102 (Czech-built Mikoyan/Gurevich UTI-MiG-15 *Midget*) trainer coded '18 Red' (c/n 612739) near Chkalovskaya AB on 27th March 1968.
6 Some sources say the conversion cost $25.3 million.
7 This Russian term is used indiscriminately and can denote any kind of testbed (avionics, engine, equipment, weapons and so on), an aerodynamics research aircraft or control configured vehicle (CCV), a weather research aircraft, a geophysical survey aircraft and so on.

Chapter Four – no notes.

Chapter Five

1 42 aircraft were struck off charge and scrapped; another 25 An-10As in reasonably good condition were transferred to the Air Force and MAP.
2 The Tu-134AK is a VIP version of the Tu-134A identifiable by the extra entry door in front of the port engine which is missing on regular Tu-134As (including those converted to VIP configuration). The Tu-134 *Balkany* (Balkans) is an airborne command post derivative of the Tu-134AK often erroneously referred to as 'Tu-135' (which was really a bomber project of 1963) and identifiable by the HF aerial 'sting' under the APU exhaust and four small additional blade aerials.
3 Called Western Group of Forces (ZGV – *Zahpadnaya groopa voysk*) in 1989-94.

Chapter Six

1 Even before that (in 1997) its flight code was reallocated to Buffalo Airways Ltd [J4/BFL] of Hay River, NWT, Canada.
2 The flight code E6 previously belonged to Elf Air.
3 The UP flight code was transferred to Bahamasair [UP/BHS] of Nassau.
4 This is an old poetic-style name for Russia.
5 Also rendered as SP Air and Spaero.
6 Formerly the COMECON Civil Aviation Centre (*Tsentr grazhdahnskoy aviahtsiï SEV*). COMECON (aka CMEA) = Council for Mutual Economic Assistance (*Sovet ekonomicheskoy vzaimopomoschchi*), the Soviet Union and its satellites' equivalent of the European Economic Council.
7 The 3P flight code was transferred to Inter Tropical Aviation [3P/TCU] of Surinam.
8 The flight code Q9 was reallocated to Interbrasil Star [Q9/ITB]; for some obscure reason this airline and Sayakhat had the same code until 1999!
9 The above colour schemes are **not** all that were used; some re-export An-24Bs and IL-62Ms had basic LOT Polish Airlines colours with Air Ukraine titles and the 'blue bird' logo!

Chapter Seven

1 Established on 18th September 1958, Interflug (a contraction of Internationale Fluggesellschaft) was originally a charter airline serving international routes which were off limits to Deutsche Lufthansa because of its name. Between 1955 and 1963 there were *two Deutsche Lufthansas* – one in East Germany and the other (the one which still exists) in West Germany. As long as the East German DLH flew domestic flights, nobody seemed to mind, but any attempt to venture outside the country would immediately result in a legal spate with its Western namesake.

2 The first General Director of the East German Deutsche Lufthansa (and subsequently of Interflug).
3 Marxwalde reverted to its original name, Neuhardenberg, after German reunification.
4 Air Pass was just a trading name; the official name was Air Cess (Swaziland), Ltd.
5 The ICAO code DYA stands for 'Democratic Yemen Airlines'.

Chapter Eight

1 VNII NP = *Vsesoyooznyy naoochno-issledovatel'skiy institoot nefteprodooktov* – All-Union Petroleum Products Research Institute.

Appendix One

1 Chronologically the manufacture dates do not always follow the c/n order; this is explained by the need to eliminate any defects discovered during the first flight and by the higher complexity of outfitting jobs on VIP and special mission aircraft as compared to Tu-154s in ordinary passenger configuration. Tu-154B-2 'Salons' CCCP-85602, '603 and '605 are a case in point; so are the final Tu-154Ms (for unknown reasons some aircraft were completed several years later than aircraft with higher c/ns).

Manufacture dates in italics come from Western sources and are not yet confirmed by Russian ones. Also, in some cases different documents give different manufacture dates for the same aircraft (such dates are given in **bold italics** in the table). For instance, the manufacture date of CCCP-85042 has also been stated as **16th** June 1973. Other 'alternative' dates are **22nd** March 1974 for CCCP-85059, 10th **March** 1976 for CCCP-85157 (which is very doubtful), **1st** November 1976 for CCCP-85180, **18th** July 1977 for CCCP-85220, **21st** September 1977 for CCCP-85231, **2nd June** 1978 for CCCP-85271, 2nd **February** 1978 (which is obviously wrong) or **20th** August 1978 for CCCP-85291, 29th **August** 1979 for CCCP-85350, 21st **May** 1980 for CCCP-85414, **25th** August 1980 for CCCP-85436, **13th** September 1980 for CCCP-85441, **24th** November 1980 for CCCP-85459, **23rd** December 1980 for CCCP-85461, **6th** April 1982 for CCCP-85537, **12th September 1986** for CCCP-85610, **2nd April** 1991 for CCCP-85693, **25th** December 1992 for RA-85759 and **8th** February 1979 for HA-LCM.

Appendix Two

1 The author uses Russian terminology here; the word 'accident' refers to fatal and non-fatal accidents when the aircraft suffers more or less serious damage to the airframe and/or engines, applying both to total hull losses and cases where the aircraft is repaired. 'Incident' means cases not serious enough to be rated as a non-fatal accident, such as avionics or systems malfunctions not causing major damage; in-flight engine shutdowns; tyre explosions; bird-strikes; lightning strikes; near-misses; departures from predesignated air routes; landings in below-minima conditions; go-around because of obstacles on the runway and the like
2 Actually a separate flight code system for domestic flights is in use in Russia, using Cyrillic letter or alphanumeric codes which, more often than not, do not coincide with the IATA codes used internationally by the same air carrier. The domestic code for Vladivostok Air is ДД (DD) and the Yekaterinburg – Vladivostok via Irkutsk service is designated in Russian documents as flight DD352.

Tu-154 Family Drawings

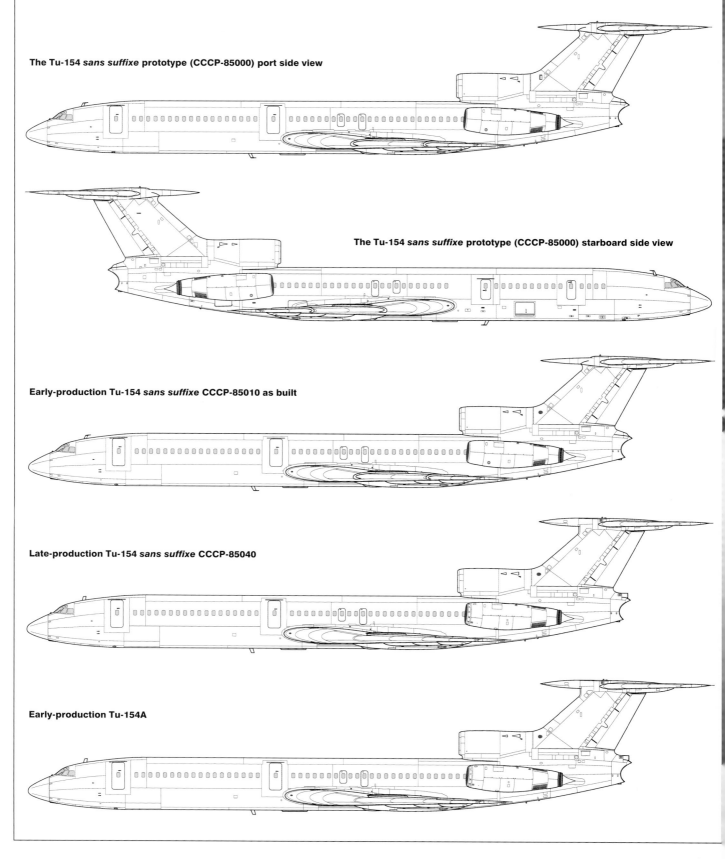

The Tu-154 *sans suffixe* prototype (CCCP-85000) port side view

The Tu-154 *sans suffixe* prototype (CCCP-85000) starboard side view

Early-production Tu-154 *sans suffixe* CCCP-85010 as built

Late-production Tu-154 *sans suffixe* CCCP-85040

Early-production Tu-154A

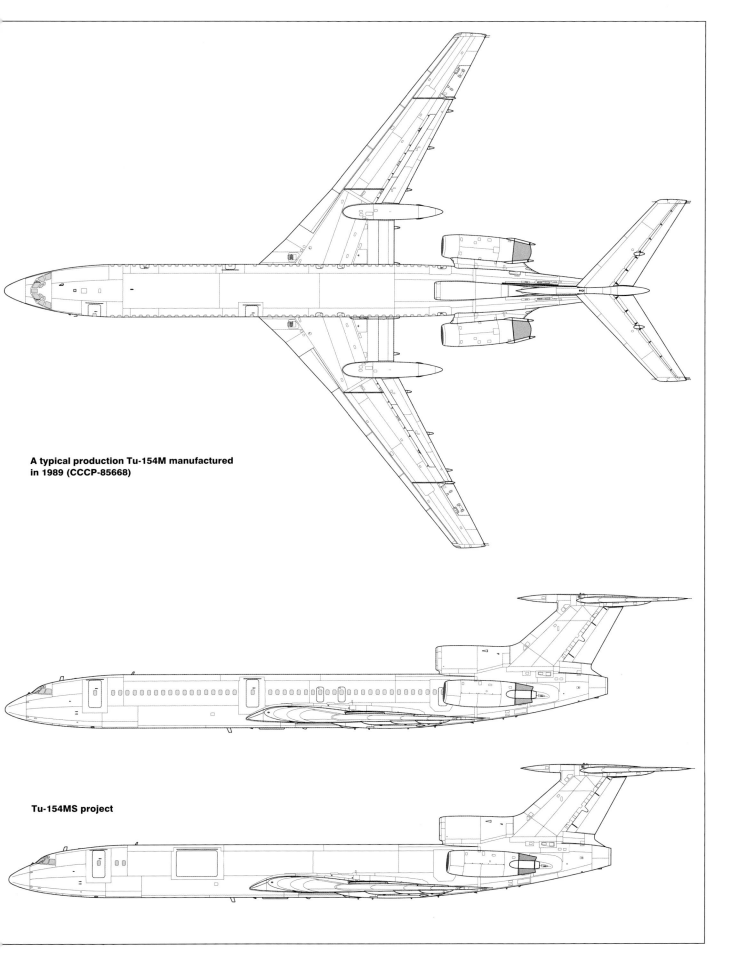

A typical production Tu-154M manufactured in 1989 (CCCP-85668)

Tu-154MS project

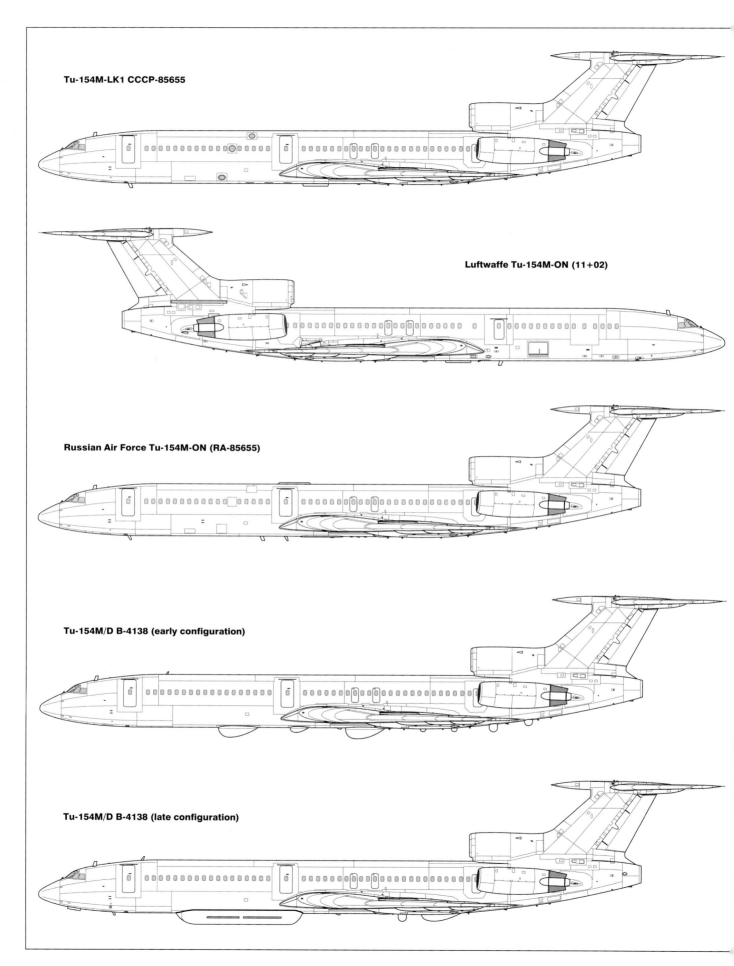

Tu-154M-LK1 CCCP-85655

Luftwaffe Tu-154M-ON (11+02)

Russian Air Force Tu-154M-ON (RA-85655)

Tu-154M/D B-4138 (early configuration)

Tu-154M/D B-4138 (late configuration)

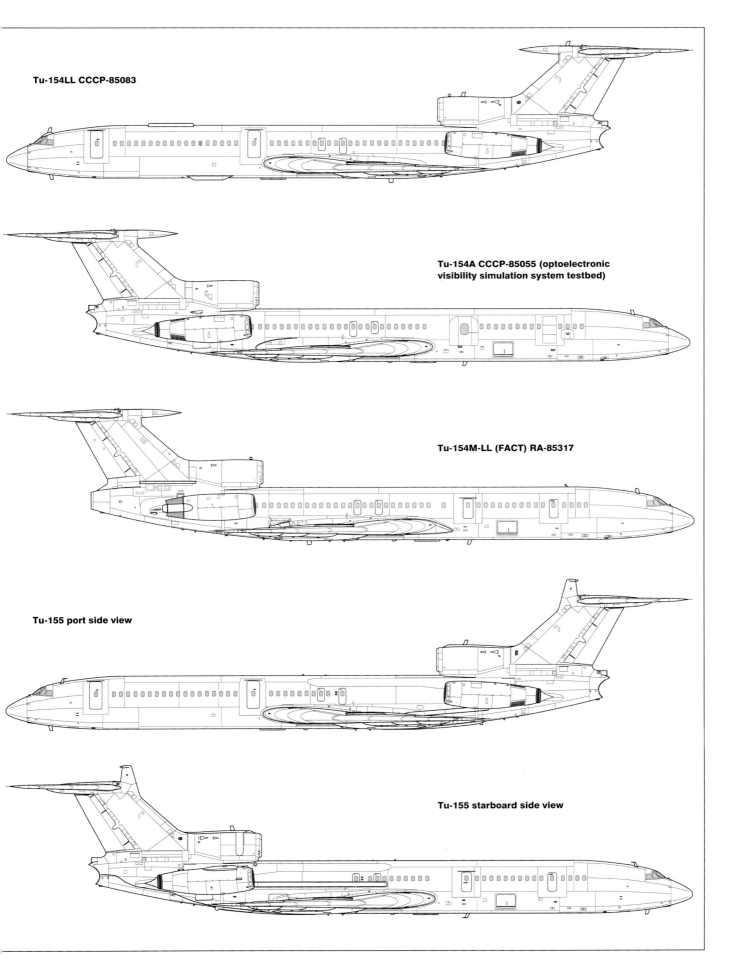

Tu-154LL CCCP-85083

Tu-154A CCCP-85055 (optoelectronic visibility simulation system testbed)

Tu-154M-LL (FACT) RA-85317

Tu-155 port side view

Tu-155 starboard side view

RUSSIAN AIRLINES AND THEIR AIRCRAFT

Dmitriy Komissarov & Yefim Gordon

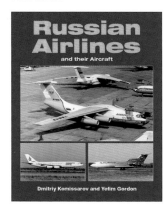

Following the ending of Aeroflot's monopoly in 1992 and the break-up of the Soviet Union, the Russian civil air transport scene has been considerably transformed.

This full-colour album covers the major airlines operating in Russia today, illustrating the types operated by each carrier, their equipment and the various colour schemes worn by them. A brief history and fleet information are provided for each airline, as are detailed photo captions.

Softback, 280 x 215 mm, 160 pages
449 full colour photographs
978 1 85780 176 7 **£19.99**

AIRLINERS OF THE 1970s

Gerry Manning

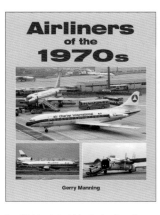

In a highly pictorial look at a decade which saw much change in the world air travel scene, well-travelled aviation photographer Gerry Manning has assembled an exciting collection of images from all over the globe. Over 60 different types are featured, from the propliners still hard at work to the newly-introduced Concorde and Tupolev Tu-144 supersonic transports by way of the first Boeing 747 services and introduction of the first Airbus product: the A300.

Softback, 280 x 215 mm, 144 pages
311 colour photographs
978 1 85780 213 9 **£18.99**

EUROPEAN AIRLINES

John K Morton

This book portrays with extended captions, a broad selection of over 100 primarily passenger-carrying airlines from 33 European countries. Starting in Ireland and continuing around the continent, the reader is taken on a 'tour' of European nations, and in each case liveries of based airlines, including all the major flag carriers, scheduled and charter airlines are included. As wide a variety of types – jets and propliners – as possible are shown and an equally-varied range of colour schemes.

Softback, 280 x 215 mm, 112 pages
188 full colour photographs
978 1 85780 210 8 **£14.99**

Aerofax ILYUSHIN IL-18/20/22

A Versatile Turboprop Transport

Yefim Gordon and Dmitriy Komissarov

The IL-18 four-turboprop airliner first flew in 1957 and was supplied to many 'friendly nations' in Eastern Europe, Asia, Africa, Middle East and the Caribbean. Its uses included passenger and cargo, VIP transportation, support of Antarctic research stations, electronic espionage and various research programmes. All versions are described, as are many test and development aircraft, the IL-20M ELINT, IL-20RT space tracker, IL-22 airborne command post, IL-24N for ice reconnaissance and IL-38 ASW aircraft.

Softback, 280 x 215 mm, 160 pages
184 b/w, 67 colour photos, plus dwgs
978 1 85780 157 6 **£19.99**

Aerofax TUPOLEV Tu-134

The USSR's Short-Range Jet Airliner

Dmitriy Komissarov

The Tu-134 has seen passenger service for over 35 years in 42 countries. Its multifarious other activities include VIP transportation, support of Air Force, Army and Navy headquarters and research and test work. The type has helped train thousands of military pilots and navigators for the Soviet Air Forces' tactical and long-range bomber forces.

Compiled from first-hand Russian sources, the book gives a full account of the Tu-134 and the type's design, test and operational history.

Sbk, 280 x 215 mm, 184pp,
204 col, 95 b/w photos, 5pp of dwgs
978 1 85780 159 0 **£19.99**

Red Star Volume 24 TUPOLEV Tu-144

Russia's Concorde

Yefim Gordon and Vladimir Rigmant

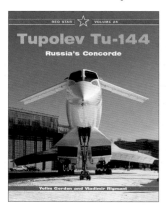

Tasked with creating a supersonic transport ahead of the West as a matter of national prestige, Andrey Tupolev met the target at the cost of a tremendous research and development effort. The Tu-144 took to the air in December 1968, ahead of the Anglo-French Concorde. This detailed account includes the reasons behind its premature withdrawal and a description of its recent use in a joint research programme with NASA.

Softback, 280 x 215 mm, 128 pages
151 b/w photos, 15 pages of colour plus drawings
978 1 85780 216 0 **£19.99**

Red Star Volume 31 TUPOLEV Tu-114

The First Soviet Intercontinental Airliner

Yefim Gordon & Vladimir Rigmant

Based on the Tu-95 bomber, the Tu-114 was the largest airliner of its time, with capacity for up to 220 passengers. It was able to fly at speeds similar to those of jet aircraft, and set a number of records, including the speed record for a turbo-prop aircraft that still stands 50 years later. 31 Tu-114s served with Aeroflot, the last being withdrawn in 1975. However, a number were subsequently converted into AWACS aircraft as the Tu-126 'Moss'.

Sbk, 280 x 215 mm, 128 pages
194 b/w, 51 colour photos, plus line drawings
978 1 85780 246 7 **£19.99**